# Global Codes
# of Conduct

## An Idea Whose Time Has Come

The John W. Houck Notre Dame Series
in Business Ethics

Also in the Series

*The Moral Imagination:*
*How Literature and Films Can Stimulate Ethical*
*Reflection in the Business World*

# Global Codes of Conduct

## of Conduct

### An Idea Whose Time Has Come

edited by

OLIVER F. WILLIAMS, C.S.C.

University of Notre Dame Press
Notre Dame, Indiana

© 2000 by the University of Notre Dame Press
Notre Dame, Indiana 46556
All Rights Reserved

Manufactured in the United States of America


*Library of Congress Cataloging-in-Publication Data*

Global codes of conduct : an idea whose time has come / edited by
Oliver F. Williams.
    p.  cm. — (The John W. Houck Notre Dame series in business
ethics)
    Includes bibliographical references and index.
    ISBN 0-268-01039-0 (alk. paper). — ISBN 0-268-01040-4
(pbk. : alk. paper)
    1. Business ethics.   2. International business enterprises.
3. Industrial policy.  I. Williams, Oliver F.  II. Series.
HF5387.G58   2000
174'.4—dc21                        99-086826

To

# Carolyn Y. Woo

*A Dean with a vision
Integrating sound ethical values with
professional excellence in business*

# Contents

## APPENDICES

# Introduction

We are living in an exciting and challenging era, characterized by what many are calling "globalization." Globalization refers to the integration of international economic activity unheard of in prior times. Not only does it involve unparalleled movements of capital but also of goods and services, technologies, and people.

Globalization is perceived as being both a *threat* and a *promise*. The promise is seen in the rising prosperity experienced by many in rich and poor countries alike in the aftermath of international linkages. The threat is the growing perception, by nations and individuals, that no longer can we control our way of life. Whether it be corporate downsizing, takeovers, bankruptcies, human rights abuses, or the loss of jobs, the pace of change and the disruption of communities is very troubling to many. Joseph Schumpeter's "Creative Destruction," described so well in his 1940 work, *Capitalism, Socialism, and Democracy*, is a double-edged sword that cries out for a humane resolution.[1]

There is no doubt that we are experiencing a growing call for a global ethic. From various parts of the world, proposals are emerging for a new global code of conduct. The Caux Round Table Principles are largely the work of Japanese, European, and U.S. business leaders; the Principles for Global Corporate Responsibility have been proposed by the U.S. Interfaith Center on Corporate Responsibility (ICCR), along with its counterparts in Canada, Britain, and Ireland. The CERES Principles are an attempt to protect the worldwide environment. There is an ever-increasing concern that human rights in developing countries be promoted and protected, highlighted in the recent code for the apparel industry, the White House Apparel Industry Code of Conduct. In

South Africa, there were the famous Sullivan Principles and in Northern Ireland there are the MacBride Principles. (See appendices for all these codes and others.)

What is the next step in this chorus of activity? Should we try to move toward one global code of conduct? What accountability structures are helpful? Where do we go from there?

To provide some insight and focus to the discussion on global codes of conduct, the University of Notre Dame Center for Ethics and Religious Values in Business invited a group of distinguished leaders from business, the academy, and civil society to offer some reflections for this volume.

Chapter 1 is authored by a business leader, Win Swenson, who argues unabashedly that good ethics means good business. Business needs predictability in order to thrive, and ethics codes insure that predictability has a chance. A global code of conduct is a requirement of our new situation, with the shrinking borders of our world compressing peoples, cultures, and economies. Technology and the internet have hastened the arrival of our global village, and the challenge to fashion a humane village is one that remains for our time.

Lee Tavis, in chapter 2, reflects on the nature of globalization and concludes that the role of the firm is being redefined as well as the role of national and global institutions. The challenge requires that business define its ethical responsibility with global standards just as it defines product, production, and employee standards. With this new relationship between business and society aborning, Tavis suggests the possibility of an international treaty between governments and multinational businesses to clarify expectations and standards.

In chapter 3, John Kline asks a penetrating question about the rights and responsibilities of business in political matters. Until recently the prevailing wisdom was that international business should not be involved in the national politics of a host nation. ITT's role in destabilizing President Salvador Allende in Chile was thought to be a clear case of inappropriate activity by a multinational enterprise (MNE).

Today the prevailing wisdom suggests that, if good outcomes are projected, politically directed activity is the responsibility of a MNE. Kline cites the Sullivan Principles as an example of this thinking (see principle 7 in Appendix 27). Kline calls for a thorough analysis and dialogue about this new thinking before principles are developed for a global code of conduct. "If MNEs bear some responsibility on political issues, do they have a concomitant right to decide whether, when and toward what objectives to act, or are they simply instruments to be used by other public or private sector actors? Which actors?"

Chapter 4, by Oliver Williams, c.s.c., discusses what the contemporary discussion on global codes of conduct might learn from the Sullivan Principles (appendix 27). While scholars may continue to debate whether international companies should have ever had operations in an apartheid South Africa, almost all would agree that the Sullivan Principles, which governed U.S. companies from 1977 to 1994, were a watershed event in the evolving relationship of business and society. Williams argues that had U.S. multinational leaders been more proactive and less reactive in their acceptance of the principles, U.S. MNEs would have fared much better than they did in the South African saga.

Garth Meintjes writes in chapter 5 as a human rights advocate. He assumes that international civil society and, more specifically, nongovernmental organizations (NGOs) will become increasingly focused on multinational business in their quest to promote and protect human rights. The essay examines the direction in which norms need to develop, outlines the strategies used by NGOs to promote business conduct, and summarizes the various efforts by national and multilateral organizations to establish more uniform and enforceable codes.

Following the practice of the U.S. Department of State in producing an annual report on human rights practices of countries, Meintjes suggests that NGOs issue reports describing the behavior of the top 500 multinational companies in the human rights area. He offers criteria for structuring such a report.

In chapter 6, James Post assumes that codes are a modern form of the social control of business and focuses on three questions to advance the dialogue. First, why are so many activists, lawyers, and business executives opting for codes of conduct as a way to meet the expectations of society? Second, what prevents us from effectively implementing a code of conduct? Third, what can we learn from management theory to implement and formulate better codes?

Prakash Sethi, in chapter 7, makes it clear that while he does not question the need for codes of conduct, he does believe that there is a pressing need for research on the effectiveness of codes. Do codes actually deliver the intended outcomes? This and other questions need much more attention. Sethi suggests that experience from earlier codes would indicate that the code development process must be carefully formulated in order that the code might be reasonably expected to achieve the desired outcomes. If business does not participate in a code formulation, for example, the code will have little promise of success.

Ann Tenbrunsel responds to Prakash Sethi's call for research and, in chapter 8, offers some psychological and behavioral research which may suggest steps to avoid undesirable outcomes of codes of conduct. How can we avoid self-interested interpretations of codes? Why do codes limit creative solutions? Both too much ambiguity and too much specificity can be problematic with codes of conduct. Tenbrunsel points the way to resolution by focusing on the underlying psychological mechanisms that are the root of the problem.

In chapter 9 Kathleen Getz analyzes the nature and causes of corruption and reviews the anticorruption codes of the major international governmental and nongovernmental organizations. The Organization for Economic Cooperation and Development (OECD), the Organization of American States (OAS), the European Union (EU), the World Trade Organization (WTO), the World Bank, the United Nations Commission on Transnational Corporations (CTC), the International Chamber of Commerce, and Transparency International (TI) are all international instruments working effectively to combat corruption. Getz reports that significant progress has been made and that she is optimistic.

Chapters 10 to 12 discuss various dimensions of the Caux Round Table's Principles for Business. In 1986 a group of senior business executives from Japan, Europe, and North America began meeting annually in Caux, Switzerland, to discuss measures to lessen trade tensions. These discussions led to further meetings about ethical issues and finally, in 1994, to the adoption of the Caux Principles for Business (see Appendix 26).

Gerald Cavanagh, s.j., in chapter 10, discusses the rationale for the Caux Principles as well as their strengths and weaknesses. Cavanagh is a champion of the Caux Principles not only because they are a set of ethical standards that hold across cultures but also because they are advocated and advanced by business leaders. The principles address the responsibilities of managers and companies from a stakeholder perspective and include all the elements that a company may want to include in its own code of conduct.

Chapter 11, by Kenneth Goodpaster, provides an insightful analysis of the origins and central themes of the Caux Principles; he uses a key point from Francis Fukuyama's *Trust* to help understand the cross-cultural moral dimension of the principles. The essay discusses some of the challenges involved in implementing the principles as well as the promises for the future.

Georges Enderle, in chapter 12, directs the reader to the magnitude of challenge of bringing an ethical dimension to the management of state-owned enterprises (SOEs) in China. Drawing on Confucian ethics, the socialist ethics as outlined by the Communist Party of China's Central Committee, as well as a development of the "goal-rights" approach of Amartya Sen, Enderle develops a number of ethical guidelines for the reform of SOEs. He does this by using the Caux Principles as a heuristic device and thus provides another experience with this code.

The next two chapters, 13 and 14, discuss a document developed by a coalition of church groups in the United States, the Interfaith Center on Corporate Responsibility (ICCR) and its counterparts in Canada (TCCR) and Britain and Ireland (ECCR). Titled the "Principles for Global Corporate Responsibility: Bench Marks for Measuring Business Performance" (see Appendix 25), this document intends "to reform the manner and means by which companies do business." Chapter 13, by Ruth Rosenbaum, asks six questions about a code which are designed to highlight the unique perspective of this new code developed by the religious community. This endeavor is an attempt to reflect on the business world in the light of religious social thought. The issue is social justice, not corporate social responsibility, says Rosenbaum: "Justice requires that we hold the faces and lives of those oppressed by poverty and oppression before us when we evaluate any code and any economy."

Chapter 14, by David Schilling, continues the discussion of the code developed by the religious communities. Schilling focuses on two issues: how to establish a credible code of conduct with viable corporate standards and how to develop effective monitoring. A strong advocate of independent monitoring, Schilling recounts how the Gap worked successfully with NGOs to build an independent monitoring system for Gap suppliers in El Salvador. Schilling discusses how the code not only has principles but also criteria and benchmarks by which a company can measure itself against this religious vision of business.

Chapters 15 and 16 discuss a code that is designed to prevent sweatshops and which includes provisions for a monitoring system. Called the "White House Apparel Industry Partnership Workplace Code of Conduct and Principles of Monitoring," the document is the fruit of a presidential task force. The task force was formed in 1996 after the outcry that followed revelations that a line of clothing bearing the name of Kathie Lee Gifford was made in sweatshops in Central America and New York.

Composed of human rights groups and apparel manufacturers, the eighteen-member task force met for more than two years before thirteen of the members finally agreed to go forward with the code in November 1998 (see Appendix 22 for code). Apparel manufacturers on the task force who agreed were: Liz Claiborne, Nike, Reebok, Phillips Van Heusen, L.L. Bean, Patagonia, Nicole Miller, and Kathie Lee Gifford. The human rights organizations signing off on the code included: Business for Social Responsibility, the Lawyers Committee for Human Rights, the National Consumers League, the International Labor Rights Fund, and the Robert F. Kennedy Memorial Center for Human Rights. The five members of the task force who did not agree to the code were primarily concerned that it did not require a "living wage" but only stipulated that the legal minimum wage be provided. Ruth Rosenbaum, in chapter 13, argues for this "living wage" when she discusses the Purchasing Power Index (see Appendix 24 for a description). Members not agreeing were also concerned about the "flawed" monitoring system included with the code; the sort of monitoring advocated by David Schilling in chapter 14 was not accepted. The most outspoken dissenters were leaders of the Union of Needle Trades, Industrial and Textile Employees; the Interfaith Center on Corporate Responsibility, represented by Schilling, was not a signatory not only because of monitoring concerns but also because the process finally agreed upon did not hold sufficient promise of moving the code toward the notion of a living wage.

Chapter 15 is by a member of the presidential task force, Linda Golodner of the National Consumers League. The chapter includes a brief history of the National Consumers League as well as a discussion of the child labor problem. Concerned that more than 250 million children between the ages of five and fourteen are forced to work, often in dangerous situations, the National Consumers League sees the code as an important step in the right direction. The ethical principle underlying its concern is clearly stated: "the consumer movement was founded on the belief that the customer who bought sweatshop goods was as much the employer of sweated labor as the boss of the shop."

Kevin Sweeney, a senior officer of the apparel maker Patagonia, offers his reflections in chapter 16. Patagonia is an original member and finally a signatory of the Apparel Industry Partnership Code. Sweeney sees the code as a first step that should eventually have the endorsement of every major manufacturer. While he agrees that the living wage is a vital issue, he does not see this coalition as the best vehicle to advance it. To reduce child labor and forced overtime is a tremendous accomplishment and he sees this as the first task which is doable in the near term. In many ways Patagonia is a model firm, and Sweeney is an articulate spokesperson for these crucial issues.

Chapters 17 and 18 focus on the responsibility of business for the environment. Lisa Newton is concerned that "our marvelous, victorious Free Market system" might very well destroy the land, the village, and the human group. In chapter 17 she outlines her concerns and advances the notion that the Japanese concept of "kyosei" may very well be our salvation. The Caux Principles are, in part, rooted in the ethical ideal of "kyosei," which the principles define as "living and working together for the common good—in a way that enables cooperation and mutual prosperity to coexist with health and fair competition." Newton notes that there are three "mute victims" of the mar-ket: the refugee, the tribesman, and the land itself. Reflecting and acting on the notion of "kyosei" may help us recover the "community of all living on the planet."

In chapter 18, the executive director of the CERES Principles (Coalition for Environmentally Responsible Economies), Robert Massie, outlines some preliminary reflections about the effectiveness of corporate codes of conduct and illustrates his points by reference to the CERES and Sullivan codes.

The final chapter, by Patrick Murphy, presents a summary of a research project investigating the content of ethics statements of companies. While the author expresses "cautious optimism," he indicates that much remains to be done. For example, "On human rights and international issues, about 40 percent of the companies provide direction in these areas."[2]

A special feature of this volume are the twenty-seven appendices which include most of the global codes that are being considered in the current discussion by business groups. For additional codes of conduct for professional societies, specific business corporations, and other groups, see "Ethics Links on the Web" on the web site of the Notre Dame Center for Ethics and Religious Values in Business (http://www.nd.edu/~ethics/).

## Acknowledgments

I am most grateful for the financial assistance provided by John Caron and William Lehr, Jr., businessmen of remarkable generosity and ethical concern. The associate editor of the University of Notre Dame Press, Jeffrey L. Gainey, deserves special thanks for his guidance and support. My gratitude goes to Deborah Coch, administrative assistant at the Center for Ethics and Religious Values in Business, for her expert assistance in preparing the manuscript. I thank Meghan Dunne, student assistant, who helped in many ways. Finally, it is only fitting that this volume be dedicated to Carolyn Y. Woo, Dean of the College of Business Administration at the University of Notre Dame. Carolyn's leadership has been an inspiration to all of us who are striving to discover creative ways to integrate sound ethical values with professional excellence in the business world.

Oliver F. Williams, C.S.C.
Academic Director
Center for Ethics and Religious Values in Business

### Notes

1. J. Schumpeter, *Capitalism, Socialism and Democracy* (New York: Harper & Row, 1940).

2. For another discussion of what remains to be done, see "Corporations Grapple With Codes of Conduct," *The Sweatshop Quandry: Corporate Responsibility on the Global Frontier*, Pamela Varley, ed. (Washington, D.C.: Investor Responsibility Research Center, 1998): 401–27.

# PART I

— ✳ —

# Why Global Codes?

*Defining a New Relationship*
*between Business and Society*

# 1

# Raising the Ethics Bar in a Shrinking World

WIN SWENSON

If we ponder the dynamic changes in our world today, advancements in technology are the most obvious. These advancements are causing two significant issues to take root, each with very strong ethical overtones. First, there is the role technology can play in the integration of global ethical values. Technology is shrinking our world and dramatically aiding the global sharing of information. The second issue, which ties closely with the first, is how business leaders need to handle the ethical *impact* of that very same technology and the information flows that go with it.

These issues present us with the unique opportunity to advance the call for a global code of ethical conduct. That's why volumes such as this one initiated by the University of Notre Dame Center for Ethics and Religious Values in Business are so important. We must begin to point the dialogue in this direction. Not only is it good for business, we have no real choice in the matter.

Let's start with the ethics of business leadership: It's the inescapable responsibility of the business leader to set the ethical tone of his or her company. While one can intellectualize the subject of ethics, for business leaders the subject of ethics must be more practical:

- It is evident in the decisions business leaders make every day;
- It is reflected in the hundreds of examples business leaders set every day;
- And, it is always visible in the actions that business leaders encourage or discourage in those who work for them. It is in these everyday realities that the "rubber of ethics" hits the road of business.

As an international operation with clients and customers in every corner of the world, KPMG Peat Marwick LLP is in a position to have a pretty broad perspective on the changes in business ethics today.

- We see the companies that just flat-out want to cheat;
- We see the companies that want to bend every law and every code to get the advantage for themselves;
- We see the clients who try to meet the letter of the law but sometimes lose the spirit;
- And finally, we see the companies who truly "walk the talk of ethics and values."

KPMG core values include:

1. Teamwork and collaboration;
2. Open and honest communication;
3. Involving everyone;
4. "Boundarylessness," which is a difficult word to pronounce but stands for a very important idea. It means doing away with stovepipes within the organization;
5. An insistence upon leaders who serve, recognizing that a key aspect of that leadership is moral leadership and the enhancement of ethics;
6. And finally, accountability.

Given the work we do, accountability is critical within our firm and within the relationships we build with our clients and the communities in which we operate; and, to help our clients achieve the highest standards and values, KPMG has established a Business Ethics practice. It's function is to help devise and evaluate management systems that, in turn, help an organization's employees *know* what's right, *do* what's right, and when they're not sure, feel confident the organization will support them if they *ask* what's right. The goal is to help clients create an environment where:

- good people aren't afraid to step forward and communicate concerns;
- where the policy and practice is not to "shoot the messenger" but to fix the problem;
- and where bad news is sought out so that small problems can be addressed before they become big ones.

Much of the work of our ethics practice centers around reviews of corporate ethics policies and programs. In those reviews, clients want to know:

- are my programs up-to-date?
- how do they compare with those of similar organizations?
- how do they stack up in view of the new federal sentencing guidelines?
- are they, in fact, working—which is a good dollars and cents question as well as an ethics one.

Interestingly, we're seeing more activity in this area on an international basis. For example, one very large multinational company has asked us to help them think about how to combine into one stakeholder's report the following factors:

- its financial audit results;
- the latest assessment of its health and safety record;
- and an audit of the company's community, environmental, and human rights record—known as a "social audit"—the standard being the company's own far-reaching standards of global conduct.

In that way, our client company will be providing its stakeholders with a comprehensive statement not only of the company's financial performance but of its ethics and corporate behavior.

Our U.S. ethics practice is also working with KPMG/Canada and members of our Japanese practice to collaborate on other international projects. There does appear to be a growing movement around the world to enhance ethical standards, and KPMG is proud to be playing an important role in it.

Before we leave the issue of ethics and values within KPMG and how we help our clients in this area, I want to say one word about judging values. When the CEO is asked to explain what kind of ethical conduct and values we are looking for at KPMG, he says: We want everyone to follow the "Glad You Asked" principle. By that, he explains, he means that every member of our firm should conduct himself or herself every day in every act as though Mike Wallace, or Dan Rather, their priest, rabbi, or minister, or even their mother and father were looking over their shoulder, questioning their every move. And, in response to any question, they could look up and say: "Glad you asked!" It is, in fact, a tough standard to meet. But I think it is at the heart of the way we want businesses to think and act. With candor, integrity, and transparency.

Now let's move to ethical values as they apply to the ever-shrinking world, a world continually being linked together in an ever-expanding web of faster and faster communications. About six weeks ago, our CEO had an experience that brought this idea home to him personally. Like many other fathers, Steve drove his daughter—in her case, to North Carolina—to begin her college career. He remembered how *he* arrived at the University of Missouri with a few reference books and some meal money. By contrast, his daughter went off to school armed with a credit card, debit card, ATM card, a phone card, and a laptop computer—complete with a modem, Internet connection, and browser. You name it, she had it—she's wired, she surfs, she is "cyber-proficient." Why is this significant?

The point is this: his daughter—a first-year freshman—has more information at her fingertips—more global news, corporate intelligence, market research, and purchasing options—than many senior corporate executives or high-ranking government officials did as little as four or five years ago. Computing and communications technologies have come a long way in a very short time. The power of a laptop built in 1997 is greater than the mainframes of the late 1970s and early '80s. Bill Gates addressed KPMG's annual meeting in August 1997, and talked about even more powerful personal computers that, as he put it, "will see, talk, listen and learn." Client-server technology, databases, desktop publishing software, electronic mail, and the Internet mean that information of all types is now available to audiences worldwide, linking people of different countries, values, beliefs, ideas, and cultures. We really are, in short, creating a global community through technology and communications.

But while technology and computing power are good, they are just tools to help us do what we do faster and more efficiently. In the end, *what we do* and *by what standards* are more important than how we do it and how fast we do it. To put that a little differently, all our technology works just as well at doing the wrong thing as doing the right thing. And frankly, there is nothing worse than doing the wrong thing faster and more efficiently. Today at KPMG, we already have a raft of technology tying our operations together. Increasingly, more and more companies are acquiring and expanding their computing power, and as a leader in the knowledge industry KPMG is helping them.

The ethical implications of all the communication and information availability, however, are staggering. The more we shrink our world to link a buyer with a seller, a business with a market, one trading partner with another, *the more we need to rely on each other to deal from the same ethical deck.* Let's take KPMG for example. KPMG is a worldwide firm with entities in 104 countries overseas. As business leaders, we're always looking for new opportunities to attract clients and to expand our relations with the clients we now serve all around the world. But in doing this, we must attend to hundreds of different rules and mores that our clients must play by. It's like playing baseball with a new umpire and rulebook every inning. Today communication and business transactions are jumping over borders like children jump cracks on a sidewalk. The technicians use common protocols and compatible hardware and software. But we are still faced with a variety of ethical standards that make it difficult to conduct business.

The *Wall Street Journal* a month or so ago featured a story about struggles that McDonald's is having in China. The thirty-four McDonald's restaurants in Beijing on average each had to pay thirty-one fees to municipal authorities. Only fourteen of the fees are legal, and the remaining seventeen illegal fees cost each restaurant more than $10,000 a year. One McDonald's was reportedly fined $1,000 for having *three* flies in the kitchen. Bureaucrats required restaurants to hire security guards or else pay the authorities $600 for the service. The fee for river cleaning was $5,000 a year despite Beijing having only a few small streams and lakes. And while there was much hoopla in the press over the fees, McDonald's reports that the authorities are still charging them. And that's only one of countless publicized examples.

The business and political environments today support the move to a global code of ethical conduct. Our CEO, as a business leader, looks for favorable opportunities to advance the interests of KPMG's business. To achieve this goal, a strong global ethical climate clearly makes good business sense. Can we make this happen? Absolutely. Now more than ever, thanks to more sophisticated technologies and greater information access, we've got the right ingredients to support such a push. If you consider a number of diverse events during the last half-century alone, there's enough evidence to suggest that when people start to appreciate that their individual interests point toward common ground, we can cooperate on just about anything. Consider the creation of the United Nations after World War II, the Bretton Woods Conference in the late '40s, and the efforts to develop stable currency markets to banish the risk of worldwide depression.

More recently, there are global trade pacts such as NAFTA, and the formation of regional trade groups such as the Association of Southeast Asian Nations. These are concrete examples of self-interest being pushed aside in favor of something larger: common ground to provide better or broader opportunity for all. Are these relationships perfect? Of course not. But the bottom line is that business counts on the predictable order of things. Good ethics means good business because it helps to lay the foundation for the predictability that business needs to thrive. If we look around at what's been going on in our world lately, you can argue that ethics is already working its way to the forefront of global discussions. Interestingly, this trend is partly in response to the global coming-together of people and markets that we've been talking about. For example:

- Surveys of executives in Japan and Korea consistently show broad support for high ethical standards and behavior in business dealings. Recent indictments of high-ranking governmental and business leaders in both countries might be thought of as reflecting only ethical lapses, *but* they are also concrete examples of a growing intolerance for serious ethical lapses, even in the face of strong political pressure to sweep them under the rug. I just returned from Japan where I had the opportunity to address the Keidanren, Japan's largest business consortium. They are very concerned about the highly publicized ethical lapses that have recently occurred there. They recognized:

- Their goals for market liberalization—especially in banking—will fall short without a strong foundation in ethics.
- Technology makes ethics breaches known in an instant around the world, yet reputations can take years to rebuild.

- A global ethics watchdog, Transparency International (which is backed by a number of international organizations) is receiving increasing recognition for its country rankings of worldwide corruption activity. Its rankings contain some of the world's most significant emerging economies as the worst offenders. Many of these countries are benefiting from greater foreign direct investment; they risk losing that investment unless they begin to clean up their act.
- Business ethics programs are now receiving greater attention in Europe. In the mid-1980s, less than 20 percent of major corporations in Germany, France, and the U.K. had a code of conduct. By the early 1990s, that figure had topped the 50 percent mark. (Incidentally, I don't believe codes, without other measures, are a panacea. But they are a start.)
- Even world economic organizations are starting to act. The Organization for Economic Cooperation and Development, a group of twenty-nine of the largest economies in the world, recently agreed to outlaw bribery of foreign officials. By taking this step, the co-signers have agreed to tackle deeply rooted corruption that has been outrightly condoned in some nations by allowing tax deductibility for foreign bribes.
- In the U.S., of course, the media have drawn increasing attention to examples of business misconduct, ranging from fraudulent Medicare billings to global sourcing from "sweat-shop" manufacturers.

So, the acceleration of *global* business relationships, spurred by technology, has generated a global sense of concern. And, while there are a lot of differences in cultures, common sense and experience will tell you that business people around the world are more alike than they are different. Business people don't like payola, they don't like bribes, they don't like influence peddling, and they don't want to be forced to deal with any of that when they do business in other cultures. As we deal together more and more, the rationale and will for global standards should only increase.

Now, let's briefly explore a second reason why the time has come for a global code of ethical conduct. Again, we return to technology. Today increasingly powerful computers and other information management technologies give people tremendous new tools. The business rewards are greater, but we've also got to acknowledge the risks. When you're shopping in many large stores these days, what's the first thing they ask you when you approach the checkout island to pay for your child's new bike or a pair of shoes for yourself? Your telephone number. How will our children's colleges keep track of them during their four years at the school? A social security number. How do telemarketers know whom to call and with what product pitch? A raft of information never before available helps them.

We live in a new age. The data gathered about people, places, events, and purchases are to today's companies what lumber, steel, rubber, and mortar were to yesterday's enterprises. They are the new raw materials of the information age. And today, that wealth of information combined with the computing power in the hands of so many, also means the possibility exists to cause real harm. We are businessmen and women, not Trappist monks, and KPMG uses information as its lifeblood. *But there has to be value-based restraint.* We know that the ethical treatment of information in a world where almost anyone can create it, steal it, manipulate it, falsify it, and move it is a very real concern today. The technological surge that we've experienced over the last 10 to 15 years *must* be met by an equally vigorous ethical awareness of how to handle this new responsibility. Recognition of this fact should further advance the call for a global code of conduct.

In a different age, the integrity of information was far easier to guarantee. If you wanted to design and test a new vaccine, for example, you sequestered the team in a research facility and you told the security guards not to let anyone in or out without permission. Information was something you found inside a person's head, not in a laptop computer as part of a corporate database, or on the Internet. The risks of someone sharing sensitive information was a real concern, of course, but sharing information wasn't as easy as it is today. As recently as five to seven years ago, there was still no practical way to move your message or share information with thousands or millions of people except through the centralized media of publishing, television, and radio.

Today, technology has changed the game. You can get your hands on highly sensitive information pretty easily. Every day, we hear growing concerns about the privacy of medical records and the sale of personal information found in consumer databases. Advances in communications have also flattened the hierarchy of *who* creates, controls, and communicates information. In one recent survey of U.S. corporate computing professionals, respondents readily acknowledged that they had opportunities to engage in unethical behavior. In another survey, 7 percent said that if they were bank programmers, they would adjust their own checking accounts to remove a service charge for a bounced check. A separate *Computerworld* magazine survey of more than 200 Information Systems (IS) professionals revealed that:

- 47 percent admit to copying commercial software without authorization;
- 15 percent sympathize with computer hackers; and
- 6 percent admit to snooping in confidential corporate files.

Interestingly, we're not talking about professionals who view the ethical rules of their professions lightly. In fact, IS professionals rank the ethical standards of their profession very highly—second only to doctors and on par with the accounting profession. And yet they're admitting activity that in many cases would violate federal law. So if there ever was a time to accelerate a global dialogue about ethics, the challenges of an information economy certainly give us the reason to do so. At KPMG, clients tell us what's important. And the issue today for a lot of them is not a lack of information but how to manage the consequences—some ethical—of too much. They're asking themselves: Who gets it and who doesn't? In what form? When? At what price? Add to the mix the rise of authoritarian governments commanding access to this information-rich technology generated by business. If governments extract bribes, will businesses be able to resist government putting their hands into the information till? KPMG clients also share a practical concern about how to ensure the integrity and security of their information and systems. Remember, this is the age when a twenty-year-old financial analyst can bring down a 200-year-old financial institution with a few keystroke trading commands.

### Conclusion

Let me close by offering four broad action steps that are on our recommended list of "must do's" to raise the ethics bar in today's shrinking world.

First, raise corporate ethics awareness. Ethics training and culturally flexible corporate codes of conduct are a big part of it. And codes and training today should also emphasize that information is a strategic asset that must be protected and carefully managed.

Second, encourage organizations to develop a broad-based value system to act as a screen for unethical behavior. KPMG's core values that I mentioned above are intended to be a "screen" that every major decision we make is passed through, and a standard by which all of our employees are evaluated. While our leadership team didn't create them solely to deter potentially unethical behavior, they clearly can have the practical effect of encouraging people to act differently. Values such as open, honest communication, teamwork and collaboration, and personal accountability are the hallmarks of strong organizations and, not coincidentally, highly ethical ones as well. In 1997 at KPMG's international partners' meeting, partners representing more than a hundred of KPMG's country practices sat down together to begin work on a common set of core values for our worldwide organization. The U.S. values are the starting point of this effort, but the international firm has the latitude to tailor them to fit its own needs. Now more than ever, we realize how closely linked we really are. Shared clients, markets, and opportunities have led to the beginnings of a shared value system.

Third, aggressively incorporate information ethics into the business school curriculum. Books such as this are one good way to continue the critical dialogue that's necessary on business and information ethics, but we can do more. And it has to go beyond academic principles and intellectual debates concerning what constitutes ethical behavior. It should include practical political, social, legal, regulatory, and technological influences. The opportunity to influence many of tomorrow's corporate managers and senior leadership is profound, particularly since U.S. business schools attract so many international students.

And fourth, hold employees accountable for violating corporate codes of conduct. If we don't, the message we send throughout our organizations will be twice as detrimental as the misdeed itself. Leaders cannot absolve themselves from taking responsibility for unethical acts by employees.

- All too often strategic goal setting occurs without reference to pressures.
- Management must *measure* and *audit* the effectiveness of its compliance and ethics initiatives. The "social audit" by the large multinational firm I mentioned is one interesting model.

You have a stake in this. In your current and future roles as teachers, executives, government and community leaders, you should help set the tone by developing ethics policies, supporting them in your personal behaviors, and giving your students, employees, or officials the tools to comply. We can and must instill the unyielding belief that ethics is "simply the way we do business." When that happens, partners and employees will *instinctively* resist courses of action that hurt others and undoubtedly tarnish the organization's own reputation.

So there's movement around the world that we can see. In some ways 1997 has been an interesting year here in the U.S. as well. The twenty-fifth anniversary of Watergate provided the backdrop for renewed reflection on a time that has since become the low-water mark for ethical behavior in this country. We've been told by the media and politicians that our level of trust in government—or in other institutions, for that matter—will never be restored to its pre-1972 levels.

The Reverend Billy Graham even said once that "everybody has a little bit of Watergate in him." If Reverend Graham is correct, then in the age of information we have some substantial challenges on our hands. Technology has changed the way we relate to each other in the course of business and many other activities. And new mediums such as the Internet are changing the way we communicate. Combined, they have had the practical effect of shrinking the borders of our world, compressing peoples, cultures and economies. Good ethics is good business and poor ethics can cost you business. There are now clear examples of this. The last time we checked, a lost sale hurts just as much in Kuala Lumpur as it does in New York City or South Bend, Indiana. People are increasingly recognizing the link between integrity and success in meeting financial objectives. Given that recognition, let's seize the moment to advance ethics globally.

# 2

# The Globalization Phenomenon and Multinational Corporate Developmental Responsibility

LEE A. TAVIS

The process that has come to be called globalization is the integration of economic activity across the world. It involves an unparalleled movement not only of capital but also of goods and services, technologies, and, even, people. The globalization of recent decades is an organic integration in contrast to the colonialism and international trade of earlier periods. It is driven by a complex of interrelated factors such as intense global competition; the technologies of communications, transportation, and production; the opening of markets in the developing countries; and the implosion of the former Soviet Union.

Global integration has led to substantial economic growth and, at the same time, an uneven allocation of the fruits from that economic growth. Supporters of globalization focus on productivity and growth:

> By enabling a greater international division of labor and a more efficient allocation of savings, globalization raises productivity and average living standards, while broader access to foreign products allows consumers to enjoy a wider range of goods and services at lower costs. Globalization can also confer other benefits by, for instance, allowing a country to mobilize a larger volume of financial savings (as investors have access to a wider range of financial instruments in various markets) and increasing the degree of competition faced by firms. (IMF, p. 45)

Evidence supports their assertion that economic growth, particularly in developing countries, has been associated with integration over the past thirty years:

> In absolute terms, living standards in most developing countries, as measured by real per capita incomes, have risen substantially between 1965 and 1995. Even excluding the successful Asian newly industrialized economies, developing countries as a whole more than doubled their real per capita income over the past thirty years. (IMF, p. 154)

Detractors focus on the inequities in the process:

> We have heard the freeing of trade and the downsizing and devolution of government held up as the ideal of progress and, incidentally, as a panacea for social ills. We have noted the paradox of a ruptured, polarizing society alongside a globalizing, integrating economy. We have witnessed the triumph of economies over politics and the elevation of finance over all economic activity. We are aware that we are living in a global economy marked by non-accountable economic power and opaque, self-serving operational practices. And we have watched economies of the North and those of the poorest nations being restructured accordingly, with windfall wealth for a small percentage of people, stagnation for many, and widespread devastating effects on the most vulnerable people in society—predominately women, children, the elderly, minorities, indigenous people, migrants, and refugees. (Hug)

The negative position is also empirically supported in that integration has led to an increase in income inequality. The dispersion of income has increased in most of Latin America and Africa. Increasing inequality is one of the striking events of the last decade for the transitional economies of Central and Eastern Europe. A number of East Asian countries, however, have managed to achieve equity with growth (Kim). The United Nations Development Program reports that the richest 20 percent of the people in the world increased their share of global income from 75 to 85 percent between 1960 and 1991. The share for the poorest 20 percent declined from 2.3 percent to 1.4 percent.

While one would expect a link between inequality and poverty, that has not been the case. In spite of the changes in income distribution, there has been a slight decrease in the proportion of people struggling to survive on the equivalent of $1 a day or less, from 34 percent of the world's population to 32 percent. We should note, however, that the absolute number of poor is increasing and over a quarter of the world's population remains in severe poverty.

In summary, the relationship between integration and economic growth is well supported. Along with that growth, we observe an increasing inequality in the distribution of income. The good news is that while the absolute number of poor is increasing, in relation to the population of the world the percentage of people living in poverty has not increased.

We should not be surprised with the favorable economic growth and the inequity of income associated with integration.[1] Given the rapid rate of market and technological change, access to the global economic/financial system is becoming more selective. Those without access become exploited and marginalized. Their human rights are easily violated, and their grievances can fuel violent conflict. Moreover, given the nature of the global economic and political changes outlined below, it is becoming increasingly difficult to intervene on the behalf of these people.[2]

Rodrik captures the tension:

> The process that has come to be called "globalization" is exposing a deep fault line between groups who have the skills and mobility to flourish in global markets and those who either don't have these advantages or perceive the expansion of unregulated markets as inimical to social stability and deeply held norms. The result is severe tension between the market and social groups such as workers, pensioners, and environmentalists, with government stuck in the middle. . . . The tensions between globalization and social cohesion are real, and they are unlikely to disappear of their own accord. . . . The broader challenge for the 21st century is to engineer a new balance between market and society. (Rodrik, pp. 2, 85)

The instruments of economic integration are multinational corporations. Integration is driven by the intense competition among large firms. (The largest one hundred multinational corporations account for one-third of the world's foreign direct investment.) These institutions focus resources from across their enterprise networks to production or service in a specific location. Multinationals deserve credit for enhancing global productivity and economic growth. At the same time, they are an inextricable component of the social maldistribution of resources. Given the power of multinationals, individually and collectively, these firms incur an increased responsibility for the systemic results. Managers are struggling to meet this new responsibility and, in the process, redefining the roles of their firms. Clearly, if the maldistribution of resources is to be ameliorated, it must involve the activities of multinational corporations.

This chapter addresses the nature of globalization, what it means for the role of the multinational firm in the developing countries, and the responsibilities it imposes on the multinational manager. The focus on developing countries comes from the weak background institutions in those areas and the resulting imbalance of power. The possibilities of exploitation are greatest in those countries, and thus the increased intensity of the corporate responsibility.

In the next three sections, specific components of the globalization phenomenon will be evaluated as they influence, and are influenced by, the activities of the multinational corporation.[3] These trends will then be synthesized in terms of the emerging role of the multinational with suggestions for how that process might unfold.

## The Decline of National Sovereignty

The idea of national economic sovereignty has changed. Much of this change is associated with marketization—the opening of national markets to international competition. There are two other trends related to this shift from government-led to market-led development: governmental decentralization and the slow but sure evolution of regional and international regulation.

### Marketization

Marketization is the reliance on markets and competitive pressures as a means of enhancing productivity. In developing countries, the most common approach has been to open domestic markets to international competition, an approach implemented by the relaxation of economic regulations, albeit under extreme market pressure supported by the World Bank and the International Monetary Fund. In this way, government-led development has given way to market-led development.

Government-led development involved tight economic control of the domestic market as well as the movement of international goods and funds in and out of that market. Internally, governments relied on taxation and other investment incentives to channel capital to specific industrial sectors and regions. Price controls were necessary to offset the distortions and monopolistic power provided to protected industries. In those sectors where governmental officials believed capital was not flowing adequately, government-owned enterprises were established. Bank credit was closely regulated with priorities and subsidies to specific subsectors.

At the interface with international markets, all-inclusive, product-differentiating, tariff and quota systems were created. Exchange transactions were closely regulated, as was foreign borrowing. For multinational enterprises, proportional limits were determined for equity ownership, performance requirements were applied, and formal approval was necessary for imported technology and planned manufacturing capacity (Tavis 1997, pp. 133–34). For the former Soviet Union and China, it was a matter of direct allocation of resources rather than control of the market and its participants.

In the shift to market-led development, these restrictions in both the domestic market and the international interface have been substantially eliminated: tariffs have been reduced, financial repression discontinued, prices and exchange controls phased out, state-owned enterprises privatized, and investment approval and requirements eliminated. Few product or financial markets, however, have become completely opened. Substantial subsidies are still in place along with the continuation of banking regulation.

Across the world, governments have forfeited their national economic regulation, most notably in the former Soviet Union and in Latin America's retreat from import substitution industrialization (ISI). This decrease in the involvement of the state in all sectors of society is unprecedented. Unfortunately, the paring back of regulatory controls too often ignored the importance of the governmental role in ensuring market efficiency through competitive structures and information flows.

Tied to the integration of product markets among countries, the creation of the Euro and the increasing use of national currency boards are further reducing national economic sovereignty. The world will undoubtedly end up with three currency blocks, the Euro, the U.S. dollar, and the yen. The previous 175 independent currencies will be tied to one of these three base currencies through monetary union, as in the case of the Euro, or self-imposed ties, as in the case of national currency boards. While monetary sovereignty is not political sovereignty, currency unification includes a substantial abrogation of economic policy independence. A mitigating factor for currency boards is that they could shift blocks to seek a different set of fiscal policies.

Developing-country governments are struggling with competitive structures that include the local activities of multinational corporations. Multinationals seek and gain monopolistic advantages in the international arena through research and development, large capital investment, brand image, and control of the channels of distribution. Multinationals also join in strategic alliances to share short-term competitive advantages. Thus, monopolistic advantages can be beyond the control of national authorities and thus continue to exist within the overall competitive international market structure.

The most serious defect in domestic markets is the lack of governmental attention devoted to information flows within the marketplace. Structural competition does not achieve its goals without informed participants. In the former Soviet Union, the requirement that efficient markets must be nurtured, and that it is not a matter of simply letting go, has been ignored.

In addition to enhancing productivity through efficient markets (competitive structure with information flowing to all participants), governments also have the responsibility to protect those injured by unfettered markets. In their drive for productivity, as governments abrogate their power to the marketplace, they have also relinquished part of their ability to serve the needs of those citizens who are unable to protect themselves.

Across the world, developing countries in their attempts to attract foreign direct investment are not supporting labor and are turning a blind eye to environmental protection. In many cases, the structural adjustment requirements of multilateral institutions have led to declines in expenditures for social safety nets and other social programs.[4]

While the focus here is on global integration enabled by marketization and its potential for exploitation and marginalization, two other trends associated with the decline in sovereignty have an important influence on the way the system is changing, particularly the redefinition of the multinational corporate role. Regulation is moving away from the national level to state and local governing bodies on the one hand, and to international regulation on the other.

### Governmental Decentralization

Before marketization, much of the private sector regulation, and most of that which applied to international transactions and thus multinational corporations, emanated from the national level. Local regulation, while significant, tended to be less dominant with an underdeveloped capacity to deliver governmental services and administer what regulatory authority it had.

In marketization, the regulatory withdrawal has been largely at the national level. In this sense, marketization is itself a form of decentralization. As decisions are transferred from typically centralized governmental agencies to individual market participants, control moves from a relatively confined set of officials to the multitude of marketplace participants.

Beyond marketization, governments are beginning to shift more of their control from national to state and local governmental bodies. There is clearly a trend toward governmental decentralization across the developing world (WDR 1997, p. 11).[5] While the motivation for decentralization tends to be country-specific, two pressures are evident in most situations.

First, there is a belated recognition on the part of governmental officials and development experts that centralized policies have failed to deliver on the promise for economic development. National governments, particularly in the developing world, have been unable to match governmental services to the needs of individual citizens and to deliver sustainable, shared, poverty-reducing development. Both international and national agencies have finally come to the understanding that local grassroots participation in both planning and implementing development projects lies at the core of success for these activities. Most observers, including this author, argue that sustainable development is a grassroots phenomenon and that the high failure rate of development projects is, in a major way, the result of failure to recognize its bottom-up nature. The top-down approach of national policies as supported by international multilateral institutions simply does not work.

A second underlying cause of decentralization is the wresting of political power away from centralized political control. Decentralization is tied to democratization. To the extent that democratization can be measured by elections, the World Bank notes, "In 1974, only 39 countries—one in every four worldwide—were democratic. Today 117 countries—nearly two in three—use open elections to choose their national leadership, and two-thirds of the adult population in developing countries are eligible to participate in national elections" (WDR 1997, p. 111). The areas of greatest change, of course, are Central/Eastern Europe and central Asia in 1989 and 1991. The decentralization associated with democratization is reflected in Latin America where, in 1994, "Close to 13,000 units of local government are electing local leaders (such as mayors) compared with less that 3,000 in the late 1970s" (p. 112).

With the possibilities of participation associated with democratization, citizens are demanding the local provision of government services. The most accessible officials are the local ones. Citizens believe that the desire for governmental legitimacy, accountability, and transparency may be available at that level.

There are three general kinds, or steps, in governmental diversification (WDR 1997, p. 121). The first is "administrative deconcentration." Here, there is a transfer of function from the national to state or local government, although the central government controls policy and budgets. A second form of centralization is "fiscal decentralization." With fiscal decentralization the subnational unit gains more control over both the revenues and expenditures. In addition to increased budgetary control, the subnational unit could gain taxing authority and the right to borrow. In the most advanced cases, this can be a substantial shift in financial power away from the national government. The final, and most advanced form of decentralization, is "devolution." Here the transfer of political and economic power would be almost complete. The subnational unit would be essentially independent of higher political authority.

Administrative deconcentration would describe most of the current observed decentralization. In some countries, such as Brazil, fiscal decentralization is well advanced where local governments now constitute half of the total Brazilian public spending (p. 125). There are few, if any, examples of devolution as defined above.

Most, but surely not all, observers view decentralization as a favorable phenomenon since it allows for local grassroots participation—the key to both economic and political development. Decentralization reflects the principle of subsidiarity. Subsidiarity argues that decisions should be made as close as possible to the issue, the source of the problem, or the opportunity. The idea of subsidiarity appeared as early as the sixth century in the Protestant Synod of Emden. It has since become a central tenant of Catholic social teaching. There are two dimensions as reflected in the papal encyclicals. One is the natural right of each individual to associate and to organize—a dimension associated with political development. The second component of subsidiarity involves efficiency. This second dimension has to do with economic as well as political development (Allsopp, p. 927).

Governmental decentralization has not proven to be an easy path. The World Bank describes the process as follows: "In many cases decentralization is not the result of any carefully designed sequence of reforms, but has occurred in a politically volatile environment in which the level of trust is low and policymakers respond unsystematically to emerging demands from below" (WDR 1997, p. 124). As noted earlier, the demand for decentralization does, indeed, generally emerge from the grassroots, often as a component of the demand for participation. And, the level of sophistication among the municipal, or subnational, governmental bodies is not great. As Glade and Tavis note, "However, most state (or provincial) and municipal governments have had minimal legislative power, little or no borrowing capacity, very limited fiscal autonomy, and a generally underdeveloped capacity to administer regulations" (Glade and Tavis, p. 1218).

If administrative deconcentration is to evolve into fiscal decentralization, and finally to devolution, there must be a substantial increase in the bureaucratic sophistication of state and municipal governments. There must be clear rules as to the specific relationship among the bureaucratic levels for national, state, and municipal governments. Recognizing the continued national role, particularly in macroeconomic fiscal and monetary policy, decentralization must be structured as a bottom-up process with optimal policy and fiscal independence at the grassroots within the need for national coordination of macroeconomic stabilization and redistribution among regions and citizen groups.

The Mexican experience is instructive in the pressures and pitfalls of governmental decentralization. Throughout her history, the political power in

Mexico has been highly concentrated. From the Aztecs, through Spanish dominance, to the Partido Revolucionario Institucional (PRI), all of the pressures have been toward centralization. Decentralization was forced upon the PRI as a political reality, following the deep recession of the late 1970s and early 1980s. In 1982, the incoming president, Miguel de la Madrid, and his advisors identified decentralization as one of the key reforms needed to enhance the popular legitimacy of the PRI and the national bureaucracy, which were under severe criticism. Among President de la Madrid's most cited statements was, "To decentralize is to democratize and to democratize is to decentralize." The following president, Carlos Salinas, during his presidential campaign adopted a slogan, "The modernization of Mexico will advance decentralization. We shall strengthen it in order to increase democracy" (Rodriguez, p. 134). It should be noted that the elite group of the PRI, not the rank and file, has been the driving force for decentralization and electoral reform.

There has been progress in Mexico. The administrative capacity at the state and local levels has improved in some instances. The national solidarity initiated under Salinas focused at the community level. Still, fiscal decentralization has not occurred. "Despite increased revenue sharing, particularly in states, the basic centralized structure of public finance remains essentially undisturbed" (Glade and Tavis, p. 1223).

In sum, the pressures toward governmental decentralization across the world are persistent. While the process is itself a slow and difficult one due to the previous centralization in most developing countries and the many diverse interests involved in decentralization, true devolution is unlikely to occur. The real danger is that the decentralization process will take place without enhancing the participation of an increased voice in policy formation from the grassroots.

### International Regulation

The opposite side of the bifurcation of regulation away from the national bureaucracy is the evolution of international regulation. As with governmental decentralization, this too is a slow process.

The complex of national laws and international agreements that constitutes international regulation is an evolving force. The UN Declaration on Human Rights is slowly being recognized as a standard. In addition, the definition of human rights is being extended beyond civil and political rights against the nation-state to the second-generation economic and cultural rights (Tavis 1997, p. 427). These second-generation rights involve nonstate individuals and institutions such as the multinational firm.

Enforcement of international standards is a clear impediment to the notion of sovereignty. One enforcement channel is through international non-governmental organizations (NGOs). These self-appointed regulators have been effective in influencing both governmental and multinational corporate actions. In this volume, Meintjes analyzes the strategies of these international NGOs and how their focus is shifting from the nation-state to multinational corporations.

Another enforcement mechanism is through national courts outside the sovereign jurisdiction of the country where the violation occurred. A number of cases against U.S. multinationals for alleged violations occurring in other countries have been heard in U.S. courts. The victims of India's Bhopal disaster sued Union Carbide in U.S. courts. Texaco was sued by a group of Amazonian Indians for environmental damage in Ecuador. An interesting case involving Shell Oil in Nigeria has been filed. This case addresses an important issue relative to sovereignty. The claimants are attempting to prove that Shell Oil is the principal and the government of Nigeria the agent (Reyes and Stern, pp. 14–25). The idea of a multinational as the principal and a sovereign nation-state as the agent is a reflection on the changing relationship between economic and sovereign power.

In sum, marketization, governmental decentralization, and international regulation all signal a major abrogation of power on the part of the national governments, particularly in developing and transitional economies. This massive shift in the balance of power signals a change in the role of these institutions relative to international resource allocations.

## The Emergence of Civil Society

Across the developing world in Africa, Asia, Latin America, and Central/Eastern Europe, the civil sector is a growing force. Fostered by the impact of marketization, and closely associated as both a cause and an effect of governmental decentralization, components of civil society are playing an increasing role in allocating the resources of society.[6]

Civil society can be envisioned as those components of a society that are not part of or represented by the state or private enterprise. The institutions of civil society are diverse, including development nongovernmental organizations, professional associations, producers' organizations, social movements, unions, religious groups (congregations, orders, or base communities), and even the mass media (Reilly 1998, pp. 176–80).[7]

Increasingly, the civil sector is joining the state and private sectors as an equal partner. Some see this as a watershed development, as described by Salamon:

> A striking upsurge is under way around the globe in organized voluntary activity and the creation of private, nonprofit or non-governmental organizations. The scope and scale of this phenomenon are immense. Indeed, we are in the midst of a global "associational revolution" that may prove to be as significant to the latter twentieth century as the rise of the nation-state was to the latter nineteenth. The upshot is a global third sector: a massive array of self-governing private organizations, not dedicated to distributing profits to shareholders or directors, pursuing public purposes outside the formal apparatus of the state. The proliferation of these groups may be permanently altering the relationship between states and citizens, with an impact extending far beyond the material services they provide.
>
> Ideological blinders have also obscured a clear assessment of the nonprofit sector's true scope and role. For much of the past 50 years, politicians on both the political right and the left have tended to downplay these institutions. The left has done so to justify the expansion of the welfare state; the right to justify attacks on the state as the destroyer of private "mediating institutions." The rise of the welfare state thus crowded out the nonprofit sector from both public discussion and scholarly inquiry even as the sector continued to grow. (Salamon, p. 110)

The growing institutional core of civil society is nongovernmental organizations (NGOs). These organizations have flourished in the industrialized world for a long time.[8] Since the 1960s, they have become a substantial force in developing countries.[9]

NGOs come in many sizes and shapes. The Commission on Global Governance notes, "Some are issue-oriented or task-oriented; others are driven by ideology. Some have a broad public-interest perspective; others have a more private, narrow focus. They range from small, poorly funded, grassroots entities to large, well-supported, professionally staffed bodies. Some operate individually; others have formed networks to share information and tasks and to enhance their impact" (Commission on Global Governance 1996, p. 254).

NGO categorization and terminology for NGOs are far from standardized. One important distinction is between those groups that form around local needs and issues (bottom up) and those that support these local initiatives (top down). The former are often called grassroots organizations (GROs). These are the local groups organized by local people to serve the special interests of their members or for more general support of local communities. Fisher estimates there are over 200,000 GROs in the developing world. Among these groups is where the greatest diversity of NGOs occurs (Fisher 1998, p. 6).

Other institutions (top down) have developed to channel resources to the GROs. These groups called Grassroot Support Organizations (GRSOs) are typically staffed by professional managers, and channel resources to local GROs. There are now at least 50,000 active GRSOs in developing countries (Fisher 1998, pp. 80–94). There is much greater similarity among the GRSOs than among GROs. In addition, there are networks of GROs and GRSOs that add to the power of the individual institutions.[10]

A large number of international organizations channel resources to indigenous GRSOs and GROs. A common term for these groups is private voluntary organizations (PVOs). The Commission on Global Governance counts 28,900 of these institutions—those with operations in three or more countries (Commission on Global Governance 1996).

The reasons for the large numbers and the increasing role of NGOs in social governance are as varied as each country's cultural and political history.[11] In most societies, the core reason for the enhanced role of indigenous NGOs is their tie to the grassroots. These organizations tend to be anchored firmly to people and issues in the local communities. As noted above, most developing-country governments have been unwilling or unable to deliver sustainable economic and social development at the grassroots.

Globalization makes the need for NGOs more urgent. They are filling the void left by marketization. The rate of change and abrogation of governmental power associated with globalization is increasing the marginalization of the poor and the creation of new marginalized groups such as sections of the middle class. Those being left out seek ways of representing their interests. These efforts start at the local level. In this sense, the growth of NGOs is part of the grassroots democratization.

There is also a close tie between grassroots participation and governmental decentralization. As noted earlier, state decisions are increasingly being transferred from national to largely under-funded and unprepared subnational governmental units. This adds to the void created by marketization. The grassroots democratic thrust leads NGOs to aggressively fill these voids. NGOs can also provide managerial and technical expertise to reinforce subnational governmental bureaucracies and enhance local efficiency (Fisher 1998, p. 68).

Reilly (1998) is positive about these grassroots relationships. "As authoritarian regimes fade and economies founder, NGO-municipal collaborative ventures, contracts, and sharing will grow more significant—for both development and democracy. . . . Negotiations, pacts, and compromise happen more readily through the propinquity principle: face-to-face encounters, while they may not guarantee good results, do require policymakers and others to at least explore accommodation, for they will meet again tomorrow" (pp. 185, 187).

Governments are schizophrenic about NGOs. Institutions of the civil society empower local peoples and make demands on governments that governmental officials are not prepared to meet. Alternatively, as noted above, NGOs can efficiently deliver services well beyond the capability of national or subnational governmental bureaucracies. While many NGOs, such as civil rights groups, came into being in opposition to the state, it is often argued that their growth in recent years reflects a more benign or even supportive attitude on the part of the state—an attitude often forced by the pressure for democratization.[12]

For their part, NGOs are changing in their activities as they relate to the state and the private business sector. The NGO leaders of today are less confrontational toward the state and less moralistic relative to business than in the past. Indigenous NGOs are now more focused on problem-solving and the delivery of services, and more likely to collaborate with the other two sectors than engage in aggressive confrontation. Part of this shift is in response to the enhanced possibility of meeting grassroots needs through collaboration with local government or business decision-making. Part of the move away from confrontation is a result of changes in funding alternatives.

Until recently, international organizations were a major source of funds for indigenous NGOs. Developing-country governments are uncomfortable about international funding. They provide NGOs independence from government control and a challenge to sovereignty. Many of these international organizations pursue specific kinds of projects or have their own political agendas (Bossuyt and Develtere 1995). For example, in Kenya, NGO funds are the largest single source of foreign exchange for the country (Fisher 1998, p. 52).

With the reduction in foreign funding, NGOs are turning more to governments that are wary of NGOs and themselves underfunded. At the subnational levels, however, the need for NGO talent is increasingly being recognized.

With governmental funding comes the pressure to be "politically correct" (Gregoire 1995, p. 63). There is the possibility that NGOs will be co-opted in this process and become more like government-owned enterprises (Reilly 1998, p. 184; Gregoire 1995, p. 68). The potential for loss of identity is the greatest in Latin America, where NGOs have been more autonomous than in Africa or Asia (Fisher 1998, p. 47). Other NGOs will be disguised as businesses in order to get funding from the state (Reilly 1998, p. 184).

As reflected in this discussion, there is a clear and increasingly important role for civil society in our economically globalizing, politically democratizing, and governmentally decentralizing world. The rapid growth in numbers and diversity of NGOs leads one to conclude that the rules of the game are not as well established for the civil sector as for either the government or the private business sector. For government, there are the rights and responsibilities of the sovereign. For the private business sector there is the acceptance of competition as the driving force. NGOs are largely self-appointed within loose legal structures. They lack the status of the sovereign and are not quite sure whether confrontation, collaboration, or competition should guide their activities with other NGOs or the other two sectors.[13]

Still, multinationals must learn to work with the institutions of civil society. They are the bridge to local communities and issues. They can be the intermediary with municipal governments.

Multinational interaction with NGOs will require a substantial change in attitude for both parties. From the multinational side, much of the interaction has been adversarial, with NGOs trying to force the multinationals into actions that the multinational managers see as contrary to the best interests of their firms. This leaves a legacy of suspicion on the part of multinational managers. The majority of NGO staff, in the author's Latin American experience, are there because they do not trust or want to participate in private business except to support microentrepreneurs as clients.

There is a remarkable level of idealism, motivation, and commitment in the NGOs. The real challenge is to maintain this intensity as these institutions move more to professional management and collaboration with the private and government sectors.

## Multinational Corporate Decision Diffusion

Multinational corporations are organized as enterprise networks. Each local business unit (subsidiary) is a component of this network with close ties to the network core and to the other business units comprising the network.[14] A fundamental component of all network policies is the balance between uniformity across the network and the flexibility of each business unit.

Following World War II reconstruction, multinationals began international integration in a period that can be termed the globalization of mass production (Tavis 1997, p. 50). During this period, most multinationals were hierarchical organizations where decisions were made at the headquarter core with close control of business units to ensure that instructions were followed. There was substantial uniformity of production process, product, and policy during this phase.

Multinationals are now well into a new phase—flexible production. Current computer and production technology has enhanced the process from design to the completed product, a process that has dramatically increased production and product flexibility without increases in unit costs (Tavis 1997, pp. 52–53).

Development of organizational networks, supported by advances in communications, has paralleled the new production processes. Multinational enterprise networks are now more likely to be heterarchical than hierarchical (Birkinshaw and Morrison 1995). In a heterarchical organization, the relationship between the headquarter core and the business units, as well as that among the business units, changes. The business units have substantially more flexibility within broad policy guidelines established by headquarters in collaboration with the business units. The business unit is judged by its performance rather than its conformity to specific instructions. The two-way command and control communications between the core and each business unit has given way to a communications network that ties the business units together, as well as with the core. This coordination among the business units is critical to taking advantage of organizational synergies. Individual business units will take on network-wide responsibilities for specific technology or products. In this way, the focus of decision-making moves from the core to the business unit (Tavis 1997, pp. 352–56, 430–31).

The process of decision diffusion in the enterprise network changes the way decisions are made in the multinationals as well as their locations. The balance between the uniqueness of local needs and the uniformity of the network is determined more by the local manager. The manager has more organizational freedom within which to negotiate local conditions.

Multinational decision diffusion, thus, matches governmental decentralization and the increasing role of indigenous NGOs to enhance the possibilities of participative, collaborative action at the grassroots.

### Synthesis

Given this confluence of globalizing trends, it can be argued that multinationals have a broader responsibility for development, that the management of this responsibility requires greater imagination than in the past, and that justice in the short term must increasingly be served by multinationals while systemic regulation in the long term must include these global enterprises as partners.

The power of the sovereign is diminishing while the economic power of the multinational increases. As the power fulcrum shifts, nation-states are less able, or less willing, to represent their disenfranchised citizens. The economic and cultural rights of these citizens are at risk.

When the deprived are stakeholders of a multinational corporation, and the host country is unable or unwilling to protect them, the correlative duty to protect from deprivation becomes that of the multinational. (Stakeholders are those influenced by, or in a position to legitimately influence, the activities of the firm [Tavis 1997, pp. 103–5, 420].) This means that multinationals must ensure stakeholder rights such as subsistence, access to opportunities through the multinational network as well as a minimum of training to use that access, and participation in the decisions affecting the stakeholders. Ameliorating stakeholder exploitation becomes the responsibility of the multinational manager.

Addressing the multinational responsibility for the needs of marginalized members of society is a more complex issue. When the individual firm has no connection with the marginalized persons, there is little normative ethical support for a correlative multinational responsibility associated with their deprivation. It becomes a moral issue for society at large.

Still, when a developing country's background institutions are weak, the firm's stakeholder net reaches farther into society. For example, in remote developing-country locations or urban slums the local business unit of a multinational is responsible not only for the employee but also for his or her family and community—a responsibility many firms accept and manage.

Another dimension of the global trends described above is the location of the multinational interface with host societies. Decision-making in the nation-state and in the multinational is drifting toward the grassroots. As recently as a decade ago, multinational corporate entry was negotiated between experienced governmental officials and multinational corporate staffs. After entry, the economic environment included government-owned enterprises and national control of market mechanisms. Increasingly, the interaction is between local multinational management interacting with local governmental officials, often with the involvement of local representatives of civil society. The sophistication of multinational decision-making set against the typical inexperience of local officials and the unevenness of indigenous NGOs tips the power imbalance toward the multinational.

So, what can be done about global resources that are being allocated to productivity and economic growth at the expense of so many that are left behind with no institution to represent them? Multinational managers need to be involved in three activities: (1) managing multinational corporate responsibility through corporate codes of conduct, (2) extending the code effort to include groups of managers from different firms joined with representatives of government and civil society for industry-wide codes, (3) participating in the development of globally uniform regulations which define and control the activities of multinational corporations, host governments, and multilateral institutions.

Multinationals must define their ethical responsibilities uniformly across their enterprise networks in the same way they establish product, production, and employee standards. Most firms use codes of conduct to achieve this moral uniformity. The shift of power in the global economic system and the transfer of the decision focus to the grassroots increase the importance of this uniformity across the network as well as the complexity of the task. At this point in the evolution of the capitalistic system, effective corporate codes of conduct are, indeed, essential. They must fill the definitional void as the system evolves.

The second suggested managerial focus is to extend codes beyond the multinational firm. Activities such as the White House Apparel Industry Partnership are particularly promising since they involve all relevant parties— multinationals, human rights groups, labor unions, and governmental representatives.

Management efforts directed to these first two activities, however, are not sufficient. In the final analysis, the specific roles of national and global institutions need to be redefined. In an insightful analysis, Reyes and Stern propose the following:

> a freestanding international treaty open to both governments and multinational corporations. The treaty will address three major cornerstone issues:
>
> a. ensure that signatory MNCs will have protection of their investment and fair national treatment with host countries.
> b. define the prerequisites to being recognized as a multinational corporation and will lay down a comprehensive code of conduct for their operations.
> c. include dispute settlement procedures and enforcement mechanisms (pp. 62–63).

The treaty would be negotiated within the structure of the World Trade Organization with enforcement linked to trade sanctions.

Whatever process occurs, a clearly defined set of enforceable global standards must be established through the collaboration of multinationals, governments, and nongovernmental organizations. As noted, the UN Declaration of Human Rights is an increasingly accepted global standard. Corporate codes of conduct reflect a search for standards as they apply to individual firms. In aggregate, these codes can be expected to converge toward a single standard.

The time of sovereign control over economic institutions is past. Capitalism is on trial because it survived the implosion of the former Soviet Union and is now the dominant economic system. The deep fault line referred to by Rodrik (1997) must be addressed.

## Notes

1. The judgment that income inequality is parallel with economic growth is broadly held. Ravallion and Chen, however, present counterevidence. They conclude, "We found no support for the view that higher growth rates in average living standards tended to accompany worsening distribution" (p. 380).

They also related poverty to economic growth and found, "There is a strong association between the rate of growth in average living standards and the rate at which absolute poverty fell" (ibid.).

2. For a nuanced discussion of the political and cultural as well as the economic effects of globalization, see Raimo Väyrynen, *Global Transformation: Economics, Politics, and Culture* (Helsinki: The Finnish National Fund for Research and Development, Sitra), 1997.

3. For an extended discussion of these trends and the nature of multinational corporate developmental responsibility, see Tavis 1997.

4. In an analysis of the relationship between market openness and the social role of government, Rodrik makes two observations. First, he states, "It is generally accepted that integration into the world economy reduces the ability of governments to undertake redistributive taxation or implement generous social programs" (1997, p. 64). As a reaction to this loss of power to the international market, however, Rodrik notes, "Societies (rich and poor alike) have demanded and received a larger government role as the price of exposing themselves to greater amounts of external risk" (p. 65). Whether this relationship between market openness and the welfare state as a means of maintaining political support for that openness will continue under the current organic global integration remains to be seen.

5. It is interesting to note that, while industrialized countries tend to be more decentralized than their developing-country counterparts, recent trends, if any, are toward more centralization (*World Development Report 1997*, p. 9).

6. The designation "civil society," drawn from Latin America, is becoming the common global terminology. In Latin American usage, civil society refers to "multiple, self-limiting organizations of citizens publicly exercising their rights and responsibilities before the state" (Reilly 1998, p. 176).

Another term, "independent sector," is used. "Once the government and private business sectors are defined, scholars argue about what to call everything else. The term *voluntary sector* tends to imply the use of volunteers. The term *third sector* coined by Nielson (1979) is confusing unless one already knows that government is the first sector and business the second. Although the term *nonprofit sector* is useful for the developed countries, it does not encompass the complex organizational reality of the Third World today. Cooperatives, for example, promote projects benefiting an entire community, in addition to making profits for their members. Therefore, I use the term *independent sector*" (Fisher 1998, p. 10).

Fisher then expands on her concept of the independent sector to include the for-profit sector in her definition of civil society (ibid.). Since the focus here is on the relationship between multinationals and Fisher's "independent" society, civil society will be equated to Fisher's independent sector by including private business.

7. While this definition views civil society as a catchall, others see it as a cohesive sector with a specific role in society. Civil society can more narrowly be defined as "a sphere of social interaction between the economy and state, composed above all of the intimate sphere (especially the family), the sphere of associations (especially voluntary associations), social movements, and forms of public communication. Modern civil society is created through forms of self-constitution and self-mobilization. It is institutionalized and generalized through laws, and especially subjective rights, that stabilize social differentiation. While the self-creative and institutionalized dimensions can exist separately, in the long term both independent action and institutionalization are necessary for the reproduction of civil society" (Cohen and Arato, p. lx). Commenting on this definition, Enderle states, "Note that this definition, first, does not identify civil society with *all* of social life outside the administrative state and economic processes in the narrow sense; rather, civil society is distinct from a political society of parties, political organizations, and political publics (in particular, parliaments), as well as from an economic society composed of organizations of production and distribution, usually firms, cooperatives, partnerships, and so on. Second, civil society does not include the whole socio-cultural life-world, but only its structures of socialization, association, and organized forms of communication to the extent that these are *institutionalized* or are in the process of being *institutionalized*. Third, civil society is *not* seen in opposition to the economy and state by *definition*, rather, they are conceived as *mediating* spheres through which civil society can gain influence over political-administrative and economic processes. Only if these mediations fail, will the relationship of civil society, or its actors, to the economy and the state become antagonistic" (Enderle, p. 206).

8. Nonpolitical labor unions would qualify as special-interest NGOs. To the extent that unions are part of the political party process, however, they would be part of the state sector. In Mexico, for example, the Confederacion de Trabajadores Mexicanos

is so closely associated with the dominant political party (PRI) that it could be viewed as more a part of the state than of civil society. In the German corporatist government, it is difficult to envision the labor federations as NGOs fitting the above-described. Alternatively, again in Germany, the work councils, with a strong voice in corporate strategy, would fit more closely with the private than the civil sector.

The influence of labor unions has been in decline over the past decades in contrast to the other institutions of civil society. This declining power coupled with their political role in so many societies may account for the paucity of discussion about labor unions in the current literature on civil society.

9. For a detailed discussion of the concept of NGOs, the origin of the term, and their legal status, see Olz 1997.

10. Fisher notes the GSO and GRSO distinction, emphasizing the importance of the vertical and horizontal networks (Fisher 1998, pp. 4–10; Fisher 1993). An early standard based on Latin America can be found in Carroll 1992. Reilly (1998, p. 181) presents the following acronyms "to guide the reader through the alphabet soup": CSO = civil society organization, increasing in use; GSO = grassroots support organizations, providing goods and services to organized poor; MO = membership organization, cooperatives, and neighborhood or ethnic organizations; PDO = private development organizations, a term of infrequent use; NGO = nongovernmental organization, term used by the UN and countries other than the U.S.; PVO = private voluntary organization, U.S. term generally used for an international NGO; QUANGO = quasi-nongovernmental organization. Tavis uses the term development intermediating organization to include the activities of grassroot support organizations in both the governmental and nongovernmental sectors (Tavis 1997, pp. 70, 283).

11. The role of NGOs differs by country and region. In the Near East, NGOs have not become as important as in other developing countries and tend to serve religious and other more traditional roles (Fisher 1998, p. 32). Near Eastern NGOs have numerically increased in democratizing countries while, in the conservative, authoritarian Arab regimes, the voluntary organizations are traditional charities rather than NGOs as defined above (Fisher, p. 59, referring to Kandil).

In Latin America, however, NGOs tend to be more autonomous than in other areas. With democratization, then, nature is changing from a focus on civil rights to sustainable development and special interests.

The activities of Asian NGOs are "largely determined by the government and its agencies" (Tandon, p. 28, as quoted in Fisher 1993, p. 48). Also governmental policy in Asia is more likely to be schizophrenic than in other regions (Fisher 1993, p. 50). In China, the government "has been omnipresent and overbearing for four decades and has left virtually no room for private voluntary organizations" (Serrano, p. 276, as quoted in Fisher 1998, p. 49).

12. Fisher argues against this generalization: "Not surprisingly, therefore, GRSOs tend to proliferate under both repressive and less repressive regimes that lack local implementation capability" (Fisher 1998, p. 60). She summarizes: "The generally positive relationship between pluralism and the proliferation of NGOs is only part of

the story. Indeed, GROs can flourish under authoritarian regimes with the ability to implement basic needs at the local level, as well as under more democratic regimes of all types. GRSO proliferation, however, provides evidence supporting Estelle James's (1987) argument that nonprofit organizations flourish when excess demand is *not* met by government, whether the government is democratic or dictatorial. In other words, GRSOs proliferate except under regimes that are both dictatorial and have considerable capacity to reach down and implement policy to local areas" (ibid., p. 61).

13. Jorge Vargas argues that the lack of uniformity in the civil sector is a function of its organizing principle. If the organizing principle for the civil sector is pluralism, then one would expect the sector to be very diverse (personal communication, March 23, 1998).

14. For a discussion of multinational corporate organizations as enterprise networks, see Tavis 1997, pp. 384–88.

## Bibliography

Allsopp, Michael E. (1994). *The New Dictionary of Catholic Social Thought.* Editor, Judith A. Dwyer (Collegeville: Liturgical Press), pp. 927–29.

Ba, Moussa (July–August 1995). "The Experience and Limitations of NGOs in West Africa." *The Courier*, no. 152, pp. 69–70.

Birkinshaw, Julian M., and Allen J. Morrison (1995). "Configurations of Strategy and Structure in Subsidiaries of Multinational Corporations." *Journal of International Business Studies*, vol. 26, no. 4, fourth quarter, pp. 729–53.

Bossuyt, Jean, and Patrick Develtere (July–August 1995). "Between Autonomy and Identity: The Financing Dilemma of NGOs." *The Courier*, no. 152, pp. 76–78.

Carroll, Thomas F. (1992). *Intermediary NGOs: The Supporting Link in Grassroots Development* (West Hartford, Conn.: Kumarian Press).

Chalmers, Douglas, Carlos M. Vilas, Katherine Hite, Scott B. Martin, Kerlanne Piester, and Monique Segarra, editors (1997). *The New Politics of Inequality in Latin America: Rethinking Participation and Representation* (Oxford: Oxford University Press.

Cohen, J. L., and A. Arato (1992). *Civil Society and Political Theory* (Cambridge: MIT Press).

The Commission on Global Governance (1996). *Our Global Neighborhood.* The Report of the Commission on Global Governance (Oxford: Oxford University Press).

Crombrugghe, Genevieve (July–August 1995). "Institutional Support for NGOs in the South." *The Courier*, no. 152, pp. 71–72.

De George, Richard T. (1993). *Competing with Integrity in International Business* (New York: Oxford University Press).

Enderle, Georges (1997). "The Role of Corporate Ethics in a Market Economy and Civil Society." Chapter 16 in *Civil Society in a Chinese Context*, Cultural Heritage &

Contemporary Change Series III, Asia, vol. 15. Editors, Wang Miaoyang, Yu Xuanmeng, and Manuel B. Dy (Washington, D.C.: The Council for Research in Values and Philosophy).

Falisse, Michel (July–August 1995). "NGOs Torn between Subordination and Independence." *The Courier*, no. 152, p. 86.

Fisher, Julie (1998). *Non-governments, NGOs, and the Political Development of the Third World* (West Hartford, Conn.: Kumarian Press).

Fisher, Julie (1993). *The Road from Rio: Sustainable Development and the Nongovernmental Movement in the Third World* (Westport, Conn.: Praeger).

Glade, William P., and Lee A. Tavis (Winter 1997). "Actualizing the Developmental Response of Multinational Corporations: The Case of Agribusiness in the Mexican Countryside." *University of Pennsylvania Journal of International Economic Law*, vol. 18, no. 4, pp. 1211–34.

Gregoire, Thibault (July–August 1995). "The Ethics of Collecting Money." *The Courier*, no. 152, pp. 83–85.

Gregoire, Thibault (July–August 1995). "NGOs." *The Courier*, no. 152, p. 63.

Gregoire, Thibault (July–August 1995). "The NGOs Refuse to Be Mere Onlookers." *The Courier*, no. 152, pp. 73–75.

Gregoire, Thibault (July–August 1995). "On the Diversity and Role of NGOs." *The Courier*, no. 152, pp. 66–68.

Hug, James, S.J., (May 16, 1997). "Covenant to Renew Community and Creation." Paper in draft.

International Monetary Fund (May 26, 1997). "Forces of Globalization Must Be Embraced." *IMF Survey*, vol. 26, no. 10, p. 154.

James, Estelle (1987). "The Nonprofit Sector in Comparative Perspective." In *The Nonprofit Sector: A Research Handbook*. Editor, Walter Powell (New Haven: Yale University Press).

Kandil, Amani (1994). "The Status of the Third Sector in the Arab World." In *Citizens Strengthening Civil Society*. Editors, Miguel Darch de Oliveira and Rajesh Tandon (Washington, D.C.: CIVICUS [World Alliance for Citizen Participation]).

Kim, Kwan, S. (November 1997). "Income Distribution and Poverty: An Interregional Comparison." *World Development*, vol. 25, no. 11, pp. 1909–24.

Kim, Kwan S., and Robert J. Riemer, SVD, editors (1997). *Economic Cooperation and Integration: East Asian Experiences*. Proceedings of the Nanzan-Notre Dame International Conference held at the University of Notre Dame in 1995 and at Nanzan University in 1996 (Notre Dame: Kellogg Institute for International Studies).

Laurent, Pierre (July–August 1995). "Emergencies and Development." *The Courier*, no. 152, pp. 89–90.

Malkin, Elisabeth (January 26, 1998). "Now, Mexico's Unions Have a Chance at Real Freedom." Editor, John Templeman. *Business Week*, p. 46.

Meintjes, Garth (October 6, 1997, and published as chapter 5 in this volume).

Miaoyang, Wang, Yu Xuanmeng, and Manuel B. Dy, editors (1997). *Civil Society in a Chinese Context*, Chinese Philosophical Studies, XV. Cultural Heritage & Contemporary Change Series III, Asia, vol. 15 (Washington, D.C.: The Council for Research in Values and Philosophy).

Nielsen, Brita Schioldann (July–August 1995). "The Dreaming Dromedaries of the Desert Meet the Bothered Bureaucrats of Brussels." *The Courier,* no. 152, pp. 81–82.

Nielsen, Waldemar (1970). *The Endangered Sector* (New York: Columbia University Press).

Olz, Martin A. (Winter 1997). "Non-Governmental Organizations in Regional Human Rights Systems." *Columbia Human Rights Law Review,* vol. 28, no. 2, pp. 307–74.

Ravallion, Martin, and Shaohua Chen (May 1997). "What Can New Survey Data Tell Us about Recent Changes in Distribution and Poverty?" *The World Bank Economic Review,* vol. 11, no. 2, pp. 357–81.

Reilly, Charles A. (1998). "Balancing State, Market, and Civil Society: NGOs for a New Development Consensus." Chapter 8 in *Poverty and Inequality in Latin America: Issues and New Challenges.* Editors, Guillermo A. O'Donnell and Victor Tokman (Notre Dame: University of Notre Dame Press).

Reilly, Charles A., editor (1995). *New Paths to Democratic Development in Latin America: The Rise of NGO-Municipal Collaboration* (Boulder: Lynne Riemer Publishers).

Reyes, David, and Ithai Stern (Spring 1998). "A New Global Power Paradigm." Research paper prepared for IIPS/MBA 611, The Development Gap and Multinational Corporate Responsibility, in the College of Business Administration at the University of Notre Dame.

Rocamora, Joel (July–August 1995). "Changing Perspectives in the Philippines." *The Courier,* no. 152, pp. 78–80.

Rodriguez, Victoria E. (1993). "The Politics of Decentralization in Mexico: From *Municipio Libre* to *Solidaridad.*" *Bulletin of Latin American Research,* vol. 12, no. 2, pp. 133–45.

Rodrik, Dani (1997). *Has Globalization Gone Too Far?* (Washington, D.C.: Institute for International Economics).

Ryelandt, Bernard (July–August 1995). "Why Does the European Community Work with NGOs?" *The Courier,* no. 152, pp. 64–65.

Salamon, Lester (1994). "The Rise of the Nonprofit Sector." *Foreign Affairs,* vol. 73, no. 4.

Stockton, Nicholas (July–August 1995). "NGOs—Subcontractors or Innovators in Unstable Situations?" *The Courier,* no. 152, pp. 87–88.

Tavis, Lee A. (Spring 1998). "Globalization and Multinational Corporate Responsibility." *Report: The Joan B. Kroc Institute for International Peace Studies,* no. 14, pp. 1–4.

Tavis, Lee A. (1997). *Power and Responsibility: Multinational Managers and Developing Country Concerns* (Notre Dame: University of Notre Dame Press).

*World Development Report, 1997, The State in a Changing World* (New York: Oxford University Press).

*World Economic Outlook* (May 1997) (Washington, D.C.: International Monetary Fund).

Yamamoto, Tadashi, editor (1995). *Emerging Civil Society in the Asia Pacific Community: Nongovernmental Underpinnings of the Emerging Asia Pacific Regional Community.* A 25th Anniversary Project of JCIE (Singapore and Tokyo, Japan: Institute of Southeast Asia Studies and Japan Center for International Exchange).

PART 2

— ✹ —

# The Past as Prologue

*Experience as a Teacher*

# 3

# Business Codes and Conduct in a Global Political Economy

JOHN M. KLINE

Discussions of global codes of conduct emerged on the international scene in the early 1970s, near the peak of antagonistic relations between multinational enterprises (MNEs) and national governments, particularly those in developing host countries. A quarter century later, much has changed. MNEs have evolved and proliferated. Many governments have changed in composition and ideology, including in their perceptions of MNEs. Nongovernmental groups have expanded their organization and activism on MNE-related issues. And finally, the meaning, methods, and motivations for seeking codes of conduct have changed, broadening but also blurring their potential role and impact in international relations.

The current context for developing global codes is, in many respects, both positive and promising. Multiple code precedents have already been established, drawing into dialogue people from various sectors of the global society. It would be an exaggeration to suggest that consensus is near, particularly in the business community, on the merits of a global code that addresses the conduct of international enterprises. However, further constructive action appears possible that could enhance mutual understanding among parties involved in the code debate. Greater attention to improving communication and cooperation among these groups may, in fact, be a practical prerequisite to agreement on a global business code of conduct per se.

The question of whether "the time has come" for global codes of conduct should not be conceptualized principally as a search for the set of normative precepts whose intellectual and emotional merits will be inherently persuasive to all parties. Alongside or perhaps even in advance of the process of evaluating, comparing, and drafting specific code text, certain core issues merit further consideration regarding both rights and responsibilities among the principal parties. In particular, a more thorough analysis and dialogue is needed to define the parameters for business responsibilities with relation to essentially political issues in an economically interdependent but politically fragmented world. This essay examines the political dynamic driving the emergence of global codes and the consequent challenge to traditional principles that sought to limit business actions on national political issues. The task of addressing this emerging conundrum regarding business rights and responsibilities in political matters should be assigned high priority among the steps being taken to develop global codes of conduct.

## A Quarter Century of Change

The origin of the contemporary debate over global codes of conduct arises from the turmoil that surrounded expanding MNE activities in the late 1960s, when foreign direct investment (FDI) became a more important vehicle for organizing and controlling the activities of international enterprises. In contrast with traditional trading relationships, FDI establishes a foreign business presence within a nation, often incorporated as a separate legal entity that becomes a "citizen" of that nation. This firm is, in essence, both foreign and domestic while its parent enterprise acquires "citizenship" in many countries throughout the world. Although MNEs engage in global business operations, they must do so through nationally regulated economies whose governments often pursue competing and sometimes conflicting objectives and interests. Without a global political authority to mediate national demands, as well as to monitor and regulate boundary-spanning enterprises, disagreements and disputes inevitably arise over the role, impact, and actions of MNEs.

Global codes can address the conduct of governments and/or business enterprises. (Conceptually, codes might cover other nongovernmental entities as well, but to date there has been less attention to this notion.) This chapter focuses principally on the idea of codes of conduct that deal with the activities of international enterprises and are voluntary in nature rather than legally binding. These two elements—voluntary codes covering international business activities or responsibilities—form the heart of the issue and shape the nature of the current challenge.

Greater progress has been made on agreements that identify and define governmental responsibilities toward foreign investors than on ones that define responsibilities of international enterprises to the societies in which they operate. Some intergovernmental agreements are binding, at least on signatory parties.[1] Other negotiations promote agreed standards that lack a legal commitment, or mix and match binding and voluntary procedures, sometimes including coverage of business as well as governmental actions.[2] The differences in these approaches reflect a fundamental reality regarding codes of conduct versus the traditional international law of enforceable treaties. Codes represent a type of "soft law" when they lack legal enforcement and generally depend upon the force of moral suasion or mobilized public opinion to spur compliance.

International "soft law" may emerge on issues that raise enough public concern and activism to gain international attention but which lack sufficient political consensus for the detailed interpretations and applications necessary for legally enforceable requirements. In the past, this situation would simply leave the issue unresolved, with the public spotlight focused on the inability of governments to agree on a course of action. During the 1970s, however, governments discovered a new type of international instrument.[3] Voluntary business codes of conduct, often backed by nonbinding governmental or intergovernmental endorsements, can shift the spotlight of attention—as well as the burden for producing satisfactory results—to the international business community.

Governmentally sanctioned business codes typically comprise a set of broad principles dealing with the activities of international enterprises. The codes lack specificity due to insufficient political consensus; if the basis for political agreement supported a detailed code of conduct, it could support a legally binding accord. As a result, parties addressed by these voluntary codes have apparent flexibility in applying the standards but are ultimately left open to the potentially divergent judgment of disparate groups interested in the issue. After endorsing a global business code, individual national governments are essentially free to sit back and evaluate business activities after-the-fact, deciding on a case-by-case basis whether to engage in public criticism (but not legal action) regarding an individual firm's performance.

While providing governments with an additional policy option, "soft law" codes also give nongovernmental groups a new way to influence business activities. On many issues, these groups might prefer new laws that would directly regulate international business behavior at the national, extraterritorial, or intergovernmental levels. However, if sufficient political support cannot yet (if ever) be mobilized to achieve the passage of new law, then nonbinding "soft law" may be viewed as a next-best alternative. Broad business-conduct guidelines can be cited in attempts to gain additional leverage to change enterprise behavior in specific cases.

For their part, MNEs tend to view the development of global codes of conduct with a skeptical if not hostile attitude, founded largely on the defensive posture adopted by corporate law departments. This position stems primarily from two interrelated concerns. First, many enterprises see code discussions as exercises aimed at laying the groundwork, if not the superstructure, for expanded legal regulation of international business activities. Therefore, executives often regard even voluntary code standards as incipient law, objecting to their imprecise formulations and potential for manipulation. This business apprehension is fed by a second, related concern that corporate critics will use, and in some cases abuse, the role of voluntary codes to attack specific corporate actions. Even with governmental assurances that voluntary business guidelines will not be used in some type of kangaroo court, business executives fear that critics will employ the codes as weapons in a battle for public opinion, interpreting and applying broad guidelines to specific circumstances in ways that will damage a corporation's image and reputation.

These two concerns highlight a dilemma for MNEs. Although the business community likes the certainty of clear standards that apply equally to all enterprises, it does not favor the passage of inflexible legal regulations. In addition, international political realities suggest that the realm of global legal regulation will expand slowly, if at all, in the near future. On the other hand, while voluntary codes of conduct permit greater flexibility for companies operating in cross-cultural environments, their inherent ambiguity and the uneven adherence of competitors can leave enterprises that comply open to damaging public challenges over code interpretations. Lower-profile competitor firms may largely avoid the costs of both compliance and public criticism.

This brief overview suggests the type of political dynamic at play among the major government, business, and other nongovernmental actors involved in the discussion of global codes. None of these groups are fully satisfied with voluntary business codes of conduct. However, as a relatively new type of instrument, global codes hold some attraction—if for no other reason than that the possible alternatives appear unrealistic or even more unsatisfying. International law to govern MNE activities will develop slowly and in piecemeal fashion because there is insufficient political consensus to permit a quicker and fuller formulation. Taking no action appears equally undesirable. The growing reach and impact of MNE activities have raised serious political, economic, and social concerns in many countries.

Perhaps "the time has come" for global business codes of conduct, but what should they cover, and how?

## Exploring Political Standards for Global Business Codes

Charges of inappropriate MNE involvement in national politics provided the initial spark for the debate on global codes of conduct. The seminal event was the overthrow of President Salvador Allende in Chile, accompanied by allegations that ITT had sought U.S. CIA support to destabilize Allende's socialist government. This event appeared to confirm widespread suspicions in many developing countries that foreign (especially U.S.) MNEs were ready, willing, and able to intervene in domestic politics to advance their own interests, at times in collusion with home country governments. In reality, this event turned out to be more the exception than the rule, but its impact helped propel code negotiations and provided an early area of apparent consensus on conduct standards. A general principle of MNE noninterference in a nation's internal political affairs emerged as a commonly cited and generally accepted principle in code discussions.

For example, the 1976 United Nations Secretariat report on *Transnational Corporations: Issues Involved in the Formulation of a Code of Conduct* states: "The prohibition of political intervention by transnational corporations in the country of operation is another principle beyond dispute."[4] The strongest condemnation was reserved for political intervention aimed at governmental overthrows. A parallel concern was that home governments might use MNEs "as instruments of foreign policy" to intervene in the internal affairs of host countries.[5] Less flagrant forms of MNE political involvement also generated opposition, leading to calls for corporations to abstain from all interference in a country's internal political affairs. This standard was "envisaged as covering pressure of various forms in support of or against a Government" as well as illegal political contributions. Particular concern was voiced regarding MNE actions that might support governments that followed racist policies or engaged in serious violations of human rights. On the other hand, the report noted that discreet public expressions of views by corporations on governmental policies such as taxes or customs duties should be permitted when such actions were routinely allowed to domestic enterprises.[6]

Broadly similar principles regarding MNE political involvement appeared in other forums. A working document prepared by a special U.S. Chamber of Commerce task force in 1975 proposed "Elements of Global Business Conduct for Possible Inclusion in Individual Company Statements." Among the suggested elements was a corporate commitment "[to] refrain from any involvement in partisan political activity." The document noted, however, that a firm could "communicate its public positions through appropriate channels on issues relating to its business operations."[7] In addition, governments and many corporations in the industrialized countries endorsed the 1976 OECD Guidelines for Multinational Enterprises. The guidelines called on MNEs to "abstain from any improper involvement in local political activities" and to refrain from political contributions, unless legally permissible.[8]

By 1980, the draft UN code section dealing with prohibited political interference was described in the following manner:

> Transnational corporations should not interfere in the internal political affairs of countries in which they operate, particularly by resorting to subversive activities, attempting to overthrow governments or to alter by pressure or coercion the political and social systems in these countries. Transnational corporations should act as good corporate citizens and abstain from activities of a political nature clearly inconsistent with the domestic legislation or established practice in such countries. Transnational corporations are further to abstain from improper interference in intergovernmental relations.[9]

The positions developed in these and other related code discussions can be summarized in the generalized principle of MNE noninterference in a nation's internal political affairs. This principle, which garnered widespread agreement, evolved several subsidiary elaborations, including:

1. MNEs should not engage in improper political activities, especially any pressure to overthrow a country's government or political system.
2. MNEs should not be used by home governments as a vehicle to interfere in another country's internal political affairs.
3. MNEs should not engage in partisan political activities, except perhaps in legally permissible political contributions.
4. MNE actions to express opinions on public policies relevant to business operations are not political interference when taken openly in a manner consistent with routine local business practice.

The distinct emphasis in these guidelines is on the restriction or prohibition of MNE activity. The elaborated basic principle seems clear—corporations should not become involved in political activities except for open, public expressions of views on policies directly related to their operations.

Subsequent developments have appeared to call into question this early agreement on a political noninterference principle. In recent cases, MNEs confronted growing pressures to assume more activist responsibilities for political matters in countries where they operate, especially where those countries have been involved in significant human rights abuses. Pressure is sometimes applied even to firms that may have little or no invested presence in the country in question. This quandary arises in part because the application and interpretation of global business codes of conduct is subject to ambiguous social and political processes. The seeming imperatives of immediate, case-specific goals can overwhelm basic principles unless there is commensurate attention to the longer-term implications of such actions. The current state of dialogue among major parties to the global code debate does not lend itself to this type of reasoned weighing of short- and long-term implications. Greater maturity and trust must be developed in this dialogue if voluntary business codes of conduct are to work effectively.

### Cases and Conundrums

The general principle of MNE political nonintervention derived largely from reaction to the ITT incident in Chile during the early 1970s. First revealed by U.S. columnist Jack Anderson and later documented in hearings by the U.S. Senate Foreign Relations Committee, this incident showed ITT involved in attempts to enlist other investors and the U.S. government, including the CIA, in efforts to prevent the electoral victory of socialist leader Salvador Allende. These revelations prompted President Allende to condemn ITT's actions before the United Nations and impelled a governmental takeover of the firm's Chilean interests.[10] The death of President Allende in a 1973 military coup added poignancy to this incident and helped spur the debate on codes of conduct.

A second, somewhat less well-known case from around the same time actually provides a better and more representative illustration of the conundrums posed by MNE involvement in political matters. Gulf Oil began exploration in Angola's Cabinda province in 1954 and struck oil in 1966. By 1971, the firm had invested $150 million and reached its production goal of 150,000 barrels per day. During this time, Angola was a colony of Portugal, occasioning protests by some U.S. religious and political groups that charged Gulf's activities supported colonial rule. Gulf responded that the firm was politically neutral and its actions aided Angola's economic development, including jobs, skills, and medical services. Gulf further argued that its withdrawal would simply turn the facility over to the government, resulting in increased rather than decreased revenue to support governmental policies.[11]

The political dynamics changed in April 1974 when a military coup in Portugal began a process whereby Angola received its independence but local warfare erupted between various groups vying for control of the new nation. These groups received support from competing foreign countries, with factions backed by the Soviet Union and Cuba on one side and the United States and South Africa on the other. Gulf attempted to remain politically neutral, but payments due the Angolan government from Gulf's oil production placed the firm in the position of aiding whichever group received the funds. For example, a two-month payment of $116 million in late 1975 effectively supported the Soviet/Cuban-backed group (MPLA) that controlled both Cabinda province and the capital city of Luanda, while the U.S. CIA was reportedly channeling $30 million to an opposing faction. Gulf's discomfort with this situation was obvious. It attempted to extract itself by temporarily suspending operations while placing subsequent tax and royalty payments in an escrow account that would go to a future Angolan government that effectively controlled the country and was recognized by the world community.[12]

These attempts to be politically neutral were, of course, neither entirely neutral nor successful. Apparent inaction still had the impact of action. By suspending operations and placing subsequent payments in escrow, Gulf was, in effect, disadvantaging the MPLA faction that was in effective control of Cabinda province and the capital city and that had benefited from the past payments. The MPLA's leader charged that Gulf acted under U.S. government pressure and was engaged in "economic war" against Angola. In the end, events "on the ground" obviated the need for Gulf's escrow option as the MPLA soon extended its control and gained enough official recognition that even the U.S. secretary of state acquiesced in a resumption of payments.[13]

In retrospect, what action could Gulf have taken that would have been politically neutral? What if one faction had controlled Cabinda and another had controlled Luanda—who gets the money? Would any change from the status quo ante have necessarily constituted political interference by Gulf in Angola's internal political affairs? Would a conscious decision not to act to change the status quo still effectively constitute action? This case points out the practical difficulty of implementing a principle of noninterference in a country's internal political affairs when an enterprise is already present and its operations are significant enough to affect domestic political dynamics, whether the effect is direct or indirect, intended or unintended.

The Angola case also illustrates the conundrum that emerges when interest groups recognize the potential influence MNEs can exert in foreign nations and seek to employ that influence to advance their chosen objectives, even if (or precisely because) such action may constitute political interference in another country. Advocates of Gulf's withdrawal from Angola when it was a Portuguese colony were seeking precisely to advance a political objective that would, in effect, overthrow the then prevailing political system. As worthy as the end of colonialism may be as an objective, the fact remains that this goal sought systemic political change through MNE action—the proposed withdrawal by Gulf was to be a means to that desired end.

The contrast with the ITT/Chile case is stark. ITT's actions (on its own or in collaboration with its home government) to influence Chile's elections were condemned as unacceptable corporate conduct (i.e., political interference), but action by Gulf that might help end a prevailing political system (colonialism) or advance the interests of a favored warring faction could be construed as acceptable or even desirable corporate conduct (even though such actions would involve interfering in the country's political affairs).

The principle of political noninterference forged in the Chilean experience clashed with calls for corporate actions to advance particular political goals. In other words, the standard for the "rightness" of MNE conduct was shifting from a process-based rule against political interference to a case-dependent evaluation of whether projected outcomes might justify such involvement. With such an outcomes-oriented standard, the real question then becomes "who chooses the desired outcomes?"

If a national or international consensus exists on the desired outcome in a specific case, then presumably the relevant political authorities could mandate corporate actions that would advance the consensus goal. If a sufficient consensus does not exist to generate binding political decisions, then the business community is left to determine its own actions, or inaction. In these cases, MNEs face increasing pressures from nongovernmental groups that seek corporate conduct to advance their favored objectives. But this leads to further questions for MNEs. Should corporate political involvement follow the dictates of market pressures instigated by activist groups, or should MNEs develop their own set of political objectives for countries in which they operate? The alternative is to return to a process-oriented standard of political noninterference, with the inherent difficulties of implementation and interpretation already discussed. This conundrum outlines the practical reality that must be addressed by a debate on global codes of conduct.

Focusing the issue even more specifically, most debate does not involve instances where MNEs take the initiative to influence a country's internal politics to their advantage. Although this type of action certainly occurs, it generally involves discrete business policy issues rather than the nature of the broader political system. The most politically controversial cases for a global code of conduct arise where the indirect impact of corporate actions either (1) supports a political system that is objectionable to significant interest groups, or (2) could help weaken an objectionable host government if the MNE altered its operations or withdrew from the country. In other words, the main dilemmas arise in cases where either the unintended, indirect effect of

MNE operations is at issue, or a proactive change in MNE operations is sought in order to alter political outcomes in a host country. Both of these situations were reflected in debates over MNE activities in South Africa.

## South Africa

Until the recent advent of representative democracy, apartheid formed the basis of South Africa's political system, infusing and enforcing racial discrimination throughout the nation's economic and social structure.[14] Despite nearly universal condemnation of apartheid outside South Africa, national governments could not achieve consensus on fully effective international actions to force an end to apartheid. Outside intervention to stop apartheid would essentially mean overthrowing that nation's government. Notwithstanding arguments regarding the illegitimacy of the South African regime, governments were unwilling to violate the principle of national sovereignty or compromise other competing political or security interests.

Trade with South Africa was progressively tightened, but most countries did not extend restrictive measures to their firms operating within the South African economy. Without a legal or clear political mandate to direct their actions, MNEs could decide individually whether or how to continue operations in South Africa. The central issues regarding corporate conduct revolved around two considerations: (1) how broadly to draw the circle of corporate responsibility beyond the core workplace, and (2) what type of political involvement was appropriate for MNEs to protest the apartheid system.

Under pressure from various groups of shareholders, employees, and other activist organizations, most firms altered their behavior to eliminate manifestations of apartheid in the immediate workplace. These firms also usually extended financial assistance to the surrounding community. The question of corporate political activity was more troublesome, however. Many foreign investors, individually and collectively, openly advocated political and social reforms in South Africa that would change the apartheid system but cautiously avoided involvement in other types of activities that could be construed as domestic political interference. This action did not satisfy critics who charged that MNE operations were contributing, even if indirectly and unintentionally, to maintaining the apartheid regime's economic base. By extension, the withdrawal of foreign investment could weaken the economy and perhaps destabilize the government. Although some investors eventually withdrew from South Africa, virtually no companies attributed their action to political motivations, citing instead the country's deteriorating economic conditions.

Should MNEs undertake actions knowing, and perhaps even intending, to destabilize a nation's economy in order to cause the overthrow of its political regime? The answer to this question, indisputably a central issue for any global code of conduct, appears surprisingly ambiguous if based on the debate over corporate conduct in South Africa. Similar to a game called *Scruples* that I sometimes play with family and friends, the answer would seem to be "it depends" rather than a clear "yes" or "no."

In the South African case, the evolution of standards for corporate conduct are reflected in the progressive expansion and final abandonment (by some) of the so-called "Sullivan Principles." At first, these conduct standards challenged firms to eliminate racially discriminatory practices in the workplace while instituting training and other programs to improve conditions for black and other nonwhite employees. Later modifications to the principles extended and elaborated these standards, including a requirement that firms oppose apartheid laws and regulations, seek their repeal, and provide legal and financial assistance to campaigns by nonwhites for equal access. Reverend Leon Sullivan endorsed this extension of the principles' corporate conduct standards as a necessary step:

> Starting in the workplace and extending to the communities, the businesses must do all they can do to help change the inequalities of and injustices against black people. And the businesses must work to influence the government to rescind its unjust racial laws. Otherwise, the multinational companies have no moral justification for remaining in South Africa and should be compelled to leave the country.[15]

Sullivan appeared to go even further when he urged U.S. business leaders to "make a united front" with South African businessmen who had called for an end to apartheid and endorsed political power-sharing after meeting outside the country with members of the outlawed African National Congress.[16] How should a global code of conduct answer a question about whether MNE executives in a country should meet with outlawed political groups actively seeking to overthrow an existing government?

In the end, the Reverend Sullivan despaired of the voluntary code approach and urged the U.S. government to make compliance mandatory. He then set a deadline for the abolition of apartheid and, when the deadline passed, disassociated himself from the principles that had carried his name and called on corporations to withdraw from South Africa. Somewhat ironically, as Sullivan moved away from his principles, the U.S. government took steps to impose a very similar set of corporate conduct standards on U.S. firms operating in South Africa. The governmental approach varied in two important respects, however. First, the principles were not imposed as direct regulation but rather as conditions for receiving U.S. government trade assistance. Second, the government-endorsed principles did not include the amplification that called upon corporations to become involved in political activities to change the apartheid system. Thus, even as the U.S. government increased its own coercive pressures on South Africa to change the apartheid system (including measures that used MNEs as instruments of U.S. policy—prohibiting sales to South African government customers, banning new investments, and setting conduct standards for operations in the country), these same political authorities were reluctant to impose or even endorse a principle urging direct business actions intentionally aimed at changing a foreign government's policy.

A similar ambiguity can be found in how South African issues were addressed in the final draft of the UN Code of Conduct, before that exercise was abandoned. The draft code contained a principle on "Non-interference in internal affairs of host countries" that proscribed interference in a host nation's internal affairs or in "activities of a political nature" that are not permitted by the country's laws or established policies and practices. This negative injunction was paired, however, with a positive declaration that MNEs "shall respect human rights and fundamental freedoms in countries in which they operate."[17]

With specific reference to South Africa (and Namibia), the draft code called on corporations to comply strictly with obligations resulting from Security Council decisions and to respect other UN resolutions. The draft code also states:

> Transnational corporations shall refrain from operations and activities supporting and sustaining the racist minority regime in South Africa in maintaining the system of *apartheid* and the illegal occupation of Namibia.

> Transnational corporations shall engage in appropriate activities within their competence with a view to eliminating racial discrimination and all other aspects of the system of *apartheid*.[18]

These formulations simply beg the question. Would *any* MNE activities in South Africa necessarily support and sustain the minority government, therefore forcing investors to withdraw from the country in order to comply with the standard? Exactly what are "appropriate activities within their competence" when MNEs are called upon to help eliminate racial discrimination; and can you undertake such activities if you must withdraw your operations? The code standards in this area lay obligations on the corporations beyond those imposed by governmental directives, while providing little guidance as to how such obligations should be met. Overall, the draft code pairs demands for restraints on MNE political activities with assertions of responsibility for activism to achieve political goals, without addressing or clarifying the conflict between these sets of standards.

The South African experience is pivotal to understanding current developments regarding MNE conduct standards in countries where unrepresentative or repressive governments engage in significant violations of human rights. The fight against apartheid drew attention to the capabilities and potential impact that MNEs can have in many host countries; it also brought a realization that individual businesses may be more susceptible to social and economic pressures than governmental institutions. The combination of these two factors, capability and vulnerability, makes MNEs an attractive target for activist groups who are not yet able to convince political authorities to take effective action to advance their goals.

The result has been a proliferation of calls for corporate actions to influence political conditions in other counties. Human rights violations in nations such as Burma, Nigeria, and China may not have sparked the same level of international community solidarity as occurred in the fight against South Africa's apartheid system, but similar calls are now heard for corporate withdrawal or other specified political activities with regard to foreign investments in those countries. But such calls do nothing to answer the questions of in which nations, and under what circumstances, MNEs should engage in such politically directed activities; and what is the appropriate range of their competence and responsibilities?

### Business Rights and Responsibilities on Political Issues

A central issue in the task of defining standards for global business conduct will be addressing the link between rights and responsibilities on political issues. The concept that rights should entail responsibilities is commonly acknowledged, if not always practiced. The reverse relationship, however, is less often discussed. Should one assign the duties and obligations that accompany responsibility statements without conceding some concomitant rights for action to carry out those responsibilities? In the global arena, MNEs are being asked to assume responsibilities for essentially political issues and conditions in countries where they operate, without much attention to the concomitant political rights that might accompany such responsibilities. Code of conduct provisions reflect this dichotomy when they prohibit MNEs from interfering in a nation's political affairs, yet still give the corporations affirmative duties to uphold and advance certain political objectives.

A danger in global codes of conduct is that their voluntary nature and often ambiguous content can obscure important relationships that would have to be addressed in a more precise, binding document. The parameters for appropriate corporate political actions must be understood and defined more specifically if global codes are to provide meaningful guidance for corporate conduct as well as a fair standard against which to evaluate business activity. In approaching this task, a number of component issues will require serious discussion and decision.

An initial issue is whether MNEs should be used as instruments by groups outside a country to influence the political conditions within that country. One aspect of this issue concerns the use of MNEs as the means of exerting home country government influence. Governments have traditionally employed external trade controls, such as embargoes, to coerce other countries to change their policies. Influence extended through a corporate entity invested and legally incorporated in another sovereign nation is more intrusive, however, and might be better characterized as internal intervention rather than external coercion.[19]

A second consideration is who assumes the responsibility for deciding whether and when to use MNEs as political policy instruments. Generally national governments bear the responsibility for conducting international relations, but the revolutions in communication and transportation technologies have given private interest-groups and individuals greater knowledge and certain capabilities to engage in international affairs. In the United States, multiple social activist groups as well as city and state governments become directly and intentionally engaged in attempts to influence political developments in other countries. This activism often seeks its expression through exerting pressure on MNEs to alter their behavior or withdraw from foreign locations in order to change political conditions in those countries. It is probably fair to say that many of these same organizations might condemn the use of corporate influence to alter another nations' political conditions if the MNEs were pursuing opposing political objectives, either at their own initiative or at the behest of others.

This dichotomy brings into focus the critical question about MNE involvement in a nation's political affairs. If MNEs bear some responsibility on political issues, do they also have a concomitant right to decide whether, when, and toward what objectives to act, or are they simply instruments to be used by other public or private sector actors; if the latter is the case, then to which actors should they respond? Pointing to a broad, general standard of respect for human rights as a guideline for corporate conduct is an insufficient answer because it begs the question of who is responsible for interpreting and applying that standard in individual cases.

Should MNEs have an acknowledged right to decide what political conditions should prevail in the countries in which they do business, and a responsibility to use their influence to bring about such conditions? Is this the societal function that we really want to assign to private business entities as a general principle? If not, then should corporations either refrain from intentional involvement in political activities, or act only as instruments under the direction of public authorities or, perhaps, private interest-groups? Many individuals may find none of these alternatives fully satisfying, but some guiding assumptions or principles must be consciously chosen if global codes are to evolve meaningful and fair standards for corporate involvement in political issues. The following section identifies some issues and suggests a few possible formulations that might be considered in discussions over how to develop a global code of conduct.

### Possible Parameters for Global Business Conduct on Political Issues

A beginning premise in defining the parameters for global business conduct on political issues is a recognition that MNEs cannot escape all connection to the political conditions in countries where they invest. MNE operations will necessarily have an impact on the local political situation, direct or indirect, intentional or unintentional.[20] This recognition places a premium on the initial foreign investment decision; it is at this point of initiation where a corporation's right to choose, and its concomitant responsibility, is greatest. Corporations should weigh the potential ethical implications of their investment in a nation just as carefully as they weigh business factors. Foreign investors expend time and resources to evaluate political conditions in a potential foreign investment site, conducting political risk assessments to ensure that their capital does not face unacceptable risks of expropriation. Equivalent care should be taken to conduct an ethical risk assessment that evaluates whether prevailing and projected political conditions present an acceptable ethical environment within which to conduct business.

Various groups already provide evaluations of political conditions in nations around the world. Governments, international organizations, and private-sector groups issue reports on human rights conditions in individual countries. Governments decide whether or not to grant diplomatic recognition to other governments, and a home government can prohibit any MNE under its effective legal control from investing in another country. For any nation in which they are legally permitted to invest, however, an MNE has a right to decide whether or not to undertake that investment and it has a responsibility to take into consideration ethical standards related to political conditions in that country.

Once invested, an MNE assumes certain citizenship responsibilities with regard to its host nation. The MNE should conform to the parameters defined by that nation's laws and established practices regarding participation in local political activities. These practices are among the political conditions that the MNE should have evaluated before deciding upon the investment. In principle, an MNE's rights and responsibilities for political participation should be greatest on those issues most immediately and directly related to its core business functions. Beyond the sphere of its own operations, an MNE would normally have few rights and responsibilities to exert political influence, particularly on issues relating to the host society's choice regarding its governing political system.

An MNEs withdrawal from a country may be justified if the nation's political climate changes to the degree that an MNE can no longer operate ethically within such a system, especially if its own operations contribute significantly to sustaining serious abuses of the population. But any withdrawal should occur in a manner that causes the least harm to innocent individuals most directly affected by the firm's operations. However, an MNE's withdrawal decision should not be undertaken for the intended purpose of overthrowing a government or damaging the nation's economy. The right and responsibility for any such overt political decision should rest with duly constituted political authorities, and petitions for such action should be directed to those institutions. To impose such a responsibility on a business enterprise is to grant it the right to engage in political activities that go beyond its appropriate role in a society.

With regard to using MNEs as instruments to influence political affairs in another country, a working assumption could be that national political authorities, acting individually or (preferably) in concert, should specify the guidelines for any such actions, including the processes for their approval. Included in this discussion should be a recognition that, if directed MNE actions are to occur within the target nation, such activity will contravene the general international principle of nonintervention. Exceptions to this principle may be justifiable in particular circumstances, but the nature of the violated principle should be openly recognized and consideration should be given to compensating the MNE (the instrument) for any harm it may suffer individually for activities undertaken at the direction of political authorities. By implication, this approach rules out both MNE political intervention on its own initiative as well as at the instigation of other private interest-groups, which should direct their entreaties to appropriate political authorities.

## Conclusion

The possible guidelines suggested above are offered as a way to encourage and perhaps focus discussion among representatives of governments, businesses, and other nongovernmental groups with an interest and a stake in developing global codes of conduct. It is perhaps ironic that areas of business conduct where standards seemed so clear at the beginning of the code debate have almost imperceptibly become blurred and confused by a series of case-specific actions. These experiences highlight the importance of undertaking a more careful and complete examination of the long-term as well as the short-term implications of business conduct standards relating to involvement in a nation's political affairs. At the core of this issue will lie difficult questions about relating rights and responsibilities when MNEs must act as good corporate citizens in a global economy where effective political authority remains nationally fragmented. The best efforts of all concerned parties are needed in a creative and cooperative dialogue to develop global codes of conduct that can effectively address this challenge.

## Notes

1. For example, the Organization for Economic Cooperation and Development (OECD) has adopted various codes on capital flows, and over 1,100 bilateral investment treaties have been signed to establish a framework of legal guarantees to facilitate investment between signatory countries.

2. An example is the OECD Declaration on International Investment and Multinational Enterprises which includes binding decisions for governments concerning national treatment and investment incentives and disincentives as well as the voluntary Guideline for Multinational Enterprises. Another example is the Tripartite Declaration of Principles Concerning MNEs and Social Policy adopted by the International Labor Organization.

3. For a discussion of these developments, see John Kline, *International Codes and Multinational Business* (Westport, Conn.: Quorum Books, Greenwood Press, 1985).

4. United Nations, Economic and Social Council, *Transnational Corporations: Issues Involved in the Formulation of a Code of Conduct*, Report of the Secretariat (New York: United Nations, 1976), E/C.10/17, p. 22.

5. Ibid., p. 31.

6. Ibid., p. 22.

7. Chamber of Commerce of the United States, "Elements of Global Business Conduct for Possible Inclusion in Individual Company Statements," Washington, D.C., January 1975.

8. USA BIAC Committee on International Investment and Multinational Enterprise, *A Review of the Declaration on International Investment and Multinational Enterprises* (New York: USA BIAC, November 1976), p. 32.

9. Alberto Jimenez de Lucio, "International Direct Investment: A View from the UN," in Charles P. Kindleberger, *A GATT for Foreign Investment* (New York: Carnegie Center for Transnational Studies, 1980), p. 28.

10. John Kline, *Foreign Investment Strategies in Restructuring Economies: Learning from Corporate Experiences in Chile* (Westport, Conn.: Greenwood Press, 1992), p. 12.

11. Thomas Gladwin and Ingo Walter, *Multinationals Under Fire* (New York: John Wiley & Sons, 1980), pp. 193–94.

12. Ibid., p. 195.

13. Ibid., p. 196.

14. This section draws from material presented in John Kline, *Doing Business in South Africa: Seeking the Ethical Parameters for Business and Government Responsibilities* (New York: Carnegie Council on Ethics and International Affairs, 1991), Case 511, Pew Case Studies in International Affairs, distributed by the Institute for the Study of Diplomacy, Georgetown University, Washington, D.C.

15. Rev. Leon Sullivan, "The Role of Multinational Corporations in Helping to Bring About Change in South Africa," in W. Michael Hoffman et al., eds., *Ethics and the Multinational Enterprise: Proceedings of the Sixth National Conference on Business Ethics* (Lanham, Md.: University Press of America, 1986), pp. 381–82.

16. Ibid., p. 385.

17. United Nations, United Nations Centre on Transnational Corporations, *The New Code Environment* (New York: United Nations, April, 1990), UNCTC Current Studies, Series A, no. 16, p. 36.

18. Ibid.

19. For a discussion of the differences between coercion and intervention as applied to international economic relations, see Charles Powers, "Ethics and United States Trade Policy," in *Trade, Inflation and Ethics*, Commission on Critical Choices for Americans (Lexington, Mass.: Lexington Books, D.C. Heath, 1976).

20. An interesting chart outlining how MNE actions influence human rights both directly and indirectly can be found in Gladwin and Walter, *Multinationals Under Fire*, pp. 144–45, 152.

# 4

# A Lesson from
# the Sullivan Principles

## *The Rewards for Being Proactive*

OLIVER F. WILLIAMS, C.S.C.

An examination of the text of the principles for the U.S. companies operating in South Africa, the Sullivan Principles, reveals a remarkable document (see Appendix 27) that has clearly been a model for many of the subsequent global codes discussed in this volume. The Sullivan Principles represent a paradigm shift, in that now ethical and human rights concerns are taken to be issues that must be factored into business decisions. What is often not understood, however, is that the principles, as stated in Appendix 27, are a product of a series of reactions to the strife in South Africa. The principles were first formulated in 1977 but only reached their final form, the form that includes concern for "social, economic and political justice," in 1986.

This chapter[1] argues that because the principles were formed in this reactive mode, they never gained widespread public support. Many U.S. citizens were never persuaded that U.S. multinationals in South Africa were doing more good than harm, that U.S. companies were concerned that basic rights of blacks in South Africa were violated; in fact, between 1984 and 1990 over 200 U.S. companies withdrew from South Africa after intense pressure from critics at home. What are the rewards for being proactive? In this case, we will never know for sure, for while the Sullivan signatory companies were courageous and did much good for the black people of South Africa, they were not proactive. The chapter will outline the development of the principles and the emerging paradigm shift in the relationship between business and society.

## Sullivan's Original Proposal: A Proactive U.S. Business Community Opposing the South African Curtailment of Rights

### Sullivan the Person

Born in 1923, Leon Sullivan was raised in a poor family in Charleston, West Virginia. Gifted intellectually, the six-foot five-inch young man also demonstrated athletic ability and won an athletic scholarship to West Virginia State College where he graduated in 1943. Enrolling in New York's Union Theological Seminary, Sullivan served in Harlem, mentored by Adam Clayton Powell. From the start Sullivan was known as a powerful and dynamic orator. After seminary education, he served several churches and finally, in 1950, settled as the pastor of Zion Baptist Church in Philadelphia. Under his leadership, the congregation grew to be one of the largest in Philadelphia, reaching some six thousand people.

Active in civil rights issues, Sullivan championed the cause of eliminating discrimination against blacks in the workplace. He argued that winning blacks civil and political rights was only half the battle and that the struggle must continue in the arena of economic rights. He reasoned that since blacks were major consumers in the Philadelphia area, they ought to have a proportionate share of the jobs. Observing that there were clear patterns of employment discrimination in the city, from 1959 to 1963 he led a campaign of "selective patronage," encouraging businesses to hire blacks or face a boycott. As opportunities for blacks in business began to increase, it became clear that often they did not have the education and training required by business for the better jobs. Again, Sullivan took the initiative and founded the Opportunities Industrialization Centers (OIC), a series of training facilities to enable blacks to acquire the skills to succeed in business. These facilities are now operating in many U. S. cities and in a number of countries in Africa.[2]

### Sullivan and Big Business

Sullivan's first position with big business began in December 1970 when the chair of the board of General Motors, James J. Roche, came to visit the Zion Baptist Church and asked him to consider joining the GM board of directors. At the May 1970 meeting, the board was lambasted by Ralph Nader's Campaign to Make General Motors Responsible for not having any black board members and for having very few black dealers; this mounting pressure may have influenced Roche's timing. In any event, Sullivan accepted board membership and attended his first board meeting in Detroit on May 21, 1971, and made a splash that was not soon to be forgotten.

It just so happened that the first shareholder resolution on South Africa from church groups that had ever come to a vote had garnered 1.29 percent of the vote and it was addressed to General Motors. The Domestic and Foreign Missionary Society of the Episcopal Church sponsored the resolution, which asked General Motors to withdraw from South Africa. Although everyone knew in 1971 that there was little prospect for a GM withdrawal, Sullivan seized the moment to make an impassioned plea to the board that they consider the moral issue involved with operating in a country that systematically denied rights to people on the basis of skin color. He argued that all international business ought to withdraw until apartheid was dismantled.[3] Needless to say, he did not carry the day but he did plant a seed that took root in short order.

In the summer of 1975, Sullivan had a brief stay in the Holiday Inn near the airport at Johannesburg while in route to Lesotho for an OIC organization meeting. Since the South African press had reported his arrival, Sullivan found a whole host of people waiting to see him and he met with them long into the night.

> They were from black groups, black individuals, labor unions, along with some business leaders. During these discussions, again and again, particularly from the blacks and labor representatives with whom I talked more than any others, I was urged to try to see what I could do to make American companies, and other companies from around the world, positive instruments for change in the elimination of segregation and apartheid.[4]

After much thought and prayer, Sullivan decided that he would attempt to get business to be an agent of change in the fight against apartheid: "Not sure myself that it could or would work, but knowing that if it did not work, at least I would have given it a try: and I knew that God would be with me."[5] Sullivan's original idea was that a code of conduct would be designed so that it would erode apartheid not only in the workplace but also in the wider society. He envisioned the U.S. companies operating in South Africa as agents of change through the use of their power by pressuring the South African government to dismantle apartheid laws, thus gradually leading to full civil and political rights for all. Emboldened by his prophetic task, Sullivan began to formulate a plan.

Frank Cary, the chairman of IBM, was on the Advisory Council for Sullivan's OIC endeavor and so he was one of the first business leaders to hear of Sullivan's South African project. After some smaller preliminary meetings,

Cary, along with Tom Murphy, chief executive officer of General Motors, hosted a meeting for nineteen top executives of fifteen of the largest corporations with South African operations. Held at the IBM training facility in Sands Point, Long Island, on January 29, 1976, the meeting started Sullivan on a journey that would finally cause a major shift in the way business views its role in society. In Sullivan's words:

> I told these business leaders of the dimensions of the crisis, as I saw it. I also told them of the moral implications to take a stand for what was morally right. I told these business leaders it was time that they took a stand against injustice in the Republic of South Africa and I urged them to join together and take a "first step" and set an example for businessmen in other parts of the world to begin doing something about the situation.[6]

As a result of the historic gathering, the business leaders agreed to consider supporting a set of principles regulating the companies' behavior in South Africa. A draft of the principles was to be formulated by Sullivan and circulated to the top executives who would then offer changes and/or deletions. The process would go on until there were enough companies agreeing to a common code.

## A Division of Thought

What became clear to Sullivan was that there was a fundamental division of thought between his vision of the companies challenging the pillars of apartheid and the business leaders' position. The business leaders argued that they could and should do nothing that opposes government law and policy. For example, in a November 1, 1976, letter to Sullivan from R. H. Herzog, chairman of the board and chief executive officer of 3M, Herzog, responding to an early draft of the principles, writes:

> The "Statement of Principles" attached to your letter reflects employment goals and practices we are supportive of worldwide and not only in the Republic of South Africa. *To the degree that South African law and South African Government policy allows,* our subsidiary there has taken aggressive action to conform to these principles. If through the offices of Dr. Kissinger the principles could receive official South Africa Government approval, it would certainly heighten our subsidiary's ability to enhance their current programs. (Emphasis added)[7]

A similar reluctance to challenge any South African laws, even those enforcing apartheid, is evidenced in a letter from J. M. Voss, chairman of the board of Caltex. Voss, writing on January 20, 1977, is responding to Sullivan's letter of December 23, 1976, which included a draft of the "Statement of Principles." Voss has no problem with the principles insofar as they concern the workplace but he registers serious reservations about challenging any South African apartheid laws.

Voss, writing to Sullivan, says:

> I returned to my desk yesterday and having studied your letter and the "Statement of Principles," would like to make the following comments.
>
> First and foremost, I reaffirm Caltex's acceptance from a moral and humane point of view of the concepts and, in our case, the utilization of fair and equal employment practices for all employees, as well as the policy of equal pay for equal work.
>
> Secondly, Caltex has training programs in place and supports programs which have as their objective, the improvement of the quality of their employees' lives outside the work environment.
>
> Finally, Caltex is, as you know, strongly opposed to Apartheid and will continue to seek to attain the establishment of the other Principles set out in the "Statement" so far *as that is possible within the laws of the Republic of South Africa. To the extent feasible to achieve these objectives*, we will also in all appropriate ways assiduously seek the requisite changes in legalization and regulations of an Apartheid character. (Emphasis added)[8]

### Announcing the Principles

After much discussion and many meetings following the Sands Point summit on January 29, 1976, Sullivan finally persuaded twelve of the fifteen companies to subscribe publicly to a version of the principles, a version which was confined to workplace issues. The document, issued on March 1, 1977, was as follows:

Statement of Principles of U.S. Firms with Affiliates
in the Republic of South Africa

Each of the firms endorsing the Statement of Principles have affiliates in the Republic of South Africa and support the following operating principles:

1. Non-segregation of the races in all eating, comfort and work facilities.
2. Equal and fair employment practices for all employees.
3. Equal pay for all employees doing equal or comparable work for the same period of time.

4. Initiation of and development of training programs that will prepare, in substantial numbers, Blacks and other non-whites for supervisory, administrative, clerical and technical jobs.
5. Increasing the number of Blacks and non-whites in management and supervisory positions.
6. Improving the quality of employees' lives outside the work environment in such areas as housing, transportation, schooling, recreation and health facilities.

We *agree* to further implement these principles. Where implementation requires a modification of existing South African *working conditions*, we will seek such modification through appropriate channels.

We believe that the implementation of the foregoing principles is consistent with respect for human dignity and will contribute greatly to the general economic welfare of all the people of the Republic of South Africa.[9]

There were two notable changes in the March 1, 1977, document from the earlier version sent out in December 1976. First, in a move to strengthen the document, Sullivan used the work "agree" rather than "wish" (see the Statement of Principles above). While the companies finally went along with "agree," there was some contention. This is reflected in a February 18, 1977, letter from William P. Tavoulareas, president of the Mobil Oil Corporation, to Sullivan:

Thank you for your letter of February 11, and the attached Statement of Principles which, of course, is in the form which we finally worked out following the larger meeting on February 9th. This statement reflects a number of practices which our South African subsidiary has been developing over the past several years. Upon reflection I believe I should say that while there may not be any important difference between the use of the words "agree" and "wish" in the penultimate paragraph of the statement, I would, if given the choice, conclude that "wish" probably is more expressive than "agree" of the precise commitment we intend. In any event, I am prepared to go along with the word "agree" if that is the desire of the group.[10]

Another more significant change was made after a meeting with the then South African Ambassador to Washington, Roelf K. Botha. The original document language was "laws and customs" and this was changed to "working conditions" (see the Statement of Principles above). Critics of Sullivan's endeavor were quick to note this change. For example, the March 7, 1977, issue of *Africa News*, discussing this change, notes that the *Johannesburg Star* "reports that Botha won concessions in wording from the group, although both Sullivan and Botha deny it."[11]

Sullivan later clarified his position, saying that he was primarily focusing on the language of the six principles at this time and thus was willing to make the proposed change.[12]

Referring to the original twelve signatories, Sullivan reminds us that "a number of the twelve were held on the list only by a shoestring."[13] Since he was not able to persuade the companies to be proactive in the wider society, to get a consensus and announce the principles program Sullivan was willing to compromise with the hope that he could incrementally expand the scope of the principles in the future. However, this particular compromise did not sit well with at least one U.S. company. W. B. Nicholson, vice chairman of Union Carbide Corporation, wrote to Sullivan on March 8, 1977, congratulating him on the March 1 announcement but quite concerned about the change.

> We conclude that the version shown to Secretary Vance is much to be preferred over the final draft submitted to Ambassador Botha.
>
> The one variance, namely the substitution of the term "working conditions" for "laws and customs" serves to weaken the statement considerably in our view. We do not have knowledge of the circumstances which gave rise to the last minute change, but we do have the described reaction and would like to let you know about it.[14]

On March 16, 1977, Sullivan answered Nicholson's objection by stating that at this time he was trying "to broaden the base and to follow through on the six principles in the Statement."[15]

From the vantage point of the 1990s, many may question why Sullivan would seek the approval of the South African ambassador. In the context of the 1970s and the common understanding of the role of business in society, it was unthinkable for the business leaders that the principles would not receive some tacit approval from South African officials before being announced. The issue debated in 1976–77 was whether this approval ought to be negotiated by the U.S. State Department or by the companies themselves. Although the 3M CEO argued for the U.S. secretary of state to negotiate approval of the principles (see note 7 above), most companies argued for a direct meeting with some of their CEOs and the South African officials. For example, in a letter from the vice president of Citibank, Robert E. Terkhom, to Leon Sullivan, dated February 22, 1977, Terkhom makes this case:

> While we agree that it is a good idea to consult the Secretary of State before delivery of the Statement to the South African Government, we do not believe the State Department should be asked to deliver this message. We prefer this effort to remain a private initiative, which the signing corporations would

communicate directly to the South African Ambassador or other appropriate representative of the South African Government.[16]

Similarly, the president of Mobil Oil Corporation writes to Sullivan on February 18, 1977:

> As to our program from this point forward, I would hope we all could conclude that it might prove counter-productive if the Statement of Principles [was] handled in such a manner as to invite government-to-government confrontation. While I think it certainly a constructive move to make what we are doing known to the Secretary of State, it is my belief that we might well impair our ability to produce the kind of conditions in South Africa which will be necessary if we are to be able to implement all of the points outlined in the statement. Since this will be an undertaking by private corporations, it seems to me we should be the parties which make it known, together with yourself, to representatives of the South African Government. An appropriate method for doing this might be a meeting of our group with the South Africa Ambassador without involvement of the U.S. Government representatives. We, as a company, would certainly be happy to be identified with the statement in an implementation program of that nature.[17]

Following this advice, IBM's Frank Cary, GM's Tom Murphy, and the Reverend Leon Sullivan met with Roelf Botha and secured his agreement with the significant caveat discussed above. They also met with Secretary of State Cyrus Vance. (Jimmy Carter was inaugurated as U.S. president in January 1977 and Vance replaced Henry Kissinger.)

The original twelve signatories to the Sullivan Principles were American Cyanamid, Burroughs Corporation, Caltex Petroleum Corporation, Citicorp, Ford Motor Company, General Motors Corporation, IBM Corporation, International Harvester Company, Minnesota Mining and Manufacturing Company, Mobil Corporation, Otis Elevator, and Union Carbide Corporation. Three companies—Motorola, Firestone, and Goodyear—represented at the original Sands Point meeting in January 1976 did not join as original signers. The reason that companies were reluctant to join is perhaps best expressed in a "Memorandum to File," written by a General Motors staff person, Larry W. Wize, after talking to Keith McKennon of Dow Chemical Company. McKennon noted that Dow had some reservations about joining the principles since "he envisions a chain reaction of proposals on a variety of subjects." There were a number of activist groups which would then be proposing "standards of behavior," initiated by "outside parties."[18] Interfering with or curtailing management's discretionary power was the issue. Another example is from the chairman and chief executive officer of Newmont Mining

Corporation, P. Malozemoff; he wrote to Sullivan on August 18, 1977, saying that while "we sympathize entirely with the objectives of your effort," the company would not join the collective effort. Malozemoff quotes the 1974 annual report where the company policy on equal employment is outlined, and then concludes:

> While we disagree in no way with the Statement of Principles which you have sent us, we prefer for the present to maintain the above as Newmont's formal statement of its position on this all important subject.[19]

For Malozemoff, only workplace issues were relevant and any move to diminish management's discretionary power was to be avoided.

### Responses to the Announcement

The response to the March 1, 1977, announcement of the principles by Leon Sullivan indicated that most critics of apartheid had little faith in the business endeavor. The American Committee on Africa, whose spokesman, ordained minister George Houser, had testified before Congress for economic sanctions against South Africa as early as 1966, called the principles "an exercise in triviality." It is important to note at this point that while mainline religious groups were, for the most part, doubtful of the helpfulness of the principles, there was some initial cooperation. For example, within three weeks of issuing the principles, Sullivan met with Tim Smith, executive director of the Interfaith Center on Corporate Responsibility (ICCR) and key members of that group. The ICCR, a coalition of major Protestant groups, and many Catholic dioceses and religious orders, had presented many shareholder resolutions asking companies to withdraw from South Africa. In fact, the very month the principles were issued, the ICCR filed such resolutions against five of the signatory companies. On the other hand, even while asking companies to withdraw, the ICCR was also persuading companies to join the principles program. Tim Smith, in a March 29, 1977, letter to Sullivan, captures the complexity of the position of most church groups at that time.

> Dear Mr. Sullivan:
>
> I was recently at a meeting in Moline with John Deere executives discussing Southern Africa. They indicated that they had not been approached to sign your set of principles but said they would be very willing to do so. Mr. William Hewitt is the Chairman and personally indicated his interest.
>
> We will also continue to raise with G.E. and ITT why they have not signed and would be pleased to raise this with any other companies you may wish, arguing that it is a minimum standard of decency in the workplace that should

be applied. However, it is also the consensus of most of the Churches that have been working on this problem that *such changes in the workplace have not and will not lead to the basic social change* that is vitally necessary in South Africa. This is one of the major points that Sally Motlana raised in her comments at the meeting. It seems to be an analysis bolstered by solid facts. However, we can all agree that companies have an obligation to act responsibly and humanely in the workplace and of course Church groups will continue to endorse this concept.

You had said at lunch that you were willing to raise some larger issues with some of the signatories, e.g., the role of Citibank's loans, G.E. attempting to sell a nuclear reactor to S.A., Union Carbide investing on the border of a Bantustan.

We look forward to hearing reports from you on the fruits of these conversations. Let's keep in touch. (Emphasis added)[20]

One important learning from the letter above is that there was a genuine cooperative spirit present in the ICCR group and *that had the 1977 principles argued for political and civil rights in the wider society and not simply for changes in the workplace, a coalition of business and the church groups on the South Africa issue might have come to pass.* Leon Sullivan's April 11, 1977, response to the above letter is very telling in that he acknowledges his desire to push for political and civil rights but judges that he must do this incrementally. As quoted above, Sullivan realizes that he is holding some of the companies in the program "only by a shoestring."

My dear Mr. Smith:

We will be having meetings during the next month with a number of companies trying to get them to sign the Statement of Principles and then to follow through on the implementation. We will be in touch with John Deere executives, as you suggest, to see if they will sign the Principles.

As you indicated in your letter, I will let you know if there are other companies with which you might be helpful to be signers, as you are doing now with G.E. and ITT. It is clear in my mind, as you have stated, that companies do have an obligation to act responsibly and humanely in the workplace. *Of course, it is my desire that much more will come out of the Statement of Principles in the longer run as we push to see how far we can go.*

Also, as you have requested, I will be willing to raise larger issues with Citibank regarding loans; with Union Carbide regarding investing on the border of Bantustans; and with G.E. regarding attempting to sell a nuclear reactor to South Africa. I do not know what successes I can have, but I will, very willingly, raise the questions. I cannot give you a time frame, but I will do this as soon as possible and will let you know the response.

I will keep in touch as you have requested.[21]

Another response to the principles, this one quite favorable, served to unite many of the church groups against the program. This most positive response was from the top officials in the South African government. Since the principles focused on the workplace, they could be easily praised by South African officials. Dr. Connie Mulder, the then Minister of Information and the Interior, spoke in Parliament in Cape Town, praising the principles. The embassy of South Africa used Mulder's comments to attempt to counter any move by U.S. groups to force disinvestment in the country. For example, in an April 20, 1977, letter, an official in the embassy of South Africa wrote to the chairman of the Endowment Committee on the Board of Regents of the University of Maryland with these words:

> Apparently, some sources expected the South African Government to respond negatively to these recommendations [i.e., the Sullivan Principles]. In fact, the South African Government has expressed its strong support for the objectives outlines in the six points mentioned above.
>
> Speaking in Parliament in reaction to the six general guidelines, Dr. Connie Mulder, Minister of Information and the Interior, publicly commended the American Business initiative launched to contribute to the well-being of black workers in South Africa. Dr. Mulder said South Africa welcomed the American companies initiative to implement and expand development programs already in operation in South Africa. He went on to say that as a result of these existing programs, the black man found himself outstripping his counterparts on the African continent and many other areas of the world in all fields of human endeavor. According to most press accounts it is clear from the tone of the South African Government's reply that the government is leaving the door open for constructive participation in the employment and welfare goals of American firms. Dr. Mulder also noted that these programs should be implemented on a non-discriminatory basis world-wide if American firms and the American Government were truly concerned with the welfare of blacks and other groups.
>
> Thus, the South African Government has endorsed the efforts by several leading American corporations to advance job opportunities and welfare of all their employees in South Africa regardless of race.[22]

To be sure, however, some South Africans were threatened by the principles, fearing that they could easily expand and become a troublesome interference in South African society. In particular, African trade unions were feared. The October 24, 1977, issue of *Business Week* reported that "a member of the S.A. Foundation, a businessmen's lobby, said that, 'if anything unreasonable, like the recognition of black trade unions come . . . , it would be most unwelcome.'" The article stated:

Fearing that African unions would quickly become lightning conductor for nationwide strikes and political unrest, the South African government has been leaning heavily on employers to ignore them and has been harassing many of their organizers.[23]

The article reported that of the more than three hundred U.S. companies operating in South Africa in 1977, the Ford Motor Company was the only one to accord black unions even a limited form of recognition.

A prominent South African business journal, the *Financial Mail,* took another tack. In its March 4, 1977, issue, an article titled "A Damp Squib Unless . . ." states that "The American business manifesto needs to go a lot further, and be followed up with determination."[24] Its key point is that trade union rights for Africans must be included in the Sullivan Principles, for "many of the problems which the manifesto seeks to tackle arise in large part from the fact that Africans are denied collective bargaining rights." The article also argues that the U.S. parent companies "should take a much closer interest in the everyday operations of the SA subsidiaries than they have done up till now." The *Financial Mail* clearly wants to see apartheid dismantled but the editors have some concern about whether the U.S. companies are serious about the endeavor. Geoffrey Windsor of Dresser SA is quoted: "It really seems to be just a lot of talk." A manager of the subsidiary of a U.S. firm, Koehring, Peter Scholtz of South Africa, says: "I expect Koehring will probably keep their noses out of what is happening." The *Mail* asks a tough question:

> There is genuine question in Washington as to whether the recent anti-apartheid gesture by the U.S. firms was aimed more at the White House and liberal American stockholder groups than at the Vorster government and its policies.[25]

## The American Public Becomes Aroused

Events in South Africa began to capture the minds and hearts of Americans. The black consciousness leader, Steve Biko, died a brutal death while in detention (September 1977) and this caused widespread unrest in the black townships. On October 19, 1977, Prime Minister John Vorster, responding to the unrest, arrested fifty black leaders and banned (outlawed) eighteen anti-apartheid organizations. President Jimmy Carter, under pressure to do something, argued for a UN embargo on arms shipments to South Africa; on November 4, 1977, the embargo was passed by the UN Security Council.

During the period of late 1977, the U.S. companies were coming under increasing pressure from the Interfaith Center on Corporate Responsibility to consider withdrawing from South Africa. For example, the CEO of Union Carbide received a letter from the ICCR, asking the company to withdraw from South Africa. Dated November 7, 1977, and signed by Sister Regina Murphy, chairperson, ICCR, along with five other members, the letter was addressed to W. S. Sneath, chairman and chief executive officer of Union Carbide. Referring to the banning and arrests in October 1977, the ICCR letter says: "we have concluded that U.S. companies are unable to act as a force for significant change but instead tend to support the status quo." The letter goes on to say:

> We call on all U.S. corporations investing in South Africa to adopt a policy to cease any expansion and begin to terminate present operations in the Republic of South Africa unless and until the South African government has committed itself to ending apartheid and has taken meaningful steps toward the achievement of full political, legal and social rights for the black majority.

> We believe this is the only responsible course of action open to U.S. investors.[26]

Universities with large endowments were also beginning to question the presence of U.S. corporations in South Africa. In 1977–78 ten universities withdrew investments from U.S. firms operating in South Africa. More and more, the U.S. companies were justifying their presence in South Africa by citing their participation in the Sullivan Principles program. For example, Tom Murphy, chairman of General Motors, in responding to an inquiry of Hugh Calkins, chairman of the Corporation Committee on Shareholder Responsibility of Harvard University, wrote as follows in correspondence dated November 22, 1977:

> Let me say that we in General Motors share your concern for the human rights of all people in that country. The recent actions of the South African government are distressing and indeed regrettable especially in light of the progress GM and others have worked so hard to achieve. I can assure you that General Motors has in the past, and will continue in the future, to avail itself of every opportunity to aggressively pursue improved conditions for General Motors' South African employees, *especially in the areas of wages, benefits, training, education, housing and recreation.*

> In this respect, we continue to strongly support the Statement of Principles developed earlier this year by Dr. Leon H. Sullivan. As you are probably aware, General Motors was one of the original twelve companies which endorsed the Principles in March of this year. (Emphasis added)[27]

It is noteworthy that, as of November 1977, the focus of the companies was still on rights *in the workplace* rather than in the wider society, even in the face of the South African government's flagrant abuses.

Sullivan's response to the sad events in South Africa was to see the glass half-full rather than half-empty. He still hoped he could eventually persuade the companies to oppose the apartheid laws and ultimately the government itself. He urged the companies to widen the circle of those involved with the principles program. In writing to Thomas A. Murphy, chairman of the board of the General Motors Corporation, on November 23, 1977, Sullivan states:

> You can expect interest around South Africa to be intensified within the next six months, as a result of the Biko exposures and the recent jailings and bannings. It is, therefore, most important that we get as much broad support behind the Statement of Principles throughout America and around the world, as possible, for the effort to maintain and gain effectiveness.[28]

### Pressure Produces Change

With the ICCR withdrawal pressure in mind, Sullivan began to move ahead with an organization strategy for the principles. After a number of meetings, finally in April 1978 Sullivan announced the formation of seven task groups which closely followed the structure of the original principles: (1) Equal and Fair Employment Practices; (2) Equal Pay; (3) Education; (4) Training; (5) Management and Development; (6) Health Care and Housing; and (7) Periodic Reporting and Economic and Community Development. The Task Groups were each composed of members of the signatory companies and were given the assignment of providing "a series of guidelines and objectives for the companies to more clearly and forthrightly pursue the aims of the Principles."[29]

Sullivan had tried unsuccessfully to include union rights in the original principles but several of the founding twelve companies opposed the idea. Now with increasing repression and the U.S. news coverage, the move to include union rights was gaining momentum. On May 9, 1978, James W. Rawlings, vice chairman, Union Carbide Africa and Middle East, Inc., wrote to Sullivan about some of the goals he envisioned for the companies of the principles program: "The government of South Africa can, I believe, be persuaded . . . to provide a nondiscriminatory legislative context for labor unions having black members and to make other changes in the law where it conflicts with the objectives to which you have applied so much energy."[30]

While it was not until May 1, 1979, that the South African Commission studying union rights, the Wiehahn Commission, published its recommendations for granting blacks the same trade union rights as whites, the task group for principle 2 took the bull by the horns and, in mid 1978, added a section advocating black union rights. Following the Wiehahn proposal, legislation was passed in 1979 in South Africa and, soon after, the Kellogg Company signed a formal union recognition agreement. (By the end of 1981, five additional U.S. companies had agreements.)

The other task groups continued their work and, within four months, all the task groups finished their first assignment and Sullivan, on July 6, 1978, announced what has become known as "The First Amplification of the Statement of Principles." The full text of that Amplification, as released in 1978, is as follows:

PRINCIPLE I   Non-segregation of the races in all eating, comfort and work facilities.

Each signator of the Statement of Principles will proceed immediately to:

- Eliminate all vestiges of racial discrimination.
- Remove all race designation signs.
- Desegregate all eating, comfort and work facilities.

PRINCIPLE II   Equal and fair employment practices for all employees.
Each signator of the Statement of Principles will proceed immediately to:

- Implement equal and fair terms and conditions of employment.
- Provide non-discriminatory eligibility for benefit plans.
- Establish an appropriate comprehensive procedure for handling and resolving individual employee complaints.
- Support the elimination of all industrial racial discriminatory laws which impede the implementation of equal and fair terms and conditions of employment, such as abolition of job reservations, job fragmentation, and apprenticeship restrictions for Blacks and other non-whites.
- Support the elimination of discrimination against the rights of Blacks to form or belong to government registered unions, and acknowledge generally the right of Black workers to form their own union or be represented by trade unions where unions already exist.

PRINCIPLE III   Equal pay for all employees doing equal or comparable work for the same period of time.

Each signator of the Statement of Principles will proceed immediately to:

- Design and implement a wage and salary administration plan which is applied equally to all employees regardless of race who are performing equal or comparable work.
- Ensure an equitable system of job classifications, including a review of the distinction between hourly and salaried classifications.
- Determine whether upgrading of personnel and/or jobs in the lower echelons is needed, and if so, implement programs to accomplish this objective expeditiously.

- Assign equitable wage and salary ranges, the minimum of these to be well above the appropriate local minimum economic living level.

PRINCIPLE IV    Initiation of and development of training programs that will prepare, in substantial numbers, Blacks and other non-whites for supervisory, administrative, clerical and technical jobs.

Each signator of the Statement of Principles will proceed immediately to:

- Determine employee training needs and capabilities, and identify employees with potential for further advancement.
- Take advantage of existing outside training resources and activities, such as exchange programs, technical colleges, vocational schools, continuation classes, supervisory courses and similar institutions or programs.
- Support the development of outside training facilities individually or collectively, including technical centers, professional training exposure, correspondence and extension courses, as appropriate, for extensive training outreach.
- Initiate and expand inside training programs and facilities.

PRINCIPLE V    Increasing the number of Blacks and other non-whites in management and supervisory positions.

Each signator of the Statement of Principles will proceed immediately to:

- Identify, actively recruit, train and develop a sufficient and significant number of Blacks and other non-whites to assure that as quickly as possible there will be appropriate representation of Blacks and other non-whites in the management group of each company.
- Establish management development programs for Blacks and other non-whites, as appropriate, and improve existing programs and facilities for developing management skills of Blacks and other non-whites.
- Identify and channel high management potential Blacks and other non-white employees into management development programs.

PRINCIPLE VI    Improving the quality of employees' lives outside the work environment in such areas as housing, transportation, schooling, recreation and health facilities.

Each signator of the Statement of Principles will proceed immediately to:

- Evaluate existing and/or develop programs, as appropriate, to address the specific needs of Black and other non-white employees in the areas of housing, health care, transportation and recreation.
- Evaluate methods for utilizing existing, expanded or newly established in-house medical facilities or other medical programs to improve medical care for all non-whites and their dependents.

- Participation in the development of programs that address the educational needs of employees, their dependents and the local community. Both individual and collective programs should be considered, including such activities as literacy education, business training, direct assistance to local schools, contributions and scholarships.
- With all the foregoing in mind, it is the objective of the companies to involve and assist in the education and training of large and telling numbers of Blacks and other non-whites as quickly as possible. The ultimate impact of this effort is intended to be of massive proportion, reaching millions.

PERIODIC REPORTING

The signator companies of the Statement of Principles will proceed immediately to:

- Utilize a standard format to report their progress to Dr. Sullivan through the independent administrative unit he is establishing on a 6-month basis which will include a clear definition of each item to be reported.
- Ensure periodic reports on the progress that has been accomplished on the implementation of these principles.

\* \* \* \* \*

Consistent with the desire of the signatory companies to contribute toward the economic welfare of all people of the Republic of South Africa, they are urged to seek and assist in the development of Black and other non-white business enterprises, including distributors, suppliers of goods and services and manufacturers.

There will be a continuing review and assessment of the guidelines in light of changing circumstances.[31]

Under heavy pressure from church groups, student activists, and others, the First Amplification of the Principles was formulated and gave some substance to the principles. The task groups—composed of all business leaders— were made part of the institution. Each task group met at least three times annually to assess what remained to be accomplished and how best to achieve those goals. The Reverend Sullivan often used those meetings to raise expectations of company performance on the various social issues and prod the groups to consider even more amplifications (by 1986 there were five amplifications). This "moving of the goalposts," as the companies liked to call it, became a permanent part of the ongoing endeavor. Unfortunately, while blacks in South Africa gained much from the principles program, perceptions by most antiapartheid groups in the U.S. were that companies were doing no more than they had to do to keep the profits rolling in.

It was becoming clear to Leon Sullivan that he had to find a way to enhance the perceived legitimacy of the principles, especially with church groups and educators. The pressure was beginning to mount on college campuses and in many church-group efforts coordinated by the ICCR. At a meeting of all the signatories on November 13, 1979, held at the Pfizer Corporation in New York City, Sullivan announced the formation of "the International Council on Equality of Opportunity Principles (ICEOP), composed of churchmen and educators, which would assess the progress made by the companies."

Three pages of minutes report on a meeting of the ICEOP, held on December 10, 1979, at the Progress Plaza board room in Philadelphia, Pennsylvania.[32] The central theme of this meeting was to develop strategies to enlist and continue the support of the clergy for the principles. It is clear from the minutes that Sullivan was skillfully building a coalition of clergy to act as spokespersons for the principles. On the other hand, Sullivan was attentive to those laypersons and clerics at the meeting who saw a need to improve upon the principles. The minutes report that Sullivan heard the following from the clergy present:

1.   Companies only do as much as they are forced to do.
2.   The much alleged progress by the present government must be carefully evaluated; while some say there are signs of progress, others call it window dressing.
3.   Immediate action is needed to avert violence; expectations have been developed.
4.   The "Principles" are being evaluated constantly by friends and critics to determine their effectiveness. Measurable progress is necessary.[33]

Unfortunately, these criticisms were a constant theme during the next seven years. Only in November 1986, in the face of massive pressure from activists, did Sullivan finally gain the consensus among the companies to add language to the principles requiring opposition to the apartheid state.

### Growing Public Pressure about South Africa in the U.S.

Examination of the level of U.S. involvement in the antiapartheid struggle from the 1950s to the 1980s reveals a close correlation with the major events of South African government repression widely reported in the media. The shooting of demonstrators in Sharpeville in 1960, the Soweto riots in 1976, and the death of African leader Steve Biko in 1977 were all catalysts that revived the dormant U.S. movement. History will perhaps remember 1984 as the year when the movement took on a whole new and powerful life. This was the year the press reported the acceptance of the new Republic of South Africa constitution with its tricameral Parliament and the intense anger of black South Africa over being denied any franchise. These events prepared the way for renewed U.S. fervor.

### No Parliamentary Franchise for Blacks

In 1983, with a proposed addition to the Republic of South Africa constitution, coloreds and Indians were to be given the parliamentary franchise when Parliament expanded from one to three chambers. A distinction was made between "own affairs" and "general affairs," with "general affairs" (foreign affairs, defense, security) being controlled by a cabinet composed of selected members of all three chambers, and "own affairs" being governed by the particular racial chamber. Although the white Nationalist Party maintained control under the new constitution, the party did, at least, acknowledge the citizenship of Indians and coloreds. To be sure, Indians and coloreds, for the most part, did not warmly receive the new constitution; the remaining 73 percent of the population, the black Africans, had yet to receive any sort of parliamentary franchise, and coloreds and Indians were understandably reluctant to accept the franchise until all could participate. Needless to say, the black population was upset.

### The United Democratic Front (UDF)

In 1983, as the President's Council was proposing the outlines of a tricameral parliament (subsequently adopted and implemented in 1984), the so-called Koornhof Bills—legislation designed to strengthen the government's control over black labor—were being discussed. Mobilized in opposition to these government moves, a number of groups came together to pool their resources and offer a united front for a free, democratic, and multiracial country. By 1985, the United Democratic Front (UDF) was a coalition of some six hundred groups—political clubs, professional societies, student organizations, community groups, and labor unions. Founded by the World Alliance of Reformed Churches president Allan Boesak, the UDF saw its role as one of coordinating the actions of the organizations. With perhaps as many as 2 million members, the group actively sought to abolish apartheid and install majority rule. The UDF called for disinvestment. Since the state of emergency was declared in July 1985, many UDF leaders were detained in jails across the nation. The government repeatedly claimed that the UDF was a front for the banned ANC since the UDF had adopted the ANC Freedom Charter.

The underlying concern of the UDF was that the Nationalist Party government was involved in an effort to modernize apartheid, not to abolish it. In the UDF's view, the Koornhof Bills attempted to divide blacks, giving urban blacks more rights and security and pushing "homeland" blacks out of the mainstream economic and political community of South Africa. In this way, the argument went, whites could appease the international community and yet still retain control. The new constitution, similarly, was seen as an instrument of neo-apartheid.

### Church Response

Pressures on the companies continued to mount. In 1983 the South African Council of Churches (SACC), a coalition of Protestant churches, passed a resolution asking the world community to refrain from investing in institutions that supported apartheid. In June 1983 Bishop Desmond Tutu, a former head of the South African Council of Churches, proclaimed the Tutu "principles." In November 1983 Sullivan announced the fourth amplification which largely followed the Tutu principles and required companies to lobby against apartheid laws. Notably, Sullivan's amplification differed from Tutu's principles in that he did not use the threat of withdrawal of all investment as leverage to move the government to dismantle apartheid.

### The Free South Africa Movement

On November 21, 1984, shortly after Ronald Reagan's landslide victory over presidential contender Walter Mondale, three prominent black leaders, concerned over the arrest of sixteen trade union leaders in South Africa, staged a protest at the South African Embassy. The three—Civil Rights Commission member Mary Frances Berry, Washington, D.C.; Congressman Walter Fauntroy; and Trans Africa executive director Randall Robinson—were arrested for demonstrating within 500 feet of the embassy. They were released, but their protest, covered by television and newspapers, caught on, and was followed by prominent blacks and whites who turned up at the embassy to be arrested in ritual fashion. Over three thousand people participated, including Senator Lowell Weicker (Republican, Connecticut); eighteen members of Congress; and such personalities as Harry Belafonte, Stevie Wonder, Dick Gregory, and Amy Carter. This ritual captured the minds and hearts of Americans or, at the very least, it tapped into the powerful moral sentiments that the anti-apartheid movement evoked for Americans.

Randall Robinson and his colleagues named the movement the Free South Africa Movement and it continued for almost two years. Robinson argued for complete disinvestment.

Meanwhile, in 1984, Bishop Tutu was awarded the Nobel Peace Prize, and his campaign for economic sanctions against South Africa was given prominent global media coverage. All this additional pressure on the companies to leave South Africa no doubt influenced them in their willingness finally to support political rights for blacks. It is noteworthy that the 1984 Arthur D. Little report on the companies' progress on the principles includes the following observation on the new requirements of the program:

> It is significant that there are today several areas in which companies are being requested to be active which would not have been tolerated by the companies when the program was initiated.[34]

### Trade Unions

Unlike labor unions in the United States, African trade unions in the apartheid era could not resort to the political arena to achieve goals that they did not gain through collective bargaining. Without the franchise, collective bargaining for Africans was their only access to the levers of power. Thus, for example, demanding (during the collective bargaining process) housing near the working site was a way for workers without the franchise to try to change the Group Areas Act. Similarly, when public policy did not outlaw discriminatory hiring and promotion practices, these matters became part of the collective bargaining agenda. Job security was another issue that took on crucial importance in South Africa; if a black African was dismissed, within seventy-two hours he or she had to leave the urban area of residence and return to a "homeland." As might be imagined, the collective bargaining process was being asked to air grievances well beyond the competence of many industrial managers. With this overburden in mind, most business leaders in South Africa were aggressively lobbying the government in the mid 1980s to improve the broad spectrum of social and political rights for the workers. For many employers, the level of black discontent was alarming.

In December 1985, thirty-six labor unions with a combined membership of more than five hundred thousand workers formed a new labor federation, the Congress of South African Trade Unions (COSATU). COSATU's president, Elijah Barayi, made it clear that the federation had a primarily political agenda, including abolition of the pass laws, *disinvestment by foreign companies*, and nationalization of the mines. COSATU member unions were some of the largest in South Africa: the Federation of South Africa Trade Unions (FOSATU), the National Union of Mineworkers, and the General and Allied Workers Union. The formation of this federation heralded a new militancy in the struggle for political rights.

### Pressure Yields Returns

In the face of an increasing spiral of violence, both the Protestant and Catholic churches actively opposed the government and even advised the global community to use economic sanctions against South Africa. Thus, in 1985, the South African Council of Churches (SACC) called for disinvestment by the world community and, in 1986, the Southern African Catholic Bishops' Conference (SACBC) issued its "Pastoral Letter on Economic Pressure for Justice." While the SACC called for outright disinvestment, the SACBC, following a characteristically cautious tack, advocated that economic pressure "be implemented in such a way as to not destroy the economy." The document expressed concern that sanctions not harm the least advantaged, but it clearly put the companies on notice.

The pressure continued to mount in the U.S. By the late 1980s, over one hundred college and university endowment funds divested stocks of companies with holdings in South Africa. While this action did not affect the bottom line of the U.S. companies involved, it did harm reputations. What was potentially very harmful to the bottom line was the selective-purchase ordinances passed by sixty-eight counties and cities and nineteen states which banned contracts with companies with operations in South Africa. This caused many companies to depart.

In May 1985, in the face of enormous pressure at home and a rapidly deteriorating situation in South Africa, Sullivan announced an ultimatum: If statutory apartheid was not dismantled in two years, he would not continue to support the principles and would call for all companies to disinvest. While most U.S. business leaders hoped that Sullivan would not issue such a call in 1987 (he did issue it in June 1987), the ultimatum pushed companies to be radical beyond their wildest dreams.

In June and August 1986 the U.S. companies, in a watershed event, explicitly and publicly championed political rights in advertisements in major South African newspapers. Organized by the American Chamber of Commerce, the advertisement proclaimed that "apartheid is totally contrary to the idea of free enterprise" and encouraged the government "to create a climate for negotiation." It listed the "urgent issues" that Pretoria must address:

Release political detainees; unban political organizations; negotiate with knowledged leaders about power sharing; grant political rights to all; repeal the Population Registration Act; grant South African citizenship to all; repeal the Group Areas Act; provide common, equal education; and equalize health services.

Finally in November 1986 the fourth amplification was expanded and designated as principle seven of the Sullivan Principles. The code was reissued on March 10, 1987 in its final form as the fifth amplification. This is the document Sullivan wanted in 1977 when it was not enacted because the business leaders thought opposing a sovereign state was impossible.

Principle seven is a remarkable change and a major paradigm shift. It is as follows:

- press for a single education system common to all races;
- use influence [to] support the unrestricted rights of Black businesses to locate in the urban areas of the nation;
- influence other companies in South Africa to follow the standards of equal rights principles;
- support the freedom of mobility of Black workers, including those from "so-called" independent homelands, to seek employment opportunities wherever they exist and make possible provision for adequate housing for families of employees within the proximity of workers' employment;
- use financial and legal resources to assist Blacks, Coloreds, and Asians in their efforts to achieve equal access to all health facilities, education institutions, transportation, housing, beaches, parks and all other accommodations normally reserved for Whites;
- oppose adherence to all apartheid laws and regulations;
- support the ending of all apartheid laws, practices and customs;
- support full and equal participation of Blacks, Coloreds, and Asians in the political process.

### Conclusion

The U.S. companies that remained in South Africa took up the challenge and began to oppose the government on various fronts. However, because most apartheid critics in the U.S. had little confidence in the principles, most companies were forced out of South Africa. Between 1986 and 1990 over 140 U.S. companies departed from South Africa under intense pressure at home. In 1990 the annual report on the activities of the U.S. companies in South Africa, compiled by Arthur D. Little, Inc., as a part of the requirements of the Statement of Principles Program, noted that only fifty-four U.S. companies continued to have operations there and that they provided more than $30 million a year to programs designed to eliminate apartheid. Some of these dollars were to assist in black educational endeavors, but many went to activities that most South Africans considered too risky because they directly challenged the South African government and its denial of political and civil rights of blacks.

What is clear is that from 1977 to 1987 a major paradigm shift was underway; the implicit social contract between business and society was being rewritten. This was largely in response to pressure; for example, by 1990 over five hundred shareholder resolutions had been presented to over ninety companies with operations in South Africa. Companies now saw the necessity of factoring human rights into business decisions. Unfortunately, because they acted incrementally and only in reaction to pressure, the business community never really got the public acclamation it might have had and, in fact, was, in large measure, pressured to leave South Africa. Many activists continue to believe, incorrectly in my view, that business was only interested in profits and that the principles were a cover story. Is there a lesson here?

## Notes

1. Sections of this chapter have been published in earlier works by the author. See Oliver F. Williams, *The Apartheid Crisis* (San Francisco: Harper & Row, 1986); and Oliver F. Williams, "The Apartheid Struggle: Learning from the Interaction between Church Groups and Business," *Business and the Contemporary World* 8, no. 1 (1996):151–67.

2. For a good account of Sullivan's work, see Leon H. Sullivan, *Build Brother Build* (Philadelphia: Macrae Smith Company, 1969).

3. Interview with the Reverend Leon H. Sullivan, July 21, 1995.

4. Leon H. Sullivan, "Speech Given to the Summit Conference of Black Religious Leaders on Apartheid," New York City, April 13, 1979, p. 7. Unless otherwise indicated, all speeches and correspondence quoted here are from the Temple University Archives, Acc. 654, International Council for Equality of Opportunity Principles, Papers from 1974–87.

5. Leon H. Sullivan, "Speech Given to the Summit Conference," p. 7.

6. Ibid., p. 8.

7. Letter from R. H. Herzog, chairman of the board and chief executive officer of 3M, to the Reverend Leon H. Sullivan, November 1, 1976.

8. Letter from J. M. Voss, chairman of the board of Caltex, to the Reverend Leon H. Sullivan, January 20, 1977.

9. Located in the Temple University Archives as indicated in note 4 above.

10. Letter from William Tavoulareas, president of the Mobil Oil Corporation, to the Reverend Leon H. Sullivan, February 18, 1977.

11. "U.S. Firms Pledge Discrimination Ban in South Africa," *Africa News*, March 7, 1977, pp. 4–5.

12. See E. J. Kahn, Jr., "Annals of International Trade: A Very Emotive Subject," *New Yorker*, May 14, 1979, pp. 137–51.

13. Leon H. Sullivan, "Speech Given to the Summit Conference," p. 9.

14. Letter from W. B. Nicholson, chairman of Union Carbide Corporation, to the Reverend Leon H. Sullivan, March 8, 1977.

15. Letter from the Reverend Leon H. Sullivan to W. B. Nicholson, March 16, 1977.

16. Letter from Robert E. Terkhom, vice president of Citibank, to the Reverend Leon H. Sullivan, February 22, 1977.

17. Letter from William P. Tavoulareas, president of Mobil Oil Corporation, to the Reverend Leon H. Sullivan, February 18, 1977.

18. Larry W. Wize, "Memorandum to File," September 6, 1979.

19. Letter from P. Malozemoff, chairman and chief executive officer of Newmont Mining Corporation, to the Reverend Leon H. Sullivan, August 18, 1977.

20. Letter from Timothy Smith, director of the Interfaith Center on Corporate Responsibility, to the Reverend Leon H. Sullivan, March 29, 1977.

21. Letter from the Reverend Leon H. Sullivan to Timothy Smith, April 11, 1977.

22. Letter from Carl F. Nöffke, Information Counselor of the Embassy of South Africa, Washington, D.C., to Mr. Hugh McMullen, chairman, Committee on Endorsements and Gifts, Board of Regents, University of Maryland, April 20, 1977.

23. "South Africa: Multinationals Are Caught in the Middle," *Business Week*, October 24, 1977.

24. "A Damp Squib Unless . . .," *Financial Mail*, March 4, 1977, p. 632.

25. Ibid., p. 634.

26. Letter from Sr. Regina Murphy, S.C., chairperson, ICCR, to Mr. W. S. Sneath, chairman and chief executive officer, Union Carbide Corporation, November 7, 1977.

27. Letter from Mr. Thomas A. Murphy, chairman of the board, General Motors, to Mr. Hugh Calkins, chairman of the Corporation Committee on Shareholder Responsibility, Harvard University, November 22, 1977.

28. Letter from Leon H. Sullivan to Mr. Thomas A. Murphy, chairman of the board, General Motors Corporation, November 23, 1977.

29. Leon H. Sullivan, "A Statement to the House International Relations Subcommittee on International Economic Policy and Trade and the Subcommittee on Africa," Washington, D.C., July 6, 1978, p. 10.

30. Letter from James W. Rawlings, vice chairman, Union Carbide Africa and Middle East, Inc., to Dr. Leon H. Sullivan, May 9, 1978.

31. Quoted by Leon H. Sullivan in "A Statement to the House International Relations Subcommittee . . .," pp. 13–16.

32. Minutes of the board meeting of the International Council for Equality of opportunity Principles, Inc., Monday, December 10, 1979, held at the Progress Plaza, Philadelphia; 3 pages.

33. Ibid., p. 3.

34. Reid Weedon, *Eighth Report on the Signatory Companies to the Statement of Principles for South Africa* (Cambridge, Mass.: A. D. Little, Co., 1984).

# 5

# An International
# Human Rights Perspective
# on Corporate Codes

GARTH MEINTJES

## Introduction

This chapter[1] offers a human rights perspective on global codes of conduct, and gives an affirmative answer to the question of whether this is an idea whose time has come? The importance of this initiative is especially evident when one considers the enormous impact that transnational corporations (TNCs) are having on the lives of people in even the most distant parts of the globe. Since this impact is rapidly increasing due to the globalization of the world's economy, the values and concerns discussed in this volume are of the utmost significance, both in terms of their impact upon the way we do business, and in terms of ensuring respect for basic human dignity.

The view presented here is that of a human rights advocate, not that of a corporate counsel.[2] Consequently, the argument put forward below is more concerned with identifying the direction in which norms need to develop than in providing a precise assessment of their current status. In particular, it is premised upon the belief that it is inevitable—in light of the dramatic shift in power brought about by the privatization of industries and economic globalization—that international civil society will become increasingly attentive to the impact of TNCs upon human rights. Indeed, there are signs that this process is already well underway, and that many of the strategies nongovernmental organizations (NGOs) have developed and implemented to promote adoption of and adherence to human rights standards by states are turning out to be just as effective against TNCs.

In presenting this perspective, the first section describes the emerging human rights obligations of TNCs; then the chapter examines some strategies used by NGOs and others to promote more responsible business conduct with regard to human rights; the next section discusses the merits of the various efforts by states and international organizations to establish more uniform and enforceable codes; and the final section recommends the preparation of an annual report to document the human rights practices of all major TNCs.

### Emerging Human Rights Obligations of TNCs

International law, traditionally, was seen as governing only the relations between states. As such, it created rights and obligations for state actors only. This does not mean that international law concerned itself only with state activities, but rather that states were expected, when necessary, to use their authority to regulate the activities within their jurisdiction which were of concern to the international community. The flaw of this approach is that one cannot always count on states to fulfill these expectations. They may lack the will to do so, or as is increasingly the case, they may lack the requisite power. One great exception to this traditional view of international law is the development since 1948 of the international human rights framework. International human rights law recognizes many specific rights for individuals, and also refers, albeit only obliquely, to the responsibilities of nonstate actors. For example, the preamble of the Universal Declaration of Human Rights adopted by the UN General Assembly, states that "every individual and every organ of society . . . shall strive by teaching and education to promote respect for these rights and freedoms and by progressive measures, national and international, to secure their universal and effective recognition and observance."[3]

Perhaps prompted by this call, NGOs around the world have taken on the task of observing, documenting, and reporting on activities—predominately by state actors—that infringe upon international human rights standards. This amorphous group of private entities generally takes as its point of departure the view that it is primarily the responsibility of states to promote and to protect international human rights. Accordingly, various strategies of NGOs have included: calling upon states to act collectively to develop clearer standards and to establish better enforcement mechanisms; urging individual states to exercise leadership in designing foreign policies which promote or even compel greater respect for human rights; and encouraging or shaming delinquent governments into improving their domestic human rights laws and practices.

The net result of these strategies is that political leaders are now obliged to include concern for human dignity among the factors influencing their decisions, or they risk losing popular legitimacy both at home and abroad. Notwithstanding this important progress, it has recently become clear to a number of these human rights NGOs that the real power to promote or to protect human rights no longer rests exclusively in the hands of states.

### Impact of TNCs upon Human Rights

As a result of increased economic globalization, TNCs now exercise significantly more power over the lives of workers, consumers, and investors around the world. Moreover, the influence of TNCs extends beyond the participants in their business activities, as TNCs often have an impact on the environment and resources of neighboring communities, sometimes displace those whose presence inhibits their business development, and at times even corrupt or unduly interfere with local political policies and decision-making.

The potential threat posed by TNCs towards human rights is especially alarming in countries where the domestic government is either unwilling or unable to regulate the conduct of TNCs. For example, Nigeria has done almost nothing to regulate the conduct of Royal Dutch Shell, which has been accused of a litany of abuses in that country, including polluting the rivers and lands of the Ogoni people, ruthlessly exploiting their natural resources, subverting the judicial process by bribing witnesses, collaborating or conspiring with the military junta to suppress opposition to Shell's activities, and rewarding soldiers for extra-judicial killings and repression.[4]

Perhaps more commonly though, TNCs are accused of abuses directly related to the production of their products. This could include "[c]oncerns such as workplace safety, environmental protection, and discrimination based on gender, disability and sexual orientation."[5] For example, Nike recently suffered embarrassment because of reports that during one day last year, a Vietnamese factory making Nike shoes disciplined fifty-six female employees for wearing nonregulation shoes to work; as punishment they were forced to run around the factory in the hot sun, until twelve of them collapsed.[6] This was not an isolated incident, as there have been other complaints against Nike involving subcontractors who pay less than the prevailing minimum wage, employ underage workers, and require 72-hour work weeks.[7] To its credit, Nike has not been unresponsive to such complaints by NGOs and in some cases it has terminated contracts with the most notorious suppliers.[8]

### The Debate over Corporate Responsibility

The demands by NGOs for greater corporate responsibility are often met by the objection from TNCs that, while human rights are a valid concern, they are the responsibility of governments and not private business entities. The best exposition of this argument is that of Nobel Prize-winning economist Milton Friedman, who called the idea of corporate social responsibility a "fundamentally subversive doctrine" in a free society.[9] According to this view, corporate executives have no right to use the funds of shareholders, customers, or employees for social interests or programs. In Friedman's view, "there is only one social responsibility of business . . . to increase its profits so long as it stays within the rules of the game."[10]

In reply, human rights NGOs insist that the rules of the game are simply inadequate and that their demand for greater accountability on the part of TNCs is justified by the global trend toward privatization and the loosening of business regulations. By relinquishing their tight economic controls, governments have created an environment in which TNCs are flourishing. TNCs have gained access to new markets, found cheaper labor, and uncovered a wealth of raw materials, and are as a result having an unprecedented impact upon people's lives.[11]

This shift in power is so dramatic that:

> Most UN Member States have economies far smaller than the annual revenues of large multinationals. As Richard Barnet and John Cavanagh point out in their book *Global Dreams,* "Ford's economy is larger than Saudi Arabia's and Norway's." And the economies of those two nations, in turn, dwarf those of nearly every nation in Africa.[12]

Accordingly, NGOs maintain that TNCs, by gaining powers that were formerly vested only in states, have also attracted the human rights responsibilities that international law currently imposes upon states.

Another argument for greater accountability is based upon the potential for enlightened self-interest on the part of TNCs. By modifying their practices to comply with international human rights standards, these corporations will benefit from improved relations with their employees and from a more positive image with their consumers and the communities in which they work. Moreover, by avoiding exploiting or oppressive business practices now, they will likely avoid the future liability which may result from precedent-setting claims being brought by NGOs and the relatives of victims.

But there is an even deeper moral aspect to this argument, namely, that "corporations are run not by robots, but by people, each of whom must confront his or her own conscience."[13] Ignoring human rights concerns might have been easy when the line between public and private activities still held meaning, but that line has now become little more than a mist which quickly vanishes in the light of scrutiny.

The strongest argument for holding TNCs accountable to human rights standards is simply that the idea of a corporation as a legal fiction without responsibilities is no more sacred or accurate than the idea of unfettered state sovereignty. In other words, just as concern for the protection of human dignity is sufficient grounds for placing restrictions upon the way in which states exercise their power, it is equally sufficient for placing restrictions upon the conduct of TNCs.

## Strategies Utilized to Promote Human Rights

### Efforts of Human Rights NGOs and Socially Responsible Business Groups

In light of the current powerful position of TNCs and their implicit role in the arena of human rights, several NGOs have started employing in their dealings with both transnational and domestic corporations strategies remarkably similar to those previously utilized in dealing with state practices and policies. These strategies include: (1) promoting adoption, both individually and collectively, of commonly acceptable human rights standards; (2) urging states and international organizations to work together to establish binding regulations or codes governing the conduct of TNCs with regard to issues such as bribery and corruption, forced labor, worker rights, production safety standards, disposal of toxic waste, and environmental protection; (3) encouraging corporations supportive of human rights to use their influence to promote human rights concerns in their business dealings with others; (4) raising the human rights awareness of stakeholders, employees, and consumers; (5) targeting delinquent corporations with leaflets, boycotts, and letter-writing campaigns; (6) marshaling shame by publicly exposing unseemly business practices; and (7) filing legal complaints, when possible, before judicial and quasijudicial tribunals. These strategies are being implemented in a number of situations, including the following.

### Standard Setting
Amnesty International, the best known human rights NGO in the world, is significantly involved in the promotion of commonly acceptable human rights standards. As an example specific to TNCs, Amnesty considered several resolutions dealing with the conduct of TNCs at its annual International Council Meeting. These resolutions extended the mandates of membership groups to work constructively with the business community in appropriate

cases and to confront irresponsible conduct when necessary.[14] This is an area where Amnesty seems to have both credibility and leverage. For example, socially responsible investors frequently turn to the expertise of groups like AI for direction regarding how to strengthen their links with companies that translate activists' concerns into demands for corporate action.[15]

### Encouraging Standard Setting through State Action

Human Rights Watch, another major NGO involved in standard setting, has been involved in challenging the Clinton administration to develop a better set of model business principles dealing with human rights and is lobbying for more hard-hitting and enforceable measures against delinquent Chinese businesses specifically.[16]

### Influence of Corporations Supportive of Human Rights

The Child Labor Coalition (CLC) is using consumer education to respond to the problem of child labor in the imported rug industry. In an effort to encourage member corporations to use their business dealings to promote human rights, the CLC orchestrated the "Rugmark" campaign, where before a company may use the "Rugmark" label it must agree to not use child labor and to allow surprise visits by inspectors.[17]

Another commendable example of the positive influence of corporations is Business for Social Responsibility (BSR)—an association of almost eight hundred firms which encourages the promotion of human rights through its consulting and clearinghouse activities. Although most of its members are small and medium firms, it also has forty firms with annual gross revenues exceeding U.S. $5 billion.[18] Some of the members are familiar names such as AT&T, Coopers & Lybrand, Dayton Hudson, Federal Express, The Gap, Home Depot, Honeywell, Polaroid, Revlon, Taco Bell, and Viacom.[19] Giving further credence to BSR efforts, its president, Robert Dunn, is former vice president of corporate affairs for Levi Strauss & Co.[20] As part of its human rights program, BSR hosted a conference focused on human rights policies, involving twenty-five companies, ranging in size from Walt Disney Studios to Noah's Bagels.[21]

### Raising Awareness

The Franklin Research and Development Corporation, a social responsibility investment firm, works both to raise corporate awareness regarding human rights issues and to encourage the promotion of human rights through business dealings. It files stockholder resolutions with companies urging them to adopt codes of conduct for their suppliers. This action has already proven effective in some important cases. For example, this group recently reached an agreement with Wal-Mart, the United States' largest retailer, setting human rights standards for all its vendors, both in the United States and abroad.[22]

### Targeting Campaigns

The story of Starbucks' code of conduct is evidence of the potential success of target campaigns against delinquent corporations.[23] In 1995, activists began asking Starbucks to impose sourcing codes—standards setting minimal working conditions and pay—on the Guatemalan plantations from which they purchase coffee beans. At first, the corporation was hesitant to take action, but the pressure to conform increased as the public became aware of their lack of compliance—for the most part as a result of informational pickets set up outside Starbucks locations. Within the year, Starbucks issued a code of conduct and specific action plans for each country from which they purchase coffee beans.[24]

### Marshaling Shame

Marshaling shame was an effective strategy used against Reebok, in helping to convince it to adopt a human rights standard. The International Labor Rights Education and Research Fund (ILRERF) publicly criticized Reebok and several other athletic footwear companies for using contractors who violated basic worker rights. To Reebok's credit, rather than simply dismissing the criticisms, it consulted with ILRERF and other human rights experts in the drafting of its "Human Rights Production Standards."[25]

### Legal Action

Recognizing the potential for taking legal action to address the impact of TNCs on human rights, the National Labor Committee (NLC) is examining the possibilities of litigation for consumer fraud against companies that claim to have codes of conduct but have not lived up to them. Although this would serve as a last resort, such litigation is an appropriate response to companies that adopt codes but then do no more, not posting them in work areas, and at times not even translating them into local languages. The NLC has also participated in public campaigns, joining forces with religious and social groups to sponsor protests targeted against The Gap. The protests resulted in a code of conduct agreed upon by The Gap, the NLC, and two Presbyterian ministers. This agreement is seen as a milestone, as it provides for independent monitoring and an inspection process "that could provide a blueprint for future agreements."[26]

One problem with the monitoring activities of human rights NGOs and the reaction of TNCs is that there is not yet a uniform set of standards that can be evenly applied. A good example of this problem involved Nike's effort to repair its tarnished public image by employing an outside reviewer to examine the factory conditions of its suppliers. The resulting report by Andrew Young is considered flimsy and shallow, and was roundly criticized for not employing a rigorous methodology and for failing to address the most critical issues.[27]

### Influence of Socially Responsible TNCs on State Actors

Successfully influencing delinquent TNCs to stop violating human rights can have consequences beyond the business sphere itself. Indeed, in certain circumstances, responsible conduct by TNCs can have a significant impact upon the overall human rights conditions of the countries in which they do business. This point was forcefully argued by the human rights movement in its struggle against apartheid in South Africa. In an attempt to respond to such arguments, the Reverend Leon Sullivan proposed one of the first and perhaps best-known sets of voluntary principles, dealing with corporate conduct in a country with poor human rights conditions.

The Sullivan principles unfortunately did not succeed in ending apartheid and were later rejected by their own author, but they were nonetheless a significant step forward, in that they acknowledged the need for corporate responsibility. They required that U.S. companies doing business in South Africa commit themselves to racially nondiscriminatory employment, to paying a fair wage, to providing managerial training for nonwhites, to providing assistance with regard to housing, health care, transportation, and recreation, and to using their influence to help end apartheid.[28]

A similar set of voluntary principles has also been adopted for U.S. firms doing business in Northern Ireland. The MacBride Principles are more limited and focus mainly on discrimination and the need for equal treatment of Catholic workers in a Protestant-majority country. In a rather unique provision, however, they require that "MacBride companies" try to protect the personal safety of their workers both at work and while commuting to and from work.[29]

Although these two examples serve as important precedent, the rapid globalization of the world's economy makes it necessary to move beyond such ad hoc standard setting exercise and to adopt more uniform and enforceable codes which apply to the conduct of all TNCs in all countries.

## The Prospects for the Development of Uniform and Enforceable Codes

In recent decades, steps have been taken in this direction by the United Nations (UN), the International Labor Organization (ILO), and the Organization for Economic Cooperation and Development (OECD), as well as by individual countries such as the United States. Unfortunately, as can be seen below, these standard-setting efforts have as yet yielded only limited results.

### United Nations

The United Nations initiative started in 1977 when the UN Commission on Transnational Corporations (UNCTC) was given instructions to draft a "Code of Conduct for Transnational Corporations." Although this code was to have been the commission's "highest priority," a draft code was not introduced until fourteen years later, and has yet to be adopted by the UN.[30]

The purpose of the Draft Code of Conduct is to guide the conduct of TNCs, and to incorporate the more specialized provisions developed by UNCTAD, ILO, and ICC.[31] As such, it is intended to be "an essential element in the strengthening of international economic and social co-operation . . . to maximize the contributions of transnational corporations to economic development and growth and to minimize the negative effects of the activities of these corporations."[32]

However, the draft code has been criticized by NGOs for the cursory and general manner in which human rights and the fair treatment of workers are discussed. For example, the draft simply requires that "[t]ransnational corporations shall respect human rights and fundamental freedoms in the countries in which they operate. In their social and industrial relations, transnational corporations shall not discriminate on the basis of race, colour, sex, language, social, national and ethnic origin or political or other opinion."[33]

Moreover, the Draft Code is regarded as weak, in that there is no formal enforcement mechanism by which to ensure compliance with its provisions. As one commentator has stated, "Without a way to force US companies' compliance with Code provisions, the UN will probably be left with nothing more than a non-binding resolution or declaration of the General Assembly."[34]

### Organization for Economic Cooperation and Development

Another intergovernmental standard-setting initiative is that of the Organization for Economic Cooperation and Development (OECD), a body of twenty-six relatively affluent nations, which established Guidelines for Multi-national Enterprises in 1976. Among other things, these guidelines recognize the right of labor to organize and bargain collectively, and also require employers to provide facilities and information to union representatives so that they may engage in meaningful bargaining. As with the UN draft code, there is no formal enforcement mechanism by which to ensure compliance with the OECD guidelines, although "workers and trade unions have occasionally achieved successful resolution of disputes through recourse to the OECD."[35] The most significant shortcomings of this initiative are that its human rights content is limited and that it covers only a small number of countries.

### International Labor Organization

The International Labor Organization (ILO) is a broader organization comprising 159 member nations. It has a tradition of pursuing consensus between business and labor. Of the ILO conventions, a number may be called its human rights "core," covering freedom of association, the right to organize and bargain collectively, minimum wages, work hours, workplace health and safety, and the elimination of forced labor, child labor, and discrimination.[36]

The ILO Code reaches areas other than those of the OECD, such as job creation, investment in the local economy, subcontracting, and others. As with the OECD, enforcement is more a matter of discreet persuasion by the officials of both bodies or of public embarrassment through the media. Although the ILO does not have the power of sanctions for enforcement purposes, it does have a structured complaint procedure, involving a Standing Committee on Multinational Enterprises empowered to investigate and make specific findings of code violations by individual companies.

Efforts of the ILO have achieved some success in recent years. They have resulted in ten thousand prisoners being freed from unlawful forced labor in an Asian state, in the release from prison of trade union and employers' organization leaders in countries of Africa and Central America, in the acceptance by countries on three continents of international aid to eliminate child labor, and in the abolition of bonded labor laws by the world's largest democracy and a pledge to free every bonded worker.[37]

Notwithstanding this success, critics of both the ILO and the OECD maintain that their guidelines are "limited and [break] little new ground, mostly reaffirming the long-standing rights of workers to organize unions, to bargain collectively, and to [have] nondiscriminatory employment."[38]

## The United States

### Legislative Initiatives

With the increased awareness of human rights issues in the 1970s, U.S. legislation came to involve more provisions concerning the rights of workers overseas. As summarized by one commentator, "[f]or the purposes of U.S. legislation, the following are specified as 'internationally recognized worker rights':

(1)  the right of association,
(2)  the right to organize and bargain collectively,
(3)  a prohibition on the use of any form of forced or compulsory labor,
(4)  a minimum age for the employment of children, and
(5)  taking into account the country's level of economic development, acceptable conditions of work with respect to minimum wages, hours of work, and occupational safety and health.[39]

Having recognized these rights, Congress has provided a unilateral enforcement mechanism, "empowering the USTR [the office of the United States Trade Representative] to impose upon US trading partners the full range of available trade sanctions in response to worker rights violations."[40] However, while this legislation focuses on ensuring that foreign governments and trading partners respect the rights noted above, it does not provide a mechanism by which the activities of U.S.-based TNCs operating overseas can be monitored and governed, except through pressure on the foreign countries in which they operate.

### Executive Initiatives

For years, human rights advocates and organizations have requested the formulation of a set of business principles that would curb U.S.-based investment and activity in countries known for human rights abuses. Finally in 1994, with the heightened public opinion about flagrant human rights abuses in China, President Clinton promised to develop such principles. In 1996, his administration introduced its Model Business Principles, which set out a minimum standard of conduct for corporations with regard to human rights.[41] This voluntary code of business ethics is intended to be used by U.S.-based TNCs "to show their commitment to upholding fundamental human and labor rights."[42]

The Model Business Principles recommend that TNCs sign onto corporate codes that would cover at least the following: (1) workplace health and safety; (2) fair employment practices, including the right to organize unions and bargain collectively, and bans on child labor, forced labor, and discrimination; (3) environmental protection; (4) compliance with laws against bribery and corruption; and (5) a corporate culture that respects free expression and does not condone political coercion in the workplace, that contributes to communities in which the company operates, and that values ethical conduct.[43]

However, human rights advocates consider the Model Principles to be too little, too late; they consider them both vague and duplicative of existing laws, with no effective method of implementation or enforcement. Indeed, it has been said that "the final draft has so many compromises that it will disappoint the human rights groups it was trying to satisfy in the first place."[44]

Businesses, on the other hand, see it as an attempt to "deputize" the TNCs, by making them moral agents of the U.S. government, thus placing them at a comparative disadvantage with competitors. In fact, "the U.S. Council for International Business issued a statement expressing its preference for the OECD and ILO guidelines of the 1970s that, it claimed, addressed most of the areas in the Administration's principles. The OECD and ILO guidelines, it noted, have the advantage of being multilateral, thus not putting U.S. based firms at a competitive disadvantage."[45]

More generally, it is presumed that "the voluntary, general code . . . is likely to be largely ignored by businesses and criticized by human rights advocates." According to U.S. Representative Nancy Pelosi, "It's a weakened, watered-down version that won't be effective, but will enable the administration to say they issued a voluntary code of conduct."[46]

As shown by the above overview, there is little prospect for a uniform and enforceable code to emerge any time soon. Nonetheless, there are already a variety of standards by which TNCs conduct may be judged and monitored. Indeed, by refusing to let the search for perfection stand in the way of positive change, NGOs can seize the initiative of developing a framework of holding TNCs accountable for the human rights consequences of their business conduct.

## Recommendation: An Annual Report on the Human Rights Practices of TNCs

In addition to the various strategies mentioned earlier, one additional mechanism could prove effective in the absence of a uniform and enforceable code. Since the late 1970s the U.S. Department of State (DOS), under a mandate from Congress, has produced an Annual Country Report on Human

Rights Practices. Although this report is primarily intended to inform Congress regarding the foreign policy matters such as the granting of aid and military assistance to other countries, under pressure from NGOs it has been transformed into a powerful monitoring tool, as well as a reasonably reliable guide for other policy and decision makers. While it is unlikely that the DOS report will soon be expanded to include coverage of the human rights practices of TNCs,[47] there is nothing to prevent NGOs from working together to prepare such a report.[48]

Conceivably, an annual report on the human rights practices of TNCs could begin by focusing on the conduct of the top five hundred TNCs.[49] While the framework for evaluating each TNC's conduct cannot yet be expected to be uniform and comprehensive, it might include the following criteria:

- Has the TNC accepted responsibility for the impact of its business practices upon the condition of human rights in the places where it does business?
- Has it voluntarily adopted a code of conduct in an effort to live up to its responsibilities?
- Is the scope of the adopted code sufficient to ensure that business practices do not have an adverse impact upon human rights conditions?
- Does the code seek to promote business practices that have a positive impact upon human rights conditions?
- Does the code include a complaint or grievance mechanism, available to workers and others impacted by the TNCs business practices?
- Is the existence of the code adequately communicated to workers and others covered by its provisions?
- How many complaints have been received during the previous year, and how have they been resolved or otherwise dealt with?
- Is the TNC open to outside scrutiny and responsive to reasonably well founded criticism?
- What general circumstances help to place the above evaluations of the TNC's business practices into context?

By compiling a report in accordance with the above criteria, human rights NGOs will be able to achieve a variety of objectives. First, the report will help raise general public awareness regarding the human rights responsibilities of TNCs. Second, it will enable consumers and investors to make informed choices regarding which products and services to support. Third, it will provide an incentive for responsible corporate leaders to keep track of the human rights impact of their business practices. Fourth, it will assist NGOs in identifying which TNCs to confront regarding irresponsible business practices. And finally, it will no doubt spur further debate regarding the appropriate standards for judging the human rights responsibilities of TNCs.

## Conclusion

While it is true that international law alone does not at present impose clear human rights obligations on TNCs, this has not prevented human rights organizations from confronting irresponsible conduct. Unfortunately, due to a lack of agreement between states and a lack of leadership among TNCs, at present the standards by which transnational business conduct should be judged are neither uniform nor effective. Nonetheless, the indications thus far suggest that strategies which human rights organizations employed against governments can, in many instances, be equally successful in confronting irresponsible TNCs. Moreover, the effectiveness of these strategies can be greatly enhanced by the preparation of an annual report monitoring the business practices of all major TNCs regarding human rights as recommended here. Together, these tools will enable international civil society to bring considerable pressure to bear upon delinquent TNCs whose practices threaten its most basic interests.

This possesses an interesting choice for business leaders and corporate counsels—they can either continue to deny any responsibility with regard to human rights and risk inviting a backlash from consumers, employees, shareholders, and, most importantly, NGOs, or they can take the initiative to help develop a uniform set of enforceable standards. The latter choice may reduce some of the profits of TNCs, but it is a choice they should seriously consider, as it will be a more morally and politically defensible position, and perhaps even serve to provide a more even playing field for international business competition.

## Notes

1. I acknowledge with appreciation the assistance of my research assistant Ms. Michelle Mack, as well as the helpful comments of my colleague Professor Robert Rodes.

2. To illustrate this difference in perspective, suppose that each is asked to give an opinion about the human rights obligations of transnational corporations. The corporate counsel might say that there is no specific international human rights treaty governing their conduct, while the advocate would probably point out that the absence

of a treaty on point does not negate the existence of obligations, especially considering it was not very long ago when many states also incorrectly claimed not to have any international humans rights obligations.

3. G.A. Res. 217 A (III) of 10 December 1948, UN Doc. A/810, at 71 (1948).

4. Whether these allegations against Shell are to be believed may soon be for a jury in a U.S. court to decide in a case being brought under the Alien Tort Claims Act by persons including the relatives of the late Ken Saro-Wiwa; see Plaintiffs' First Set of Interrogatories and Requests for Production of Documents to the Royal Dutch Petroleum Company, Wiwa v. Royal Dutch Petroleum Co. (S.D.N.Y. 1997) (96 Civ. 08386 (KMW)). The deceased, an internationally renowned author, and human rights and environmental activist, was hanged on November 10, 1995, after being convicted of treason in a sham trial for activities which included organizing protests against Shell.

5. Simon Billenness, *Beyond South Africa: New Frontiers in Corporate Responsibility* 86 BUSINESS AND SOCIETY REVIEW, Summer 1993, at 28.

6. Bob Herbert, *In America: Brutality in Vietnam*, N.Y. TIMES, March 28, 1997, at A29.

7. See *Nike ends contracts with four Indonesian factories*, AGENCE FRANCE PRESSE, September 23, 1997.

8. *Id.*

9. Milton Friedman, *The Social Responsibility of Business Is to Increase Profits*, N.Y. TIMES, Sept. 13, 1970, at 32, 125.

10. *Id.*

11. Billenness, *supra* note 5, at 28.

12. Douglass Cassel, *Corporate Initiatives: A Second Human Rights Revolution?* 19 FORDHAM INT'L L.J. 1963, 1979 (1996) (citation omitted).

13. *Id.* at 1978.

14. See *AIUSA AGM 1997 Resolutions: Sunday Voting Plenary Final Draft*, Amnesty International report (Amnesty International, New York, N.Y.) (on file with author); 1997 *International Council Meeting (ICM) Resolutions*, Amnesty International report (Amnesty International, New York, N.Y.) (on file with author).

15. Billenness, *supra* note 5, at 28.

16. Cassel, *supra* note 12, at 1975.

17. Lance Compa & Tashia Hinchcliff-Darricarrere, *Enforcing International Labor Rights through Corporate Codes of Conduct*, 33 COLUM. J. TRANSNAT'L L. 663, 673 (1995).

18. Cassel, *supra* note 12, at 1973.

19. *Id.* at 1973–74.

20. *Id.* at 1974.

21. Dominic Bencivenga, *Human Rights Agenda: Corporations Weigh Benefits of Voluntary Plans*, 7/13/95 N.Y.L.J. 5 (col. 2).

22. Billenness, *supra* note 5, at 31.

23. Cassel, *supra* note 12, at 1976.

24. Jennifer Click, *New Business Standards Focus on Human Rights*, H.R. MAGAZINE, June 1996, at 65.

25. Billenness, *supra* note 5, at 29.

26. Ken Cottrill, *Global Codes of Conduct*, JOURNAL OF BUSINESS STRATEGY, May/June 1996, at 55, 59.

27. See *Report on Nike Work Force Glossed Over Issues*, Letter to the Editor, N.Y. TIMES, June 30, 1997, at A10; Steven Greenhouse, *Nike Shoe Plant in Vietnam Is Called Unsafe for Workers*, N.Y. TIMES, Nov. 8, 1997, at A1, D2.

28. Cassel, *supra* note 12, at 1970–71.

29. *Id.*

30. Mark Baker, *Private Codes of Corporate Conduct: Should the Fox Guard the Henhouse?* 24 U. MIAMI INTER-AM. L. REV. 399, 410 (1993).

31. *Id.* at 411.

32. *Id.* at 410.

33. Compa & Hinchcliff-Darricarrere, *supra* note 17, at 670. See generally, Development and International Economic Cooperation: Transnational Corporations, UN Economic and Social Commission, 2d Sess., Agenda Item 7(d), at 1, UN Doc. E/1990/94 (1990).

34. Baker, *supra* note 30, at 413.

35. Compa & Hinchcliff-Darricarrere, *supra* note 17, at 671.

36. *Id.* at 665 n.2. See *Human Rights—A Common Responsibility*, International Labor Organization (1988) (report of the ILO Director General).

37. *ILO: Human Rights in the Working World*, I.L.O. Report to the World Conference on Human Rights, Vienna, Austria, June 14–25, 1993 (obtained from <gopher://gopher.igc.apc.org:70/00/peace/hr/hr.gopher/8>).

38. Cassel, *supra* note 12, at 1970.

39. Harlan Mandel, note, *In Pursuit of the Missing Link: International Worker Rights and International Trade?*, 27 COLUM. J. TRANSNAT'L L. 443, 446–47 (1989).

40. *Id.* at 446. "The USTR is empowered to suspend, withdraw or prevent application of trade agreement concessions, impose duties or other import restrictions on goods, impose fees or restrictions on services, and restrict the terms and conditions of any service sector access authorizations granted or pending after the time a petition is filed or an investigation is initiated." *Id.* at 446 n.15 (citing Trade Act of 1974 §301(c), 19 U.S.C.A. §2411(c) (Supp. 1997)).

41. Barbara Frey, *The Legal and Ethical Responsibilities of Transnational Corporations in the Protection of International Human Rights*, 6 MINN. J. GLOBAL TRADE 153, 172 (1997).

42. *Id.*

43. Cassel, *supra* note 12, at 1974.

44. David Sanger, *Clinton to Urge a Rights Code for Business Dealing Abroad*, N.Y. TIMES, March 27, 1995, at D4.

45. Cassel, *supra* note 12, at 1975.

46. Robert Greenberger, *Code for Firms Selling Abroad Arrives Soon*, THE WALL STREET JOURNAL, March 24, 1995, at A2.

47. Although, it should be noted that there is ample precedent for monitoring the practices of nonstate actors such as guerilla groups in countries where their conduct is believed to have a significant impact upon the overall human rights assessment.

48. The idea for an annual report on the human rights practices of TNCs arose during a conversation with my colleague Professor Dinah Shelton.

49. Determination regarding which TNCs to monitor may be based either upon the total value of their assets or the amount of their annual revenues.

— ❋ —

## PART 3

# Codes as a Contemporary Form of the Social Control of Business

*Prospects for Success*

# 6

# Global Codes of Conduct

## *Activists, Lawyers, and Managers in Search of a Solution*

JAMES E. POST

Do global codes of conduct represent an important pathway to a future or an "impossible dream"? Current interest in codes reflects the social and political view that codes are utilitarian—they meet a goal. It is less clear whether or not codes have a more significant economic and/or moral purpose? Do examples of "mature" codes of conduct provide any useful lessons to the development and nurturing of "emerging" codes? Is there a learning curve for practitioners of code creation—activists, lawyers, and managers—and, if so, are there ways in which academic research can contribute to the learning process?

## Introduction

Like Cervantes' fabled Don Quixote, many of my colleagues and I have tilted at many windmills. We have sought to make a difference in our organizations, our communities, and our professions. Our commitments may have stemmed from frustrations, recognition of an injustice, or issues so fundamental to our beliefs and values as human beings that we felt compelled to act. Such "calls" may perplex and puzzle our colleagues, neighbors, and families. But I suspect that most people reading this essay will recall the sense of anger or anguish or pain that first prompted us to say, "this is wrong and it *must* change!"

The people interested in global codes are more than riders on old horses, jousting with old injustices. Most of us are actively engaged in a world of human affairs in which we have demonstrated some ability to get things done.

As teachers, executives, lawyers, or activists, we have shown that we are "practical people" who know how to change the world, if only a little. Our worldly knowledge is extensive and we possess a broad repertoire of practical skills. The editor of this volume obviously hopes that these essays will help to accomplish something others can also use in their efforts to shape a world in which human beings can live in proper relation to one another, their communities, and the natural environment. That is a fancy way of saying someone else also thinks *our* windmills matter!

Codes of conduct occupy an interesting place in the picture of social commitment, action, and change. There are dozens of codes of conduct in the modern business world. By one count, there are more than eighty multiparty formal codes attempting (or aspiring) to guide corporate behavior.[1] These are a clear response to the challenge of harmonizing corporate behavior with social goals.

The codes are a modern form of "social control of business." The idea that business needs "social control" lost its cachet in the early 1980s, but times have changed and there are signs that this idea is once again timely as the twentieth century closes. Simply stated, codes of conduct exist because we need them, and we need them because many "gaps" exist between public expectations of responsible business conduct and the performance of individual firms or industries. Codes of conduct signal the existence of serious problems of corporate behavior and the commitment of interested parties to move towards standards embodied in the code.

My objective is to address three questions that seem central to the discussion of codes of conduct. In framing these questions, I take as a starting point the idea that we need to examine two distinct processes: the *formulation* of the code of conduct, and the companion process, *implementing* the conduct's provisions.

1. First, why have so many activists, lawyers, and business executives embraced codes of conduct as a useful means to achieve better relations between business and society? Do these motivations make a difference in the type of code that is created or its ultimate effectiveness?

2. Second, what problems do efforts to operationalize a code of conduct encounter when the language of a code is translated into a "living document" for organizations and people? What barriers and obstacles challenge the effective implementation of codes?

3. Third, what ideas do various management theories suggest be taken into account in the development and implementation of *effective* codes of con-

duct? Does management theory have anything to offer regarding the formulation or implementation of codes of conduct?

The answers to these questions are complex and the remainder of this chapter attempts to address these issues. In summary, I wish to suggest these conclusions:

1. Activists, lawyers, and executives find codes of conduct to be a practical way to create reasonable forums for articulating principles, policies, and practices to guide socially acceptable conduct of business in the modern world. While codes differ in form and expression, they have in common the commitment of authors and signatories to a level of business practice that recognizes important problems, relationships, and ethical concepts.

2. Codes of conduct typically encounter a "translation problem," as the well-intended words of a code are transformed into actual behavior. There are many pitfalls and obstacles to be overcome in operationalizing any code of conduct. Some barriers are institutional, existing within the culture of a business or industry or within the legal and political mechanisms of society. Other barriers exist at the individual level where human beings have to meet objectives, alter behavior, and reconcile emotional responses to new realities. Good code design takes these problems into account, and code advocates—activists, lawyers, and executives—must recognize that designing a good implementation process is central to effective code development.

3. Management theory has not been a major influence in the development of most codes. There are however, theories of stakeholder relations, resource dependence, and institutional behavior that are relevant to these questions. There are a number of propositions that should be examined in the hope of determining ways in which codes can be made more effective as mechanisms for harmonizing economic and social goals. Accepting the proposition that there is nothing so useful as a good theory, perhaps we have, or can create, theories that are useful to tilting at windmills.

### Why Codes?

Codes of conduct enjoy great appeal as we come to the end of the 1990s. Several factors help explain this popularity. Most notable is the great change in global economic conditions. We live in a world that has resoundingly endorsed capitalism and free markets as means through which improvements in the human socioeconomic condition can be effected. The last quarter of the twentieth century will surely stand as an era in which the shackles of government regulation, central planning, and trade barriers came off in North America, Europe, Asia, and much of the developing world, thereby unleashing a great burst of entrepreneurship and economic growth. Old institutions collapsed or were destroyed in favor of a new economic order. But the new order has been chaotic and it has left many gaps between peoples' needs for freedom and their need for security. The old security that government regulations or bureaucratic processes once provided is gone, exposing society to risks from which it had once thought itself safe. Even vigorous proponents of free trade have been forced to recognize the obvious problems. C. Fred Bergsten, director of the International Institute for Economics and past chairman of the American Competitiveness Policy Council, a pro-free-trade group, wrote:

> On balance, globalization is good for every country, but many governments have been slow to erect the necessary domestic complements. Without adequate safety-nets to cushion *adjustment burdens* . . . political support for globalization may be impossible to sustain.[2] (Emphasis added)

The new order has also encouraged business practices that were impossible or infrequent under old regimes. Relatively few companies pursued global production capacity in developing nations with extremely low labor costs until trade barriers fell and global sourcing became a reliable approach to serving global markets. Global manufacturing begets global finance, and the explosive growth of capital markets has produced innovations in currency trading that can sharply affect a country's ability or inability to manage economic development according to its own model.

This was at the core of the bitter conflict between international financier George Soros and Malaysian Prime Minister Mahathir Mohammed. In a series of speeches and articles in the *Asian Wall Street Journal*, Mahathir has charged currency traders like Soros with being "criminals" for their alleged manipulation of financial markets. In late September 1997, Mahathir said in an interview with the *South China Morning Post*, "Why should we [allow] something which is damaging to us?" "Currency trading will be limited to financing trade."

Mahathir's statement sent shock waves through Southeast Asian markets. The Malaysian currency—the ringgit—plunged against the dollar. The U.S. dollar gained 22.8 percent in two months, and signaled the precipitous fall of the ringgit. Worse, turmoil in the trading of Asian currencies also hurt Thailand, Indonesia, and the Philippines.

Soros called Mahathir "a menace to his own country" and claims he has made "vile, false" statements about Soros in order to cover up his own mismanagement of Malaysia's economy. Mahathir added more fuel to the rhetorical fire when he likened currency speculation to abuses such as monopolies and insider dealing. "With these self-serving systems," he wrote, "the big players can wreak havoc in the stock market. And that is precisely what they did in Southeast Asia." The conflict shows few signs of letting up. Speaking at the Asia-Pacific regional meeting in Santiago, Chile, on September 30, 1997, Mahathir gave a speech in which he said, "I would like to suggest that we do away with trade in currency as a commodity."[3]

In short, we are witnessing a high uncertainty amidst the chaotic conditions following the present historic shift in economic and political freedom. Codes may not solve the international currency crisis, but they do represent one attempt to impose an element of order on the chaos and to introduce some stability into the froth of change.

The second factor propelling our current enthusiasm for codes is the visibility of the social costs. It may be that social costs are an inevitable part of a nation's economic development. The truth of that assertion should not obscure the fact that many of the social costs that attended development activities in the past are better understood and can be minimized with little long-term negative effects on economic growth. This is especially clear in the areas of pollution control, protection of natural resources, and provision of safe working conditions.

As the social costs of economic growth and free market development become more pronounced and visible, it is inevitable that those at risk, and interested observers, will challenge the assumption that those burdens must be borne by the innocent. It is an assumption of convenience that sweatshops and child labor are inevitable in the garment industry or that a hazardous factory floor is "normal." It is also an assumption of convenience to say that plants cannot operate without unfiltered air emissions or that timber cannot be harvested without despoiling a nation's forests. As my high school world history teacher often said, "history is a pendulum and no pendulum ever swings just one way!" The drive to open markets and expand global economic activity has been powerful and sustained. But the externalities of economic behavior have become more pronounced and visible, and have begun to slow the pendulum's historic swing. In many industries, businesses now face the prospect of new regulation and restraints on competitive behavior. The impact of such actions is felt in a loss of corporate discretion, flexibility, and the freedom to make decisions. In the world of politics, voluntary action can deter more onerous forms of regulation. That is an important incentive for industry to design codes of conduct with which member firms can live. It provides an important motivation for business executives.

Activists have learned that codes can be a useful device as well. The world is not ready for a new wave of widespread government regulation. Extreme situations such as the 1997 tainted meat episode involving Hudson Foods create a widely perceived need for expanded regulatory authority (e.g., USDA did not have the power to directly order Hudson to close its operations, only to remove USDA inspectors, thereby eliminating the safety seal of approval). But a more recent episode of tainted produce from Guatemala did not produce similar pressure despite scientific assertions that this represents a broader threat to U.S. consumers.[4] For activists, an industry's willingness to consider "voluntary" standards of behavior may be an irresistible opportunity to "raise the bar" to an improved, if still imperfect, level of performance.

The third stakeholder group of importance in code formulation is the legal community, especially those corporate counsels and activist counsels whose role is essential in modern business negotiations. Because U.S. antitrust law, in particular, reflects a historic suspicion of voluntary standard-setting among competitors, the opinion of legal counsel is vital before a company or its executives and directors will commit to a multiparty code of conduct. Code language has become more formal and legalistic, reflecting the seriousness with which the parties view the commitment. It has also created pressure for more generally framed codes of principles or values as alternatives to specific outcomes or behavioral standards. As the permutations of codes of conduct increases, code design is becoming a growth area of lucrative legal innovation and practice.

### Obstacles—from Formulation to Implementation

Winning a code is not the same as winning the war! *A code of conduct does not settle a complex public issue.* It is a way station on the road to resolution, even though it may masquerade as a "solution." This point becomes clear if we examine the World Health Organization's international code for the marketing of breast-milk substitutes.

The WHO Code was promulgated in 1981 and formally adopted by 118 member nations of the World Health Assembly. The pressure to create this code came from public health advocates who saw the aggressive marketing behavior of infant formula manufacturers in developing nations as encouraging practices that undermined child health and safety. Direct pressure on manufacturers such as Nestlé, the industry leader, failed to effect significant change in industry marketing behavior. Frustrated at the lack of response, activists—including many church organizations—launched an international boycott of Nestlé products. Activists called the company a "baby killer" and engaged in a variety of confrontational tactics. The boycott campaign built momentum for several years and successfully mobilized thousands of people in North America and Europe. In time, pressure from many quarters produced a call for WHO to use its "good offices" to facilitate a conflict resolution process. The idea of a code of conduct had emerged in the late 1970s and gained credence as a viable means to bring adversaries together for a common purpose. The drafting process was lengthy and elaborate, involving several formal drafting rounds and the involvement of activists, industry, public health specialists, and consultants. WHO's director-general and staff provided important leadership through many conflicts and crises.

Adoption of the WHO code closed one chapter of the infant formula marketing controversy; it also opened a new chapter regarding the implementation of commitments embodied in the code (see Exhibit 1). The formulation of the WHO code required great political will and determination by all parties. The code that was adopted was weakened by compromises, especially those following from a change of presidential administrations in the United States. When political fortune shifted, and Ronald Reagan defeated President Jimmy Carter in the 1980 election, the relative strength of the adversaries shifted as well. The new administration was ideologically hostile to international regulation, and industry opponents of the code saw an opportunity to use the new administration to weaken the code. Proponents of the code—both inside and outside the U.S. government—struggled to keep the code process on track. The weeks leading up to the May 1981 vote were filled with intrigue and charged with intense activity. By the time the code was adopted in May 1981, collective exhaustion swept over the players, especially the WHO staff which had borne much of the responsibility for fashioning the compromises over the final weeks.

Having been involved on both sides of the code process—helping to create the language, then working to implement its provisions—I can testify that the work that followed the code's adoption was no less vexing and challenging than the work that went into creating the code.

Winning the code vote (despite the opposition of the United States) ended the formulation phase of the process but it foretold what would happen during the implementation phase. First, the political costs to WHO were very

EXHIBIT 1. *The World Health Organization Code for the Marketing of Breast-Milk Substitutes*

---

- Adopted by members (national governments) of World Health Assembly in May 1981
- Developed by staff of the World Health Organization (WHO)
  * Preparation of draft documents from 1980 through 1981
  * Recommended to members of the World Health Assembly by its Executive Committee
- Adopted as a "recommendation to members" (national governments)
- National governments have adopted the code in whole or in part
  * Adoptions often involve amendments to meet local conditions
- Firms in the industry were divided about the desirability of such a code in 1980 and 1981
- Following adoption by the WHO, Nestlé (industry's largest seller) made a stated commitment to implement the code in developing nations
- Nestlé established NIFAC (Nestlé Infant Formula Audit Commission) as an independent audit commission to oversee and publicly comment on its efforts to meet its stated commitments to the code
- NIFAC operated from 1981 through June 1990

---

high and thereby limited its ability to press for aggressive implementation. WHO needed resources to provide substantial technical assistance to developing countries, for example, but could not secure them from key member countries. Second, the industry's opposition to the code produced a "go slow" approach to operationalizing the code in the field. Third, activists were so incensed by the last-minute switching behavior of WHO, industry members, and government officials that many felt betrayed, isolated, and empowered to hold the moral high ground against all others. In retrospect, the code development process had failed to inspire meaningful collaboration because of the trust-shattering "end game" behavior that preceded the vote.

Ironically, one supporter of the code, immediately following the May 1981 vote, seemed to be Nestlé. The code gave the company a chance to urge others to judge its marketing activities in developing nations against the more "objective" code standards rather than the "subjective" standards of activist groups. To facilitate this process, Nestlé developed a set of marketing instructions for its field staff based on the WHO code provisions. Although criticized as being "watered down" code language, this effort to translate code language into behavioral guidelines for sales staffs in many different countries was an important step toward implementation.

### The Enforcement Problem

*A code without teeth is not worth the commitment.* Enforcement is essential for an effective code of conduct. Failure to create a working enforcement mechanism can doom a code to failure in the world of practice. If a code consists of a statement of behaviors or actions or principles that individuals and/or organizations would not freely adopt as being in their self-interest, some mechanism must be created to reinforce and support those terms. This point was well stated by President Ronald Reagan, who said, in reference to the Soviet Union's commitments on arms reduction, *"Trust, but verify!"*

The WHO code had no built-in enforcement mechanisms. Since the code was actually a "recommendation" to national governments, the enforcement of code provisions depended on national adoption of the code language and creation of an enforcement mechanism. This set in motion a series of country-specific lobbying battles over code adoption. Thus, advocates and opponents had new opportunities to continue the battle. In the years following the creation of the WHO code individual countries have repeatedly been the sites for intense skirmishes over national legislation.

One of the most interesting aspects of code enforcement involved the work of the Nestlé Infant Formula Audit Commission (NIFAC), an independent group created by Nestlé to monitor the company's stated commitments to the WHO code. Chaired by former U.S. senator and secretary of state, Edmund Muskie, NIFAC's membership included leaders of churches that had supported the Nestlé boycott, several public health specialists, and other "eminent people." One of the commission's first tasks was to comment on the marketing instructions Nestlé's Swiss headquarters staff prepared for its marketing staff.

Leadership is a requirement for both code formulation and effective code enforcement. Senator Muskie's leadership of NIFAC is a worthy case-study of code-related leadership. Senator Muskie not only chaired, but truly *led,* the commission. He ensured that the commission operated on a "rule of law" basis and insisted on the need for due process and clear procedures to handle complaints about Nestlé's behavior in the field. Most importantly, he understood the unique role of the commission as source of credibility to verify Nestlé's claim of code compliance. Anything other than genuine independence was unacceptable. I personally saw how skillfully Muskie used this argument in dealings with Nestlé senior executives who might have otherwise sought to influence NIFAC's actions.[5]

In time, NIFAC's consistent handling of complaints, its public reporting, and the demonstrated effectiveness of its dialogue with Nestlé senior management about the changes in the company's performance, created a record of note. NIFAC proved to be the most important enforcement mechanism specifically created to enforce the code. As an innovation in code governance, the NIFAC example of an independent commission stands virtually alone. Independent audit commissions have been considered by parties involved in other conflicts, but have been rejected for a variety of reasons including cost and institutional complexity. Still, in situations where public credibility is essential, and the company involved has little or nothing on which to draw from its "reputation bank," an independent commission is a viable means of code enforcement.

### Building Trust

*Precise commitments build trust.* Codes that emerge from conflict and adversarial processes are often drafted in terms other than those each stakeholder would have preferred. To transform a code into a "living document" requires a process by which the adversaries can acknowledge the progress that is being made toward the code's objectives. This measurement of progress is basic to building trust.

Two options exist for assessing progress. One option is to establish *benchmarks* of implementation progress and collect appropriate and relevant information. For example, Nestlé had to distribute its field instructions to staff in dozens of countries. Regular reports were provided to NIFAC detailing the "roll out" of these marketing policies and practices. The more precise the commitment, the more specific the implementation objectives.

A second option is to count the "results" of activity prompted by the code. For example, NIFAC established a complaint procedure to receive and review charges of Nestlé marketing violations. Thousands of complaints were received over the commission's life (1981–90). Each was given an identification number and processed through a staff investigation and commission review procedure. NIFAC regularly reported on the number of complaints received, and their disposition, in its quarterly reports. It became publicly evident, for example, that Nestlé moved to a high level of compliance with the media advertising and labeling provisions of the code much faster than it did with provisions relating to free samples and free supplies. Nevertheless, the public record illuminated the progress made by the company in meeting its public stated commitments. Over time, this helped narrow the range of unresolved issues between NIFAC and the company. Indeed, this publicly documented record of progress was an essential ingredient of the commission's plan to "wind down" its activities in 1990.

Codes need a process to improve, upgrade, and advance the level and degree of commitment among participants. (The CERES code provides an especially interesting current example of this process concept.) Although the WHO code per se did not have a process improvement mechanism in place, the Nestlé marketing instructions provided a focus for NIFAC, the activist community, and other interested parties to debate appropriate improvements. Over time, Nestlé's publicly stated commitments were "ratcheted up" through the process of dialogue between the company and its key stakeholders.

### Can Management Theory Help?

Theories of management offer a number of useful concepts to those seeking to better understand issues surrounding codes of conduct. Stakeholder theory, for example, is a source of propositions about the engagement and willing involvement of individuals, groups, and institutions in formulating and implementing codes of conduct. As Patricia Werhane has written,

> A stakeholder approach sorts out descriptively who in a particular context is affected and how, and, normatively, what responsibilities each party has to the other. Stakeholders are any persons, social groups, collectives, institutions, political/economic systems, or even the ecosystem that affects, participates in, or is affected by, a particular situation, dilemma, or action.[6] (Freeman and Gilbert, 1988)

Institutional dependencies affect both code creation and implementation processes. Resource dependence suggests plausible reasons why, and to what extent, adversaries are willing to consider the use of codes. Robin et al. (1989) provides a useful framework for thinking about various types of codes. As shown in Exhibit 2, codes vary in terms of the type of guidance provided (value-based or rule-based) and the degree of guidance (low specificity to high specificity) regarding conduct. Among adversaries, we can hypothesize that the strong will prefer rule-based or value-based guidance depending on which best suits their competitive and institutional interests. Nestlé, for example, lobbied for a value-based code during the WHO drafting process. Once a rule-based framework seemed inevitable, the company shifted its argument in favor of a preamble that would reflect principles rather than rules. This would subsequently set off a conflict with NIFAC as to whether the preamble or the specific language controlled the company's provision of free supplies to health institutions. Rule-based systems may tend to limit a company's flexibility to respond to new market conditions whereas a value-based system would enable a company's executives to design specific responses that meet competitive needs and are consistent with values expressed in the code.

EXHIBIT 2. *Different Forms of Code Design*

|  | Low<br>(little specificity) | High<br>(very specific) |
|---|---|---|
| Rule-<br>Based<br><br>TYPE<br>OF<br>GUIDANCE | Cell 1<br>Unlikely | Cell 2<br>Highly likely |
| Value-<br>based | Highly likely | Unlikely |

*Source:* Based on Donald Robin, Michael Giallourakis, Fred R. David, and Thomas E. Moritz, "A Different Look at Codes of Ethics," *Business Horizons,* Jan–Feb., 1989, pp. 66–73.

Finally, even rule-based codes might vary in the number and specificity of stated rules in the code. The WHO code itself had a relatively limited number of rules which were quite specific (e.g., no free samples to be distributed to mothers or health workers). When Nestlé issued its marketing instructions, however, they issued a much more elaborate statement of rules to guide field staff behavior. In that instance, the high degree of specificity was directly tied to knowledge of field conditions.

A third area in which management theory can improve our thinking about codes involves corporate culture. In the infant formula case, an understanding of the unique corporate cultures of the firms involved in the infant formula industry was useful to both code formulation and code implementation. Early thinking about code provisions, for example, failed to take into account the different ways in which food companies and pharmaceutical firms promoted and sold their products. An effective code needed to address both the health promotion and the mass-market promotional channels used by industry members. Had that not been done, the code provisions would have favored one group of competitors over the other. Similarly, when NIFAC was developing a plan to bring its activities to a close, the commissioners prepared a set of organizational change requirements (including field staff education programs) that were prerequisites for a final NIFAC sign-off.

Modern corporations operate in ways that are unlike their predecessors' ways. Today's executives are viewing stakeholders, resource dependencies, alliances, and cooperation in decidedly new and different ways. The design of effective social control mechanisms must take this into account. Codes of conduct can be useful to this process. For some problems, and some industries, they are the right tool at the right time.

## Conclusion

This chapter has focused on lessons learned from one of the great "stories" in the history of the business and society field. It is a story of normal business conduct (marketing of consumer products) which, when applied on a global scale (developing nations), produced unintended (tragic) consequences for intended beneficiaries (infants).

The "simplicity" of this social issue is deceptive of course. First, the fortunes of great corporations, emerging nations, and a global health-policy system were intricately entwined in the infant formula controversy. Second, the number of interested stakeholders grew to the dozens as media, churches, governments, and activist organizations engaged the issue in various ways. Third, the issue persisted for decades without full resolution. The controversy continues as of 1997, twenty-two years after my first involvement, and twenty-five years since the first formal institutional action was taken to address the underlying market behavior that prompted the controversy.

Anyone who believes that a code of conduct "settles" a social issue has not studied the history of the infant formula controversy. Still, the WHO code was a milestone in both the evolution of the controversy and the evolution of social issues in the management field. Infant formula became the "never ending story," the intractable issue that tarnished the careers of dozens of executives, the issue whose solution proved elusive to the best lawyers, public relations consultants, and media advisors that money could buy. Fifteen years after the WHO code was adopted, and seven years after the Nestlé Infant Formula Audit Commission issued its final report, this controversy still speaks to us about corporate responsibility, social control, and the usefulness—and limitations—of codes of conduct.

## Notes

1. I am grateful to Susanna Khavul, a doctoral candidate at Boston University, for valuable research assistance on this subject.

2. "Bergsten on Trade," *The Economist,* Sept. 27–Oct.3, 1997, pp. 23–26; quote on page 24.

3. "Asians Suffer Further Damage on Malaysian's New Remarks," *New York Times,* Oct. 2, 1997, p. D13.

4. Jeff Gerth and Tim Weiner, "Imports Swamp U.S. Food-Safety Efforts," *New York Times,* Sept 29, 1997, pp. Al, A10.

5. I became a member of Nestlé Infant Formula Audit Commission in 1984. The Nestlé boycott had been "suspended" by the international boycott committee. One of the discussion topics between the boycotters and Nestlé was the composition of NIFAC membership. Shortly after the suspension was announced, Angela Blackwell, an attorney who headed Public Advocates, a San Francisco-based public-interest law firm, and I were invited to meet with NIFAC members to discuss possible membership. Formal invitations to become members followed shortly thereafter. The meetings that followed were not smooth. Ms. Blackwell and I questioned a number of internal procedures and encountered Senator Muskie's legendary temper. I have described these tensions in an unpublished paper entitled "A Commission Is Not a Team: Cooperation v. Public Credibility."

6. Patricia H. Werhane, "Commentary: The Business Ethics of Risk, Reasoning, and Decision-Making," in David M. Messick and Ann E. Tenbrunsel, eds., *Codes of Conduct: Behavioral Research Into Business Ethics,* New York: Russell Sage Foundation, 1996, pp. 332–33. The reference is to R. E. Freeman and D. R. Gilbert, *Corporate Strategy and the Search for Ethics,* Englewood Cliffs: Prentice-Hall, 1988.

## 7

# Gaps in Research in the Formulation, Implementation, and Effectiveness Measurement of International Codes of Conduct

### S. PRAKASH SETHI

## MNC Codes of Conduct

International codes of conduct, or more specifically codes of conduct that attempt to redirect and monitor the behavior of multinational corporations (MNCs) in emerging economies, have become the focus of intense public scrutiny and debate. The drive for enactment of these codes is most pronounced in the United States with other industrialized countries, notably those in Western Europe, following the U.S. lead at a somewhat slower and reluctant pace. In the United Sates, the primary drive for codes has come from public interest groups—notably religious institutions, human rights activists, and groups concerned with Third World countries.

The need for codes emanates from two developments in the last quarter of the twentieth century: the emergence of market economies and the growth of capitalism. With the collapse of the centralized economic system of the former Soviet Union, and the never-ending poverty in large parts of the Third World, centralized command economies have been shown to fail in meeting the needs of their people. Thus erstwhile communist and socialist countries are falling over each other in their haste to embrace the new religion of capitalism as a panacea to their eternal problems of poverty, underdevelopment, and despotic and corrupt governments.

Multinational corporations, after falling into disrepute in the '60s, have again emerged as the engine of growth because, unlike development assistance from industrially advanced countries and international lending agencies, MNCs alone can provide all the ingredients necessary for growth and development, i.e., capital, technology, management skills, and access to international markets. It is no wonder, therefore, that the growth of the world economy during the last twenty-five years and more has been accompanied by an ever-faster growth in international trade, private capital flows, and emergence of MNCs as the dominant institution at the apex of this process.

MNC's dominance has been buttressed by three factors. First, the control of the enormous amounts of capital and markets. Second, developing countries compete intensely among themselves to seek MNC investments within their borders and consequently yield enormous bargaining leverage to MNCs. Finally, there is relative lack of international oversight and regulating mechanism, or what Professor Presten calls "the new policy regimes," which allows MNCs to exercise enormous discretion in conducting their global operations. It is no wonder, therefore, that MNCs often exercise this discretionary power in the marketplace in a manner that often creates unintended adverse second-order effects in terms of environmental degradation, political corruption, erosion of basic human rights, hazardous working conditions, and decline in the quality of life in the affected communities.

While the clamor for greater oversight and control over the conduct of MNCs continues to escalate, multinational corporations, as yet, do not seem to have come to grips with this phenomenon especially in terms of what it entails in the sphere of nonmarket activities, i.e., the second-order effects of their actions in the economic arena. Resorting to the old cliché of "sticking to one's knitting"—which in practice they rarely do especially when it affects their own bottom line—they have tended to ignore the social consequences of their market actions, especially in the emerging economies of the world.

This posture of "benign neglect," however, cannot be sustained. Evidence of abuse of their relative bargaining power, although anecdotal and unsystematic, and the reluctant repercussions from affected groups, is all around us. There are increasing and ever-more insistent calls on MNCs to prevent human rights abuses in developing countries where they do business, and especially among their own foreign operations and those of their subcontractors and suppliers. There have also been calls for creating universal codes of conduct which the multinationals must adopt or face boycotts and protests from public interest groups in their home markets.

## Development and Implementation of Codes of Conduct: Flaws in Current Approaches

From one perspective, code development is a growth industry. One could easily write a book by merely describing the vast variety of codes that are being advocated by groups of all likes and persuasions. However, one would be hard-pressed to write more than a few pages if one were to report the research evidence of the effectiveness of these codes, as to intended outcomes, verification of claims made by various parties with regard to alleged wrong-doings by MNCs and their casual relationship to solutions recommended by code proponents, and above all, evidence of their sustained relevance and viability under various cultural and political frameworks, economic and competitive industry conditions, and institutional organizational constraints.

I have devoted a large part of my professional working life to analyzing business-society conflicts, domains of congruence, and possible approaches to conflict resolution. I have also spent a significant portion of my research effort on the issues related to MNC codes of conduct. I must admit that the current state of affairs with regard to MNC code development leaves me with a sense of despondency. My own experience with some of the more recent major code initiatives is not encouraging. The proponents of the codes invariably resort to anecdotal and episodic evidence of wrongdoings and project the total magnitude of the problem in a manner which can only be justified in terms of divine guidance and inspired vision. MNCs and other critics of codes respond in similar terms by questioning the validity of the proponents' claims and, at the same time, offering platitudinal statements of commitment couched in equally moral terms tempered with pragmatic economic explanations that are devoid of specifics and independent monitoring of actual conduct and outcomes. There is little evidence, and little research on the part of all parties to generate verifiable evidence. Ironically, this situation has been allowed to exist because both the advocates and critics of these codes stand to gain from this void. It is an unintentional but unholy alliance. Both sides have colluded to avoid conducting any serious research because it allows each side to claim victories and to avoid facing the tough issues of relevance, substantiveness, and effectiveness.

Let me emphasize here that I do not question the need for codes of conduct—or some new forms of extra-legal mechanisms—that would create a more level playing field in the international trade and investment arena. I also seek mechanisms that would provide a more equitable participation in the decision-making process, and a fairer distribution of the benefits to all stakeholders who are at the nexus of this "new" market-oriented global economic activity.

## Failure of Current Code Development Process

A brief discussion of the three most important recent codes dealing with MNCs would illustrate my point. Consider first the debacle of the UN Code of Conduct for Transnational Corporations. After an effort of more than ten years, millions of dollars in expenditures, and thousands of hours in negotiations and deliberations, the resultant document could best be described as full of empty rhetoric and devoid of any practical usefulness, with the result that everyone involved is only too willing to forget its very existence.

The reason for the failure of this code is all too apparent from hindsight but should have been equally apparent before the fact, if those involved had only bothered to consider the implications of the process they had chosen to create the code. The UN-initiated process was almost entirely political and controlled by member states. Code provisions were designed primarily to meet the agenda of developing countries who were at the same time unwilling to correct any of their own shortcomings with regard to multinational corporations or offer any guarantees for their conduct and accountability. MNCs were not about to yield to such a one-sided arrangement. MNCs also held significant resources that they could withhold from recalcitrant countries. And finally, given the often disparate and competing interests of the countries involved, the process was doomed to failure.

The second case pertains to the enactment in 1981, at the WHO, of the International Code of Marketing of Breast-Milk Substitutes, or the Infant Formula Code. The code called for, among others, significant restrictions in marketing and promotion of infant formula products on the part of multinational corporations. Admittedly, there was considerable, albeit anecdotal evidence, as to the misuse of infant formula among people in developing countries leading to infant malnutrition, morbidity, and mortality. The magnitude of the problems, and its one-to-one correspondence with the products and marketing practices of the companies involved, remains uncertain because the corporate critics did not have the resources to gather such information. The companies, on their part, claimed the critics' assertions to be highly exaggerated, and yet disclaimed any need to gather such information and make it available to the public.

The biggest problem, however, was to demonstrate how such a code, if it were to be made fully operational, would solve the problem. The countries involved, despite their claims to the contrary, could have easily banned any and all practices on the part of multinationals that they deemed undesirable. A great many countries actively participated in the distribution of infant formula products which they procured as foreign aid. Many developing countries also had significant domestic producers whom they sought to protect from foreign competition.

Is it any wonder, therefore, that even sixteen years after the passage of the code, a great many countries have yet to create enabling legislation to implement the code, or to set up mechanisms to enforce it? Similarly, WHO, in its infinite wisdom, has refused to monitor the performance of these countries or make its findings public. And in a conspiracy of silence, the activists have also avoided chastising these nations and have thus contributed to the failure of the mechanism to yield any measurable results. The paramount question, therefore, remains unanswered and is unlikely to be resolved any time soon. What, if any difference has been made in reducing infant sickness and deaths in Third World countries as a consequence of the infant formula code? Could not all the resources expended in creating this code have been spent more productively to achieve this end?

The third case pertains to the Sullivan Principles and their application to the operations of U.S. companies in South Africa. In many ways, the Sullivan Principles were a success story. They constituted the first voluntary code of ethical conduct to be applied under realistic operating conditions, involving a large number of corporations, recipient constituencies, and an institutional framework for project implementation, monitoring, and performance evaluation. The principles had a large measure of moral authority to validate corporate actions, and where necessary, to exhort companies to undertake activities that they might otherwise consider ill-advised. During the seventeen years of operation, the companies subscribing to the code spent over $400 million in the areas of health, education, housing, training, and support for black entrepreneurship. These companies were also model employers and operated according to the highest standards of good corporate citizenship. At the same time, however, faced with constant pressure, an increasing number of companies opted to withdraw from South Africa. Over a short period of four years, the number of U.S. companies in South Africa declined from over 160 to less than 52.

Despite its apparent success in funneling badly needed funds to community-related causes, it is doubtful that the Sullivan Principles contributed more than marginally to the abolition of apartheid, or left a lasting legacy in terms of improving black economic empowerment. Notwithstanding, the operations of the Sullivan Principles offer an excellent laboratory to examine the efficacy of various modes of corporate actions when confronted with hostile socio-political environments, conflicting economic and social goals, and even lack of total support from their host country managers both as to the rationale for the principles and the manner in which they were being applied to local subsidiaries.

### A Research Paradigm for Evaluating the Appropriateness and Effectiveness of MNC Codes of Conduct

Both the corporate critics and MNCs must move beyond the current state of rhetoric, claims and counterclaims, and accusations and assertions of innocence, if codes of conduct are to fill the current lacunae in creating a new set of "rules of the game" that would govern the conduct of all major stakeholders—including MNCs and host country governments—in a competitive marketplace.

Such a paradigm must meet three criteria:

1. It must provide an analytical framework that offers a rational and intellectually defensible structure linking various perceived problems to be resolved; the process of their resolution; and, their linkage with the intended outcomes. Furthermore, the framework must provide a logical explanation linking individual variables, i.e., actions, to some causal or associational relationship with other variables. And lastly, the entire structure and framework of relationships should be empirically testable to ensure the validity of the constructs and the saliency and viability of asserted results. In research terminology, the first element would be described as theory formulation, the second element hypothesis development, and the third one empirical testing and validation.
2. The second important element is related to the process. The system must involve all major stakeholders in the decision-making process. Otherwise, it would fail to yield optimum results even if it succeeded in operating at all.
3. The third element has to do with the transparency of the system and independent monitoring of the activities of major stakeholders to engender mutual trust and to keep everyone honest.

It should be apparent that all three codes discussed above failed the first criterion on almost all three elements. The transnational code for multinational corporations clearly failed the other two criteria as well. The infant formula code failed the other two criteria in terms of participation in the decision-making process and independent monitoring and performance accountability on the part of all major stakeholders. The Sullivan Principles fell short in the area of inclusive decision-making process but did an excellent job in terms of independent monitoring and performance accountability.

## Core Values of Stakeholders as a Potential Problem Source

An important, but generally overlooked, source of problems with regard to lack of success of these and most other codes is to be found in the core values that various groups hold and seek to implement through codes of conduct. These core values are rooted in moral and ethical concerns, economic and competitive constraints, and organizational-institutional dynamics.

### Moral and Ethical Concerns

A large number of highly innovative proposals for MNC codes of conduct have been made by religious groups or those who lay claim to the necessity of codes on moral and ethical grounds. Imbued with a sense of moral outrage emanating from evidence of apparently unethical or inhumane conduct, these codes and their advocates seek "universality of conduct" in terms of "absolute or moral minimum." To be sure, this description is overly simplistic and does not do justice to many refinements incorporated in some of these codes. Nevertheless, this explanation is quite valid in terms of the core values on which the justification for these codes is based.

Unfortunately, the proponents of these codes and the intensity of moral offense and violation of some universal ethical standards to which they respond to also spell the death knell of these codes.

a) The sponsors of these codes rarely, if ever, are among the stakeholders that form the nexus of activities and institutional arrangements to be covered under the proposed codes. They also rarely, if ever, directly represent any group of core stakeholders. The most they can claim is that they represent a "constituency" of ideas or speak for the people who are otherwise disenfranchised and, therefore, are unable to speak for themselves.

b) Their code proposals are often couched in absolute terms and seldom take into account real economic and competitive concerns of the corporations and other stakeholders.

c) They are inconsistent in their choice of culprits and imposition of sanctions. Quite often their victims are not the companies or countries that are most intransigent, but those who are open to reform and, therefore, susceptible to pressure.

### Economic and Competitive Constraints

Codes of conduct that affect operational costs, productivity, and output cannot be constructed without taking into account economic environment and competitive constraints. Minimum standards, whether they are operating costs or working conditions must take into account alternative opportunities of employment available to workers and competitive conditions confronted by employers.

Even in the worst of the worst-case scenario of "sweat shops" employment conditions, no matter how repugnant to people in the industrially advanced countries, such shops offer a better option and a first step up the economic ladder to the poor and unskilled people in a developing country. To these people, the choice may not be between higher- and lower-paid employment, but between some form of wage-based employment and a life of utter poverty and destitution. The children we are trying to save from bondage in a rug factory may also be the children we are condemning to work in back-breaking brick manufacturing or highly hazardous factory manufacturing match boxes.

And let's not forget that today's economic tigers, including Japan and South Korea, were yesterday's poor countries where unskilled workers put long hours at low wages and inhumane working conditions. Remember also that many of the countries that are objects of our scorn and condemnation are not controlled by oppressive and corrupt dictators but are stable and functioning democracies. It would be the height of arrogance for us to assume that only we have the keys to the Kingdom of Heaven, and only we are entitled to speak for the poor and oppressed in those countries when they have not even asked us to do so.

The situation from the perspective of the MNCs raises similar concerns. It is only partially relevant as to what proportion of a product's final price at the retail end is reflected in labor costs. What is equally relevant is the cost structure of a firm's competitors. A highly competitive market effectively limits a firm's options in passing higher costs to its customers. Similarly, a highly competitive financial market effectively limits a firm's ability to raise capital if its cost structure and profit margins are higher than those of its competitors.

Let me emphasize unequivocally that I am not arguing against the need or the desirability of seeking better working conditions and protection from exploitation for the workers in poorer countries. What I am arguing is that these standards must take into account the realities of economic and social conditions as they exist in those countries and not be based on what we feel those conditions ought to be.

### Organizational-Institutional Dynamics

Institutional dynamics and organizational constraints play an important role as to how various codes would be formulated and implemented. This applies equally to both the public interest groups and corporations. The activist leader is pulled by two competing forces in his/her drive for developing codes of conduct. At one end, there are pressures from professional reformers in parallel organizations whose support must be garnered to create a broader constituency among activists toward the choice of issues and institutions to be targeted. Unfortunately in this case, it is the radical and the most uncompromising among the activists that set the tone and pace of demands—and thus inevitably steer the code process to a self-defeating end. Conversely, leaders must also seem to appear to be "reasonable and practical" to the general public if they are to secure their support, without which no code is ever likely to become a reality.

MNCs are also confronted by a similar set of conflicting forces. A corporation taking the lead in accepting a new code of conduct must make every effort to build consensus among otherwise competing corporations so as not to be placed at a competitive disadvantage. Ironically, in this case, it is the most obstreperous company that often sets the pace for accepting new reforms. Internally, the corporate leadership faces resistances from those who view "outsiders" as the enemy who seek unwarranted intrusion into management's prerogatives. A CEO runs a serious risk of alienating both its internal and external constituencies if the pace of advocated reforms is too fast and resisted by large segments of these constituencies.

### Conclusion

Let me conclude by paraphrasing the theme of this volume, namely, the time has indeed come for global codes of conduct. Nevertheless, the current process is in a sorry state and must be made to work if we are to avoid evermore destructive confrontation and are forever lost in a thick fog of empty rhetoric.

Multinational corporations cannot escape this challenge unless they are willing to confront even greater societal conflict and universal public protest that must eventually lead to increased governmental regulation at the national and international levels. This is especially true of the multinational corporations based in the United Sates. They cannot and must not abdicate their responsibility to play a more proactive role in the world arena. American values and culture will not tolerate a posture of benign neglect. Nor would they be allowed to do so in the face of the vast infrastructure of nongovernmental organizations (NGOs) that are steeped in the tradition of social activism and voluntary action.

Public interest groups—and those who seek changes in corporate conduct in the marketplace that alters competitive behavior—must take cognizance of market-competitive conditions to fashion codes that are realistic in their objectives and pragmatic in operational approaches. Otherwise, they would have less and less legitimacy in speaking for the people they seek to represent, and would only hear voices that are echoes of their own.

It would be the height of arrogance to presume that all corporate leaders are bereft of conscience and indifferent to society's concerns. Similarly, it would be equally egregious to label all public-spirited groups as made up of radicals who are bent on destroying "capitalism" and the market economy.

A successful code formulation process must build on the consensus of all core stakeholders and address their legitimate concerns. It must (a) understand business-society conflicts within a normative, economic, and contextual framework, and (b) evaluate the likelihood of success or failure of various strategic options and implementation formats that might be available for use in a given situation.

At the macro level, this process should look at:

a)   The social-political environment that gives a particular issue of public policy its ideological-moral legitimacy, emotional intensity, and political potency; the role different groups play in creating ownership of such an issue; and, the process through which a supportive public opinion environment is created.

b)   The linkage between domestic events and international events that are likely to enhance or weaken the saliency of a public policy issue and the process through which these linkages are strengthened by advocacy groups.

c)   The linkage between ethical-moral values and economic considerations that define the optional characteristics of the social conflict especially as it pertains to who does what to whom and with what effect and how it would affect other parties, who are otherwise uninvolved in the controversy.

d)   What is the impact of the industry structure, competitive intensity, and level of profitability for the companies involved and how would these factors influence their willingness to cooperate with various advocacy groups or resist their demands?

e)   What are some of the different approaches that might be considered in developing codes of conduct, their voluntary vs. mandatory character, and systems of monitoring and evaluation? Are there specific approaches that might be suitable for specific types of issues and external sociopolitical conditions?

At the micro level this process should look at:

a)   What happens to the parent-subsidiary economic relationships when the MNC head office imposes certain moral/ethical operational rules on the local subsidiary? Available research in the area of MNC parent-subsidiary relations suggests that there is strong tendency for the subsidiary management to conceal information from the head-office staff when such information would adversely affect the operational autonomy of the local subsidiary even though it might be beneficial for the MNC's home country and/or global operations.

b)   Adhering to parent MNC's social policy goals might generate peer group hostility against the local managers. It would also engender adversarial reaction from the local governmental agencies where such support is vital to the successful operations of the local subsidiary, and where an aggressive pursuit of the parent MNC's social goals might result in a weakening of the local subsidiary's competitive position.

c)   How might the parent MNC resolve the issues of performance measurement and evaluation, and management compensation, where pursuance of social policy goals might adversely affect the subsidiary's economic performance? Alternately, how might a company develop monitoring and evaluation measures where performance on social policy goals is considered an integral part of the subsidiary's overall performance?

d)   What are some of the measures that companies can take to ensure that they are not held hostage by the advocacy groups in their home country, and by recipient groups in the host country, to ever-escalating standards of performance without regard to the company's vital strategic interests in its global operations?

# 8

# A Behavioral Perspective on Codes of Conduct

## *The Ambiguity-Specificity Paradox*

ANN E. TENBRUNSEL

The challenge to develop global codes of conduct raises many important normative questions. What values are to be emphasized? What constitutes ethical behavior when different cultures are involved? How will agreement be reached?

While these questions are deserving of serious thought and attention, finding answers and solutions to them is not sufficient to promote ethical and just behavior. It is critical to define the principles that constitute global codes of conduct, but it is equally important to understand how individuals will respond to these principles. Thus, in addition to the issues raised above, other questions about the interpretation and implementation of codes need to be addressed. How might psychological and behavioral responses reduce the effectiveness of codes? What factors may foster self-interested interpretation? Why might codes limit creative solutions?

It is in the search for answers to these questions that a behavioral approach can be of some value. Such an approach can provide insight into how individuals may react to codes and standards and, in this way, highlight factors that are important to consider in their development. One factor worthy of consideration is the specificity of the code. Drawing on psychological and behavioral research on the effects of goals, standards, and laws, this chapter identifies the problems that arise from too much ambiguity on the one hand, and too much specificity on the other. The chapter concludes with recommendations for dealing with this apparent paradox in the development of codes of conduct. Rather than searching for the optimal degree of specificity, these recommendations focus on addressing the underlying psychological mechanisms responsible for the undesirable outcomes.

## What Does This Mean? The Case Against Ambiguity

Global codes of conduct are often positioned as a benchmark for individual organizations and countries to use in the development of their own specific codes and standards. For example, discussions of the Caux Principles have resulted in the recommendation that they "are intended to serve as a framework within which individual organizations operating in foreign countries can draft their own freely-chosen codes of business conduct." Similarly, the Principles for Global Corporate Responsibility state that "the company observes a code or codes of best practice or has drawn up its own comprehensive corporate code."

Company and country-specific codes offer the advantage of principles which are tailored to specific situations and cultures. Potential problems can arise, however, because of the necessary ambiguity required to express the intent of the global framework. In order to allow for individual interpretation, the global framework must be written somewhat loosely. The situation is similar to that faced at the organizational level, where it has been asserted that organizational values may be purposefully lacking in precision to allow for individual interpretation (Eisenberg, 1984). It is argued, however, that the resulting vague language required for such interpretation can in turn promote self-interested and perhaps unethical behavior.

Uncertainty has been linked with self-focused behavior and outcomes. Pfeffer, Salancik, and Leblebici (1976) assert that uncertainty increases the prevalence of social influence attempts and political behavior. Gilmore and Ferris (1989a and 1989b), for example, suggest that recruiters' lack of knowledge about job candidates may result in self-promoting political behavior on the part of the candidate. In this sense, then, uncertainty and ambiguity can allow for the effective management of meaning (Ferris, King, Judge, and Kacmar, 1991) and the opportunity for self-interested behavior (Ralston, 1985; Ferris, Russ, and Fandt, 1989).

Hsee (1995) provides an interesting discussion of the effect of uncertainty on one's behavior. He presents a scenario that depicts a salesman who has a choice between two cities in which to market and sell his product. City A has more buyers than City B, but City B is a more enjoyable city to visit.

Hsee argues that the salesman wants to travel to City B but does not feel that choosing this more enjoyable city over city A which has more buyers is acceptable or justified. He further argues, however, that uncertainty may provide the salesman with the opportunity to act as he wants to, in this case by giving him the freedom to select City B. In a test of this assertion using a similar (but not identical) scenario, Hsee finds that uncertainty does promote the more desirable, but less justifiable, decision. Extending his results to the above scenario,

Hsee says that these results imply that when the number of buyers is fixed—60 buyers for City A and 40 buyers for City B—the salesman feels that he must choose City A. However, when the number of buyers is uncertain, such that City A is described as having somewhere between 40 and 80 buyers with an expected average of 60 and City B is described as having between 20 and 60 buyers with an expected average of 40, the salesman would feel free to select City B. The reason for this, Hsee asserts, is that uncertainty allows the salesman to interpret the data as he wishes, (mis)judging the number of buyers in City B to be closer to the higher end of the range (i.e., 60) and (mis)judging the number of buyers in City A to be closer to the lower end of the range (i.e., 40). The uncertainty thus makes it more likely that individuals will base their decisions on self-interest.

Other research supports the contention that uncertainty may provide individuals with the flexibility to behave as they wish to do so. In an extension to a particularly relevant context, Wade-Benzoni, Tenbrunsel, and Bazerman (1997) argue that the management of international environmental resources is fraught with uncertainty which may promote egocentric interpretations of fairness and encourage self-favored rather than other-favored interpretations and actions. Particularly problematic in the environmental domain, they argue, are the various dimensions by which fairness can be judged. Asymmetries in power, inputs and outputs among the various constituents are argued to create differing perceptions about potentially fair solutions. The uncertainty about what constitutes the "fair" solution in turn encourages egocentric interpretations of fairness, where parties focus on the solution that is most advantageous to them. Their discussion of global warming demonstrates this problem.

> Two activities that are argued to contribute to $CO_2$ emissions and the greenhouse effect are the burning of fossil fuel and deforestation. The Northern Hemisphere, which is responsible for more fossil fuel burning, believes that eliminating deforestation is the best way to address the problem. The Southern Hemisphere, on the other hand, which engages in deforestation, is more in favor of reducing fossil fuels as a potential solution. Furthermore, the North, which has contributed more green house gas in the past, would be more likely to support equal reduction in emissions; in contrast, the South, which is expected to increasingly contribute to the problem in the future, is likely to suggest that equality in economic development must exist for equal reductions in emissions to occur and therefore the North should stop development until this equality is achieved.

This example demonstrates how asymmetries—whether in the form of contributions to the problem, power, or motivation—introduce uncertainty and promotes self-interested perceptions. Asymmetries introduce multiple dimensions of the problem, creating many possible causes and solutions. Both parties focus on contributions to the problem that are associated with the other party and ignore their own contributions, which in turn generates different perceptions on how to solve the problem. The resulting uncertainty about what constitutes the "fair" solution results in each party proposing solutions that are slanted in an egocentric or self-interested direction, with the environment paying the ultimate price.

More detrimental than promoting self-favored choices, uncertainty has also been linked with unethical behavior. In a study designed to investigate the effect of uncertainty of information on misrepresentation, Tenbrunsel (1995) asked individuals to assume the role of a sales manager who was under great pressure to secure an order from at least one new customer. The manager had located only one such customer who showed interest in placing an order and was in the process of negotiating with this customer. During this negotiation, the customer had asked the manager for an honest estimate on the expected lead time. The manager was told that the customer preferred a shorter lead time, such that the longer the lead time, the lower the probability of obtaining the sale. While all individuals were told the honest estimate was a thirty-day lead time, half of the individuals were told that they were very certain of this number because of meticulous records that had been kept (low uncertainty condition), while the other half of the individuals were told that they were very uncertain of this number because detailed records were not available (high uncertainty condition). The managers were then asked to provide the customer with an estimate of the lead time. Results supported the assertion that managers who were more uncertain would be more likely to engage in self-serving misrepresentation by deviating more from the honest estimate, with those individuals providing an average lead-time estimate of 27.4 days versus 29.2 days provided by individuals in the low uncertainty condition.

Drawing on behavioral and psychological research, we thus see that ambiguity and uncertainty, while allowing for the development and expression of organization and country-specific principles, may also act as a catalyst for self-serving and perhaps unethical behavior. We must be attentive, therefore, to principles and codes which will foster this type of behavior. In the Caux principles, for example, it is asserted that it is our responsibility to "seek fairness and truthfulness in all of our activities." Similarly, the Principles for Global Corporate Responsibility "call for fundamental fairness in all agreements." It is important to recognize the uncertainty surrounding these principles and the potential for individuals to select self-focused definitions of fairness which may not correspond with the normative intent of the global framework. In a similar vein, an implementation of the Caux principle stating that we should

"promote competitive behavior that is socially and environmentally beneficial" needs to take into consideration the asymmetry and uncertainty introduced by the various constituents, and the resulting tendency for individuals to
promote those beneficial solutions which are most advantageous to themselves. As an additional example, the expressed desire to have organizations
"share information with suppliers" (Caux principles, p. 6) is a sound principle, and yet it must be recognized that the truthfulness of information that is
shared may depend on the quality of each organization's information.

It is thus argued that while principles and codes may be of sound normative logic, we must take a further step and consider the manner in which they
may be interpreted. Uncertainty surrounding such codes provides individuals
with a justification for behaving in a self-serving manner (Hsee, 1995; Tenbrunsel, 1995). The end result is that individuals do what they effectively want
to do, rather than what they normatively should do (Bazerman, Tenbrunsel,
and Wade-Benzoni, 1998) and the effectiveness of the codes is diminished.

### "I Did What I Was Told to Do": The Problems with Specificity

The above discussion seems to imply that global codes of conduct should
do away with any ambiguity and replace vague language with very specific principles and required behaviors. Indeed, some psychological research
supports this view, suggesting that ambiguous "do your best goals" are inferior to specific, challenging goals (Locke, Shaw, Saari, and Latham, 1981). Before such an approach is implemented, however, we should be cognizant of the
problems associated with specific objectives and directions. Such specificity
may result in a focus on the principle itself rather than on the objective behind
the principle, causing a neglect of anything not specified by the principle and
potentially increasing the undesirable behaviors that the codes are attempting
to eliminate.

Research on the effects of specific goals and standards suggests that these
guidelines do such a good job focusing individuals on the goal or standard that
anything not specified by the standard or goal is ignored. The goal-setting literature supports this assertion. While goals help to target behavior and direct
and focus one's attention (Staw and Boettger, 1990), this focus may result in
attention being drawn away from areas not specified by the standards. Shalley
(1991), for example, asserts that the presence of a goal will lead to decreased
performance on other dimensions not specified by this goal. In support of this
assertion, Ilgen and Moore (1987) found that a focus on quality slowed down
the time it took to complete a task whereas a focus on the speed of the task re-

sulted in a performance of lower quality. Staw and Boettger (1990) found a similar result in an examination of subjects who were presented with the task of improving a paragraph. They found that individuals who were given specific goals relating to grammar were less likely to improve the content of a paragraph than individuals who were given more general goals to do the best that they could.

Research on the effects of specific standards on judgments demonstrates a similar finding, suggesting that the standards exert such a powerful influence that they may cause suboptimal outcomes. In a study of the influence of standards on judgments, it was found that the presence of an environmental standard distorted judgments of various emission proposals, such that proposals that were on the same side of the standard—either above it or below—were inaccurately judged to be more similar than proposals which fell on opposite sides of the standard (Tenbrunsel, Wade-Benzoni, Messick, and Bazerman, forthcoming). In addition, the standard was found to exert an independent influence on the judged acceptability of environmental proposals, above and beyond that exerted by the emissions levels, with the assessment of the same emissions-level proposal changing, dependent on the placement of the standard.

While the above research is demonstrative of the influence that standards can have, a more important question is whether this influence can potentially produce less than optimal outcomes. Additional studies by Tenbrunsel et al. (forthcoming) suggest that standards are so powerful that they may produce a preference for actions that conform to the standard, rather than actions that do not conform to the standard but do a better job of achieving the purpose behind the standard. In one of the studies, subjects were asked to assume the position of an advisory board member who was to evaluate a copper smelter emission proposal(s) from a local plant. The plant had three component processes which emitted arsenic. Subjects were told that emissions and arsenic-related cancers were linear, such that an increase in emissions would result in an increase in arsenic-related cancers. To reduce the arsenic-related cancers, the EPA had set an environmental standard that specified that each component process should emit no more than 100 tons of arsenic.

Individuals, in the capacity of the advisory board member, were either asked to evaluate a single arsenic-reduction proposal or to choose between two such proposals. The "standard achieving" proposal conformed to the EPA standard with the three component processes emitting 97, 91, and 95 metric tons for a total of 283 metric tons. The "purpose-achieving" proposal, with plans for emissions of 108, 115, and 9 metric tons, did not completely conform to the EPA standard but did achieve a lower overall emissions level (232 metric tons versus 283 metric tons). Of those individuals who assessed whether the standard-achieving proposal should be approved, 87 percent recommended approval. In contrast, only 51 percent approved the purpose-achieving proposal when it was evaluated by itself. This preference reversed itself when the plans were evaluated simultaneously, with 20 percent recommending the standard-achieving plan and 76 percent recommending the purpose-achieving plan (4 percent did not recommend either plan). Thus, specific goals and standards can create such a focus that achieving the purpose behind the standard takes a back seat to standard conformance.

The above research suggests that behavior or values that are not specified by a code of conduct may be ignored and, consequently, the objective behind the code may be forgotten. Of more concern is the research suggesting that specific directives and standard-based systems may actually encourage the undesirable behavior that the code is intended to reduce or discourage the behavior that the code is intended to promote. The formalization of procedures and rules in a legal sense has been argued to potentially undermine the goals that the formalization was designed to pursue (Sitkin and Bies, 1993). Kerr (1975), for example, suggests that the standard of sending soldiers home at the end of a tour of duty in Vietnam, rather than when the war was over as was the case in World War II, created a situation whereby obedience was desired but it was disobedience that was actually rewarded. Darley (1991), in a discussion of teaching practices in high schools, asserts that multiple-choice tests, which are designed to promote knowledge, focus students' attention on finding the right answers, rather than on solving problems.

Research on standards and goals thus suggests that specific codes, while useful in directing attention toward what is specified by the code, may create unintended and undesirable consequences. One consequence may be a focus on the code, rather than the spirit of the code. Although the Caux principles encourage individuals to go beyond the letter of the law, very specific codes may decrease the probability that this actually occurs. For example, Principle 7 addresses illicit operations that should be avoided, including bribery, money laundering, arms trades, drug traffic, and organized crime. While this specific list should be useful in discouraging these activities, it may send the message that other illicit activities not listed are not as important. An increase in specificity may also result in individuals "gaming" the system (i.e., appearing to meet the standard without really doing so) which would only undermine the purpose of the codes. Furthermore, specific principles may decrease the creativity and adaptiveness that is necessary to keep pace with an ever-changing global environment, such that the behavior specified by the target increases while more innovative activities decrease (Staw and Boettger, 1990). In this sense, then, codes of conduct may fall prey to the same pitfalls as legal procedures, where it is argued that they foster a "superficial reliance on that which has an acceptable rationale over that which is more socially or economically rational" (Sitkin and Bies, 1993).

### Resolving the Specificity-Ambiguity Paradox

The above discussion seems to leave us in somewhat of a quandary in the development of global codes of conduct, with too much ambiguity and too much specificity both capable of producing undesirable results. Kerr (1975) points out this apparent paradox, suggesting that in the realm of politics, politicians are faced with espousing vague goals, which tend to be more acceptable but of lower quality, or operative goals, which are of higher quality but lower acceptability. One resolution is to search for the optimal degree of specificity. This task, however, will not only be extremely difficult, involving much trial and error, but may also be impossible. It has been asserted that standards distort judgments, independent of where that standard is set (Tenbrunsel et al., 1997). Similarly, guidelines for behavior, whether in the form of codes of conduct, goals, or standards, may result in dysfunctional outcomes for any level of ambiguity or specificity.

A more effective approach involves identifying and addressing the underlying mechanisms responsible for the suboptimal psychological and behavioral responses. As discussed above, codes that are too specific may result in a focus on the codes themselves rather than the meaning behind the codes, perhaps because the intrinsic motivation to follow the spirit of the codes decreases as specificity increases. Conversely, ambiguity in the development of such principles may foster self-interested behavior with a disregard for others. Thus, in order to realize the full potential of global codes of conduct, steps must be taken to promote a focus on the objective behind the principles, increase intrinsic motivation to adhere to the codes, and decrease the tendency for self-favored decisions to win out over other-favored decisions.

### Promoting a Focus on the Underlying Objectives

Research on standards identifies the important role that multiple options can play in promoting a focus on the purpose behind the standard rather than on the standard itself. Recall that, in the study of environmental emissions, individuals who evaluated proposals separately were more likely to approve a proposal that adhered to the EPA standard than a proposal that did a better job of achieving the purpose behind the standard (i.e., reducing overall emissions).

This pattern of results was reversed however, when the proposals were viewed simultaneously (Tenbrunsel et al., forthcoming). These results suggest that the presentation of multiple options may be one way to highlight the objective of a code or standard of behavior. Attention should thus be directed toward methods which encourage a variety of solutions and perspectives, such as brain-storming, NGT, and the Delphi techniques. Individual organizations and countries should be encouraged to utilize these idea-generation techniques to generate multiple ways by which they can comply with the stated principles. To further prevent the "tunnel vision" and static nature that can characterize responses to behavioral guidelines, it may also be useful to encourage innovative ideas from a variety of factions. A tolerance for deviation and minority opinion has been shown to affect the decision process of individuals by forcing them to more thoroughly identify the various aspects of a decision and to reexamine the decision premise (Nemeth and Kwan, 1985; Nemeth and Wachtler, 1983; Staw and Boettger, 1990). More directly, the principles themselves should promote creativity. Indeed, setting a creativity objective has been shown to prime individuals to be more creative, independent of coexisting productivity goals (Shalley, 1991). By explicitly calling for innovative approaches in the design of the principles themselves, it is hoped that the true spirit of the codes will be realized.

### Increasing Intrinsic Motivation

The presence of codes of behavior, while calling attention to the values that promote corporate and social responsibility, may have the unfortunate drawback of undermining the intrinsic motivation to behave in a responsible and ethical fashion. The mere formalization of principles that have been successfully operating on an informal basis has been argued to remove the interpersonal responsibility that was the reason for their success (Macauley, 1963; Smitka, 1994). In this sense, codes of behavior can lead people to attribute their behavior to the codes themselves, rather than to their own inherent desires (Cialdini, 1996; Deci and Ryan, 1987). The decrease in intrinsic motivation means that individuals become less interested in the positive behavior itself and more interested in code conformance, including gaming the system to lend the appearance of acceptable behavior. As described earlier, the end result is an increase in the undesirable behaviors that the codes were designed to suppress.

One way in which to increase intrinsic motivation is to include as many individuals as possible in the development phase. Goal-setting theory, often referred to as a motivational technique (i.e., see McCormick and Ilgen, 1985) provides support for this assertion. This research has demonstrated a positive relationship between participation and performance, suggesting that when people were allowed to participate in setting their own goals, their performance was higher (Earley and Kanfer, 1985; Mento, Steel, and Karren, 1987). Recognizing that it is not possible to include everyone, attention should be paid to identifying the individuals who are most influential in the organization. Research on communication networks suggests that only a few key people are active communicators of informal information, with estimates indicating that only 10 percent of a firm's employees act as information liaisons (Davis, 1953; Robbins, 1994; Sutton and Porter, 1968). Armed with this knowledge, companies should identify and include these key employees in the codes of conduct development group so that the resulting values and motivations underlying the codes are more effectively transmitted.

### Decreasing Self-Interest

To promote a healthy balance between solutions that favor the self and solutions that favor society, it is important to address the underlying reasons for self-interest. As discussed, one reason that decisions are often tipped toward the self is that there is uncertainty about what constitutes fair or ethical actions. Often, many different solutions are possible and individuals naturally gravitate towards those that are most favorable, believing that these solutions are the most fair. Encouraging open communication between the various parties (i.e., suppliers, customers, organizations, the community) has been shown to be useful in reducing these egocentric interpretations of fairness (Wade-Benzoni, Tenbrunsel, and Bazerman, 1996). Communication exposes individuals to other "fair" solutions, which may cause them to reassess their own self-focused judgments and increase the probability that individuals will be able to reach a consensus (Wade-Benzoni et al., 1996). Furthermore, communication increases the development of commitment norms and the salience of the group identity (Van Lange et al., 1992) and produces a more cooperative atmosphere in which solutions that maximize overall benefit are generated (Dawes, McTavish, and Shaklee, 1977).

It is also important to make salient the individuals who would be adversely affected by the unethical behavior. In a discussion of the skewed trade-offs between a manager's personal well-being and that of others, Loewenstein (1996) asserts that the statistical nature of victims of unethical behavior promotes a self-favored choice by the decision-maker, such that victims who are statistical are less likely to receive differential treatment (i.e., empathy) than victims who are more identifiable. He argues that the "smokers who eventually contracted lung cancer, workers and their families who died of asbestos poisoning, drivers and passengers who were incinerated in Pintos, and women who suffered high rates of infertility and miscarriage as a result of DES were all statistic victims," which increased the probability that self-interest would dominate over societal interest. Individualizing the potential victims of socially irresponsible behavior to the relevant decision-makers by putting a "face to the name," is an additional step that should be useful in preventing these skewed tradeoffs.

## Conclusion

This volume raises the important question of whether it is time for global codes of conduct. The question is timely and deserving of serious thought. If the answer is yes, the first step in this development is to determine the basic principles that should underlie these codes. The creation of these principles will involve intense normative debate that addresses difficult questions. While finding answers to these questions represents a major step forward, it would be a crucial mistake to assume that our work is over once we have done so. In order to realize the potential that these codes represent, it is essential to also understand how individuals respond to guidelines and codes. Utilizing a behavioral approach to gain this understanding will be useful in recognizing and identifying unforseen obstacles in the implementation of these codes. The purpose of this chapter is to use the ambiguity-specificity dimension to highlight potential pitfalls that may occur and to challenge researchers and practitioners to conduct research that investigates this and other relevant dimensions. It is hoped that future discussions on this topic encourage interplay between normative and behavioral perspectives, which will not only help to ensure that the transition from theory to practice is a smooth one but will also enable us to develop principles whose full potential is realized.

## Bibliography

Bazerman, M. H., Tenbrunsel, A. E., and Wade-Benzoni, K. A. (1998). "Negotiating with yourself and losing: Making decisions with competing internal preferences." Academy of Management Review, 23, 225–241.

Cialdini, R. B. (1996). Social influence and the triple tumor structure of organizational dishonesty. In D. M. Messick and A. E. Tenbrunsel (eds.), *Codes of Conduct: Behavioral Research into Business Ethics*. New York: Russell Sage.

Darley, J. (1991). Setting standards seeks control, risks distortion. *Public Affairs Report*, 32, 3–5.

Davis, K. (1953). Management communication and the grapevine. *Harvard Business Review*, September–October, 43–49.

Dawes, R. M., McTavish, J., and Shaklee, H. (1977). Behavior, communication, and assumptions about other people's behavior in a common dilemma situation. *Journal of Personality and Social Psychology*, 35, 1–11.

Deci, E. L., and Ryan, R. M. (1987). The supports of autonomy and the control of behavior. *Journal of Personality and Social Psychology*, 53, 1024–37.

Earley, P. C., and Kanfer, R. (1985). The influence of component participation and role models on goal acceptance, goal satisfaction, and performance. *Organizational Behavior and Human Decision Processes*, 36, 378–90.

Eisenberg, E. M. (1984). Ambiguity as a strategy in organizational communication. *Communication Monographs*, 51, 227–42.

Ferris, G. R., King, T. R., Judge, T. A., and Kacmar, K. M. (1991). The management of shared meaning in organizations: Opportunism in the reflection of attitudes, beliefs, and values. In R. A. Giacalone and P. Rosenfeld (eds.), *Applied Impression Management: How Image-Making Affects Managerial Decisions*. Newbury Park, Calif.: Sage.

Ferris, G. R., Russ, G. S., and Fandt, P. M. (1989). Politics in organizations. In R. A. Giacalone and P. Rosenfeld (eds.), *Impression Management in the Organization*. Hillsdale, N.J.: Lawrence Erlbaum Associates.

Gilmore, D. C., and Ferris, G. R. (1989a). The effects of applicant impression management tactics on interviewer judgments. *Journal of Management*, 15, 557–64.

Gilmore, D. C., and Ferris, G. R. (1989b). The politics of the employment interview. In R. W. Eder and G. R. Ferris (eds.), *The employment interview: Theory research and practice*. Newbury Park, Calif.: Sage.

Hsee, C. K. (1995). "Elastic Justification: How Tempting but Task-Irrelevant Factors Influence Decisions." *Organizational Behavior and Human Decision Processing*, 62, 330–337.

Ilgen, D. R., and Moore, C. F. (1987). Types and choice of performance feedback. *Journal of Applied Psychology*, 72, 401–6.

Kerr, S. (1975). On the folly of rewarding A, while hoping for B. *Academy of Management Journal*, 18, 769–83.

Locke, E. A., Shaw, K. N., Saari, L. M., and Latham, G. P. (1981). Goal setting and task performance: 1969–1980. *Psychological Bulletin*, 90, 125–52.

Loewenstein, G. (1996). Behavioral decision theory and business ethics: Skewed trade-offs between self and other. In D. M. Messick and A. E. Tenbrunsel, (eds.), *Codes of Conduct*.

Macauley, S. (1963). Non-contractual relations in business: A preliminary study. *American Sociological Review*, 28, 55–67.

McCormick, E. J., and Ilgen, D. (1985). *Industrial and Organizational Psychology*. Englewood Cliffs: Prentice-Hall.

Mento, A., Steel, R., and Karren, R. (1987). A meta-analytic study of the effects of goal setting on task performance: 1966–1984. *Organizational Behavior and Human Decision Processes*, 39, 52–83.

Nemeth, C. J., and Kwan, J. L. (1985). Originality of word associations as a function of majority vs. minority influence. *Social Psychology Quarterly*, 48, 277–82.

Nemeth, C. J., and Wachtler, J. (1983). Creative problem solving as a result of majority vs. minority influence. *European Journal of Social Psychology*, 13, 45–55.

Pfeffer, J., Salancik, G. R., and Leblebici, H. (1976). The effect of uncertainty on the use of social influence in organizational decision making. *Administrative Science Quarterly*, 21, 227–45.

Ralston, D. (1985). Employee ingratiation: The role of management. *Academy of Management*, 10, 477–87.

Robbins, S. P. (1994). *Management*. Englewood Cliffs: Prentice-Hall.

Shalley, C. E. (1991). Effects of productivity goals, creativity goals, and personal discretion on individual creativity. *Journal of Applied Psychology*, 76, 179–85.

Sitkin, S. B., and Bies, R. J. (1993). The legalist! organization: Definitions, dimensions, and dilemmas. *Organization Science*, 4, 345–51.

Smitka, M. (1994). Contracting without contracts: How the Japanese manage organizational transactions. In S. B. Sitkin and R. J. Bies (eds.), *The Legalistic Organization*. Newbury Park: Sage.

Staw, B. M., and Boettger, R. D. (1990). Task revision: A neglected form of work performance. *Academy of Management Journal*, 33, 534–59.

Sutton, H., and Porter, L. W. (1968). A study of the grapevine in governmental organization. *Personnel Psychology*, Summer, 223–30.

Tenbrunsel, A. E. (1995). "Justifying unethical behavior: The relationship between uncertainty and misrepresentation." Working paper.

Tenbrunsel, A. E., Wade-Benzoni, K. A., Messick, D. M., and Bazerman, M. H. (1997). The dysfunctional aspects of environmental standards. In M. H. Bazerman, D. M. Messick, A. E. Tenbrunsel, and K. A. Wade-Benzoni (eds.), *Environment, Ethics, and Behavior*. San Francisco: The New Lexington Press.

Tenbrunsel, A. E., Wade-Benzoni, K. A., Messick, D. M., and Bazerman, M. H. (forthcoming). "Understanding the Influence of Environmental Standards on Judgments and Choices." *Academy of Management Journal*.

Van Lange, P. A. M., Liebrand, W. B. G., Messick, D. M., and Wilke, H. A. M. (1992). Social dilemmas: The state of the art: Introduction and literature review. In W. B. G. Liebrand, D. M. Messick, and Wilke, H. A. M. (eds), *Social Dilemmas: Theoretical Issues and Research Findings* (pp. 3–28). Oxford, UK: Pergamon Press.

Wade-Benzoni, K. A., Tenbrunsel, A. E., and Bazerman, M. H. (1996). Egocentric interpretations of fairness in asymmetric, environmental social dilemmas: Explaining harvesting behavior and the role of communication. *Organizational Behavior and Human Decision Processes*, 67, 111–26.

Wade-Benzoni, K. A., Tenbrunsel, A. E., and Bazerman, M. H. (1997). Egocentric interpretations of fairness as an obstacle to the resolution of environmental conflict. *Research on Negotiations in Organizations*, 6, 189–206.

# 9

# International Instruments
# on Bribery and Corruption

KATHLEEN A. GETZ

Opponents of bribery and corruption in international business must feel as though they are riding a roller coaster. There are reasons for elation and reasons for distress. In the past few years, there have been significant developments at several international organizations which are intended to cleanse the world of the international business of bribery. Actions have been taken by the Organization for Economic Cooperation and Development (OECD), the Organization of American States (OAS), the International Chamber of Commerce (ICC), the World Bank, and the European Union. However, scandals ranging from petty sleaze to substantial bribery have erupted around the globe. Without doubt, bribery in international business continues to be widespread.

Bribery and corruption are thought by many to be part and parcel of international business. Business persons from the industrialized countries of the West assert that it is impossible to do business in certain parts of the world without paying bribes. Time and again people seeking to find excuses for paying bribes attribute their action to local foreign cultures. However, that bribery is tolerated in some countries more than in others says much more about politics and legal systems than it does about deeper matters of culture. In virtually all cultures, corruption is illegitimate and repugnant. Politicians and officials cannot claim to be legitimately empowered to corrupt acts. Therefore corruption is necessarily accompanied by secrecy. Corruption cannot prosper in highly transparent environments. OAS Secretary General Cesar Gaviria said recently, "Corruption deprives all of us: our governments of their legitimate functions; our citizens of their resources and rights; and the international commerce of its balance and transparency."[1]

There are many international instruments, most in the form of voluntary codes or guidelines, that are intended to combat bribery in international business. Early prohibitions against bribery were embedded in broader codes for multinational enterprises (MNEs), such as the Guidelines for Multinational Enterprises of the OECD, and the Code of Conduct of the United Nations Commission on Transnational Corporations. There are no documented cases of any formal enforcement efforts regarding bribery under these voluntary codes.

However, as international business has grown, international organizations, often under pressure from the United States, have pushed for recommendations that focus solely on the issue of bribery and corruption. During the past four years, new recommendations, guidelines, and conventions have been proposed, and many of them have been signed by a majority of member countries. In this chapter, I will review the requirements and prohibitions regarding bribery and corruption for business and for government under each of the new international instruments. I will also provide analysis and recommendations regarding the most promising avenues for reducing bribery via cooperative international action.

## Corruption in International Business

Some analysts define corruption as the use of public office for private gains (Bardhan, 1997; Goudie & Stasavage, 1997; Shleifer & Vishny, 1993). Others suggest that there ought to be two definitions, based on the type of private gains obtained through corruption. Administrative or bureaucratic corruption involves the use of public office for pecuniary gain, and political corruption involves the use of public office by politicians both for pecuniary gain and for purposes of remaining in office (Rose-Ackerman, 1978; Tanzi, 1994). It is interesting that these sorts of definitions focus on the action of public officials. However, a corrupt transaction cannot occur if only one party is involved.[2] At least two actors make bad decisions in a corrupt transaction: the receiver (public official) and the payer (in international business, a representative of a private organization). Thus those of us interested in corruption in international business always speak of bribery and corruption in one breath.

In a recent speech, then U.S. Trade Representative Mickey Kantor noted that "Corruption has existed as long as there have been people in power and money to influence them." Though it is unlikely that the world will ever be corruption-free, he said, we "have a legal, moral, economic and political responsibility to pursue this problem in every possible forum and with every tool at our disposal" (Kantor, 1996). Kantor's attitude regarding the prevalence of corruption is widely shared by leaders in business and government worldwide. So, too, is his belief that corruption and bribery are unlikely to be eradicated. Even his opinion that there is a broad responsibility to fight corruption is generally shared, at least among leaders in the U.S. In order to understand these attitudes, we must understand the causes of corruption.

### Causes of Corruption

Understanding the causes of corruption begins by dispelling the myth that corruption is a matter of culture (TI Source Book, 1996). It is, of course, true that in some cultures social norms emphasize an individual's allegiance to collectivities over his responsibility to act as a rational bureaucrat (Ekpo, 1979; Gould & Amaro-Reyes, 1983; Tanzi, 1994). However, vocal opposition to corruption and anticorruption campaigns have existed in many countries that traditionally are thought to have "corrupt cultures." For example, Nigerian culture includes a strong anticorruption sentiment despite Nigeria's ongoing problems with corruption (Smith, 1979). Also, norm-based arguments are tautological: analysts observe corruption and then conclude that a country's norms must favor corruption (Goudie & Stasavage, 1997). Finally, as documented by Transparency International (TI Source Book, 1996) and others, bribery is illegal and criminal under the laws of virtually every country, even those with cultures that supposedly support corruption. Furthermore, the people who live in those societies do not approve corruption, they resent it. Were this not the case, secrecy would not be a necessary part of corrupt transactions. In fact, participants in corrupt transactions prefer not to disclose their actions precisely because their actions are seen as repugnant and illegitimate, regardless of culture and social norms.

With respect to the "receiver" side of the corrupt transaction, Goudie and Stasavage (1997), citing Rose-Ackerman (1978) and Klitgaard (1988, 1995), argue that corruption is essentially a problem of imperfect agency. The principal is the top level of government, and the agent is the government official designated to carry out a task. The agent does not always act in the interest of the principal, due to three institutional structures that create opportunities for corruption. (1) Monopoly power exists when a certain official is the only person charged with performing a certain task. The official can extort payment without worry that a competing official will step in to perform the task, at a lower (or no) cost. Dishonest officials may compete for such assignments (Shleifer & Vishny, 1993). (2) The greater the amount of discretion given to a government official, the more opportunities there will be for agents to give favorable interpretations of government rules and regulations to businesses in exchange for illegal payments. However, rules that are too rigid or too unrealistic may incite noncompliance, and allow a large amount of de facto discretion for officials (Tanzi, 1994). (3) Institutional imperfections in monitoring allow corrupt officials to act without fear of being held accountable. Goudie and Stasavage also note that, in many cases, there are reasonable questions regarding the incentives offered for staying honest, particularly the level of pay and the opportunities for advancement in the public sector.

With respect to the "payer" side of the corrupt transaction, separate explanations are given for the international and the national contexts. Here, we are most interested in the international context. Many analysts maintain that the competitiveness of international markets promotes corruption. For competing companies, the cost of bribing officials is seen in the context of exploiting market opportunities (Shleifer & Vishny, 1993). Competitive bribery may be a more cost-effective strategy than competing on the basis of price or quality, whether companies are from developed or developing economies. Furthermore, once relationships with key public officials have been established through a series of bribes, companies have an incentive to resist reform. Also, given the (actual or perceived) prevalence of bribery, a company may be reluctant to refrain from bribing because of the loss of competitiveness it will likely experience unless its competitors also abstain (Windsor, 1997). Layered on top of the competition at the enterprise level is competition at the national level. To the extent that industrial competitiveness is representative of the competition among nation-states, governments have an incentive to support businesses in their international activities. With respect to corruption, this has often resulted in explicit approval of corruption: governments permit tax deductibility of bribes paid outside the home country.

### Moral Arguments against Corruption

Most scholarly and journalistic analyses of corruption begin with the assumption that bribery and corruption are morally wrong. Few explain the immorality in any detail, preferring to address the economic arguments against corruption (see below). For example, Michael Hirsh, a leader of the anti-corruption organization Transparency International, states that "Corruption is not *just* a moral problem" (Hirsh, 1995:56; emphasis added). The Organization for Economic Cooperation and Development begins with the assertion that *bribery* is wrong, because it cannot occur without *corruption,* but it makes no effort to explain the immorality of corruption (OECD Letter, 1996).

Virtually all methods of ethical analysis lead to the conclusion that bribery is wrong or bad. Two primary moral costs of bribery and corruption have been identified. First, bribery is antidemocratic. Donaldson (1989) has shown that the right to political participation is a fundamental human right, regardless of nationality. By paying a bribe to a public official to act in the interest of the company, a firm violates its obligation to honor citizens' right to political participation. Second, corruption spreads, infecting large groups of people, and even whole societies with widespread moral decay and fatalism, resulting in hopelessness and inaction (Transparency International, 1996).

### Economic Counterarguments

Some scholars use utilitarian analysis to argue that bribery in international business can be economically useful, regardless of the political and social implications. The economic benefits of bribery, according to the argument, obtain both for the bribe payer and for the host country. For example, Nye (1979) asserts that businesses seeking to operate in hostile or indifferent countries may succeed *only* through the payment of bribes. The business that results from the bribe payment may stimulate the development process. Many developing country governments have imposed excessive bureaucratic controls on their economies, and such regulations can create uncertainties for foreign enterprises. Bribery encourages bureaucrats to circumvent the regulations and to minimize uncertainty regarding enforcement (Nye, 1979).

Bribery has other potential advantages. In cases where several companies may be competing for a single government permit to operate, corruption becomes an "auction mechanism" whereby the most efficient firm will be able to pay the highest bribe and will be awarded the permit (Leff, 1979). Thus the government awards the permit using rational, rather than ad hoc, criteria. Furthermore, the criterion used is a good proxy for efficiency, so allocative efficiency is improved: the lowest-cost firm wins due to its ability to pay the highest bribe. Leff's argument, of course, ignores the possibility that the most efficient firm might also be honest, and therefore unwilling to participate in the corrupt auction.

Empirical studies have attempted to test the hypothesis that corruption accelerates development. Several studies have supported the hypothesis (see, e.g., Brunetti, 1995; Mauro, 1995). However, these studies have been criticized on the basis of methodology and model development, leading Goudie and Stasavage (1997) to conclude that the effects of corruption depend in part on how corruption is organized and on the country's level of efficiency at the outset.

### Economic Arguments against Corruption

While some economists have attempted to make a utilitarian argument in favor of corruption and bribery, others have used the same sort of argument against corruption. It is, in fact, difficult to quantify the economic costs of corruption, because the transactions are made in secret. Generally, there are two types of economic arguments against bribery.

First, bribery has distortionary effects (Goudie & Stasavage, 1997). It has opportunity costs, because the money paid in the form of a bribe is not put to productive use, and because it is probable that the most efficient firm is not the firm that pays the highest bribe. Furthermore, the secrecy surrounding bribery may lead government officials to bias their activities towards companies with which the risk of detection is lowest. Thus officials may collude with a group of established firms, and be unwilling to admit innovators (Alam, 1990) or be willing to contract for inappropriate technology or activities (Shleifer & Vishny, 1993). More broadly, bribery leads to distortion in multiplier effects, competitiveness, fiscal functions, debt effects, and growth and investment (Goudie & Stasavage, 1997).

Second, bribery has disincentive effects. It increases risk and uncertainty for firms, related to the probability that a corrupt act will achieve desired goals and the probability of detection and/or punishment. Such uncertainty can deter investment. The cumulative effect of corruption, thus, can be that economic development is hindered (Goudie & Stasavage, 1997). Of course, this argument is in direct contrast to the favorable analysis presented above.

Recent research offers some support for the hypothesis that corruption is a disincentive to investment. Researchers from Emory University developed and tested the Market Discipline Corruption Model (MDCM). They found a significant relationship between media exposure of corruption and foreign direct investment in corrupt countries. Exposure of corruption, combined with the perception that the government was unable or unwilling to change, was associated with a decrease in investment (Busse et al., 1996).

Of course, all these economic arguments, legitimate though they may be, do not make a *moral* case against bribery:

> Those who attempt to establish a correlation between good ethics and successful business, and then use it as the principal reason for taking ethics seriously, forget that the economic downside of, say, bribing a publicly elected official, cannot count as a moral reason for refusing to bribe. They forget, in other words, that the moral reason for not giving a large bribe to a publicly elected official in Brazil is simply that it is wrong. . . . They forget, in short, that moral reasons are required in support of moral conclusions. (Donaldson, 1989: 147)

### Recent International Instruments

Over a quarter-century ago, members of the international economic community began to build an anticorruption regime. However, until quite recently, it appeared that regime-building had stalled (Windsor, 1997). Recent actions by international governmental organizations have given anticorruption advocates cause for hope. Organizations that have taken action include the OECD, OAS, EU, WTO, and World Bank.[3]

### Organization for Economic Cooperation and Development

The Organization for Economic Cooperation and Development (OECD) is the major economic policy-making body for the industrialized democratic countries. Currently, there are twenty-nine member countries: the nations of Western Europe, the nations of North America, and the industrialized democracies of the Pacific. The OECD is home to a majority of the world's multinational corporations. The OECD has explicitly stated its opposition to bribery and corruption since the mid-1970s. In 1976, the OECD adopted the Guidelines for Multinational Enterprises, which provide very broad guidance on appropriate social and economic behavior for businesses. The Guidelines include one general antibribery statement repudiating bribery and extortion.

More recently, the OECD has taken a much more active anticorruption stance. In May 1994, after four years of preparatory work, the OECD issued the nonbinding Recommendations on Bribery in International Business Transactions (Transparency International, 1996). This was the first multilateral agreement among governments to combat bribery of foreign officials. The OECD called upon member countries to take steps nationally and internationally to deter, prevent, and combat the bribery of public officials in foreign countries. This included reviewing criminal, civil, administrative, tax, business accounting, and banking laws, searching for provisions that directly or indirectly favor bribery. The recommendations also called for strengthening international cooperation in identifying and combatting bribery. The OECD allowed two years for member states to review their own laws and prepare reports (1995–96). Beginning in 1997, members were expected to take action to change their laws where necessary.

While the state-by-state review process went forward, the OECD worked to formulate more detailed recommendations. For example, in October 1995 the Committee on Fiscal Affairs issued a Recommendation on the Tax Treatment of Illicit Payments, suggesting that member states which allowed the tax deductibility of bribes discontinue this treatment (Transparency International, 1996). In May 1996, OECD members agreed to criminalize the bribery of foreign officials (OECD Letter, 1996), and recommended that governments take action to introduce anticorruption provisions into contracts funded by their aid budgets.

In May 1997, OECD ministers adopted a program to bring together all the recommendations it had issued since May 1994 (Sanger, 1997). There are two critical elements in this program: (1) an agreement that the next stage of policy-making should rely on a binding treaty, rather than nonbinding recommendations; and (2) a detailed and ambitious timetable for each stage of the treaty-making process. According to the timetable, the treaty would be ready for signature by the end of 1997 and would enter into force by the end of 1998 (Heimann & Boswell, 1997). Furthermore, the treaty would allow member countries to monitor compliance by other member countries (Sanger, 1997).

Current or expected elements of OECD anticorruption policy include: (1) criminalizing the bribery of foreign public officials; (2) implementing civil, commercial, and administrative laws and regulations to make bribery illegal; (3) changing tax laws so they do not favor bribery (e.g., ending tax deductibility of bribes); (4) changing business accounting to require recording of relevant payments; (5) creating banking, financial, and other record-keeping requirements for relevant payments; and (6) implementing laws and regulations related to public subsidies so that they could be denied if bribery occurred. The OECD also recommends international cooperation in investigations and legal proceedings, including extradition (OECD, 1997).

The significance of OECD action is threefold. First, it represents the first broad multilateral effort to create a binding anticorruption treaty. Second, since the OECD members are home to most of the world's MNCs, most MNCs will be subject to the treaty and national laws, once they come into effect. Third, the agreement of certain OECD members, notably France, Germany, and Japan, to participate in these anticorruption efforts is remarkable, as these countries (and others as well) have been reluctant to take any actions that might reduce the success of their corporations' overseas activities (Blustein, 1997; Noonan, 1984; Sanger, 1997).

### Organization of American States

The Organization of American States (OAS) currently has thirty-five member states, all of the independent republics of the Americas except Cuba. An additional thirty-seven states and the European Union have been granted Permanent Observer status. The basic purposes of the OAS are to strengthen the peace and security of the continent, to promote representative democracy, and to promote economic, social, and cultural development.

In December 1994, at the Summit of the Americas, the OAS adopted a plan of action aimed at strengthening democracy and combating corruption (OAS Homepage, 1997). In 1995, spurred on by Venezuela, a Working Group on Honesty and Public Ethics drafted the Inter-American Convention Against Corruption, which was signed in March 1996 by twenty-one members (Babbitt, 1996). The first-ever regional treaty against corruption, the convention is not an agreement to outlaw bribery. Rather, it makes recommendations for policies and practices that ultimately would make bribery or corruption more transparent and less appealing. Specifically, the convention calls for raising public awareness of the effects of corruption. It also calls for measures to bring recipients of bribes to justice, suggesting ways in which offenders might be detected, and including extradition and confiscating on the national and international levels of money or property gained through corrupt practices. In addition, the convention calls upon the OAS General Assembly to devise a strategy for implementing preventive measures (OAS Homepage, 1997). The intention clearly is to outlaw bribery at some point. The convention entered into force in March 1997, though not all OAS members have yet ratified it (Transparency International-USA, 1997a).

The significance of OAS action is twofold. First, it has come in the form of a binding treaty, rather than a set of nonbinding recommendations. While it does not ban bribery, it does require that members cooperate on developing antibribery practices. Second, there is a widespread perception that many OAS member countries condone bribery and corruption, at least by custom (McGugan, 1995). Active participation in OAS anticorruption efforts may help to dispel this perception, especially since the convention gives explicit attention to the recipients of bribes.

### European Union

The European Union is the most advanced regional economic area in the world, with integration including common trade policies among its fifteen members, harmonized economic policies, monetary cooperation, and extensive political integration. Despite its policy cooperation in a wide variety of issues, including some which are controversial, the EU has been a particularly reluctant participant in international anticorruption efforts. Until recently, it had opted to allow member countries to act independently. However, under pressure from private business leaders and America, the EU has now taken some modest steps.

In December 1995, following a summit meeting between President Clinton and representatives of the EU, a statement was issued which included a commitment to implement the 1994 OECD recommendations regarding bribery and corruption. A few days later, the European Parliament adopted a report on combating corruption in Europe. In September 1996, the European

Council adopted a protocol making it a crime in each member state to bribe an official of the EU or of any EU member state, provided the financial interests of the EU are damaged. Then in May 1997, the EU Commission adopted a program for action. Points include criminalization of bribery of officials of the EU and of member states and cooperation with the OECD in criminalizing bribery outside the EU. The report also criticized tax deductibility of bribes and urged the EU to develop a program to abolish it (Heimann & Boswell, 1997).

While the EU's initiatives are quite modest in comparison with the actions of the OECD, they are significant in that they represent a turnaround. Whereas in the past, the EU cast a blind eye toward bribery and corruption, it has now acknowledged the need to discourage such behavior in business.

### World Trade Organization

The World Trade Organization (WTO), established in 1995 as the successor to the General Agreement on Tariffs and Trade, is the legal and institutional foundation for trade relations among countries. Its objective is to liberalize global trade on the premise that trade accelerates development. Compared to the OECD, OAS, and EU, the WTO has a somewhat narrower mission. Therefore its interest and involvement in anticorruption efforts is clearly subordinate to its other activities. However, modest anticorruption action has been taken. In December 1996, the WTO ministerial created a procurement working group which is currently assessing the procurement practices of the World Bank, the UN, and other international organizations, with the idea of discovering and adopting the best practices (e.g., those least likely to create opportunities for corruption). U.S. officials anticipate negotiations on a WTO transparency agreement in 1998 (Heimann & Boswell, 1997).

### World Bank

The World Bank Group comprises five organizations; the International Bank for Reconstruction and Development (IBRD) and the International Development Association (IDA) are the two organizations that engage in lending to governments. The money loaned by the World Bank is used to pay for development projects, such as building highways, schools, and hospitals, and for programs to help governments change the way they manage their economies.

The World Bank's role in the anticorruption regime is different from those of the other international organizations in this list. The World Bank is not a policy-making body, per se. However, it does dispense advice regarding fiscal, monetary, and economic policies, along with its loans. The bank has come to recognize that by failing to take explicit measures to eliminate corruption, it has, in effect, contributed to corruption.[4]

Beginning in 1996, the leadership of the World Bank began to take steps to purge corruption in bank-funded transactions. New guidelines are intended to eliminate opportunities for corruption by replacing administrative mechanisms with market mechanisms, simplifying tax systems, reforming regulations to enhance transparency, and strengthening institutions, both in government and in civil society. Furthermore, new procurement guidelines provide that the bank may cancel a loan if key actors engaged in corrupt or fraudulent practices to secure the loan. There are also procedures for blacklisting offending corporations, procedures for investigating allegations of corruption, and a new requirement for the disclosure of commissions paid to agents (Heimann & Boswell, 1996; World Bank Homepage, 1997).

### Other International Action

A number of other international organizations, both governmental and nongovernmental, have offered anticorruption resolutions or agreements. While these are less significant than those listed above, they deserve mention. Some general-purpose codes of conduct for multinational corporations include statements against corruption. The United Nations Commission on Transnational Corporations (CTC) is a global organization created in 1974 as a forum for comprehensive and in-depth consideration of the full range of issues relating to MNCs. Its initial mandate was to prepare a code of conduct. The CTC Code of Conduct for Transnational Corporations states that MNCs should neither pay nor offer to pay a bribe to any public official. Founded in 1986, the Caux Roundtable is a private organization of business executives from Europe, Japan, and the U.S. In 1994, the roundtable issued the Caux Principles, a brief document which outlines proper conduct for international business. Principle 7 asserts that a business should not participate in or condone bribery, and should seek cooperation with others to eliminate corrupt practices.

In addition, there have been specific anticorruption statements from some organizations, including the UN, the Council of Europe, the International Chamber of Commerce, and the Organization for African Unity. For example, in December 1996, the UN issued a Declaration Against Corruption and Bribery in International Commercial Transactions. The declaration reaffirms the anticorruption provisions of the CTC Code of Conduct, and urges countries and companies to eradicate corruption.

In 1994, the Council of Europe established a Multidisciplinary Group on Corruption, and instructed it to begin to draft a program of action against international corruption. The Council of Europe's active interest in combating corruption is significant because its membership is much broader and more diverse than the membership of either the European Union or the OECD. (There are thirty-nine members, including all Western European countries and almost all Central and Eastern European countries.)

The International Chamber of Commerce (ICC) is a private employers' federation operating at the international level. In 1977, it issued its first set of Rules of Conduct on Extortion and Bribery. In 1995, the ICC substantially revised the rules and produced suggested corporate codes of conduct for member organizations. The rules are intended as a method of self-regulation, though the ICC also asserts that they should be supported by governments. The specific provisions prohibit direct and indirect payment or offer of bribes and require accurate accounting of all transactions supported by independent auditing of accounts.

Finally, some international organizations have pledged to combat corruption by working cooperatively with other IOs. For example, in 1994, the Organization for African Unity (OAU) called upon its member governments to adopt measures against bribery and to work closely with the OECD. To date, the OAU has done little beyond making this commitment, in part because the leader of the movement, General Olusegun Obasanjo, former president of Nigeria, has been illegally imprisoned in Nigeria (TI Newsletter, 1996b).

### Levers against Corruption

A review of the codes, as well as general consideration of the issue of bribery and corruption, reveals that there are three basic points against which to act to eliminate the problem: the supply-side; the demand-side; and the intermediaries (Wedgwood, 1996). Bribery is an act that must involve two parties, the payer and the payee. Depending upon the size of the bribe, and the payee's wants, bribe money might be laundered, thus involving a third party, international banks.

### Supply-Side

The most common way that international organizations try to thwart corruption is to target suppliers. This follows the example of the U.S. Foreign Corrupt Practices Act, which makes paying a bribe to a foreign government official illegal. FCPA does not criminalize the *receipt* of the bribe, for this would without question involve an extraterritorial application of U.S. law. Most countries, both advanced and developing, have laws against the payment of bribes to their own officials, regardless of the citizenship of the payer (Noonan, 1984). Thus the recommendations by international organizations focus on eliminating incentives and opportunities for payment of bribes to foreign officials.

The steps taken, recommended, or expected against bribe payers are several. First, the IOs call for an end to blatant support of bribes, such as tax deductibility (OECD, EU). Second, the IOs call for an end to more subtle support of bribes. They recommend increased transparency, such as disclosure requirements for payments made to agents as well as those made directly to foreign officials (OECD, WTO, World Bank). Third, the IOs call for denial of certain benefits for the payers of bribes. For example, public subsidies might be denied (OECD), or corporations might be made ineligible for certain types of contracts (World Bank). Fourth, the IOs call for civil and criminal sanctions against the payers of bribes, including possibly fines and imprisonment (OECD, EU). Fifth, the IOs call for international cooperation, including sharing information for investigations and extradition (OECD).

### Demand-Side

A less common way that international organizations have recommended to thwart corruption is to target the officials who receive or demand the bribes. There are two reasons that this method is less common. First, as noted above, for one country to criminalize the receipt of a payment in another country would represent an extraterritorial application of the first country's laws, something which is generally proscribed in international law. Second, most countries, both advanced and developing, already have laws that make it illegal for public officials to take payments for favors. In fact, some of the new recommendations are aimed at strengthening the enforcement of existing laws.

The steps taken, recommended, or expected against bribe recipients are several. First, IOs recommend increasing public awareness of the cost of corruption, and thereby increasing public outrage (OAS). Second, IOs recommend ways to detect guilty parties. In particular, they recommend that governments question increases in the assets of a government official that cannot be explained (OAS). Third, the IOs recommend ways to reduce the opportunities for corruption, by reducing bureaucracies, simplifying tax systems, and strengthening civil and public institutions (OAS, WTO, World Bank). Fourth, the IOs call for direct penalties, both for individuals and governments. For individuals, money and property gained through corrupt practices should be confiscated (OAS). For governments, loans should be cancelled if the proceeds are mismanaged by corrupt government officials (World Bank). Fifth, the IOs call for international cooperation, including sharing information for investigations and extradition (OECD, OAS).

## Intermediaries

The least common way that international organizations have recommended to thwart corruption is to target the intermediaries, chiefly international banks, which do not participate directly in the bribe transaction but nonetheless facilitate it. This technique is used regularly in the drug wars, with some success (Wedgwood, 1996), and could likewise be used against corruption. At present, there is only one IO action that specifically addresses the issue of money laundering. The OECD recommends that member countries create banking, financial, and other relevant record-keeping requirements.

## Implementation Efforts

The extant literature on multilateral regulation and international organizations tends to assume that implementation is difficult or impossible because of the strictly voluntary relationship between sovereign states and IOs (e.g., Kindleberger, 1986; Nadlemann, 1990; Preston & Windsor, 1992; Reynolds, 1985; Sanders, 1982). Recent analysis specifically focused on anticorruption efforts is similarly pessimistic regarding effective implementation (Klitgaard, 1996; Windsor, 1997). Nonetheless, it is possible to affect implementation, using a variety of levers (Getz, 1995a).

Implementation of multilateral regulatory policies is a three-step process, involving communicating requirements, monitoring behavior, and sanctioning behavior (Getz, 1995a). The purpose of communication is to assure that affected firms know what they are expected to do; the purpose of monitoring is to observe and evaluate the behavior of firms with respect to policy requirements; and the purpose of sanctioning is to encourage compliance with requirements and to discourage noncompliance through the promise of rewards and the threat of punishments. International policies may include explicit requirements regarding these three steps, either for the international organization itself or for signatory states, but often they do not. The new international instruments described here explicitly remark on a few aspects of implementation. In addition, nongovernmental organizations have voluntarily assumed a role in implementing these international anticorruption instruments.

## Official Implementation Efforts

The anticorruption instruments include no requirements regarding communication, either for the IOs or for signatories. However, some communication efforts are evident. The most typical IO communication tactic is to publicize widely, through press releases, and library and Internet publications. This is the tactic used by each of the IOs with respect to the issue of corruption. For example, the OECD, the OAS, and the World Bank have published their policies for wide dissemination, in hard copy and electronically. These organizations have also issued repeated press releases, which have received widespread coverage. (This is particularly true of OECD actions.) A second communication tactic for IOs is to hold meetings or seminars at which new or pending recommendations or treaties are explained or discussed. The IOs interested in corruption have held such meetings. For example during 1995, the OAS organized seminars in many member countries to promote and explain the Inter-American Convention Against Corruption. There is less evidence of active efforts to communicate requirements by signatory states. Press releases have been issued when states have signed on to these agreements, but beyond that, little active effort to communicate with affected firms is apparent.[5]

Implementers use two key tactics, inspections and reports, to monitor firm behavior. The anticorruption instruments include just one type of requirement regarding monitoring. Two of them (OECD and OAS) explicitly permit signatory states to monitor compliance in other signatories. This is a rather unusual provision for international agreements, since cross-border monitoring could be interpreted as a violation of the principle of international comity. There is little evidence that this cross-border monitoring has yet occurred, perhaps because the OECD treaty is still being drafted and the OAS treaty has been in effect for only a few months. Although there are few explicit measures regarding monitoring, states are developing some monitoring tactics. For some states, anticorruption efforts are new. Their monitoring begins with establishing new offices or agencies. For example, Algeria recently created the Observatoire National de Surveillance et de Prevention de la Corruption. Its objective is to collect and process information concerning corruption (TI Newsletter, 1996a). Some states are instituting programs which encourage citizens to monitor public officials. Pakistan recently started a monitoring program involving citizens. Rewards of 10 percent of recovered proceeds are promised to people who report corruption in government to the anticorruption agency (TI Newsletter, 1997b). In South Africa, a register of the financial interests of members of parliament was recently released. For a fee, citizens may review a report for each MP (TI Newsletter, 1997c). (Other countries do not require citizens to pay a fee for this type of information.)

Sanctions are intended to effect rational cost-benefit calculations: positive sanctions should increase benefits while negative sanctions should increase costs. Typically, international organizations threaten trade sanctions for non-complying signatory states, while states use fines, imprisonment, and tax incentives as sanctions. The anticorruption instruments are atypical in two ways. First, there are some IO sanctions that apply directly to MNEs, rather than to signatory states. The World Bank and the World Trade Organization both threaten to blacklist corporations that engage in bribery or fraudulent practices in their efforts to obtain procurement contracts with these IOs. Second, IO sanctions against states are not related to trade. The World Bank (and a number of regional development banks) threaten to withdraw financing from projects in which public officials of the debtor country are found to be corrupt. Beyond these IO efforts, the instruments call directly for sanctioning by signatories. Most importantly, the OECD recommendations, and the pending convention, call for criminalization of the bribery of foreign officials. Thus sanctions applied by governments will include fines and imprisonment. For example, Triton Energy Ltd. recently agreed to pay $300,000 to settle charges that it had paid hundreds of thousands of dollars in bribes to Indonesian public officials. The former president of Triton Indonesia also agreed to pay a fine of $50,000 in settlement of similar charges (TI Newsletter, 1997d).[6] Other state-applied sanctions recommended by the international agreements include blacklisting corporations that contribute to corruption by paying bribes and extradition of those accused of bribery or corruption to the country leveling the charges.

### Nonofficial Implementation Efforts

Nongovernmental organizations can play a significant role in communicating expectations to MNCs, monitoring MNC behavior, and sanctioning MNCs (Getz, 1995a; Jacobson, 1992). In fact, a role for representatives of the public interest has been advocated or documented for many aspects of social responsibility, domestically or internationally (see, e.g., Mahon & Waddock, 1992; Stone, 1975). Several nongovernmental organizations have demonstrated a strong interest in combating corruption, either in cooperation with international governmental organizations or on their own. Two organizations deserve mention: the International Chamber of Commerce (ICC) and Transparency International (TI). Both organizations are private. Both have as members high-level individuals representing business; TI also has government officials among its members. Transparency International is a very new organization, formally constituted in 1993. Its mission is to build international and national coalitions against corruption. The ICC was described above.

Both the ICC and TI have been actively engaged in trying to communicate with affected parties about international anticorruption codes and about corruption in general. The ICC has held meetings and seminars to promote its own code and the OECD recommendations. It has published its code both in hard copy and electronically. TI has published extensive information about progress on the codes, treaties, and recommendations, via its newsletters, memos to supporters, annual reports, and articles written by its members. It has also posted the OECD recommendations as an annex to one of its electronically published press releases. TI and its country chapters have held seminars and meetings all over the world to discuss corruption and the requirements of the codes. Members of TI also engage in one-on-one communications, acting essentially as evangelists, at every opportunity. Finally, TI has taken active steps to communicate with governments, and to encourage them to implement the OECD recommendations. This type of communications, essentially a lobbying effort, has been carried out by chapters in Australia, Denmark, Germany, Switzerland, and other countries (Transparency International, 1996).

Nongovernmental organizations do not have the authority to demand reports from firms or to inspect firm records regarding their compliance with anticorruption instruments (or with any other regulations). However, NGOs can monitor the compliance behavior of MNCs through direct inquiries to firms, open or under-cover investigations, or audits. TI has tried very hard to avoid active monitoring of firm-level behavior, disclaiming a role in investigation or exposure of corruption (Transparency International, 1995). However, TI and several of its national chapters actively monitor media reports of corruption and record them.

NGOs can provide negative sanctions, such as negative publicity or boycotts, and they can provide positive sanctions, such as positive publicity. The efforts of TI to communicate about corruption in general and about the international recommendations in particular result in a form of sanction for some firms and for some countries. Although TI believes its role to be one of providing information and proselytizing on the evils of corruption, its actions and communications inevitably involve naming specific firms and countries, in a negative or positive light. To the extent that TI is considered a reliable source of information (and it is), the reputations of firms or countries named in communications efforts are affected. TI does make an effort, in its face-to-face communications, to convince individual business executives to commit to eradicating corruption in their own organizations and the countries in which they do business.

## Analysis of Implementation Efforts

There are two bodies of literature that may contribute to understanding the implementation of these international anticorruption instruments. The scant literature on multilateral regulation suggests variables which contribute to MNCs' compliance decisions. The better-developed literature on moral development identifies the criteria individuals use in making decisions on moral issues.

### Multilateral Regulation

The literature on multilateral policy tends not to address the issue of implementation (see, e.g., Adelman, 1988; Fejfar, 1983; Grieves, 1979). However, a preliminary theory of the implementation has been developed by Getz (1995a). Based on the implementation framework of Sabatier and Mazmanian (1980), Getz's theory suggests that implementation effectiveness is dependent on variables related to the tractability of the problem addressed by the multilateral policy and on specific provisions written into the policy.

Of five variables related to tractability, there are two related ones which should be important for the issue of corruption. Getz argues that the relative size and power of the target group is an important issue. The larger the group, the more intractable the problem and the greater the difficulty of successful implementation, in part because of higher costs of communication, monitoring, and sanctioning. Powerful targets are also negatively associated with implementation, given the ability of powerful actors to resist and even hinder efforts to monitor and sanction. For the issue of corruption, the target group is large. Widespread corruption among government officials in many parts of the world is assumed, and there is some evidence to support the assumption. Furthermore, many of the actors involved in corrupt exchanges are powerful. The government officials who accept or extort bribes are very powerful locally, and the MNCs whose employees or agents offer or pay bribes are often powerful both locally and internationally. Thus, according to Getz's theory, the size and power of the target group in anticorruption policies decrease the likelihood of successful implementation.

Of five policy variables, there are two which should be important for the issue of corruption. Getz argues that a policy with unambiguous directives is easier to implement than one in which objectives are unclear or conflicting. Communication is facilitated because the message to be delivered is well developed in the policy itself. Monitoring is also easier because clearly stated objectives help implementers determine which aspects of behavior to monitor. Sanctioning is eased because unambiguous policies tend to be perceived as legitimate (Reynolds, 1985). Getz also asserts that implementation is positively associated with policies that provide a means of access to nonstate actors (i.e., interest groups). Access which includes some participation in the policy-making process also increases the likelihood that interest groups will perceive IO expectations as legitimate. Communication is enhanced because interest groups better understand the policy. Firms which respect the involved interest-groups may be more open when implementers attempt to monitor their behavior, and may come to value the approval of implementing officials, thus increasing the utility of normative sanctions. For the issue of corruption, policy objectives are unambiguous. Also, access for interest groups is relatively high, though most of the access is informal rather than encoded in policy. The importance of interest-group access is highlighted further below.

### Moral Development

There is an extensive literature on the antecedents of corporate social performance. Important variables include organizational climate, top management commitment to good behavior, and structures and processes that guide behavior, such as ethics codes, ethics training, and social audits. In addition to organizational variables, individual variables affect organizational behavior. In particular, the moral development of decision-makers is important.

Research on moral development helps explain why individuals "do the right thing." Moral behavior can be triggered by fear of punishment or desire for reward, by reference to and desire for approval of a particular group (family, friends), by a general understanding of the needs of society as a whole, or by a clear commitment to principles of good and bad or right and wrong. For most adults, moral reasoning is guided by consideration of what is desired by and good for a reference group or for society at large (Kohlberg, 1981; Rest, 1986). Thus norms are more important as drivers of behavior than fear of punishment and desire for reward. They are also more important than broad ethical principles. However, there is variation across individual situations. Thus one good approach to the deterrence of bribery and corruption would be to assure that an effort is made to trigger each type of moral reasoning. That is, there should be a credible threat of punishment for wrongdoing; there should

be appeals based on small-group and social norms; and there should be identification and advancement of universal principles.

Preconventional moral reasoning is characterized by avoiding punishments and seeking rewards. There has been no apparent effort by any interested actors to offer rewards for good (noncorrupt) behavior. However, in the
new anticorruption codes, the punishment system is much better developed
than it is in many other international codes. Noncomplying states may lose
their access to development loans. Noncomplying firms may lose their access
to lucrative procurement contracts with IOs, and may be assessed hefty fines.
Noncomplying individuals may lose the proceeds of their extortion or be imprisoned. These and other punishments are specified in the anticorruption
instruments.

Despite these well-articulated and credible punishments, the desire to
avoid punishment may not be the best driver of moral behavior. For individual
decision-makers, social-group or social norms may be more relevant. The
progress of the IOs in writing recommendations and treaties, combined with
the significant efforts of the NGOs, especially TI, are in essence creating a
change in international norms regarding corruption and bribery. These activities are relevant for individuals whose moral reasoning has developed to the
conventional level.

Conventional moral reasoning is characterized by attempts to conform
with the expectations of direct relationships and consideration for the good
of the larger social system. In order for conventional moral reasoning to lead to
noncorrupt behavior, there must be small-group expectations and social norms
that proscribe bribery. Transparency International is working to create such
expectations and to promote such norms. TI has as members and spokespersons high-level individuals whose behavior others are likely to emulate and
whose approval and esteem others desire. The individuals who lead TI are well
known and respected in their own and other countries, particularly among
business and government leaders. For example, Peter Eigen, the founder and
chairman of TI, is a former executive of the World Bank. He has achieved a high
level of accomplishment that is recognized not only in his native Germany but
virtually around the world. TI supporters include such prestigious companies
as Arthur Andersen, Boeing, Bristol-Myers Squibb, Ciba-Geigy-Stiftung, Coopers & Lybrand, Deutsche Telecom, Enron, IBM, Merck, Nestlé, Pfizer, Ray-
theon, Schering, Westinghouse, and Zurn Industries. TI also receives support
from public-sector agencies in Canada, Denmark, Ecuador, the EU, France,
Germany, the Netherlands, Norway, Sweden, Switzerland, the U.K., and the
U.S., as well as from some regional and global governmental organizations.

Furthermore, TI has an extensive system for disseminating information,
ranging from newsletters and Internet sites to speeches and presentations to

large and small audiences. Publications and presentations by TI and its representatives are informative and highly persuasive. There is a growing consensus that TI is successful (Kaltenhauser, 1996; McGugan, 1995; TI Newsletter, 1997a). In the U.S. press and in official government circles, TI is almost never mentioned in a negative way.[7]

The important work of TI reinforces norms and expectations. However, it is itself supported by an even more widespread (though probably more subtle) phenomenon: a global recognition that corruption and bribery violate the intrinsic social contract between government officials and ordinary citizens. A universal anticorruption ethic is emerging throughout the world. This phenomenon is relevant for individuals whose moral reasoning has developed to the postconventional level.

Postconventional moral reasoning is characterized by reference to basic rights and universal ethical principles. In order for postconventional moral reasoning to lead to noncorrupt behavior, there must be accepted international norms against bribery and corruption. There is a growing body of literature which provides an analysis of international norms (e.g., Donaldson & Dunfee, 1994; Frederick, 1991; Getz, 1995b; Nadlemann, 1990), including descriptions of the sources of such norms.

In a powerful analysis, the purpose of which was to integrate the empirical and normative branches of business ethics research, Donaldson and Dunfee propose the concept of hypernorm. Hypernorms "entail principles so fundamental to human existence that they serve as a guide in evaluating lower level moral norms" (1994:265). A clue to the existence of a hypernorm can be found in "a convergence of religious, philosophical, and cultural beliefs" (1994:265). As Donaldson and Dunfee argue, there is evidence of such convergence for international business (e.g., Frederick, 1991; Getz, 1995b; Nadlemann, 1990; Preston & Windsor, 1992). Several of the sources cited here and/or by Donaldson and Dunfee as providing evidence of convergence do not refer directly to religious, philosophical, or cultural beliefs. In fact, many of them refer to international policies or international regimes. Thus, it seems, the very fact that IOs are successful in writing recommendations or treaties is evidence that there is broad consensus about appropriate norms.

Recent attention to bribery and corruption by international organizations, therefore, is momentous. The consensus achieved simply to write the recommendations or treaties, or even to conduct studies and hold conventions, is reason for optimism. While the consensus on norms regarding corruption evidenced by these new instruments may not translate directly into reductions in corrupt behavior, it is *at the least* the beginning of a regime. A regime, which can as easily be based on norms as on explicit rules, provides guidance for behavior (Krasner, 1983). Thus the emerging anticorruption regime may be expected to affect MNC behavior; MNCs will conform to the norms of the regime.

## Conclusion

As mentioned earlier in this chapter, analyses of international regulatory efforts, and particularly of international codes of conduct, are often characterized by pessimism regarding likely effectiveness. This pessimism is based in part on the legalistic view that IOs cannot forcibly extract compliance from unwilling MNCs, because they have no direct authority over MNCs. Furthermore states may fail to enact or to enforce needed laws, and some states are not even signatories to the international agreements.[8] As Windsor states: "collective international standards that must be enforced by national action are especially ripe with free riding opportunities in which many countries can continue to enjoy the fruits of noncompliance" (1997:1). I have attempted to show in this chapter that such pessimism is misplaced in the case of anticorruption codes. In fact, because of many related developments, there is reason for optimism.

1. The codes have been carefully written, focusing on a specific issue, articulating fairly precisely the sorts of behaviors that are prescribed and proscribed. The codes have also made allowance for active participation by nongovernmental organizations.

2. The combined efforts of governmental and nongovernmental organizations to combat bribery and corruption have relevance for individuals at all levels of moral reasoning. There is a punishment system. There is an articulation of interpersonal and social expectations. And there is a growing consensus on an international anticorruption ethic.

In sum, significant progress has been made in combating corruption. Much more remains to be done. I am hopeful that over the next several years the overall level of corruption in the world will be reduced.

## Notes

1. TI Newsletter, September 1996, p.4.

2. Goudie & Stasavage (1997) acknowledge this by explicitly excluding unilateral theft from consideration.

3. Many of the international instruments have a broader focus than just international business. They address bribery and corruption in international and domestic transactions, and in business and non-business relationships.

4. The realization was a long time in coming. As recently as 1990, the World Bank explicitly forbade a director working in Africa from becoming involved in anti-corruption activities, on the grounds that such activities went beyond the mandate of the bank. The director, Pete Eigen, soon retired from the World Bank and founded Transparency International, now the leading nongovernmental anticorruption organization in the world.

5. This generalization may be unwarranted. I have not reviewed the news accounts of signatories other than the U.S. and Great Britain.

6. These charges were filed under the FCPA. Under the OECD recommendations, other countries will pass legislation similar to the U.S. law.

7. I was unable to find any negative references.

8. Indeed, this is not an uncommon problem. For example, China, a significant producer of chloroflurocarbons, has failed to sign the Montreal Protocol on Substances that Deplete the Ozone Layer.

## Bibliography

Adelman, Carol C. (ed.). 1988. *International regulation: New rules in a changing world order.* San Francisco: ICS Press.

Alam, M. S. 1990. Some Economic Costs of Corruption in LDC's. *Journal of Development Studies,* 27 (1).

Babbitt, Harriet C. 1996. Outlawing corruption in the Americas. *Washington Post.* March 21: A16.

Bardhan, P. 1997. *The Role of Governance in Economic Development: A Political Economy Approach.* Paris: OECD Development Centre.

Blustein, Paul. 1997. Pact to bar bribery is reached. *Washington Post.* May 24: F1+.

Brunetti, A. 1995. Political Variables in Cross-Country Growth Analysis. Harvard University working paper.

Busse, Laurence, Noboru Ishikawa, Morgan Mitra, David Primmer, Kenneth Doe, & Tolga Yaveroglu. 1996. The Perception of Corruption: A Market Discipline Approach. Emory University working paper.

Donaldson, Thomas. 1989. *The ethics of international business.* New York: Oxford University Press.

Donaldson, Thomas, & Thomas W. Dunfee. 1994. Towards a unified conception of business ethics: Integrative social contracts theory. *Academy of Management Review,* 19: 252–84.

Ekpo, Monday. 1979. Gift-giving and bureaucratic corruption in Nigeria. In Monday Ekpo (ed.), *Bureaucratic corruption in sub-saharan Africa: Causes, consequences, and controls,* Washington, D.C.: University Press of America.

Fejfar, Mary A. 1983. *Regulation of business by international agencies.* St. Louis: Center for the Study of American Business.

Frederick, William C. 1991. The moral authority of transnational corporate codes. *Journal of Business Ethics,* 10: 165–77.

Getz, Kathleen A. 1995a. Implementing multilateral regulation: A preliminary theory and illustration. *Business & Society,* 34: 280–316.

———. 1995b. Trans-ideological business values in international codes of conduct. *International Journal of Value-Based Management,* 8: 117–34.

Goudie, Andrew W., & David Stasavage. 1997. *Corruption: The Issues.* Paris: OECD Development Centre.

Gould, D., & J. Amaro-Reyes. 1983. The Effects of Corruption on Administrative Performance: Illustration from Developing Countries. World Bank Staff Working Paper #580.

Grieves, Forest L. (ed.). 1979. *Transnationalism in world politics and business.* New York: Pergamon Press.

Heimann, Fritz, & Nancy Zucker Boswell. 1996. Memorandum to TI-USA supporters. August 6.

———. 1997. Memorandum to TI-USA board and supporters. May 27.

Hirsh, Michael. 1995. Graft Busters. *Newsweek,* December 23: 56+.

Jacobson, R. M. 1992. Responsible care: A public commitment. Paper presented at the Conference of the Center for the Study of Business and Public Issues, The Pennsylvania State University.

Kaltenhauser, Skip. 1996. When bribery is a budget item. *Worldbusiness,* 2 (2): 11.

Kantor, Michael. 1996. Remarks prepared for delivery to the emergency committee for American trade, March 6, found at <webmaster@ustr.gov>.

Kindleberger, Charles P. 1986. International public goods without international government. *American Economic Review,* 76: 1–13.

Klitgaard, Robert. 1988. *Controlling corruption.* Berkeley: University of California Press.

———. 1995. Institutional adjustment and adjusting to institutions. World Bank Discussion Paper #303.

———. 1996. National and international strategies for reducing corruption, 37–54 in OECD Working Papers: Symposium on Corruption and Good Governance. Paris: OECD.

Kohlberg, Lawrence. 1981. *The philosophy of moral development.* San Francisco: Harper & Row.

Krasner, Stephen (ed.). 1983. *International regimes.* Ithaca: Cornell University Press.

Leff, Nathaniel. 1979. Economic development through bureaucratic corruption. In Monday Ekpo (ed.), *Bureaucratic corruption in sub-saharan Africa: Causes, consequences, and controls.* Washington, D.C.: University Press of America.

Mahon, John F., & Sandra Waddock. 1992. Strategic issues management: An integration of life cycle perspectives. *Business & Society,* 31: 19–32.

Mauro, P. 1995. Corruption and growth. *Quarterly Journal of Economics,* 109: 681–712.

McGugan, Ian. 1995. Greed, si, but adios to bribes. *Canadian Business.* 68 (2): 93.

Nadlemann, Ethan A. 1990. Global prohibition regimes: The evolution of norms in international society. *International Organization,* 44: 479–526.

Noonan, John T., Jr. 1984. *Bribes.* New York: Macmillan.

Nye, J. S. 1979. Corruption and political development: A cost-benefit analysis. In Monday Ekpo (ed.), *Bureaucratic corruption in sub-saharan Africa: Causes, consequences, and controls.* Washington, D.C.: University Press of America.

OAS Homepage. 1997. <http://www.oas.org>

OECD Letter. 1996. December issue, vol. 5/10.

OECD. 1997. Recommendations on bribery in international business transactions. Paris: OECD.

Preston, Lee E., & Duane Windsor. 1992. *The rules of the game in the global economy: Policy regimes for international business.* Boston: Kluwer.

Rest, James R. 1986. *Moral development: Advances in research and theory.* New York: Praeger.

Reynolds, Thomas H. 1985. Clouds of codes: The new international economic order through codes of conduct: A survey. 1–40 in Kenneth R. Simmonds (ed.), *Multinational corporations law: The United Nations and transnational corporations.* Dobbs Ferry: Oceana Publications.

Rose-Ackerman, Susan. 1978. *Corruption: A study in political economy.* New York: Academic Press.

Sabatier, Paul, & Daniel Mazmanian. 1980. The implementation of public policy: A framework of analysis. *Policy Studies Journal,* 8, Special 2 (4): 538–60.

Sanders, Pieter. 1982. Implementing international codes of conduct for multinational enterprises. *American Journal of Comparative Law,* 30: 241–54.

Sanger, David E. 1997. 29 Nations agree to a bribery ban. *New York Times,* May 24: 1+.

Shleifer., A., & R. Vishny. 1993. Corruption. *Quarterly Journal of Economics,* 108: 599–617.

Smith, M. 1979. Historical and cultural conditions of political corruption among the Hausa of Nigeria. In Monday Ekpo (ed.), *Bureaucratic corruption in sub-saharan Africa: Causes, consequences, and controls.* Washington, D.C.: University Press of America.

Stone, Christopher. 1975. *Where the law ends.* Prospect Heights, Ill.: Waveland Press.

Tanzi, V. 1994. Corruption, governmental activities, and markets. IMF Working Paper #94/99.

TI Source Book. 1996. Linked to Transparency International homepage at <http://www. transparency.de>.

TI Newsletter. 1996a. Algeria creates an anticorruption observation office. December: 5.

———. 1996b. Free Obasanjo activities. December: 7.

———. 1997a. Editorial. June: 1.

———. 1997b. Pakistan: Rewards for tip-offs promised. June: 4.

———. 1997c. South Africa: A price on access to MPs ethics. June: 4.

———. 1997d. U.S.: Triton pays fine for "systematic corruption." June: 9.

Transparency International. 1995. Building a global coalition against corruption. Berlin: TI.

———. 1996. Sharpening the responses against global corruption. Berlin: TI.

Transparency International-USA. 1997a. Newsletter. 1 (2): 3.
————. 1997b. Program highlights. April.
Wedgwood, Ruth. 1996. Stop the greedy "kleptokrats." *Washington Post.* June 4.
Windsor, Duane. 1997. Illicit foreign payments: Toward an international regime. Paper presented at the Eastern Academy of Management Meeting, Dublin.
World Bank Homepage. 1997. <http://www.worldbank.org>

PART IV

— ✻ —

# The Caux Round Table's Principles for Business

*A Framework for Company Codes*

# 10

# Executives' Code of Business Conduct

*Prospects for the Caux Principles*

GERALD F. CAVANAGH, S.J.

This chapter examines global codes of business conduct, and specifically the Caux Round Table's Principles for Business, by responding to five questions:

1. Why should we be concerned about global business ethics now?
2. What are the Caux Round Table's (CRT) Principles for Business?
3. Are these Principles for Business practical?
4. How do the Caux Principles compare with other global codes?
5. What are the prospects for these Principles for Business? Can they be implemented?

### Global Free Markets in the Twenty-first Century

The answer to the first question is clear to most people. With the collapse of communism and the advance of communications and transportation, the market system has rapidly become both global and dominant in our world. This market system has immense strengths. It provides goods and services for billions of people, and it also is the source of jobs and family income for most of these same people. Not only does that system provide rewarding work for many, it also enables people to lead a humane life, both through the products and services it produces and the incomes that support families in all of the countries of the world. Moreover, the market system rewards hard work, entrepreneurship, innovation, and flexibility. In the smaller world in which we now live, business bridges nations, cultures, and peoples. It is essential for managers to understand other cultures if they are to be a success in international business.

Global firms have operations overseas; thus countries and firms are "interlinked."[1] We see examples of such linkages in the North American Free Trade Agreement (NAFTA), the European Union (EU), the economic treaties of the "tigers" of Southeast Asia (ASEAN Union), and many other cases.

In the wake of the success of free markets it is tempting for citizens and government officials alike to think that the market, operating without restrictions, will itself solve current and future economic and social problems.[2] Nothing could be further from the truth. There are widespread inequities that the market not only does not solve but in many cases exacerbates. When some people, lands, and natural resources are treated unfairly, it creates serious problems for people and for business itself. It is not a favorable environment for doing business; it is "not a level playing field."[3]

Let us examine some of the inequities that we experience with the market system. The first is corruption and bribery. Korean courts recently convicted two former presidents of Korea and four corporation presidents for bribery.[4] In Mexico, often government officials must be paid off, along with individual policemen. In order to do business in Indonesia, the global firm had to cut President Suharto, or one of his relatives, in on the deal; they had to be made partners, major shareholders (without any investment), or made directors or consultants with immense mandatory payments.[5]

Sweatshops recently have received much attention in the U.S. Many manufacturers have subcontracted sewing of clothes and shoes to firms that hire children who often work ten to fourteen hours a day and six or seven days a week.[6] Nike's shoes are stitched in Indonesia and Vietnam by young women making a base wage of $2.23 a day. It takes $2.40 to feed one person three meals a day, let alone provide for a family. Total Nike labor cost is $2.50 for a shoe that sells in the U.S. or Europe for up to $150.[7] It is sobering to recognize that such working conditions are similar to those of U.S. workers a hundred years ago.[8] In the 1990s such sweatshop conditions with illegal immigrants have even been exposed in both New York City and Los Angeles.

Another difficult global problem is the piracy of trade secrets. China does not recognize intellectual property rights as Western nations do. Individuals in China have copied videos, CDs, and software in record numbers, and then sell them, not only in China, but throughout the world.

Pollution and the exploitation of the environment (oil, minerals, logging tropical rain forests) is another problem. Great profits can be made by such mining, logging, and polluting, and government officials in, for example, Brazil, Malaysia, and the Philippines are often bribed in order to permit such exploitation. The question that faces all of us is: what kind of a world will we leave to our children?

The increasing disparity of income between developed and developing countries and within all countries is also a cause of great concern. Global firms contribute to this by their huge compensation to a few and by forcing lower wages on the less skilled. As Lee Tavis puts it, "While readily apparent in all countries, this bifurcation becomes overpowering in the developing countries of Africa, Asia, and Latin America, and increasingly so in Central Europe and what was the USSR."[9]

These inequities will not be addressed by international law within the foreseeable future. Nation states, and especially the United States, are too chauvinistic. Moreover, the actions of a single firm or a single country have a limited impact. Some firms have excellent codes of ethics that they live by, but those codes influence only that one firm. Some countries have enacted antibribery or antipollution legislation, but that, too, has a limited impact. When the U.S. Congress passed the Foreign Corrupt Practices Act in 1977, making it illegal to bribe foreign officials, the U.S. thought that other developed nations would follow. Only now are some other nations acknowledging the problem. Since, at the present time, no international body has the ability to enact and enforce global business codes, dealing with these problems initially must be done in a voluntary fashion by business leaders themselves.

The stakes are very high. At a minimum, without some common ethical standards, an immense portion of a country's wealth will be drained off into the hands of corrupt politicians, a wealthy elite, and criminals. A worse case would be that the system will collapse, through either peaceful or bloody revolution, because of such injustices to people. Such a collapse could bring either anarchy on the one hand or stifling government policing on the other hand.

All of the above scenarios are bad for business, especially in the long run. Corruption increases costs and thus makes a country less attractive for investment. Beyond corruption, pollution and the oppression of working people also increase the cost of doing business, and might even make ordinary, legitimate business impossible. Hence, there is an increasing realization that global ethical standards that will hold across cultures are essential.[10] Global codes are an attempt to specify those standards.

## The Caux Global Code of Business Conduct

Codes of business ethics can be classified according to purpose and content.[11] Codes of the first type are aspirational. That is, they are ethical principles to which people can aspire. Such codes provide goals and are intended to inspire people to right actions. A second type of code is more specific, relating to an individual firm, country, or situation, and such a code provides specific guidelines or proscriptions with regard to business practice. Such codes are more detailed and cover specific situations, such as precise limits on gifts that purchasing agents can accept from suppliers. Ninety percent of U.S. firms have codes of ethics. Those codes cover business practice and employee actions; some of the codes are aspirational. Let us now turn our attention to the aspirational code that was developed by the Caux Round Table.

The Caux Round Table (CRT) was founded in 1986 by senior business executives from Japan, Europe, and North America. Initially the group came together in an effort to lessen trade tensions. The Round Table is named after Caux, the town in Switzerland where it meets annually. The Steering Committee of the Caux Round Table is made up of executives from: Siemens, Chase Manhattan Bank, Canon, Matsushita, Ambrosetti Group, 3M, Dana, Nissan, Ciba-Geigy, Philips Electronics, Sumitomo, and others.[12]

The Minneapolis-St. Paul business community, with executives from 3M, Honeywell, Dayton-Hudson, Medtronic, and other firms, has been meeting since 1978 as members of the Minnesota Center for Corporate Responsibility. Business leaders of Minneapolis-St. Paul have long held a leadership position nationally among U.S. business executives on issues of social responsibilities. In 1991, after determining that they wanted some unity amidst the chaos they were experiencing in world markets, these leaders designed and supported the Minnesota Principles: Toward an Ethical Basis for Global Business.[13]

In 1992 the Caux Round Table realized that "sound ethical and moral principles" were essential for efficient global business operations. The leaders sought to develop a global code of business conduct built upon accepted ethical norms. They then learned that the Minnesota Center for Corporate Responsibility had developed a global code of ethics a year or so earlier. Caux met with the Minnesota group in Tokyo and Minneapolis to discuss the code. Caux adopted the Minnesota code, but added a preamble emphasizing (1) living and working together for the common good from the Japanese tradition ("Kyosei"), and (2) human dignity from the Western tradition.[14]

The Caux Principles for Business, published in 1994 (see Appendix 26), addresses the responsibilities of managers and firms from a stakeholder perspective. This takes into account the interests of customers, employees, suppliers, owners/investors, and communities. When one reads the Caux Principles for Business, one notes that the principles call for, among many other items: respect for both international and domestic laws and rules; going beyond the letter of the law to what is ethically required; working for sustainable development and improving the environment; and avoiding all corrupt practices and also refusing to trade in armaments or other materials that assist terrorism, drug traffic, or organized crime.

### The Caux Principles for Business Compared to Other Codes

We have considerable experience with various types of global business codes. The United Nations, and some of its agencies, have developed ethical codes. William Frederick examined the content of six "landmark multilateral international codes that were developed from 1948–1988."[15] They are:

1. United Nations Declaration of Human Rights (1948)
2. European Convention on Human Rights (1950)
3. Helsinki Final Act (1975)
4. The Organization for Economic Cooperation and Development (OECD) Guidelines for Multinational Enterprises (1976)
5. International Labor Office Tripartite Declaration (1977)
6. The United Nations Code of Conduct on Transnational Corporations (1972–90)[16]

The major issues that Frederick finds in these multilateral compacts are:

1. Employment practices and policies (e.g., fair pay, nondiscrimination, health, and safety issues)
2. Consumer protection (e.g., safe products and packaging, truthful labeling, accurate advertising)
3. Environmental protection (e.g., monitor and protect air, water, and soil)
4. Political payments and involvement (e.g., bribes, interference)
5. Basic human rights and fundamental freedoms (respect rights, protection of law, choice of job, etc.)

These compacts have had only spotty success. They are designed as ideals. For example, the Universal Declaration of Human Rights has been widely quoted and used as a guide throughout the world. Nevertheless, the compacts have no teeth in themselves. Many government and business officials pay little attention to these international compacts.

In addition to the United Nations multilateral compacts, other, more specific, global pacts have been written. We will outline and summarize some of the better-known codes. Most of these codes are discussed in detail elsewhere in this book.

The World Health Organization compact for marketing infant formula (breast-milk substitutes) was forced on the infant formula industry by U.S.

investors. While the producers signed the code, they did so under pressure. When they were able to circumvent the code, they often did so. There were no penalties set up for violators, and developing nations did not support these standards with local law. Dr. James E. Post discusses this code in this book.

The Sullivan Principles for U.S. firms operating in South Africa were agreed to by U.S. firms. They were the result of pressure by investors, largely religious groups, who wanted to change the racist apartheid regime in South Africa. The investors had sufficient influence to demand an audit of the actions of firms that signed the Sullivan Principles and this increased the effectiveness of the principles. John Kline and Oliver F. Williams, c.s.c., discuss the Sullivan Principles and their effect on modern South Africa in this volume.

The Organization for Economic Cooperation and Development (OECD) code prohibits bribery.[17] This code has strong prospects for significantly lessening bribery in the world, but it is so new that it is yet difficult to determine its effectiveness. Dr. Kathleen A. Getz discusses the OECD code in this volume.

The Coalition for Environmentally Responsible Economies (CERES) Principles on environmental pollution (also called the Valdez Principles) are voluntarily signed by U.S. firms. They were achieved, again, through considerable pressure from environmental groups and investors. There is an audit mechanism, since the firms who sign must report on their activities.

The Interfaith Center on Corporate Responsibility's (ICCR) Principles for Global Corporate Responsibility: BenchMarks for Measuring Business Performance were published in draft form in 1995 and in final form in 1998. They are aspirational, comprehensive, and also detailed. The ICCR Principles, unlike the above codes, apply to the entire universe of potential ethical issues facing a firm. They are written by people connected to church groups in the U.S., Britain, Canada, and Ireland. They follow a stakeholder approach, as do the Caux Principles.

The ICCR Principles may have been inspired by the earlier work of religiously rooted Vesper International (San Leandro, California) and the Hinksey Centre (Oxford, England). After a meeting in England in 1989, they published a comprehensive and useful "Declaration of Guidelines for International Corporations" based on the stakeholder model.[18]

However, the Vesper-Hinksey guidelines, as well as those of ICCR, while international and ecumenical, are written by people from only English-speaking Western countries. Another limitation is that both the Vesper-Hinksey and the ICCR Principles are written, not by business executives, but by people largely outside of business. A valuable feature of the ICCR code is the inclusion of eleven additional codes as appendices, including CERES, General Motors Board Guidelines, and International Labor Organization conventions.

Another type of code that has rapidly gained acceptance among the business community is the ISO 9000 Standards. These standards generate a worldwide system of common standards on production inputs and outputs. Without such standards global trade would be hobbled because of varying dimensions and quality standards. Suppliers who sign on to ISO 9000 are certified as such if they submit to an audit of their products and processes. By March 1995 there were more than 95,000 registered sites around the world, 8,100 of them in the U.S. Many large- and medium- sized firms in the U.S. are now certified.[19] Such acceptance of the ISO 9000 Standards, and now the further development of the ISO 14000 Standards, demonstrates that worldwide standards are recognized as essential for global commerce. If there is a recognized need for common production standards, is there not a parallel need for standards by which business deals with people?

The ISO 9000 Standards are spreading rapidly, with many firms seeking to be certified. Following certification these firms are audited regularly to insure continuous compliance. China, with an export value of $16 billion in toys, has now allowed itself to be audited.[20] While the ISO Standards do not treat most ethical issues, they do deal with quality. These standards began in Europe and the U.S., but they are now spreading worldwide.

The Caux Principles for Business are also aspirational and also apply to the entire universe of potential ethical issues. However, unlike the ICCR Principles, the Caux Principles were written by business executives themselves. They also have a broader base of support, since they were written by executives from Europe, Japan, and the U.S. Moreover, the Caux Principles now have the support of many business schools in Latin America and Asia in addition to Japan. Thus, they are more likely to be regarded favorably by business executives of various countries.

In sum, the Caux Principles for Business are aspirational, cover the entire array of issues, and are also the most likely to be regarded favorably by business executives and firms. But the question remains: what is the prospect for the implementation of these principles?

### Prospects for the Caux Principles for Business

The Caux Principles have a better chance of being implemented than most global codes of business conduct because the Caux code was written by business leaders. The Principles have a running start, since they have already been implemented in dozens of large firms in Europe, Japan, and the U.S. Moreover, business executives designed the Principles and they support them worldwide because they recognize that it is only with some common understanding of the ethics of business relationships that global business can be successful.

The Caux Round Table began by asking firms to endorse the Principles for Business.[21] Initially, some firms did so. However, other CEOs sent the principles to their legal counsel before endorsing. These lawyers maintained that endorsing the Principles would increase the liability of the firm to outside parties, who could claim that the firm did not live up to its own guidelines.

After further reflection, CRT decided that to be effective a code should not be merely endorsed but should be written by persons within the firm in their own words to meet the firm's own situation. So, CRT sent the Principles to a thousand of the largest firms, suggesting that these Principles be used as a framework and foundation for fashioning or updating their own missions and codes.

Many firms have done just that. Bank of America now issues its code of business practices and prints the CRT Principles alongside to show how they parallel each other. Several firms in the Netherlands have also used Caux as a guide. Smaller firms in Australia and Malaysia have simply included the Caux Principles for Business in their articles of incorporation when they began. India reproduced the Principles in their national business newsletter for firms to use as a guide. Many Chinese are concerned with corruption and have turned to Caux for help in developing their codes. The Hong Kong Ethics Center has published the Principles in both English and Chinese and has helped as many as five thousand large and small firms in Hong Kong and Shanghai use them as guides.

Russian business leaders recognize the need for such principles, and the CEO of the largest bank in St. Petersburg has approached Caux for aid in helping Russian firms use the Principles as a framework for codes of conduct. Business leaders in Lebanon have translated the Principles into Arabic and are distributing them throughout the Middle East. These leaders would like Beirut to again take leadership as the commercial capital of that area, and they intend to encourage using CRT Principles as a part of that effort. Some African business leaders have come to Caux asking for help, also.

The Caux Principles have received considerable favorable attention among university faculty, in spite of the fact that they were written as recently as 1994.[22] Many business school faculty support and have been involved with the Caux Principles. Kenneth Goodpaster, Koch Professor of Business Ethics, University of St. Thomas, helped to formulate the Minnesota Principles. Moreover, he was involved in the discussions with Caux executives to adopt the Principles as their own. Several other academic scholars have become involved with the Caux Principles because of their work as the principals in the

Alfred P. Sloan Foundation project: "Redefining the Corporation: An International Colloquy." Thus, Thomas Donaldson, University of Pennsylvania, gave a keynote address at a Caux meeting in Washington, D.C., in 1996; Lee E. Preston, University of Maryland, attended the 1996 Caux annual meeting, as did Max B. E. Clarkson, University of Toronto. Thomas Dunfee, University of Pennsylvania, attended the 1997 Caux annual meeting.

Support for the Caux Principles came from a large number of business schools in 1995. The International Association of Jesuit Business Schools (IAJBS) consists of more than eighty business schools on six continents. IAJBS, at their 1994 annual meeting in Recife, Brazil, decided to devise a global code of business ethics. The executive director, Thomas Bausch, asked Gerald Cavanagh, University of Detroit Mercy, to lead this effort. After some inquiry, he found that the Caux Principles seemed to fit the need. The Caux Principles for Business were presented to the IAJBS at their 1995 meeting in Yogyakarta, Indonesia. Representatives of sixty business schools from six continents opted to support these Principles. In sending the Principles to member universities, IAJBS appended a section showing how the Caux Principles are consonant with Catholic principles of social justice.

As a result of this support, the Caux Principles for Business have been taught to business students and programs presented to alumni in Barcelona, Bogota, Buenos Aires, Detroit, Mexico City, Milwaukee, Monterrey, New Orleans, and many other cities.[23] Members of the Caux Round Table are happy with the support of IAJBS, since the Round Table does not have representatives or visibility in Latin America, Africa, or Asia, outside of Japan.

However, there are omissions in the Caux Principles, reflecting the positions of the authors, which might limit their acceptance among some groups. There are some issues that are not treated in the CRT Principles, which one might expect to be a part of such principles. For example, there is no mention of:

1.  Truthful advertising, safe packaging, and proper labeling;
2.  Right of employees to join trade unions;
3.  Advance notice of plant closings;
4.  Adopting preventive measures to avoid environmental harm;
5.  Rehabilitating environments damaged by operations;
6.  Promoting international environmental standards.

Since there are omissions in the Caux Principles, we can readily judge that the Principles are not complete. They can be amplified over time. On the other hand, now having available a comprehensive, written statement of global business aspirations, based upon sound ethical principles, is a major step forward.

In addition, the Principles are more acceptable to business people. Business people authored the Principles, not academic, religious, or advocacy groups, so there is a better chance of global ethics being taken seriously and eventually implemented.

So, then, what are the prospects for the further implementation of the Caux Principles for Business? Implementation of voluntary business codes, as is true of any ethics strategies, is not an easy task. We do, however, have some experience with the implementation of ethical codes and with social audits, and this experience can be of value to us in this endeavor.[24]

We see elsewhere in this volume the effectiveness of other global codes addressed to specific issues: the WHO infant formula code on breast-milk substitutes, the Sullivan Principles for U.S. firms operating in South Africa during apartheid, various treaties on bribery, the antisweatshop agreement, CERES on the environment, and ISO 9000 standards.

We have learned that codes are more likely to be observed when they are voluntarily undertaken by business people themselves and when there is some sort of an audit mechanism in place. We have examples of global codes that have been implemented. The CERES Principles on the natural environment have been adopted by nine of the largest firms in the U.S., including General Motors, Bank of America, ITT, Bethlehem Steel, and Polaroid. Levi-Strauss decided not to manufacture their clothing in China or in Burma because of human rights violations that are so common in those two countries. Moreover, Levi-Strauss has fifty overseas monitors on its own payroll who are charged with auditing subcontractors on working conditions, wages, treatment of workers by supervisors, and more.

An internal or external audit mechanism has also proven to be an aid to implementation. Eight hundred firms organized as Business for Social Responsibility (BSR) have sponsored workshops to train auditors of corporate codes of conduct.[25] As a further means of implementation, the members of the Caux Round Table also advocate that the major elements of the Principles be enacted into law in both developed and developing countries.

An audit of perceptions of corruption, country by country, was done by Transparency International (TI). TI has published an annual "Corruption Perception Index" each year since 1995. Founded in 1993, TI is a nongovernmental agency, headquartered in Berlin, Germany, which attempts to support global integrity systems. TI today has more than sixty national chapters worldwide. In the 1997 listing, TI ranked fifty-two countries on the basis of seven international surveys on the extent of perceived corruption. In the 1997 ranking Denmark is listed least corrupt, Nigeria is perceived to be the most corrupt; the U.S. ranks sixteenth out of fifty-two nations.[26] Reflecting the importance that global firms place on this issue, TI has received major encouragement and financial support from many nations, nongovernmental aid agencies, and firms such as GM, Exxon, Ford, Boeing, Bristol-Myers, Arthur Andersen, Coopers & Lybrand, GE, IBM, Merck, Motorola, and United Technologies and Westinghouse.[27]

Perhaps because of the attention received by the TI rankings, there has been some progress in generating antibribery treaties, at least among the industrialized countries. Dr. Kathleen Getz discusses this issue in this volume.

### Future Agenda and Research on the Principles for Business

At their 1997 annual meeting, the Caux Round Table decided to focus on four areas in the future: The Employment Dilemma; Sustainable Practices and Values; Trust, Honesty and Transparency; and Collaboration and Partnerships for Action. The employment dilemma includes the need for job creation and the gulf between the rich and the poor. Sustainable practices and values addresses energy efficiency, resource management, human exploitation, employee development, and the encouragement of sound values in the family and society. Trust, honesty, and transparency is to be encouraged in media, advertising, and in all business dealings—including eliminating bribery. Collaboration and partnerships for action with nongovernmental organizations (NGOs) takes Caux into a new, more active role in working with other groups that can bring about the above.

There are two principle objections to the Principles for Business. The first is that the principles are too general to be of much value. They provide general principles, not specific prescriptions. However, the Caux Principles are designed as broad aspirations. They are not intended to be specific rules. Moreover, the more specific such principles become, the more difficult it is to obtain agreement from business people in varying countries and cultures. As we have seen, even the present Principles are sometimes objected to by company lawyers, who fear that they would increase the liability of the firm that acknowledges them.

The second objection is that, since there are no enforcement provisions, the Principles are useless. However, the Caux Round Table has no juridical authority; it only has moral authority. Any enforcement mechanism must be enacted by affected nation-states. That is precisely the role of the nation-state. Perhaps one day we will see some international mechanism for enforcement.

Additional research is required to better understand and to fully spell out the potential of the Caux Principles. Some questions might be:

1. What will be the result of the recent focusing of Caux efforts on the four above priorities? Will this help with the implementation of the Principles?
2. Are there issues omitted that should be included in this set of global principles of business conduct?
3. How many individual firms have taken the Caux Principles as a framework and foundation for their own firm's codes?
4. How much consensus is needed to make a global code effective?
5. Since business acknowledges the need for global ISO 9000 Standards, is there not a parallel need for global standards and an audit for ethical business conduct?

### Conclusion

Over the past few years there has been increasing agreement that the new global marketplace demands a common understanding of what constitutes responsible business conduct. The Caux Round Table's Principles for Business are an early, and perhaps the best, foundation upon which such common understandings can be built.

Although only written in 1994, the Principles are already widely known and supported on six continents. We are still a long way from full recognition and implementation, but the Caux Round Table Principles for Business are the best foundation that we have for placing all people and future generations first on the list of business's responsibilities.

### Notes

1. Kenichi Ohmae, *The Borderless World* (New York: Harper, 1990), p. 55.

2. It should be noted that many of these markets are not really free. They are dominated by one or more players that set the terms for operating. These few firms often act to exclude new entrants into their markets. For critical views, see David C. Korten, *When Corporations Rule the World* (San Francisco: Barrett-Koeller, 1995), and Richard J. Barnet and John Cavanagh, *Global Dreams: Imperial Corporations and the New World Order* (New York: Touchstone, 1995).

3. For a more detailed treatment of the strengths and weaknesses of the global market system, see chap. 1, "A Free Market for Ethical Values," pp. 1–31 in Gerald F. Cavanagh, *American Business Values: With International Perspectives* (Upper Saddle River, N.J.: Prentice-Hall, 1998); implementation of codes and corporate social performance is discussed in chap. 8, "Ethics and Performance Measures," pp. 227–60.

4. "Unfinished Business: Kim Sends the Chaebol a Message," *Business Week*, September 9, 1996, pp. 56–57.

5. "Family Ties that Bind Growth: Corrupt Leaders in Indonesia Threaten Its Future," *New York Times*, April 9, 1996, pp. C1, C2; "Irate at Subsidy Program, GM Halts Investment in Indonesia," *Wall Street Journal*, June 12, 1996, p. C6.

6. "Pangs of Conscience: Sweatshops Haunt U.S. Consumers," *Business Week*, July 29, 1996, pp. 46–47.

7. "An Indonesian Asset Is Also a Liability," *New York Times*, March 16, 1996, pp. 46–47.

8. See Gerald F. Cavanagh, S.J., "Children and Immigrants in Nineteenth-Century Factories," in *American Business Values: With International Perspectives*, pp. 139–41.

9. For a thorough treatment of this issue, see Lee A. Tavis, *Power and Responsibility: Multinational Managers and Developing Country Concerns* (Notre Dame: University of Notre Dame Press, 1997), and his, "Bifurcated Development and Multinational Corporate Responsibility," in *Emerging Global Business Ethics*, ed. Michael Hoffman et al. (Westport, Conn.: Quorum, 1994), pp. 255–74.

10. See the excellent collection of examinations of international business ethics from Western, Eastern, and Islamic perspectives, *Business Ethics Quarterly*, 7 July 1997, pp. 1–70.

11. Patricia Werhane classified codes as: (a) general, usually moral, prescriptions or proscriptions, and (b) specific cultural, ethnic, country, religious, or social prescriptions or proscriptions. *Global Codes of Business Conduct: Impact on Business Behavior, Teaching and Research*, Symposium at the Academy of Management, Boston, August 12, 1997.

12. See the Caux documents: *Principles for Business*, Caux Round Table, 1994; *A World That Works: Priorities for Business Leadership*, Caux Round Table, 1996; and the position papers: "The Caux Round Table: An Introduction," 1997 and "The Critical Role of the Corporation in a Global Society: A Position Paper of the Caux Round Table (CRT)," 1997.

13. For more information, contact Robert W. MacGregor, President, Minnesota Center for Corporate Responsibility, 1000 LaSalle Ave., Minneapolis, MN 55403-2005; Phone: (612) 962-4121.

14. See Ryuzaburo Kaku, "The Path of Kyosei," *Harvard Business Review* (July–August 1997), pp. 55–63. Kaku, chairman of Canon, is a member of CRT, and he defines Kyosei as cooperating for the common good.

15. William C. Frederick, "Moral Authority of Transnational Corporate Codes," *Journal of Business Ethics* 10 (1991), pp. 165–77.

16. For two discussions of this code, see Duane Windsor, "Toward a Transnational Code of Business Conduct," and Franklyn P. Salimbene, "Equity, UN Development Efforts, and the Code of Conduct on Transnational Corporations," both in *Emerging Global Business Ethics*, ed. W. M. Hoffman, J. Kamm, R. Frederick, and E. Petry (Westport: Quorum, 1994), pp. 165–76, 177–90.

17. "29 Nations Agree to a Bribery Ban: Global Accord to End Payoffs to Foreign Officials in '98," *New York Times*, May 24, 1997, p. 1, 34; also "2 Global Lenders Use Leverage to Combat Corruption," *New York Times*, August 11, 1997, p. A4.

18. Leo V. Ryan, "Incorporating 'Just Profit' Guidelines in Transnational Codes," in *Emerging Global Business Ethics*, ed. W. Michael Hoffman et. al. (Westport: Quorum, 1994), pp. 191–200.

19. Mustafa V. Uzumeri, "ISO 9000 and Other Meta-standards: Principles for Management Practice?" *Academy of Management Executive*, 11 (March 1997), pp. 21–36.

20. Ken Cottril, "Ethical Codes of Conduct on New Agenda for Companies with Global Operations," *Traffic World*, 246 (May 20, 1996), p. 18.

21. For information on the Caux Round Table actions to implement the Principles, I thank CRT member Robert W. MacGregor, president of the Minnesota Center for Corporate Responsibility.

22. See, for example, Charlene Marmer Solomon, "Put Your Ethics to a Global Test," *Personnel Journal*, 75 (January 1996), pp. 66–68.

23. Gerald F. Cavanagh, S.J., "International Codes of Business Conduct and Jesuit Schools of Business" and "Working With Business to Develop Codes of Conduct," *Proceedings of Third World Forum of International Association of Jesuit Business Schools* (Yogyakarta, 1995); "Task Force: The Caux Principles in Action— Success in Implementation," *Proceedings of Fourth World Forum of IAJBS* (Los Angeles, 1996).

24. For examples, see Francis J. Aguilar, *Managing Corporate Ethics: Learning from America's Ethical Companies How to Supercharge Business Performance* (New York: Oxford University Press, 1994). Two older, but still excellent, aids to doing a corporate social audit are the handbook *The Measurement of Corporate Social Performance* (New York: American Institute of Certified Public Accountants, 1997) and the case histories in *Corporate Social Reporting in the United States and Western Europe* (Washington, D.C.: U.S. Department of Commerce, 1979).

25. Ken Cottril, "Ethical Codes of Conduct on New Agenda for Companies with Global Operations," p. 18.

26. "Survey Ranks Nigeria as Most Corrupt Nation," *New York Times*, August 3, 1997, p. 3.

27. "Executive Summary," *Transparency International USA* (Washington, D.C., August, 1997).

**11**

# The Caux Round Table Principles

## *Corporate Moral Reflection in a Global Business Environment*

KENNETH E. GOODPASTER

There is a close relation between "infusion with value" and "self-maintenance." As an organization acquires a self, a distinctive identity, it becomes an institution. This involves the taking on of values, ways of acting and believing that are deemed important for their own sake. From then on self-maintenance becomes more than bare organizational survival; it becomes a struggle to preserve the uniqueness of the group in the face of new problems and altered circumstances.

—Philip Selznick, *Leadership in Administration*

### Introduction

Selznick's observations about the role of the leader in helping an organization to acquire a distinctive identity apply with special importance in today's global business environment. For global competition clearly means "new problems and altered circumstances" for the corporations involved. Are there ways to support those organizations which seek, in Selznick's words, to incorporate "the taking on of values, ways of acting and believing that are deemed important for their own sake"? I believe the answer is *Yes*, and that for this reason global codes of conduct, along with realistic approaches to implementation, are indeed an idea whose time has come.

In this chapter I will discuss, first, the origins and central themes of the Caux Round Table Principles for Business; second, some challenges associated with their implementation; and third, an implementation project just getting underway. I will conclude with some remarks about the promise of the Caux Principles as we move into a new century. The actual text of the principles is included as Appendix 26.

### Origins and Central Themes

The Caux Round Table Principles for Business were officially launched in July 1994. Their content emerged from discussions among Japanese, European, and American executives and were fashioned in substantial part from a document called the Minnesota Principles. The Minnesota Principles were formulated in 1992 at the University of St. Thomas by a working group representing about a dozen Minnesota-headquartered corporations under the auspices of the Minnesota Center for Corporate Responsibility.[1]

The aspiration of the Caux Principles, and the Minnesota Principles before them, was to articulate a comprehensive set of ethical norms that could be embraced by businesses operating internationally and in multiple cultural environments. The preamble of the Caux Principles (adopted verbatim from the Minnesota Principles) expresses this aspiration clearly:

> The mobility of employment and capital is making business increasingly global in its transactions and its effects. Laws and market forces in such a context are necessary but insufficient guides for conduct. Responsibility for a corporation's actions and policies and respect for the dignity and interests of its stakeholders are fundamental. And shared values, including a commitment to shared prosperity, are as important for a global community as for communities of smaller scale. For all of the above reasons, and because business can be a powerful agent of positive social change, we offer [these] principles as a foundation for dialogue and action by business leaders in search of corporate responsibility. In so doing, we affirm the legitimacy and centrality of moral values in economic decision making because, without them, stable business relationships and a sustainable world community are impossible.

I have explained elsewhere that the Caux Round Table Principles are inspired by two key concepts—kyosei and the moral point of view—that afford a bridge between Eastern and Western moral philosophy.[2] Each concept includes subthemes of interest-based, rights-based, and duty-based ethics, and each contributes to the justification of the Caux Principles as they were finally articulated (see Appendix 26).

The challenge that the Caux Principles sought to meet, the challenge of facilitating a truly global, ethically-based business system, with regular, meaningful dialogue, meant formulating core values in such a way that both Eastern and Western mindsets could find them accessible and intelligible. Some examples of practical arenas within which the ideals of kyosei and the moral point of view might be expected to manifest themselves in the decision-making of the organization are:

- unemployment and retraining of employees whose jobs are made redundant by technological and competitive pressures;
- environmental impacts of corporate production including pollution, conservation of resources, and preservation of biological species;
- work and family issues, including the impact of work demands on marriage relationships, the education of children, physical and mental health, and social harmony;
- trust, honesty, and transparency in international and host country transactions;
- collaboration between corporations and local communities, partnerships for action in arenas like education and emergency services.

A conviction that both lies behind and is to some degree warranted by the Caux Principles is that there is a shared "moral sense" among human beings which, despite significant differences of cultural circumstances and norms, allows for accountability in discussions of ethical values. Without such a moral sense, we would be left with power as a substitute for reason, and might in place of right. Participants in the Caux Round Table were well served by an affirmation at the outset of a shared "moral sense" to which appeal could be made in ethical discussions and debates both within and between cultures. While it is apparent that social norms and legal expectations differ from one cultural setting to another, the "moral sense" does not. It is the moral sense that we share as human beings which accounts for common ground, while differing circumstances account for the social differences. This moral sense includes such things as sympathy, a sense of duty, a sense of fairness, and an attitude of self-development.[3]

I say that this notion of a shared moral sense lies behind the Caux Principles, because it is clear to me that the parties at the table believed it from the beginning. But I add that this conviction or faith in a shared moral sense is to some degree warranted by the Caux Principles because the process of debate and eventual agreement was a kind of empirical test of the realism of the participants' convictions.

To be sure, the fact that a culturally diverse group of reflective leaders agreed on a set of ethical propositions does not itself prove that there is a cross-cultural moral touchstone, much less that their agreed-upon propositions articulate that common touchstone. But surely the discovery of common ground offers some reinforcement for the participants' moral ideal and a reasonable approximation to its content. The emergence of consensus on the Caux Principles seems to illustrate a point made recently by Francis Fukuyama in his book on trust:

> There is no doubt that human beings are, as the economists say, fundamentally selfish and that they pursue their selfish interests in a rational way. But they also have a moral side in which they feel obligations to others, a side that is frequently at cross-purposes with their selfish instincts. As the word culture itself suggests, the more highly developed ethical rules by which people live are nurtured through repetition, tradition, and example. These rules may reflect a deeper adaptive rationality; they may serve economically rational ends; and in the case of a few individuals they may be the product of rational consent. But they are transmitted from one generation to another as irrational social habits. These habits in turn guarantee that human beings never behave as purely selfish utility maximizers postulated by economists.[4]

The structure of the Caux Principles—a preamble followed by seven broad philosophical propositions followed by six stakeholder principles— invites progressively more specific consensus on matters of business behavior. Nevertheless, these principles still leave unanswered many questions about how specific administrative challenges are to be handled. Because of this "behavioral underdetermination," cynics might argue that accepting the Caux Principles carries no real substantive commitment.

My own view is that while "behavioral underdetermination" is a matter of some concern, it must be understood in context. Certainly consensus on the preamble and the general principles is something, not anything; but just as certainly, consensus on the stakeholder principles represents a further step in the direction of corporate decision-making behavior. This being said, there can be no question that the Caux Principles—without a serious effort on the part of their subscribers in the direction of more specific behavioral implications—will not realize their full promise and potential.

## The Challenges of Implementation

Let me now turn to some of the management challenges that might be involved in implementing the Caux Round Table Principles in corporate policy. I have elsewhere indicated several broad approaches to implementation available to organizational leaders who seek to bring values and principles into action. Let me here mention three: *dictation, surrogation,* and *institutionalization.*[5]

*Dictation* is simply a matter of an authority figure laying down a set of rules—along with some guidelines for interpretation. Penalties for disobedience or noncompliance are enforced firmly, and behavior (often because of fear) is influenced. In effect, the bridge between principles and practice becomes the will of the one in power, the will of the strongest.[6] In the present context, this approach might mean senior management presenting the Caux Principles to employees as a set of corporate rules with some interpretations and sanctions attached. The watchword would be *compliance.*

The *surrogation* approach consists in identifying *systemic substitutes* for a set of principles—substitutes different from the will of the corporate authority figure. Adam Smith looked for such a substitute in what he called the "invisible hand" of the free-market system. Others have found a substitute in the "visible hand" of the state—whether in the executive, legislative, or judicial branches. What these latter two approaches have in common is reliance upon a *process*, either economic or political, to act as a *surrogate* for the realization of principles and ideals. It is as if we cannot trust the leadership of organizations or the insights of ordinary people with the capacity to build the bridge to action. To shift the metaphor, it is insisting that flying the airplane of morality cannot be trusted to the pilot. It must be governed by a surrogate— an autopilot. In connection with the Caux Principles, the surrogation approach would amount to adopting the principles but leaving it to geographic market forces, host country laws, regional trade agreements, or perhaps regulatory bodies like the United Nations to provide substance in their implementation. On this approach, the implementation of ethical principles is essentially *outsourced* by the organization.

The third approach, *institutionalization,* is the one I believe is the most acceptable. It involves two subtypes: *macro*-institutionalization and *micro*-institutionalization. Macro-institutionalization means creating support systems between and among organizations willing to self-impose kyosei or moral principles. Affiliation among such like-minded organizations may be essential if the risks of unilateral adoption of such ideals are to be minimized. The Caux Principles and the support system implicit among organizations endorsing them can lead to international efforts at removing competitive pressures for unethical behavior. Endorsement by the Caux Round Table for the antibribery treaty among twenty-nine countries currently being negotiated by the Organization for Economic Cooperation and Development (OECD) would be an example of macro-institutionalization.[7]

By micro-institutionalization, I mean a sequence of activities designed:

- to articulate a corporate philosophy,
- to assign special responsibility for transforming it into action,
- to educate employees about its meaning,
- to audit operations with attention to conflicts between the corporate philosophy and other organizational incentives that undermine it,
- to report on difficult cases to the corporate leadership, so that finally reintegration and clear communication can be restored.

In effect, this amounts to creating an organizational analogue of personal conscience: a feedback loop of ethical awareness that involves articulating, communicating, motivating, monitoring, and learning. It is interesting to note in this context that the 1991 U.S. Federal Sentencing Guidelines for corporations define a credible organizational compliance system in similar terms.[8] On this model, the Caux Principles might serve either directly as an articulation of the subscriber company's norms of conduct, or indirectly as a template for assessing a company's pre-existing norms.

The essence of this micro-institutionalization approach is that it involves ethical awareness—"flying" rather than using some kind of automatic pilot. Organizational leaders acknowledge the importance of authority, of market signals, and of governmental regulation—but they go further. They seek to carry the Caux Principles into action and to sustain their presence as action-guides by creating an organizational cycle of ethical awareness that addresses the realities of the decision-making environment. These measures foster a living conversation between employees and executives. And if we reflect on the ideals of kyosei and the moral point of view—living and working together for the common good—we may be persuaded that the best way to apply ideals lies not in dictation or surrogation, but in institutionalization. The challenge for corporations that would build this bridge is to undertake alliances (externally) and foster moral conversation (internally). These are the principal defenses against competitive forces (outside) and hypocrisy (inside) that might lead a company to abandon its ethical ideals.

In summary, kyosei and the moral point of view offer broad ethical ideals that are congruent with one another in their deep structure. Each seems to be anchored in three avenues of ethical reflection: interest-based, rights-based, and duty-based thinking. Each also finds application on multiple levels, e.g., family, group, organization, state, region, and globe. When we bridge from these ideals to *action*, the most promising path lies not in dictating or relying on surrogates, but in what we have called institutionalization (internal as well as external). Let us hope that this broad foundation for dialogue between

Eastern and Western thought can lead to improved business and government behavior in the twenty-first century.

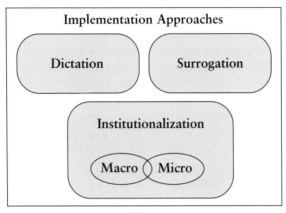

Figure 1

## An Implementation Project

Recently the Minnesota Center for Corporate Responsibility initiated a project that has the potential to advance what I have been calling the institutionalization approach to the Caux Principles. The first phase of the project is to develop a structured inventory of case studies that will shed light on implementation challenges faced by companies subscribing to the Caux Principles. By "structured inventory," I mean a set of case studies whose themes would represent the principal regions (North America, Europe, and Asia) and each of the Caux Principles (preamble, general, and stakeholder). These case studies would serve several purposes. They would be of direct use to the management, education, and training departments of the participating corporations. They would also be of use to business schools that sought to make the Caux Principles an element of their business ethics curriculum. Most importantly, however, the completed inventory would provide a platform for serious and practical discussions of implementation policies, the objective of the second phase of the project.

The idea, then, is to fill the matrix displayed in figure 2 below with well-written cases on the themes and in the geographical regions indicated by each cell. These cases will then serve as pedagogical tools for discussing realistic implementation norms that participants in the Caux Round Table could jointly adopt. The conviction at work here is that practical corporate proposals for the future must be patiently arrived at and pedagogically sophisticated.

It is our expectation that the University of St. Thomas will take the lead in this case-development effort, since as an institution it brings to the table an application-oriented research agenda, along with an emphasis on working closely with the practitioner. The magnitude of the task, however, filling a 14-by-4 matrix with 56 quality cases sited in different regions of the world, will no doubt call for wider academic participation. The most natural coordinating body for this undertaking would be the Minnesota Center for Corporate Responsibility, since its relationship to the Caux Round Table has been long and fruitful.

## A Structural Inventory of Case Studies

| | Global Illustration and Application | North America (Canada, U.S.A.) | Europe (Western and Eastern) | Asia (Japan, China, SE Asia) | Other Regions (S. America, Africa . . .) |
|---|---|---|---|---|---|
| *The Caux Principles* | | | | | |
| I. Preamble | Legitimacy of MPV | | | | |
| II. General Principles | | | | | |
| 1 | Beyond Shareholders toward Stakeholders | | | | |
| 2 | Economic and Social Responsibility | | | | |
| 3 | Beyond Letter of Law toward Trust | | | | |
| 4 | Beyond Trade Friction toward Cooperation | | | | |
| 5 | Beyond Isolation toward World Community | | | | |

| | | | | | |
|---|---|---|---|---|---|
| 6 | Beyond Environmental Protection toward Enhancement | | | | |
| 7 | Beyond Profit toward Peace | | | | |
| III. Stakeholder Principles | | | | | |
| 1 | Customers | | | | |
| 2 | Employees | | | | |
| 3 | Owners/ Investors | | | | |
| 4 | Suppliers | | | | |
| 5 | Competitors | | | | |
| 6 | Communities | | | | |

Figure 2

## The Promise of the Caux Principles[9]

So far, I have offered a historical sketch and an implementation analysis of the Caux Round Table Principles. I have also described a project in its initial stages that holds some hope for taking the Caux Principles from their current "aspirational" role to a much more concrete commitment with reasonably clear behavioral implications. As a tool for the institutionalization of ethical values in global corporations—both macro-institutionalization and micro-institutionalization—the Caux Principles may eventually realize their full potential and promise. In this concluding section, it might be helpful to reflect further on what that full potential and promise really might amount to. I believe there are five components that deserve mention.

### The Promise of a Socratic Forum

Sam Goldwyn once said: "For your information, let me ask you a question." This is a healthy attitude to adopt as the Caux Principles are further interpreted through concrete case discussion. It is essentially a Socratic attitude—pursuing knowledge and understanding by a process of questioning, of examining the value foundations as well as the factual assumptions behind policies and decisions. Like the Academy in Athens, Caux-sur-Montreux in Switzerland may become a place that helps witness to the responsibility and the health of a republic. This is not necessarily to identify with Plato's answers to the basic questions, only to respect his methods and to suggest their utility in our twenty-first century search for a "global republic" of commerce and communication.

Caux Round Table participants have understood from the beginning that values drove their questions, their research agendas, their information nets, and their audit priorities. They have been and continue to be convinced that in a complex, information-hungry world, core values are the principal drivers of research, data-gathering and applied science generally. In the end, we track what we care about—and our priorities are often visible in our information nets. Values shape questions, and questions shape our convictions about relevant answers.

### The Promise of Openness in the Forum to Nonbusiness Voices

As the Caux Round Table follows out its mission, it is well advised to include voices in the dialogue that go beyond business leaders to include leaders in labor, government, education, religion, and other institutional pillars in a global environment. To quote Fukuyama once again:

> Workers are never merely counters in a company's table of organization; they develop solidarity, loyalties, and dislikes that shape the nature of economic activity. In other words, social, and therefore moral, behavior coexists with self-interested utility-maximizing behavior on a number of levels. The greatest economic efficiency was not necessarily achieved by rational self-interested individuals but rather by groups of individuals who, because of a preexisting moral community, are able to work together effectively.[10]

This counsel is important because the institution of business in the twenty-first century will be interdependent with these other institutions. The basic focus of the Round Table will continue to be business, but the voices in the conversation need to be more diverse for that very reason.

### The Promise of Teachability (conceptual economy)

It is helpful, when possible, to apply a principle of economy or parsimony in the formulation of core principles for any person or institution. A set of principles must be rich enough to be useful in complex situations, of course, but unnecessary multiplication of principles undermines their long-term practicality. One reason for this is *teachability*, which includes the memorability of the core list, along with a clear understanding of the relationships among the items on the list. The communication of the Ten Commandments across generations has been aided, at least in part, by the economy of the list. The "Twenty Commandments" would, one suspects, have had a harder time of it. Similarly, the New Testament consolidation of the ten into two (*Love of God* and *Love of Neighbor*) enhanced the teachability of these core values. The relative economy and elegance of the Caux Principles increases their potential both pedagogically and pragmatically.

### The Promise of Mutual Reinforcement among Core Values

Sometimes systems of values lead to conflicts requiring tradeoffs between and among them, but not always. We must be alert to possibilities of mutual reinforcement or synergy among the core values affirmed by the Caux Principles. Wealth creation, for example, may make justice *more* achievable in many ways—leading to more community as well. In turn, productivity born of a sense of fairness and community might well be higher than it would be in the absence of these social virtues.

It can happen, of course, that core values conflict in certain concrete circumstances. Acting to enhance one value might by the same token lead to a diminution of a second value. Caux Round Table chairman Win Wallin suggested an example of this in his remarks about the need for companies to pay attention to whether free trade policies (which enhance wealth creation in a macro sense) overlook job *replacement* responsibilities that companies incur by shifting production across borders (justice, community).

Wallin believed that a principle of "mitigation" or "remediation" might be invoked in tradeoff situations, namely, when policies or actions are undertaken by an organization or a government in pursuit of one of its core values, an audit of the ethical "side-effects" with respect to the other core values should be undertaken. This would allow for balance-preserving conditions to be imposed on initiatives—like support for skilled workers not easily outplaced from manufacturing to service-sector jobs.

### The Promise of Increased Trust in Global Business

Perhaps the principal touchstone of the Caux Round Table mission is its desire to increase the trust of people and organizations worldwide in the institution of business. This desire is again echoed in the work of economist Francis Fukuyama:

If the institutions of democracy and capitalism are to work properly, they must coexist with certain pre-modern cultural habits that ensure their proper functioning. Law, contract, and economic rationality provide a necessary but not sufficient basis for both the stability and prosperity of postindustrial societies; they must as well be leavened with reciprocity, moral obligation, duty toward community, and trust, which are based in habit rather than rational calculation. The latter are not anachronisms in a modern society but rather the *sine qua non* of the latter's success.[11]

And as Fukuyama goes on to point out—moving from necessary conditions to predictable consequences—the economic significance of trust in global business transactions is large:

If people who have to work together in an enterprise trust one another because they are all operating according to a common set of ethical norms, doing business costs less. Such a society will be better able to innovate organizationally, since the high degree of trust will permit a wide variety of social relationships to emerge. Hence highly sociable Americans pioneered the development of the modern corporation in the late nineteenth and early twentieth centuries, just as the Japanese have explored the possibilities of network organizations in the twentieth. . . . By contrast, people who do not trust one another will end up cooperating only under a system of formal rules and regulations, which have to be negotiated, agreed to, litigated, and enforced, sometimes by coercive means. This legal apparatus, serving as a substitute for trust, entails what economists call "transaction costs." Widespread distrust in a society, in other words, imposes a kind of tax on all forms of economic activity, a tax that high-trust societies do not have to pay.[12]

Trust is both a laudable goal and a challenging one for the framers of the Caux Principles. For there is no road to trust that does not pass through *trustworthiness*. In the end, an institution (like an individual) is trusted when its core values are seen to be sincerely ethical, concerned for the well-being of those whose trust is sought.[13]

We have come full circle to Philip Selznick's understanding of the role of organizational leadership as a form of institutionalization. We can slightly modify Selznick's words, applying them to a group of companies—those participating in the Caux Round Table—rather than simply to a single company:

As a group of organizations (like the Caux Round Table) acquires a distinctive identity, it becomes an institution. This involves the taking on of values, ways of acting and believing that are deemed important for their own sake. From then on self-maintenance becomes more than bare organizational survival; it becomes a struggle to preserve the uniqueness of the group in the face of new problems and altered circumstances.

## Notes

1. Joe Skelly, "The Rise of International Ethics," *Business Ethics Magazine* (March/April 1995).

2. Goodpaster, "Bridging East and West in Management Ethics: Kyosei and the Moral Point of View," Indian Institute of Management, *The Journal of Human Values* (January 1996).

3. See James Q. Wilson, *The Moral Sense* (New York: The Free Press, 1993), p. 246.

4. Fukuyama, *Trust: The Social Virtues and the Creation of Prosperity* (New York: The Free Press, 1995), p. 41.

5. See Goodpaster, "Bridging East and West in Management Ethics: Kyosei and the Moral Point of View."

6. The cover story in *Business Week* (October 9, 1995) was entitled "Blind Ambition," and it described the problems recently faced by Bausch & Lomb because its chief executive officer dictated commands without checking out their concrete implications in the world of work.

7. Neil King, Jr., "Momentum Builds for Corporate-Bribery Ban," Wall Street Journal, September 30, 1997, p. C14.

8. *U.S. Sentencing Commission Guidelines Manual* (1993), chapter 8, pp. 337–38.

9. See Apendix 26 for the text of the Caux Principles.

10. Fukuyama, *Trust: The Social Virtues*, p. 21.

11. Ibid., p. 11.

12. Ibid., pp. 27–28.

13. "Not all economic action arises out of what are traditionally thought of as economic motives. . . . Human beings act for non-utilitarian ends in irrational, group-oriented ways sufficiently often that the neoclassical model presents us with an incomplete picture of human nature" (ibid., pp. 18, 21).

## 12

# Ethical Guidelines for the Reform of State-Owned Enterprises in China

GEORGES ENDERLE

### Relevance and Assumptions

State-owned enterprises (SOEs) undoubtedly play a unique and pivotal role in the process of economic reform. They epitomize a large number of crucial issues affecting both the enterprises and the economic system as a whole: the independence and social obligations of economic organizations; social ownership; a level playing field for all types of companies; the role of government organs; and the relationship with international business. How these issues are dealt with will shape the economic and social future of China.

So far, however, economic and legal considerations have dominated discussions about the reform of SOEs. The ethical dimension of this highly complex problem is barely addressed explicitly, much less developed systematically and integrated into a broader analytical framework for companies in China. This serious lack of attention entails far-reaching consequences, i.e., the exclusion of any ethical considerations and their factual replacement by ethical arbitrariness, and greatly contrasts with the practice of SOEs where ethical problems abound.

In a 1996 colloquium in Beijing, I presented a proposal which attempts to introduce these kinds of ethical considerations by applying the framework of "a balanced concept of the firm" (Enderle, forthcoming). Its relevance may lie in the following characteristics:

1.  The relationship between state-owned enterprises and their macro-context is close, yet differentiated. For reasons of fairness and economic

efficiency, a strong institutional framework must guarantee a level play-ing field for all types of enterprises.

2. SOEs are independent economic actors that enjoy freedom and, corre-spondingly, bear responsibility. This necessarily involves an ethical dimen-sion which can be understood as the "depth dimension" of the "freedom and responsibility" of enterprises.

3. Enterprises reflect the multipurpose reality of society, which is not neatly divided into purely economic, political, and sociocultural spheres. Rather, these spheres partially overlap at the societal level and thus cannot be totally separated at the corporate level. Therefore, three partially over-lapping realms of corporate responsibilities can be distinguished: eco-nomic, social, and environmental.

4. A common ethical bottom line for all types of enterprises is necessary for both ethical and economic reasons.

5. Given this common ethical ground, there is room for a wide range of pos-sible variation within which the individual enterprise can strike its own balance of economic, social, and environmental responsibilities.

To point to the ethical dimension of the reform of SOEs and to characterize it by the key term "responsibility" is a first step of developing corporate ethics in China. Many questions regarding content and justification of responsibility, however, remain open. To some extent, the following sections will address these questions.

### Three Sets of "Ethical Resources" for Ethical Guidance in China

In order to substantiate the meaning of corporate responsibility in China, I propose to start from the present sociocultural situation of the country, which is determined by a twenty-five hundred-year legacy of Confucianism, a fifty-year history of a socialist regime, and, due to China's "Open Door" policy since 1978, a multitude of international, Western, and non-Western influences. Ac-cordingly, I will draw on: (1) Confucian ethics as it is currently understood in a fairly comprehensive and modernized way; (2) Socialist ethics as it is iden-tified by the recent Resolutions of the Communist Party of China Central Com-mittee; and (3) the "Goal-Rights-Approach" that reconciles deontological and consequentialist traditions in the non-Chinese ethics discussion.

### Confucian Ethics in a Comprehensive and Modernized Sense

As the history of Confucianism shows, many traditions and interpre-tations of Confucian ethics exist, some of which are quite controversial. For instance, Max Weber held that Confucianism as a religion in China did not provide any help towards modernization (such as the rise of capitalism), but obstructed the rise of the instrumental rationality needed for modern economic and social development. On the other hand, given the economic successes in Taiwan, South Korea, Hong Kong, and Singapore, Confucian ethics is often portrayed as the spiritual source and resource of these developments. Because there is no room to address these issues in this chapter, I only refer to Antonio Cua's fundamental discussion of Confucian Ethics (Cua 1992) and adopt Chung-ying Cheng's view that Confucian ethics should be transformed and modernized and then used creatively and productively (Cheng 1996). Cheng identifies seven elements that constitute the internal factors of the economic development in Taiwan and other East Asian societies (which, moreover, should be understood as closely interconnected and related to the external factors of international business and Western ideas and culture). These elements are the following (Cheng 1996, 37–43):

(1) Facing the hardship of survival, Chinese people tend to have a strong consciousness of "misgivings" or "profound care" (*yu-fan yi-shih*) that engenders the virtues of patience, toleration, and seeking harmony, and promotes a spirit of self-reliance and perseverance. (2) The need for adaptation to a changing environment brings about a general sense of flexibility among common people and a sense of creativity among Chinese intellectuals. (3) The Confucian emphasis on education strongly motivates Chinese people to learn from others and absorb Western knowledge and Western values. (4) Through this learning process, all Confucian values receive a new valuation according to their potential contribution toward maintaining individual integrity and social harmony or national coherence: *hsing* (faithfulness), *li* (propriety), *cheng* (sincerity), *ching* (respect), *chung* (loyalty), *hsiao* (filial piety); also the less dominant virtues of *ch'ien* (thriftiness), *lao* (hard-working), and *ching* (arduousness). (5) The conspicuous virtues of *jen* (benevolence) and *yi* (righteousness) are given universal and modern meanings, and interpreted as policy-generating and decision-supporting virtues that provide the moral foundation for economic institutions and regulations. Therefore, governmental policies and managerial decisions should be guided by *jen,* understood as unselfishness and care for the people, and *yi,* as fair play and fairness or reasonableness. (6) The virtue of *zhi* (wisdom) obviously matters to modernization, not only with its moral dimension, but also with its cognitive dimension, particularly for strategic and tactical planning. (7) A highly significant element contributing to economic development is the popular pragmatism of profit-seeking among the general public. How does this relate to Confucian ethics? Confucius observes that, as a matter of fact, the "small man" seeks profit and the "superior man" seeks rightness, and he would like to see everyone become a "su-

perior man." But he does not reject profit-seeking as either base or undesirable, provided that the right means to seek profit are used and priority is always given to the public good (*kung-li*). While Confucius stresses the fair distribution of wealth, Mencius and *The Great Learning* mention the importance of creating wealth in order to make people well-provided for—an aspect of Confucian ethics that is often mistakenly denied and insufficiently recognized. Thus both the "small men" and the "superior men" have their roles to play in the process of economic development.

To summarize Cua (1992), Confucian ethics is an ethics of virtue. It aims at a well-ordered society based on good government that is responsive to the needs of the people, to issues of wise management of natural resources, and to just distribution of burdens and benefits. Guided by the ethical ideal of a good human life as a whole (*tao*), Confucian ethics stresses character, formation or personal cultivation of virtues (*te*): first the basic, interdependent virtues of *jen* (love and care for one's fellows), *li* (a set of rules of proper conduct), and *yi* (reasoned judgment concerning the right thing to do); then the dependent virtues of filiality, respectfulness, trustworthiness, and others.

### Socialist Ethics According to the Resolutions of the CPC Central Committee

On October 10, 1996, the Communist Party of China (CPC) Central Committee adopted the "Resolutions Regarding Important Questions on Promoting Socialist Ethical and Cultural Progress" (CPC 1996) to provide guidance for "building socialism with Chinese characteristics" from 1996 to 2010 (no. 20). What is particularly striking about the Resolutions is the Committee's vigor and directness in emphasizing the crucial role of ethical and cultural progress (no. 20). After almost twenty years of reform and opening-up to the world, it seems necessary to counterbalance the heavy stress on material progress, given the fact that "the standard of moral conduct has been lowered in some spheres" (no. 22), and a great number of serious moral problems exist, such as "worshiping money, pornography, . . . drug abuse, . . . production of shoddy and fake goods, . . . fraud, . . . corruption." Although already stated in 1978, "the strategic principle of placing equal emphasis on material progress and ethical and cultural progress" (no. 20) has now become even more important.

Both the reform and opening-up are called for to promote ethical and cultural progress (no. 20):

- "to form the socialist concept of justice and interests that places the interests of the State and the people above all and fully respects the legitimate personal interests of the citizens, and form norms for a healthy and orderly economic and social life" and

- "to absorb and learn from advanced sciences and technologies, management expertise, and all other useful knowledge and cultures for the promotion of ethical and cultural progress."

After discussing the paramount importance of ethical and cultural progress at this point in China's history, the Resolutions then turn to the question of the norms and values that should guide this progress. In this regard, two sections are especially relevant. Section 4 recalls the official CPC doctrine that forms the general guiding ideology and the overall requirements of promoting ethical and cultural progress. In particular, the Resolutions state that "the promotion of socialist ethical and cultural progress must take as its guides Marxism-Leninism, Mao Zedong Thought and Deng Xiaoping's theory of building socialism with Chinese characteristics" (no. 23).

Section 11 is more explicit and gives an extensive list of values and norms of socialist ethics, including: "service to the people as its nucleus, collectivism as the principle, and love for the motherland, the people, labor, science and socialism as the basic requirements" (no. 25). The Committee further states that "education in social moral standards, professional ethics and family virtues should be carried out so as to form in all aspects of society a relationship among people that is characterized by unity and mutual help, equality and affection, and common progress."

The Resolutions emphasize family virtues, define the role of the state in economic activities, and give high priority "to promoting progress in professional ethics and rectifying unhealthy tendencies in all professions" (no. 26). Furthermore, the Resolutions conclude that "all trades and professions . . . must offer education to their employees on professional responsibilities, ethics, and discipline, strengthen job training, standardize professionalism, and create new work standards in their respective trades" (no. 29), whereas "those who violate professional ethics should be criticized and educated" (no. 31).

If we look at the document as a whole, it seems fair to say that the Committee makes a compelling case for the need for ethical progress while remaining very general and rather vague in providing ethical guidance. This lack of precision and concreteness surprisingly contrasts with the almost Confucian insistence of the Resolutions that the promotion of ethical and cultural progress should be of high practical relevance. For example, Section 20 states that "All activities involving promotion of ethical and cultural progress must be closely related with solutions to the practical problems that people are generally concerned about, and with the promotion of economic development and social progress" (no. 29).

### "Goal-Rights-Approach" as a Normative-Ethical Framework

A Western ethics discussion might offer a third "ethical resource" to cope with the ethical challenges regarding the reform of state-owned enterprises. Instead of choosing between either a deontological approach (such as Kantian ethics) or a consequentialist approach (such as Utilitarianism), a proposed third approach better takes into account the complexities of moral life. Amartya Sen developed this "goal-rights" approach, which is discussed further in my own work (Enderle 1996). This approach aims at integrating the two seemingly opposing perspectives because both the deontological and consequentialist approaches contain concepts of irreplaceable value. The deontological view insists that the dignity of human beings should be recognized as intrinsically important and should never be used or manipulated as mere means to achieve other ends. The consequentialist view requires that the outcome of human action and institutional behavior be considered and those goals which improve their outcome be identified and pursued.

More specifically, the respect for human dignity is commonly expressed in the Western tradition by the "language of rights," which includes three sets of rights: civil and political, economic and social, and cultural. With regard to business and corporate ethics, of particular interest are "economic rights," such as production-related rights (the rights to work, property, and entrepreneurial initiative) and consumption-related rights (the rights to subsistence and welfare). Despite the historic significance of various international declarations of human rights in the last fifty years, human rights are not unquestionably recognized all over the world. Not only economic rights, but also the universal validity itself of human rights is not infrequently put into question. Therefore, it appears to be necessary to pay closer attention to what the philosophy of human rights really means and to distinguish its content from the language which expresses it. Consequently, a clearly limited list of human rights should be established, and corresponding duties and responsibilities should be emphasized. The contents of human rights should be unambiguously determined and distinguished from the various ways they can be justified, be it from an individualistic or collectivistic, philosophical or religious point of view. Given these qualifications, it seems that a wide international and intercultural consensus about "the core issue" of human rights is feasible, even if it is expressed in a language different from the common "human rights language." The indispensable "core issue" lies in the fundamental anthropological assumption that human beings necessarily need a basic endowment of capabilities in order to live and act decently in society.

As for the specification of the consequentialist view, it is imperative to determine common goals insofar as collective action is required. This is obviously the case for each country that needs a broadly accepted national identity for survival and development. It is also required for undertaking collective action at the international level and for each organization and enterprise that wants to be successful. Moreover, at the level of individual agents, the cooperation in groups demands a fairly clear understanding of their common objectives. In sum, the discussion of goals is indispensable whenever collective action is inescapable or desirable, and involves a normative-ethical dimension. It renders the manipulation of social relations more difficult, strengthens motivation and discipline, and improves the flexibility and efficient allocation of means.

Sen proposes to integrate the deontological and consequentialist perspectives into a "goal-rights" approach (discussed in Enderle 1996). Although this approach certainly needs further development, it is still one of the few contemporary attempts to overcome the traditional division between these opposing schools and sets a number of crucial benchmarks in the ethics discussion.

### Ethical Orientation for the Reform of State-Owned Enterprises

From the discussion thus far, I now allow some tentative conclusions to establish a number of ethical guidelines for the reform of SOEs, thereby using the Caux Round Table Principles for Business Conduct as a heuristic device (*Principles for Business* 1994). This undertaking is fairly daring, given the multiple uncertainties involved in the transition from the planned economy to a market economy and the intended transformation of the SOEs from primarily "social" to primarily "economic" organizations. In order to reduce these uncertainties, the building and enforcement of an unambiguous and comprehensive legal framework is of paramount importance. Such a legal framework does not suffice, however, because it is itself inspired and supported by a certain moral philosophy and practice and cannot fully determine business conduct, leaving a certain discretionary freedom for ethical decision making.

Similar to the Caux Principles, three levels of ethical "input" can be distinguished: basic ethical ideals, general principles that help to clarify the spirit of these ideals, and more specific ethical guidelines that represent a practical way to apply the ideals.

### Individual Integrity and Social Harmony as Two Basic Ethical Ideals

By comparing the three sets of "ethical resources" just described, one can identify two basic ethical ideals that are involved in each of these sets, yet weighed somewhat differently: individual integrity and social harmony. Individual integrity can be expressed by the Confucian ethical ideal of a good human life as a whole (*tao*) or by the more Western concept of "human dignity" that includes, in one "language" or another, the content of a limited set of human rights. It is also contained, though significantly less articulated, in what the CPC Resolutions call "the legitimate personal interests of the citizens" (CPC 1996, no. 8 ). As for social harmony, the Confucian ethics of virtue aim at a well-ordered society based on good government. Socialist ethics place the interests of the state and the people above all and declares "the service to the people as its nucleus, collectivism as the principle, and love for the motherland, the people . . . as the basic requirements." (CPC 1996, no. 25). In the goal-rights-approach, social harmony is what John Rawls calls a "well-ordered society" based on "an overlapping consensus of reasonable comprehensive doctrines" (Rawls 1996, 35–40, 133–172). Interestingly, the two basic ethical ideals of the Caux Principles come close to social harmony and individual integrity. The Caux Principles state: "The Japanese concept of 'kyosei' . . . means living and working together for the common good [and] . . . 'human dignity' refers to the sacredness or value of each human person as an end, not simply as a means to others' purposes or even—in the case of basic human rights—majority prescription."

Obviously, these two basic ethical ideals must be placed in the context of modern societies at the national and international levels. Thus they are challenged by, and must stand the test of, ever more functionally differentiated and pluralistic societies. The wholeness of the human person and the harmony in the society are inescapably exposed to and must confront these problems. Therefore, both extreme views are not acceptable. The absolute separation of different functional spheres (the economic, political, and sociocultural) and the roles of individuals and institutions would lead to the breakup of the unity of individuals and societies. The close entanglement of these spheres, roles, and institutions would seriously hamper the efficiency of modern societies and render the decentralization of power impossible.

Related to the economy and to business, the two basic ethical ideals involve the ethical core values of prosperity, justice, and community (which are also emphasized by Goodpaster in his interpretation of the Caux Principles; Goodpaster 1999). They mean the efficient creation and fair distribution of wealth, in which all members of the community should be included and take part. As discussed above, the comprehensive and modernized understanding of Confucian ethics particularly stresses both prosperity and justice, which is also the core issue of Rawls' *Theory of Justice*. With regard to community, socialist ethics appear to be more articulated than the other two sets of "ethical resources": Confucian ethics and Western ethics as a "goal-rights-approach."

### General Principles: The Responsibilities of Economic Organizations

What is proposed above in general terms applies more specifically to economic organizations. Individual integrity and social harmony, as well as prosperity, justice, and community, are to be translated to and substantiated at the corporate level. This means that discussing and defining the role and objectives of the economic organization must avoid the extreme views of being either a highly entangled politico-socio-economic organization or a purely economic one. Accordingly, the CPC Resolutions require "to strictly prevent the rules on commodity exchange in economic activities from being introduced into the political life of the Party, the political activities of government departments and institutions" (CPC 1996, no. 11). On the other hand, the slogan "the business of business is business" should not govern either. Furthermore, the economic organization is not only an efficient device of creating wealth, but includes a distributional and a communitarian dimension as well, which are interconnected with the productive dimension.

This understanding lays the foundations of "balanced concept of the firm" that distinguishes economic, social, and environmental responsibilities (see above, pp. 196–97). The Caux Principles also advocate the stakeholder approach in Principle 1, which states: "The value of a business to society is the wealth and employment it creates and the marketable products and services it provides to consumers at a reasonable price commensurate with quality. To create such value, a business must maintain its own economic health and viability, but survival is not a sufficient goal. Businesses have a role to play in improving the lives of all their customers, employees, and shareholders by sharing with them the wealth they have created."

A number of "General Principles" further characterize the Caux Principles:

a. to contribute, as responsible citizens, to the economic and social development of the communities in which corporations operate;
b. to respect the rules of fair competition;
c. to avoid illicit operations such as bribery, money laundering, and other corrupt practices;
d. to go beyond the letter of law and build a spirit of trust in all business activities;
e. to support multilateral trade and the international agreements regulating it; and
f. to take a proactive stand in promoting sustainable (ecological) development.

These principles can be grouped as relating to economic responsibility (a), social responsibility (a, b, c, d, e), and environmental responsibility (f). Although primarily designed for multinational corporations, they can provide guidance to state-owned enterprises as well. An especially important feature of these General Principles is the implication that free markets need well-designed institutions and clearly established rules that must be actively supported by corporations and enterprises. As mentioned previously, such a support can be provided by the Confucian ethics of virtue, particularly by the basic virtues of *jen* (unselfishness and care for the people), *yi* (fairness or reasonableness), and *li* (a set of rules of proper conduct). Moreover, the virtue of *zhi* (wisdom) is highly relevant to environmental responsibility. The Resolutions also call for forming "norms for a healthy and orderly economic and social life" (CPC 1996, no. 22).

### Ethical Guidelines for the Reform of State-Owned Enterprises

It would be unfair and unrealistic to demand radical reforms from the SOEs without radically changing the macro-context in which they operate. As long as the various types of enterprises in China (state-owned enterprises, urban collective enterprises, township and village enterprises, privately-owned firms, joint ventures, foreign-owned firms, and others) are subject to considerably different legal and regulatory treatments, in terms of publicly stated and actually demanded requirements, the markets cannot produce the intended efficient and fair outcomes. In addition, major social obligations, honored until now by SOEs, reflect important needs of the people. If SOEs cannot any longer meet these needs, other governmental and nongovernmental institutions must be put in place and take on these responsibilities.

Therefore, the following guidelines for the *nationwide SOE reform policy* (GN) are proposed:

GN 1: Creating and enforcing a level playing field of laws and regulations for all types of enterprises in China.

GN 2: Strengthening the economic and financial autonomy of SOEs in order to enable them to assume their corresponding responsibilities.

GN 3: Establishing fair and efficient systems of social security for retired, disabled, sick, and unemployed people.

These guidelines point to several necessary conditions for a successful reform of SOEs. They must, however, be supplemented by a number of guidelines (GE) which directly concern the responsibilities of SOEs themselves.

They can be grouped in three partially overlapping sets of economic, social, and environmental responsibilities.

*Economic responsibilities of SOEs:*
Regarding the SOE as an economic organization:

GE 1: Enhancing considerably efficiency and productivity.

GE 2: Taking full financial responsibility for the management of the SOE, even at the risk of bankruptcy.

GE 3: Reducing the social obligations for surplus employment, social security, health care, housing, education, and other activities *to the extent* that these services are being provided by other, governmental and private, institutions.

GE 4: Competing with honesty and fairness.

Regarding managers and employees:

GE 5: Respecting the human dignity of every manager and employee.

GE 6: Being innovative in creating and preserving productive and meaningful jobs.

GE 7: Clearly determining the roles and responsibilities of managers and employees, and establishing a fair and effective system of reporting and accountability.

GE 8: Setting and implementing reasonably high standards of a "work ethic" in terms of thriftiness (*ch'ien*), hard-working (*lao*), and arduousness (*ching*).

GE 9: Providing safe and healthy working conditions, and paying fair wages and salaries.

GE 10: Promoting professional ethics (related to *yi* and *li*).

GE 11: Separating the work life of managers and employees from their private life.

Regarding other stakeholders:

GE 12: Serving the customers who directly purchase the SOEs' products and services, and who acquire them through authorized channels.

GE 13: Honoring the trust of the SOEs' owners and investors.

GE 14: Paying mutual respect to the suppliers.

*Social and environmental responsibilities:*

GE 15: Respecting the letter and spirit of laws and regulations (related to *yi* and *li*).

GE 16: Honoring the social obligations which remain in the realm of SOEs.
GE 17: Fostering cultural heritage and innovations.
GE 18: Promoting sustainable business that "leaves the environment no worse off at the end of each accounting period than it was at the beginning of that accounting period" (UNCTAD definition quoted in Schmidheiny et al. 1996, 17).

In conclusion, these guidelines attempt to indicate an ethical direction for the reform of SOEs. Admittedly, they are incomplete and need a great deal of discussion and further specification (particularly GE 12–18). It is hoped, however, that they can contribute to the learning process in which managers, employees, SOEs as organizations, and society as a whole must engage in order to pursue and achieve the successful reform of state-owned enterprises in China. In *Analects* 17:8 (Cleary 1992, 45) Confucius aptly expresses the importance of learning.

> If you like humaneness but don't like learning, it degenerates into folly.
> If you like knowledge but don't like learning, it degenerates into looseness.
> If you like trust but don't like learning, it degenerates into depredation.
> If you like honesty but don't like learning, it degenerates into stricture.
> If you like bravery but don't like learning, it degenerates into disorder.
> If you like strength but don't like learning, it degenerates into wildness.

## References

Cheng, Chung-ying. 1996. "Totality and Mutuality: Confucian Ethics and Economic Development." In *Confucianism and Economic Development*, edited by the Faculty of the Chinese Institute of Economic Studies, Taipei, Taiwan.

Cleary, T. (ed.). 1992. *The Essential Confucius.* San Francisco: Harper.

CPC 1996. Resolutions of the (CPC) Central Committee Regarding Important Questions on Promoting Socialist Ethical and Cultural Progress. *Beijing Review* 20, November 4–10.

Cua, A. S. 1992. "Confucian Ethics." In Becker, L. C., Becker, C. B. (eds.), *Encyclopedia of Ethics.* New York: Garland, 194–202.

Enderle, G. 1996. "Towards Business Ethics as an Academic Discipline." *Business Ethics Quarterly,* January, 43–65.

Enderle, G. Forthcoming. "Integrating the Ethical Dimension into the Analytical Framework for the Reform of State-owned Enterprises in China's Socialist Market Economy: A Proposal." *Journal of Business Ethics.*

Enderle, G., and Tavis, L. A. 1998. "A Balanced Concept of the Firm and the Measurement of Its Long-Term Planning and Performance." *Journal of Business Ethics* 17, 1129–1144.

Goodpaster, K. E. 1999. "The Caux Round Table Principles for Business: Presentation and Discussion." In Enderle, G. (ed.). *International Business Ethics: Challenges and Approaches*. Notre Dame, Ind.: University of Notre Dame Press.

*Principles for Business*. 1994. The Hague: Caux Round Table Secretariat.

Rawls, J. 1996. *Political Liberalism*. Second edition. New York: Columbia University Press.

Schmidheiny, S., and Zorraquín, F. 1996. *Financing Change: The Financial Community, Eco-efficiency, and Sustainable Development*. Cambridge: MIT Press.

— ✺ —

## PART V

# Principles for Global Corporate Responsibility

*The Point of View
of Church Groups*

# 13

# In Whose Interest?

## A Global Code of Conduct for Corporations

RUTH ROSENBAUM, T.C.

Scarcely a week, even a day, goes by without seeing the words "globalization of the economy" in the various news media. I would be willing to wager that nary a month goes by without one or another group sponsoring a conference on some aspect of this move towards economic globalization. For the sake of utility, I would divide these conferences into two major groupings.

In one group, there are the people and groups who seem to assume that this globalization is inevitable. For them, the globalization forces are like a force of nature that cannot be molded, shaped, perhaps even undone in areas. This is a failure to recognize, or to acknowledge that this globalization is the result of human beings making human decisions, not for the good of the world but primarily for the good of certain groups of people, for the good of certain countries—often to the exclusion, whether purposeful or by design, of the majority of humankind inhabiting the earth.

In the second group are those who raise questions about this globalization, questions concerning the human decisions by which this globalization is being designed. Who benefits from the globalization and who decides who benefits? How much do they benefit? How is it that some are included in the benefits and so many are excluded? Is this by chance or by design? How is it possible to have growing economies at the same time that there is a growing number of people living in poverty, in destitution, in so many countries? How is it possible that as the Dow continues to go up, the standard of living for more and more people continues to go down?

As an adjunct to these two sets of conversations comes the talk of codes of conduct. These codes originate from a variety of sources. There are corporate codes of conduct coming from companies who want to be seen as "socially responsible." Companies as diverse as Nike, General Motors, and IBM have codes governing all sorts of activities within their corporate operations. These company codes can be coupled with industry codes, which seek to apply standards of operation to their company members. The Chemical Manufacturers Association would be a prime example. The Caux Principles would also fall into this category since they are sourced in the corporate community although they purport to have a "global" context to them.

Then there are the government codes, which vary from regulating industries to demanding standards from companies doing business with the government. In this last group we have municipalities who require compliance with codes such as the MacBride Principles for Northern Ireland (see Appendix 21), or not doing business in Burma before contracts with the government are possible. In the past, we had the Sullivan Principles, which became the Principles for South Africa (see Appendix 27). More recently, we have seen living-wage laws being passed in various cities, requiring anyone doing business with the city to pay their workers a living wage rather than that destructive standard we usually see, the minimum wage. From another direction come codes seeking to address an issue. The most prominent one would be the CERES Principles, a set of environmental principles formulated after the Valdez disaster in Alaska a number of years ago (see Appendix 2).

The final group of codes falls into the "global" category, that is, they seek to formulate a set of global standards by which companies would be measured and by which companies would be asked to measure themselves. Into this category comes the Global Principles: Benchmarks for Corporate Social Responsibility from the collaborative work of the Interfaith Center on Corporate Responsibility (ICCR) in the U.S., and its counterparts: the Ecumenical Committee for Corporate Responsibility (ECCR) in the United Kingdom and the Task Force on Churches and Corporate Responsibility (TCCR) in Canada. The starting point for this code is radically different from all those above. This time, the starting point is not a particular sector of the business establishment or a specific company. Rather the whole direction of accountability is changed with the starting point moved from the corporation to the community, from the business world to humanity as a whole.

In addition, the faith communities represented by ICCR, ECCR, and TCCR move the questions being asked from the notion of "corporate social responsibility" to the idea of social justice. Within the justice context, it is not enough to talk about economic growth without raising the need for more equitable distribution of the benefits from that growth. Justice requires that we hold the faces and lives of those oppressed by poverty and oppression before us when we evaluate any code and any economy.

All codes need to be compared in terms of both content and context. In order to understand both the content and context of these codes, I suggest a number of key questions need to be asked and answered.

### Question 1: What "Stake" Is Seen as the Starting Point for the Code in Question?

This reorientation of thinking is key to any global code of conduct. Traditionally, the emphasis has been on a stakeholder model, defined by the corporations, in which various community groups are defined in terms of their importance to the corporations. In this traditional model, shareholders, employees, consumers, community groups, etc. are seen as stakeholders in the corporation, thereby making the corporation the center of the model and the center of concern. This has been true as corporations have developed from local and national businesses through international, multinational, and transnational forms. The changing names reflect the importance that the corporations have come to hold in the lives of communities around the world.

In a reenvisioned stakeholder model, I proposed a redefinition of the corporation in which each and any corporation is asked to recognize itself and be willing to be recognized by others as one among the many stakeholders in a community. This is not as radical as it may seem, but rather a return to the commitment that corporations made to be "good corporate citizens" in the original charters of incorporation granted by the various states. Under this revised stakeholder model, all segments of the community are equal stakeholders in the community, along with the corporations. In addition, this revised stakeholdership places the sustained community as the prime goal of the interactions, inter-relationships, and operations of each community segment (First Principles for Analyzing Corporate Business Responsibility by Faith).

Through the building of relationships among the various stakeholders within the communities, as well as the building of constructive relationships between communities, steps towards sustainable development can be undertaken as part of a long-term approach that has as part of its vision the sustaining of resources for future generations. This redefined stakeholder model is therefore seen as integral to the possibility of sustainable economic development, "the process of building equitable, productive and participatory structures to increase the economic empowerment of communities and their surrounding regions." The benefits to the corporation would include a more stable work force, a stable community in which to operate, and a community which can aspire to own the products which are produced within the community.

The Global Principles for Global Corporate Responsibility: Benchmarks for Measuring Business Performance have as a constitutive element the revised stakeholder model, moving the corporations from the center of concern to their rightful place among us all in the community.

## Question 2: Who Stands to Benefit from This Code?

Code statements bring benefits in a number of ways. The first is that the group presenting the code gets to control the conversation. The question then becomes compliance with that code, rather than what is included in the code or, conversely, what has been omitted. This is true however limited or extensive the code is. The second benefit is that the group proposing the code looks good in the media and in the eyes of the public. This can continue unless and until the content of the code is examined and explained by those practiced in code interpretation.

One only has to look at the assorted corporate codes of conduct to illustrate. Of the more than one hundred codes which have come across my desk in the past twelve months, it would be difficult to find more than a minimal list of common issues which they cover. Just the fact that each company seeks to have a unique code rather than developing common codes illustrates the point.

A unique exception to this has been the recent Workplace Code of Conduct developed by the Apparel Industry Partnership. It will be interesting to see how long it takes for each member of the apparel industry to sign on to a common code and lose control over the enforcement of the code and how that plays out in the public eye.

This is connected to another advantage, that is, what is addressed and what isn't. Again the Apparel Industry Partnership stands as an illustration. While the code developed by the AIP includes many issues, one glaringly omitted is that of adequate wages to allow workers to meet their needs. (This issue of adequate wages will be discussed in a later section.) Once a code is enacted, it is difficult to get it amended or extended.

In response to the codes in existence, questions then need to be raised: Who writes the code where the workers are the primary beneficiaries? Who writes the codes where human rights and labor rights, where children's rights and social rights are the starting place?

The writers of the Global Principles for Global Corporate Responsibility: Benchmarks for Measuring Business Performance have used two lenses through which to evaluate each principle, benchmark, and criterion. The first has been the collective lens provided by the various international documents on human rights, labor rights, children's rights, rights of indigenous peoples, etc. The second lens has been the question: will this principle, this criterion, this benchmark address the needs of the workers, the men, the women, and, yes, the children, around the world who toil to produce much of what the world produces?

### Question 3: Who Is Responsible for the Enforcement of the Code?

Certainly a corporation is responsible for its own operations. However, if that were sufficient, there would be no need for corporate codes of conduct in the first place. Companies would be able to do whatever they do, and say that they are doing so according to their own corporate ways or standards. In the larger community concerned with the questions of corporate social responsibility, the issue of monitoring of codes of conduct is an important one. If we define monitoring as regular on-site inspection during which the facility and its operations are evaluated, then we need to make sure that the evaluation is done in reference to two sets of norms. The first is the specific code of conduct established by the retailer or corporation involved. The second set of norms is equally if not more important; these are the relevant human rights and labor rights established by international norms.

Operating from these two reference points, there are three types of monitoring usually discussed: internal monitoring, external monitoring, and independent monitoring. Internal monitoring is the on-site inspection as done by the corporation and/or retailer (or their immediate agents) involved. External monitoring is the on-site inspection done by a party or parties hired by the retailer or corporation involved. The external monitors report to the corporation. In contrast, independent monitoring is the on-site inspection done by selected monitors who are financially independent and report not only to the parent company/retailer, but also to the consumer communities, and to other interested parties. Funding for such monitoring needs to done in such a manner as to leave the monitors truly independent of the companies whose factories are being monitored. In the world of human rights and labor rights, internal monitoring is expected of companies; however, it is third-party, independent monitoring which is considered the only acceptable form to guarantee the rights of the workers involved.

An associated issue should be added: where does the money spent on monitoring accrue? In the larger corporate community? Or in the community where the monitoring is needed? For monitoring to be not only effective but a contribution towards sustainability in countries and communities where development is critically needed, the monies used for the monitoring need to accrue to the communities themselves; monitoring should not involve corporate money flowing to other corporate entities, again bypassing the local developing communities.

The Global Principles for Global Corporate Responsibility: Benchmarks for Measuring Business Performance calls for the use of independent monitoring groups in each and all of the communities where corporations operate. As more and more industries move towards the use of contract suppliers or vendors to produce their goods and supply their services, this need becomes ever more critical. In the U.S. and in other industrialized countries, this role is usually done by governmental regulatory agencies. However in developing countries, the government is often part of the problem. Hence the need for the involvement of labor groups, human rights groups, and religious groups.

### Question 4: Does the Code Talk about Development, That Is, Real Development Which Leads Towards Sustainability? Or Is It Really Talking about Industrialization?

For our purpose here, let us describe development as the establishment of an industrial base, including industry but not limited to it or solely dependent upon it, where the purposeful design of the interrelationship between labor, management, resources, energy, products, marketing, land use, costs, profits, physical infrastructure, social infrastructure, etc. is for the benefit of the people of the community, their communities, and the country. The purpose of development is the empowerment of the people, communities, and country over their own future, not the creation of a self-perpetuating system of dependency on outside funding which must eventually, at great price, be paid back with interest.

In contrast, industrialization is the setting up of any industries that will do the following:

a)   allow for the creation of goods,
b)   provide centers for creating these goods,
c)   hire workers.

This industrialization has the following consequences:

1)   workers congregate in the area of the industrial center,
2)   requiring the development of systems of physical infrastructure such as housing, sanitation, roads, electricity, etc.,

3) and the development of systems of social infrastructure such as schools, medical facilities, community services, religious facilities, etc.

In reality, the problem is that what is required is not necessarily provided, or, if provided, is not necessarily adequate. Sustainability issues revolve around development, not around industrialization.

The Global Principles for Global Corporate Responsibility: Benchmarks for Measuring Business Performance uses the need for sustainable development as a central underlying foundation. Industrialization that does not lead to sustainability is definitively challenged.

This leads directly to the next question(s).


### Question 5: Where Are the Profits Made?
### Where Do the Profits Accrue from Corporate Activity?
### How Is It Decided How the Benefits Will Be Distributed?

Because the marketing of the products of industrialization rarely occur at the centers of production, decisions are made regarding the distribution of those profits. A recent case in point might be the Stanley Works Company in Connecticut. Headlines in the *Hartford Courant* in July told us that the company was shutting some operations in Connecticut and moving the jobs in question to China, where the costs of production would be lower. The company was described as having always been profitable, never failing to have profitable quarters for many years.

If we look at the accrual of the benefit of profits, we could describe the Stanley Works movement in the following manner. First of all, we have to note the change in how wages are described. Previously, the ability to pay workers was seen as a benefit of profits made. These profits were shared with workers, whether management or other men and women working for the company. The benefits of the profits accrued to the communities where the workers lived. There they paid taxes, as well as spent their wages, helping to ensure the sustainability of their communities.

Now labor is seen as a cost, a negative. Therefore jobs are moved to minimize these costs. Because lower wages can be paid at the site where the new workers engage in the company business, there is a double loss to sustainability. First, the wages that were paid in the Connecticut community are lost to those communities. Yes, most likely those workers will find other jobs. However, one of the realities of our times is that having replacement jobs is not the same as earning replacement wages or salaries. Those workers on whatever level they operate do most jobs that replace old ones at the sacrifice of income. Second, the new community, in this case China, does not receive the benefit of these wages because the wages are so much lower that the ripple effect caused by wages being spent in a community is much lower.

This highlights the way in which we now talk about profit. Profit is acknowledged only when it accrues away from the company, away from the community where it operates, away from the community where its products are made. Profit is now seen only as what accrues to shareholders.

Central to any discussion about profit is the question of wages. The establishment of quantifiable standards for wages must be addressed. Minimum wages are not enough. Even the Apparel Industry Partnership's Workplace Code of Conduct clearly states that "wages are essential to meeting employees' basic needs." These basic needs include the needs of dependents, either children or elderly who cannot themselves work. If wages are essential to meeting needs, the question then arises as to how the wage scales in use in each country and in regions within a country are quantified to actually meet the needs of workers and their families.

The minimum wage is cited as an "at least" or a "floor." In too many countries, this minimum wage is often the acceptable standard wage in the assembly sector occupied by contract supplier plants. With rare, if any, exceptions, countries have established minimum wage standards which have nothing to do with meeting basic needs of workers and their families. This is, unfortunately, also true in the U.S.

We hear talk of "real" wages, by which is meant how today's wages, in any country, relate to wages paid in some past year which is used as a standard. I suggest that what is "real" about wages is what a worker is able to buy with those wages in a particular location within a particular country.

Rather than talk about "real wages" we need to talk in terms of the purchasing power workers in any country can earn by working a set workweek at the wage levels in that country. Purchasing power as determined by the Purchasing Power Index (PPI) (see Appendix 24) is measured in terms of the number of minutes workers need to work at their wage rate to buy the items necessary to meet basic needs. The PPI does not decide what a worker will buy. It measures what workers are *able* to purchase based on the earned purchasing power during a given workweek. The PPI is the only transnational, transcultural, and transtemporal index measuring the combined effects of wages, prices, and inflation. It allows us to see, with a clear focus and great accuracy, how workers are effected by wages paid in Indonesia, Haiti, Vietnam, China, even the cities and villages of our industrial countries.

From a justice point of view, rather than the corporate viewpoint, the problem with the entire contract supplier system is that little of the profits accrue in the country or countries where the majority of the work is done. The system is designed so that assembly-plant workers are paid ever-lower wages; it is also designed so that the major part of the price paid for an item does not even stay within the country of assembly. Let's take Disney or Nike as illustrations. Disney was sourcing in Haiti; Nike sources in Indonesia, among other places. Yet the factories where the workers assemble the goods for Disney and/or Nike are not owned by Haitians in Haiti or by Indonesians in Indonesia. In country after country, we find that assembly plants are being set up in free-trade zones (called by a variety of names but still free-trade zones) by persons not native to the country where the assembly takes place. Let's play "follow the profits."

Disney signs a contract with a plant owner who operates a plant in Port-au-Prince. In order to attract assembly-plant owners to Haiti, where people are desperate for jobs, the Haitian government, pressured by the Structural Adjustment Program (SAP) designed for Haiti by the IMF and World Bank, has had to agree to tax indemnities for extended numbers of years, sometimes more than ten years. So, Disney signs the contract for shirts with the plant management. The management hires sewers to make the shirts. The workers are paid a few cents per shirt. Disney sells the shirts for highly inflated amounts at its various commercial outlets.

Disney receives its profit from the high prices charged for the shirts. The management receives the bulk of the payment from Disney as "profit" and transfers that profit back to its home country. Disney does not pay taxes in Haiti. The assembly-plant owner does not pay taxes in Haiti. The profits of both Disney and the assembly-plant owner are not spent in Haiti. Nothing stays in Haiti except for a few cents per shirt.

Now taxes are talked about these days as though they are the ultimate evil. I suggest to you though, that taxes are the way in which we return to the community in proportion to what we have received. Taxes are how we provide for the common good. Taxes are how we contribute to the development of the physical and social infrastructure of our communities. When a tax system is designed to not provide adequate monies for this physical and social infrastructure, development cannot occur.

A related issue is, how do the value of resources "show up on the books" of a country or a corporation? How is it that when resources have yet to be removed from the earth, be they oil or gold or natural gas, they do not show up in the financial ledger of that country as an asset? How is it that these only become as asset when they are removed from the earth, where they have belonged to the people of that community or country, and are now listed as "assets" in the financial ledgers of the corporation which has removed them while they are never recorded as a debit for the community which has lost them?

The Global Principles for Global Corporate Responsibility: Benchmarks for Measuring Business Performance call for the establishment of wages in each and every country, based on country-specific, systematic, and ongoing Purchasing Power Index studies. In addition, it calls for the establishment of sustainable living-wage scales in each country, not based on minimum standards but on what is necessary for workers to be able to meet both immediate *and* long-term needs as well as support their community.

### Question 6: Is the Code a Statement of Minimization, a Set of Minimum Standards Which Are Then Deemed to Be Acceptable Because They Are Met? Or Does the Code in Question Talk about Responsibility to Return in Proportion to What One Has Received?

This last question to be raised here regarding codes brings us almost full circle to where we started. What is the purpose of any code? Is it to create minimum standards by which any corporation can pull out of a community what it needs or wants and then abandon that community when there is no more to extract? What will corporations do when there are no more places to exploit? When there are no more places to which assembly can be moved? Even in the arena of corporate self-interest, what will the corporations do when there are no more people who can afford to buy their products and services? How then will corporations expand their markets?

The Global Principles for Global Corporate Responsibility: Benchmarks for Measuring Business Performance move the conversation from what is legal, through what is ethical, on through what is socially responsible and into the area of what is just. The groups which have engaged in the writing of the Global Principles have taken upon themselves the task of moving the conversation beyond that of company profits to that of being a company of prophets, that is, holding the truth before us about the need to reform the manner and means by which companies do business.

# 14

# Making Codes of Conduct Credible

## *The Role of Independent Monitoring*

DAVID M. SCHILLING

### Introduction

The globalization of the international economy poses fundamental challenges for corporations as well as for local, national, and international communities. As the global marketplace expands, corporations are faced with the question of what values should guide their operations since companies and their suppliers now operate in places where basic human rights and labor rights are not guaranteed and workers face abusive conditions that violate their lives and compromise their dignity. The ability to move production quickly from one country to another and the growing reliance on contract suppliers means that, in addition to their traditional business focus, corporations need to address global concerns about fair wages and safe working conditions, child and forced labor, the environment, and sustainable community development. The global supply system demands it.

Corporations also are pushed to deal with worker rights from the consumer side since an increasingly aware and conscientious public does not want to buy goods made by children or adults working under abusive conditions. The question of how to regulate the operations of corporations and their suppliers around the world requires that corporations carry within themselves self-regulatory mechanisms that were once thought to be intrinsic to the nation-state. Attempts to incorporate labor and human rights standards into the company and supplier relationships brings forth two sets of linked questions: how to establish credible corporate codes of conduct and how to make sure those codes are consistently applied. This chapter is devoted to these two issues, the question of corporate standards and the question of effective monitoring.

## Global Codes of Conduct

By the early 1990s, transnational corporations controlled 25 percent of the world's productive assets, 70 percent of the products in international trade, 80 percent of the world's land cultivated for export crops; the major share of the world's technological innovations.[1] Corporations now have the capacity to shift resources—finances, machinery, technology, personnel—anywhere in the world to maximize their competitive position. Traditional methods of regulating corporate activities based on an old nation-state model are simply not adequate when applied to transnational and supranational corporations.

By the 1970s multinational corporations came under attack from governments and nongovernmental groups (NGOs) in developing countries because of a failure "to operate in harmony with local economic, social and political objectives."[2] Pressure grew to formulate codes of conduct that would regulate business activity to ensure that basic human and labor rights were not violated. Early United Nations attempts to create a global code of conduct failed because individual governments were not able to reach legislative assent to a "Code of Conduct for Multinational Corporations." Many companies opposed the attempt.

The "Tripartite Declaration of Principles Concerning Multinational Enterprises and Social Policy" was approved by the International Labor Organization (ILO) in 1977. The International Labor Organization is a United Nations-related organization that predates the UN and is made up of representatives from three sectors: government, business, and labor. The Tripartite Declaration is a universal voluntary instrument provided to guide governments, employers, and workers in adopting policies and taking measures within multinational enterprises that would minimize conflict and promote cooperation. The principles described in the declaration should be respected by all international corporations and by the countries in which they operate. The Tripartite Declaration of Principles contains mechanisms for reporting abuses and problems, but the principles are not enforced because of their voluntary and nonlegally binding status.

In the 1990s the reporting of labor abuses in supplier factories dramatically increased and the public's awareness increased as a consequence. Although sweatshop conditions in factories throughout the world are not new, they became headline news when the public learned that clothes made under Kathie Lee Gifford's label were sewn by children at Global Fashions, a maquiladora factory (where products are made for export) in Honduras. Gifford, a television talk-show celebrity and children's advocate, was appalled when the National Labor Committee announced that clothes bearing her name were made by girls ages 12 to 14 who were forced to work 13-hour shifts under armed guard for 31 cents an hour. When she found that the charges were true, she convinced Wal-Mart to withdraw its contract from Global Fashions. Press attention given to this situation led to greater public awareness and pressure on companies to take action to ensure that their products were not made by children or under other abusive labor conditions. Conversations are now taking place with increased urgency among community, religious, and human rights groups, shareholders, and corporations. Some corporations have responded by adopting global codes and guidelines for their own operations and the operations of their contractors and suppliers. All corporations, whether local or global, have the potential to play a positive role in communities where they operate. If global guidelines and codes lead to building partnerships among those who have a stake in the health and well-being of communities in which they operate, then they can prove to be useful tools for sustainable economic and human development.

### Principles of Global Corporate Responsibility

Three faith groups—Interfaith Center on Corporate Responsibility of the United States, Ecumenical Committee for Corporate Responsibility of the United Kingdom, and Task Force on the Churches and Corporate Responsibility of Canada—published the "Principles for Global Corporate Responsibility: Benchmarks for Measuring Business Performance" (Global Principles) in 1995 to contribute to the discussion of global codes of conduct.[3] The Global Principles, which received wide resonance in the press, are rooted in the faith and experience of these three groups and their member communities, which have a long record of working for socially responsible business practices. The document was circulated for comment to groups around the world including human rights, indigenous, labor, women's, consumer, and environmental groups and corporations. Following this, the three faith groups drafted a new version based on the feedback they received. The new version was published in the spring of 1998.

In its "Context of Faith" the three groups spell out their perspective on corporate social responsibility:

- Faith communities evaluate companies, not only by what they produce and their impact on the environment, but also by how companies contribute to sustainable community and protect or undermine the dignity of the human person. We believe these companies carry responsibility for the human and moral consequences of their economic decisions.
- We believe the challenge for both companies and individuals in the global economy is to ensure that the distribution of economic benefits is equitable, supports sustainable community and preserves the integrity of creation.
- We believe the promotion and protection of human rights—civil, political, social, religious, cultural and economic—are minimum standards for all social institutions including companies.

In the Preamble, the three groups state their belief that:

The community, rather than the company, is the starting point of economic life. For the community to be sustainable, all members need to be recognized, i.e., consumers, employees, shareholders, the community at large and corporations. Respect for each group's essential role in the economic and social life of the community will facilitate more just relationships locally and globally.

The Global Principles were put forward to challenge companies to formulate strong, enforceable codes of conduct and to establish systematic ways in which corporations can more productively relate to people, communities, and the environment.

## Voluntary Company Codes of Conduct

Because of the failure to create an enforceable global code through international institutions like the United Nations, pressure on companies to be more socially and environmentally responsible has led to the adoption of voluntary company codes of conduct. Codes of conduct are statements that encompass the company's core beliefs related to its ethical practices and its responsibilities to uphold human rights, labor, and environmental standards in all its operations and the operations of its suppliers. During the past six years, some companies have formulated codes to be used as guidelines for relations with suppliers and to inform shareholders and the public what its standards are. In 1991, Levi-Strauss was the first multinational company to establish comprehensive global sourcing and operating guidelines. Gap, Liz Claiborne, Reebok, Phillips-VanHeusen and L. L. Bean are examples of companies which have adopted codes of conduct and have revised them based on their experience. Individual company codes vary widely in terms of the standards affirmed and the level of monitoring of compliance with those standards.

Company codes are voluntary and can be formulated as serious company policies or as public relations gestures. A *USA Today* article quoted a Hong Kong trade lawyer as saying that many importers "just think it's wrong to have their goods made under conditions considered offensive. Others . . . don't want to be exposed on *60 Minutes* or *20/20*."[4]

Companies spend substantial resources on developing a positive brand image and good will with consumers and the public. Allegations that their operations employ abusive labor practices can quickly lead to the tarnishing of a "good corporate citizen" image which can damage the company in economic terms. When tapes of Texaco officials making racist and anti-Semitic remarks were made public in 1996, the value of shares dropped precipitously and Texaco lost an estimated $800 million in one day along with its image as a "good corporate citizen." In the aftermath, Texaco met with ICCR members who had filed shareholder resolutions and discussed with the company, for the past five years, concerns regarding the company's employment policies and practices related to women and people of color. Texaco met with other groups, including the NAACP, and came up with a detailed action plan designed to address discrimination in the company.

## Code Credibility Check List

Because codes are drafted and adopted by a company voluntarily for a variety of motives in a variety of ways, the credibility of the code must be addressed. In assessing the credibility of a company's code of conduct, a number of factors must be taken into account. Here is a checklist to help rate code credibility:

- *Was the code discussed, drafted, and adopted by top management, or was it the product of the public relations or communications office?* If codes are not the statement of the company's core vision, values, and standards and fully operationalized in its programs, policies, and practices, it will be viewed as a public relations gesture with little impact on its employment practices and the practices of its suppliers.
- *Does the code include essential areas covered by key international human rights, environmental, and International Labor Organization standards?* In the Interfaith Center on Corporate Responsibility's corporate accountability work, we have found that very few companies explicitly include the right of freedom of association in their codes. It took public pressure and filing shareholder resolutions with companies like Disney and Nike before they agreed to include this international right in

their company code of conduct. It is essential to address the issue of freedom of association given the endemic problem of workers fired for exercising their rights to form a union, especially in export processing zones around the world.

- *Does the code succumb to the "Tyranny of the Minimum" or does the code stake out territory that contains higher standards?* If the code reflects minimum standards, it has the advantage of being achievable within current competitive realities, but it is unlikely to raise labor or environmental standards and practices in the company's operations. "Tyranny of the Minimum" thinking is most evident by assessing company wage standards. The vast majority of company wage standards are based on paying the minimum wage required by local law or the prevailing industry wage. The problem with this formulation is that the minimum wage in most countries is set so low that "minimum" does not mean a wage level that enables a person to survive. Instead of companies paying the minimum established by the government of a country or the prevailing industry standard, we suggest that they should analyze the purchasing power needed for workers to meet their basic needs and then use that figure as the minimum standard. An important consequence of raising labor and wage standards elsewhere is that it makes U.S. workers more competitive in the global economy.

  The Global Principles document states a higher standard which addresses the basic right of a worker to get a fair day's pay for a fair day's work: "The company pays sustainable community wages which enable employees to meet both the basic needs of themselves and their families, as well as to invest in the on-going sustainability in local communities through the use of discretionary income." Dr. Ruth Rosenbaum, Center for Reflection, Education and Action, has developed the Purchasing Power Index study which companies can use to determine the wage level that equals a sustainable living wage.[5] How a company answers the question, "Does it pay a sustainable living wage?" communicates a great deal about its status as a socially responsible company.

- *Is the company's code made real through concrete implementation strategies?* The standards may speak for themselves but they must be accompanied by detailed plans of action in order to ensure that code standards are being applied. The Gap has developed detailed "Sourcing Evaluation and Compliance Monitoring" instruments and a "Vendor Guide to Factory Evaluation" to assist in the implementation of its Code of Vendor Conduct. Some other companies have developed similar auditing instruments. A company seeking to make compliance with its code more effective and credible could begin by implementing the following: hire and train company personnel to monitor code compliance; require its business partners to abide by their standards as a condition for doing business; develop detailed audit instruments and use on-site (particularly unannounced) inspections; interview workers away from the plant to get their perspective on workplace conditions; and develop working relationships with local human rights, labor rights, and religious organizations that have the trust of workers.

- *Does the company effectively monitor its code of conduct?* Monitoring makes a significant difference in determining whether or not plants are in compliance with codes of conduct and national law. The U.S. Department of Labor's 1996 study of garment shops in Los Angeles found that a shop is three times more likely to be in compliance with wage/hour laws if the shop is monitored. Twenty-seven percent of monitored shops had some violations, while 64 percent of nonmonitored shops had violations.[6]
- *Does the company accept independent monitoring of its code of conduct by respected local religious, human rights, labor rights organizations in the areas where it or its suppliers operate?* Independent monitoring of codes of conduct is emerging as the key issue in providing public credibility on code compliance. It is to this issue we now turn.

### Independent Monitoring of Codes of Conduct

A number of companies have utilized consulting firms to aid them in the auditing of compliance with their codes of conduct. While this strategy may produce valuable information on whether or not a supplier is in compliance, third-party audits of this type rely largely on infrequent on-site inspections. In a promising development, the Gap agreed in 1995 to work with nongovernmental organizations to build an independent monitoring system at Mandarin International, a Gap supplier in El Salvador.

### The Gap Example

The National Labor Committee Education Fund in Support of Worker and Human Rights in Central America (NLC) had found violations of the Gap's "Sourcing Principles and Guidelines" at Mandarin International, a maquiladora shop owned by a Taiwanese firm and located in the San Marcos Free Trade Zone in San Salvador. Workers had complained to the National Labor Committee about the use of child labor, forced overtime, unsafe working conditions, threats to prevent workers from organizing, and firing of union leaders. After six months of leafleting at stores, letter-writing by religious and community groups, and face-to-face discussion, Gap agreed to explore independent monitoring at Mandarin International and to urge Mandarin to rehire union leaders who had been fired.

On December 15, 1995, Gap, the NLC and several religious leaders met to discuss the issues at Mandarin. The outcome of this meeting was a resolution in which Gap agreed to work with the Interfaith Center on Corporate Responsibility, Business for Social Responsibility, and the National Labor Committee to explore the viability of independent monitoring at Mandarin International. In January 1996, these groups formed the Independent Monitoring Working Group (IMWG) and began to define independent monitoring, its goals and scope. As a part of its exploration, some members of the IMWG traveled to El Salvador in February 1996 and visited the Mandarin facility, met with factory managers and workers, and conferred with representatives of various local religious, labor, government, and human rights organizations. In an effort to develop a working model for independent monitoring in El Salvador, the IMWG also solicited input from more than seventy-five U.S. and international human rights, labor, religious, academic, and business groups.

### Definition and Goals of Independent Monitoring

The Independent Monitoring Working Group developed the following working definition of independent monitoring: "An effective process of direct observation and information-gathering by credible and respected institutions and individuals to ensure compliance with corporate codes of conduct and applicable laws to prevent violations, process grievances, and promote humane, harmonious and productive workplace conditions."

The IMWG set the following goals for independent monitoring at Mandarin: detect violations of the Gap's Code of Vendor Conduct and applicable law; promote practices leading to the suppliers' compliance with the Gap's code and applicable local law; deter abuses against workers; provide a safe, fair, credible, and efficient mechanism for dispute resolution; foster a productive, humane work environment; and promote utilization of existing processes within the factory to resolve problems as soon as possible.

### Respected Local NGOs Step Forward

The independent monitoring project took a major step forward in February 1996 when four respected institutions agreed to form the Independent

Monitoring Group of El Salvador (IMGES). The monitoring group includes representatives of the Secretariat of the Archdiocese of San Salvador; Tutela Legal, the Human Rights Office of the Archdiocese of San Salvador; The Human Rights Institute of University of Central America (a Jesuit institution); and Center for Labor Studies, a labor research organization. These institutions are widely respected in Salvadoran society because each has a proven track record on the promotion and protection of human rights, familiarity with the labor situation in El Salvador, and all are working to create a society where conflicts are resolved nonviolently.

On March 22, 1996, a historic meeting took place with the Independent Monitoring Group of El Salvador, managers and current workers at Mandarin, and former union leaders (of Sindicato de Empresa des Trabajores Mandarin International—SETMI) where a resolution was signed pledging each party to focus on worker-management relations and create "a productive, stable and successful business at Mandarin." The resolution committed the signers to the following:

1.  That the six former SETMI union leaders be the first employees to be hired by Mandarin International when the factory receives sufficient orders to do so.
2.  When the necessity to hire more people comes about with sufficient new orders, the first employees to be hired will come from a list of 250–400 workers who lost their jobs at Mandarin International during 1995 and 1996.
3.  A Team of Independent Monitors will be formed to ensure that the parties conform first to the Salvadorean Laws and second to Gap's code of conduct.

This resolution of the conflicts at Mandarin is unprecedented. Mandarin pledged to rehire former union leaders. The typical pattern facing workers who attempt to organize is firing and "blacklisting," making it difficult for them to find work in the industry. Mandarin pledged to work with IMGES to monitor the factory's operations, giving total access by nongovernmental organizations to the plant. Gap and Mandarin became the first company and supplier to agree to independent monitoring.

### Monitoring Progress Report

The Independent Monitoring Group of El Salvador issued a public report on its work in April 1997, one year after the monitoring project began. The monitoring group stated that the March 22 resolution's three points had been largely fulfilled. After sufficient orders returned to Mandarin, some former

SETMI leaders who wanted to return to the factory were rehired in October 1996, and in 1997 additional workers were rehired from a list developed for recalls. IMGES continues to monitor the hiring of new workers, based on the second number in the agreement.

IMGES has been a major influence is resolving disputes arising at Mandarin, enabling the reintegration of former SETMI members back into the workforce in a way that has mitigated against renewed conflicts. IMGES has developed a number of methods to monitor the March 22 agreement and Mandarin's compliance with the Gap's code. They include: "bilateral meetings with the management of Mandarin International to discuss compliance with the resolution and the solution to the problems that were being detected; meetings with leaders of ATEMISA (company-sponsored association of workers) and former leaders of SETMI; meetings/assemblies with all of the Mandarin personnel; field visits to verify the intensity of the work being done and currently existing working conditions at the factory; meetings and conference calls with the Independent Monitoring Working Group and with representatives of the Gap, and responding to people who approach the IMGES with complaints about conditions at Mandarin, including follow-up on complaints which are received."[7]

IMGES has conducted several systematic worker surveys and found that there have been no reported cases of abuse or mistreatment once the monitoring system was put in place, and that the physical facilities were clean and spacious, although there was a need expressed for better ventilation. Women workers did report their opposition to pregnancy testing as a basic prerequisite for obtaining work. IMGES raised this issue with Mandarin management and Mandarin took the unprecedented step of eliminating the pregnancy testing requirement, the first to do so in the maquiladora sector in El Salvador. IMGES also found that while it is true that the company did not formally place obstacles to the freedom to organize, there is a climate of mistrust on this issue.

IMGES has been successful in addressing complaints, solving problems, and helping to create a humane and productive workplace at Mandarin. What was once a conflict-ridden factory with workers facing arbitrary military-style discipline, labor abuses, and firings of workers that was costly to the company is now a place where worker rights are respected, productivity is high, and practices are carefully monitored by Gap and IMGES. In the spring of 1997, Mandarin advertised in newspapers to identify and notify former workers to return to work. "It is worth noting," states the IMGES Report, "that several of the people who approached the factory to express their interest in returning were working in other factories located in the same free trade zone. According to them, the treatment and working conditions at Mandarin are now better than what they have in other neighboring factories. . . . Mandarin has come to be an attractive place for workers due to clear improvements in working conditions, which shows the advances which have been achieved."[8]

This major advance in supplier monitoring and corporate accountability resulted from the Gap's participation in the process and its ability to encourage Mandarin management to improve its worker standards, and from IMGES's persistence in responding thoroughly to worker complaints, resolving conflicts, and proposing doable solutions to improve working conditions. Now that Mandarin is up and running, IMGES will be able to focus more of its energies on regular monitoring of the workplace rather than on crisis management and dispute resolution. IMGES plans to monitor the supplier facilities of other companies, bringing their experience and expertise to bear on the maquiladora sector in El Salvador.

### Learning from IMGES's Experience

The Independent Monitoring Group of El Salvador provides credibility to the Gap's code of conduct (1) because it is rooted in the communities where the factories are located; they work and live and are accountable to those communities, not to the company, and (2) because IMGES is made up of respected nongovernmental organizations that have unique skills in human rights, labor rights, and a demonstrated knowledge of the local social, cultural, legal context, and the trust of workers. If a company gives itself good marks on the code compliance report card, there is room for questioning its validity. If a company gets good marks from a monitoring group made up of respected local religious and human rights groups and/or individuals, the rating is more credible to consumers, shareholders, human rights, labor, and community groups. It is simply more believable coming from a source independent of the company's control.

### Independent Monitoring, The Heart of the Debate

Human rights and religious groups have pressed companies to include independent monitoring of their codes of conduct as a crucial part of making codes credible. Given reports of severe abuses of supplier factories around the world, in 1997 ICCR members filed shareholder resolutions with Disney, Nike, and Wal-Mart, calling on these companies to establish independent monitoring programs in conjunction with local respected religious and human rights groups in the countries where they contract their work. Several years ago, independent monitoring was a new and controversial concept. Today, independent monitoring, though still controversial, is at the heart of the debate concerning how to identify labor abuses and eliminate sweatshop conditions at home and abroad.

### Who Are the Independent Monitors?

Today, there is a struggle going on over the definition of independent monitoring and who can qualify as an independent monitor. The pressure created by nongovernmental organizations for companies to adopt independent monitoring has created a new industry. Accounting, auditing, and consulting firms, such as Coopers & Lybrand, Ernst and Young, KPMG Peat Marwick, and Price Waterhouse have moved into the independent monitoring field and developed social audit instruments to measure compliance with company codes of conduct. These firms, many with long experience in financial auditing, have little, if any, experience auditing labor rights standards. Yet, big auditing firms are offering their services to companies as "independent monitors" of their codes of conduct, codes which are based not only on international labor standards that require an extensive knowledge of international labor rights and conventions but also on an understanding and ability to gain reliable information about local labor conditions.

The big accounting firms have considerable appeal to companies as their monitors. They have the financial resources to design and implement a monitoring program with global reach; they can hire human rights and labor rights experts to do the monitoring; and they are likely to be perceived as "easy to work with" by companies who have dealt with them as financial auditors in the past and see them as sharing similar values and work styles.

These perceived advantages to the companies may well become disadvantages in the company's quest to establish credible independent monitoring for their codes of conduct. Large accounting and consulting firms are too close to the company and too far from the local workers in plants in El Salvador, Indonesia, or China where labor violations occur. These firms are well suited to look at pages of figures, analyze data, and check for quantifiable code violations. They are ill suited for the kinds of on-the-ground detection systems needed to uncover violations of worker rights. Serious violations of freedom of association and common forms of harassment of workers often go undetected by auditors who come into an area, visit a plant for a short period, then leave. Independent monitors made up of local, respected nongovernmental groups—rooted in local communities and having the trust of employees—are better qualified to detect the essential, but less easily observed, elements in the workplace which relate to human respect, nondiscrimination, the right to freely associate and to work in a safe environment free from fear. Local human rights and religious groups know the local social and cultural context, speak the local language(s), are likely to have the trust of local workers, and are ultimately accountable to their community, not the company. Because of this relationship of accountability, local NGO groups provide a valuable asset to companies and contractors precisely because they are not beholden to the company, have the trust of workers, and have a credibility which can carry weight with consumers, investors, labor, human rights groups, and the public.

The problem of outside monitors was highlighted in a *New York Times* editorial:

> The sneaker manufacturer Nike recently sent a civil rights leader and former United Nations representative, Andrew Young, to tour some of its factories in Asia. Mr. Young surely had the best of intentions, but his report, which concluded that Nike had done "good job," revealed the problems with this kind of monitoring. His factory visits were mainly scheduled in advance and done with Nike's own translators. The better way is local, truly independent monitors who speak the language, can make unannounced visits and enjoy the trust of a largely young, female, vulnerable work force.[9]

### Independent Monitoring and the Apparel Industry Partnership

On April 14, 1997, the White House Apparel Industry Partnership—a unique task force of apparel and footwear companies and nongovernmental organizations, including the Interfaith Center on Corporate Responsibility—announced a step in the struggle to end sweatshop conditions in apparel industry factories. The partnership includes eight companies (Liz Claiborne, L. L. Bean, Nicole Miller, Nike, Patagonia, Phillips-Van Heusen, Reebok, and Tweeds) and Business for Social Responsibility; Interfaith Center on Corporate Responsibility; International Labor Rights Fund; Kathie Lee Gifford; Lawyers Committee for Human Rights; National Consumers League; Retail, Wholesale and Department Store Union; AFL-CIO; CPC; Robert F. Kennedy Memorial Center for Human Rights; and Union of Needletrades, Industrial and Textile Employees. The partnership issued a Workplace Code of Conduct and Principles of Monitoring for the apparel industry.

The White House Apparel Industry Partnership (referred to in the press as the Presidential Anti-Sweatshop Task Force) was formed in August 1996 largely because of former Department of Labor Secretary Robert Reich's leadership on the sweatshop issue. President Clinton appointed the task force and gave it a two-pronged mandate: "To ensure that the products companies make and sell are manufactured under decent and humane working conditions, and to develop options to inform consumers that the products they buy are not produced under exploitative conditions."

The first step was to establish the Workplace Code of Conduct and Principles of Monitoring. In receiving the Apparel Industry Partnership's (AIP) report in April 1997, President Clinton said, "It is not enough to establish tough rules. We must ensure that they are enforced, and that American consumers know they are being followed. That is why the apparel industry is forming a special association to make sure companies and contractors live up to the Code of Conduct, using independent monitors." Now, the second, much harder task is to develop monitoring systems that ensure the Code of Conduct is applied.

The AIP worked on the design of a "Fair Labor Association," which would (among a number of tasks) oversee the certification and supervision of independent monitors of the Workplace Code of Conduct. The AIP had serious, often heated, discussions about independent monitoring: who will do it and how will it be administered. Companies on the task force tend to prefer the use of auditing firms as their "independent monitors." The AIP's Principles of Monitoring is a compromise agreement on independent monitoring. Local nongovernmental organizations themselves can be the independent monitors of plants in their area, verifying that the workplace standards are indeed being followed. A participating company, however, could choose its independent monitor from a list of organizations or firms certified by the association. Auditing firms could qualify as independent monitors as long as they follow the obligations established by the agreement, including involvement of local NGOs in the actual monitoring of workplace standards.

What powers and functions the association will have are currently being discussed. Questions being addressed include: Who hires and pays for the independent monitors—the company or the association? Are the independent monitors accountable to the association, the company, or both? Are the reports of the monitors made available to the public? Whatever is included in the final agreement of the presidential antisweatshop task force, the association needs to effectively oversee independent monitors in order to provide credible information to consumers and the public as to which companies are seriously addressing the problems in the industry and which are not.

### Building Public Trust

Independent local NGO monitors are indispensable to the task of building public trust and credibility in the process of eliminating abusive labor conditions in the apparel industry. The key to establishing public trust is independence. Consumers and other stakeholders want information on labor practices from sources independent of the company. Because local NGOs stand outside of the company's sphere of control and are likely to have the trust of workers, their participation in monitoring plants will provide greater assurance that the Workplace Code of Conduct is indeed being applied and standards are improving. The experience of the Independent Monitoring Group in El Salvador can be drawn on to create effective monitoring programs in other locations.

### Emergence of New Independent Monitoring Projects

Already there are independent monitoring projects emerging in various parts of the world. A new independent monitoring project has begun in Guatemala. A number of religious, human rights, and labor rights groups have formed the Commission for the Independent Verification of Codes of Conduct. The group includes local institutions—the Pastoral Social Department of the Catholic Archdiocese, the Latin American Evangelical Center for Pastoral Studies (a Protestant organization), and the Center for Human Rights Legal Action—and individuals with expertise in labor law, development, child labor, sociology, and anthropology. This newly formed commission is negotiating with Liz Claiborne to begin monitoring two or three of its supplier plants, eventually to expand to cover all eight of its contractors' factories in Guatemala. Liz Claiborne has updated its code of conduct, learned from its experience, and has taken leadership in the AIP. The commission is also discussing with Starbucks Coffee (the first company to draft a code of conduct in agriculture) the possibility of monitoring its coffee suppliers.

Levi-Strauss is exploring the possibility of initiating an independent monitoring pilot project in a small number of locations. Other companies are likely to join the Gap and Liz Claiborne in working with NGOs to form on-going independent monitoring projects with respected religious and human rights groups.

### Challenges Facing NGOs

In order for nongovernmental religious, labor, and human rights organizations to take on the task of monitoring codes of conduct, extensive planning and coordination needs to take place within the NGO community. Not all NGOs are qualified to monitor. Many have little or no expertise and experience in the areas of labor and human rights. Not all have the respect and credibility within a broad sector of the community. The Gap's experience with the Independent Monitoring Group of El Salvador suggests that, to succeed, independent monitoring groups should consider two essential aspects:

1.  Monitoring teams should be composed of institutions and individuals with a track record based on the investigation of human rights and labor rights abuses and protection of basic human rights.
2.  Monitoring teams should seek to include institutions representing important sectors of the local community such as, religious, human rights, and labor rights organizations.

Monitoring teams made up of experienced, respected nongovernmental organizations from key sectors can significantly help monitor company codes of conduct, detect areas of noncompliance, and suggest remedial action. The prospect of local NGOs participating in independent monitoring projects will require serious discussions between local NGO groups leading to the decision to use valuable resources and time to undertake this endeavor, and the formation of local committees to handle the task.

In countries like China where nongovernmental organizations are almost nonexistent, it will be important (until local NGOs develop) to rely on nongovernmental organizations removed from local communities where supplier plants are located. Groups could include the Asia Monitor Resource Centre based in Hong Kong and the Hong Kong Christian Industrial Committee. Both organizations have issued reports on labor conditions based on the survey of workers on site in factories producing for U.S. companies. A nonprofit organization in the U.S., Verite, also has done surveys in China, based on worker interviews done by Chinese-speaking staff.

### Challenges Facing Companies

Difficult challenges face companies in accepting independent monitoring of their codes of conduct. Here are a few areas that will require flexibility and change if independent monitoring will succeed:

1.  Companies need to give up some degree of control. This is the single, most difficult challenge for companies who want to control the monitoring. By definition, independent monitors are outside the control of the company, outside of the company's chain of command, and in a position to make independent judgments on code of conduct compliance. This independence initially makes many companies hesitant about using them. However, in a long-term perspective, companies will need to understand

this distance as an asset in providing credibility and accurate detection of code violations.

2. Companies need to find effective ways to encourage their suppliers to co-operate with independent monitors made up of local NGOs. It took concerted attention and action on the part of the Gap to get the cooperation of Mandarin management. Gap pressure is what finally convinced Mandarin management that the Independent Monitoring Group of El Salvador was an essential resource in the establishment of labor peace and a productive, harmonious workplace.

3. Companies need to learn how to relate to nongovernmental organizations as valued partners and to recognize the expertise they have to offer in resolving abusive labor conditions that damage the company's reputation.

### Potential to Make a Difference

Codes of conduct can raise labor standards in the thousands of factories around the world manufacturing goods for U.S. companies. Independent monitoring that involves respected local NGOs has tremendous potential in making codes credible and convincing consumers that the products they purchase are made under fair labor conditions. Independent monitoring is no replacement for independent local unions, controlled by workers, that can address workplace violations in a systematic and effective way on the shop floor. Independent monitoring can provide another level of accountability crucial to the companies themselves as well as to workers and their communities. The next few years will be rocky as companies learn to work with NGOs and NGOs learn more about business operations from companies. As is always the case in pioneering movements, there will be false starts, setbacks, and a variety of competing monitoring models will emerge that try to address intolerable working conditions. In the process effective codes and monitoring systems can be established that keep in the forefront the primary concern of this project, that is, the persons who work in factories in this country and around the world deserve to be paid fairly and treated with dignity and respect. That is the final measure of the worth of codes of conduct.

### Notes

1. *Criteria For Sustainable Development Management*, United Nations Center on Transnational Corporations, New York, 1991.

2. James Michael Zimmerman, *Extraterritorial Employment Standards of the United States: The Regulation of the Overseas Workplace*, New York: Quorum, Books, 1992.

3. Interfaith Center on Corporate Responsibility et al., "Principles for Global Corporate Responsibility: Benchmark for Measuring Business Performance," *The Corporate Examiner*, vol. 24, no 2–4, Sept. 1, 1995.

4. "U.S. Retailers Put Pressure on Foreign Factories," *USA Today*, September 4, 1996.

5. Ruth Rosenbaum, *In Whose Interest? Using the Purchasing Power Index to Analyze Plans, Programs and Policies of Industrialization and Development in Haiti*, January 1996.

6. U.S. Department of Labor Study, September, 1996.

7. "First Public Report of the Independent Monitoring Group of El Salvador," 11 April 1997: 2.

8. IMGES Report, 11 April 1997: 6.

9. Editorial, "Watching the Sweatshops," *New York Times*, August 20, 1997.

## PART VI

# An Experiment

*The White House Apparel Industry
Partnership Workplace
Code of Conduct and
Principles of Monitoring*

# 15

# The Apparel Industry
# Code of Conduct

## A Consumer Perspective
## on Social Responsibility

LINDA F. GOLODNER

Long before consumers united for product, food, and drug safety and myriad other issues with direct consumer impact, they cast their influence unselfishly to improve conditions for the workers who produced the nation's goods.

The 1890s were a time when industrialization in the United States burgeoned, when workers eked out an existence on starvation wages. Corporations—replacing family firms, partnerships, and proprietorships—showed little interest in those they employed. Cheap labor made higher profits, and profit was the name of the game.

### Consumers Movement Founded on Social Responsibility

The consumers movement was founded on the belief that the customer who bought sweatshop goods was as much the employer of sweated labor as the boss of the shop. Consumers leagues became the central force in the social justice movement. In 1891, Josephine Shaw Lowell, founder of the New York City Consumers League, stated the challenge well.

> It is the duty of consumers to find out under what conditions the articles they purchase are produced and distributed and to insist that these conditions shall be wholesome and consistent with a respectable existence on the part of the workers.

For ninety-eight years, the National Consumers League has represented consumers who are concerned about the conditions under which products are manufactured. To illustrate the philosophy, an early league motto was the following: *To live means to buy, to buy means to have power, to have power means to have duties.*

In July 1940, Mary Dublin described the League's work as

> an expression of the conviction that consumers have a far-reaching responsibility to use their buying power and their power as citizens to advance the general welfare of the community. Substandard wages and depressed industrial conditions impose a burden not on labor alone but on consumers as well. What is not paid in wages, the community is called upon to pay in relief; in wage subsidies; in contributions to meet the cost of illness, dependency, delinquency, and numerous other social ills which these conditions produce.

Since those early years, the consumers movement has blossomed into many areas of interest—from food/product standards and quality to consumer rights to consumer protection and more. New consumer organizations have expanded the scope and definition of consumer. But the consumers movement's history and mission (for some like the National Consumers League) reflect the continuing commitment and sense of responsibility for the conditions under which products are produced and for the decisions consumers make in the marketplace.

> Fifty years ago today a brilliant, though basically simple, idea was born. This was that the people who buy goods in stores could have a say as to the conditions under which those goods were produced. By their economic and political pressure they could fight child labor, they could protect women against exploitation, they could make the ideal of the minimum wage a living fact.[1]

Consumer pressure significantly influenced the passage in the U.S. of child labor laws, minimum wage, and overtime compensation, as well as shorter workdays and workweeks. Such efforts culminated in the 1938 Fair Labor Standards Act. The league's nearly one hundred years of experience in fighting sweatshops and child labor underscores some basic truths, which are applicable today.

    1. Consumers should not expect a problem to be solved just because a law has been passed. When various industries, responding to the National Industrial Recovery Act of 1933 established codes prescribing maximum hours, minimum wages, collective bargaining, and abolition of child labor, the National Consumers League hoped its major work was accomplished. When the codes went into effect, the league kept in close touch with workers to find out

how they were affected. It was soon apparent that in industries where unions were strong, workers benefited through higher wages and shorter hours. But in unorganized industries, while there was improvement in hours and wages, unscrupulous employers used every possible device to rob workers of what was due them legally. (On May 27, 1935, the U.S. Supreme Court declared the NIRA unconstitutional.)

2. Consumers want an uncomplicated, easy means to identify products made under decent conditions. As consumer demand increased for such products during the early 1900s, the league developed and oversaw the use of the White Label. The label was attached to women's and children's stitched cotton underwear if the factory guaranteed that it obeyed all factory laws, made all goods on the premises, required no overtime work, and employed no children under age sixteen. Representatives of the league inspected factories to assure compliance. Originating in New York City, use of the label spread to thirteen states. In 1918, the league discontinued the label as union leaders began developing labels that guaranteed labor standards enforcement. Consumers see labels as an easy point-of-purchase tool to use in the marketplace.

3. Consistency and integrity of the message or claim is the key to consumer understanding and confidence. This can be seen through numerous consumer disclosure and labeling initiatives from past and recent years. A contemporary example is the consumer confusion and misinformation over the inconsistent use of words like "low fat," "fat-free," "less fat," and others, which were not governed by standardized definitions and usage. In the presence of inconsistency in message or claim, the integrity of the claim is lost upon the consumer and confusion among the public is likely to result.

4. Consumers expect transparency in order to verify corporate responsibility. Consumer confidence in the integrity of the company's claim is tied to the vigilant oversight of working conditions. Transparency must be through external, independent monitors from the nongovernmental and nonindustry communities.

## Global Expansion of Social Responsibility: Consumers Avoiding Personal Collusion in Repression

The concluding years of the twentieth century have witnessed the expansion of the global marketplace and the propelling of companies to a transnational playing field. The consumers movement has responded with increased action and awareness outside of its own national borders to consider social responsibility on a global level.

Consumers who are educated about exploitative working conditions and feel a sense of responsibility to act upon this knowledge find frustration in the marketplace. As a reaction to a lack of information and labels to help the conscientious consumer identify products made under decent conditions, many consumers are taking personal action, including, even, personal boycotts of certain products, companies, and countries.

Some detractors claim that personal boycotts are doomed to failure through lack of massive consumer participation. The facts, however, suggest that consumers choose a personal boycott as a means of expression because they find a company's, industry's, or nation's policies or behavior morally objectionable. In other words, their personal action is based on their commitment to not be an accomplice, even with a few dollars, in support of offensive policies. Thus it is not the consumer's worry whether their action will similarly motivate other consumers, but it justly can be the worry of the offending company, industry, or country.

According to the 1997 Human Rights Watch survey, "Because the goods purchased in one country may be produced by victims of repression in another, the very act of consumption can be seen as complicity in that repression." The expansion of the global economy is creating "new and immediate connections among distant people," and is thereby spawning "a surprising new source of support for the human-rights cause." To avoid personal complicity, many consumers "are insisting on guarantees that they are not buying the products of abusive labor conditions."

### Consumer Activism: Examples of Power

Over the years, consumer activism has influenced many industries. The results have been new product offerings, new labels, and new packaging. For example, the automobile industry was disinterested, often hostile, to providing airbags, antilock brakes, and other safety features until consumer demand necessitated their change of heart.

Similarly, before the early 1990s, who had ever heard of "environmental-friendly" labeling? Or, "not tested on animal" labeling? These were both an often-reluctant industry response to consumer demand.

And the list goes on. Consumer pressure for more healthy alternatives in fast food restaurants has culminated in consumers being able to go into any McDonald's today and get a salad. Consumers wanted more nutrition information on packaged foods—especially detailed fat and saturated fat information—and they got it.

These examples reinforce the tremendous power that consumers have over industry. The same influence has been and can continue to provide improvements in social issues such as child labor and sweatshop exploitation.

Karl E. Meyer raised an interesting analogy to today's consumer efforts at social responsibility.

> As Hong Kong reverted to China on July 1, 1997, we were reminded of a bit of history known as the Opium War between Britain and China from 1839 to 1842. Western protests against the war mark it as the beginning of a concern with international human rights. Along with the slave trade, the traffic in opium was the dirty underside of an evolving global trading economy.
>
> In America as in Europe, pretty much everything was deemed fair in the pursuit of profits. In 1839, the Emperor of China responded to the epidemic addiction to opium in his country by naming an Imperial Commissioner to end the trade, which in a large part was conducted by American companies, which brought opium from India to China through Turkey. Outrage was expressed by British and American press and the pulpit, forcing the businesses to pull out of the opium trade.
>
> We no longer believe that anything goes in the global marketplace, regardless of social consequences. It is precisely this conviction that underlies efforts to attach human rights conditions to trading relations—to temper the amorality of the market.[2]

## Industry Codes of Conduct: Evolution, Reality, and Shortcomings

Media and consumer outrage over child labor and sweatshops spurred many companies to initial action within the last decade. In the early 1990s, industry leaders who developed corporate codes of conduct (primarily targeting their overseas contractors) were Levi Strauss, Reebok, and Liz Claiborne. Other companies followed, each emphasizing its own list of abusive practices that it would not tolerate.

On several levels, the company codes of conduct proved problematic. They fell short of their intentions, and thus lost their credibility among consumers.

- *Variation between company codes and standards bred confusion:* Using child labor as an example, as it is one of the issues most commonly addressed in codes of conduct, compare these differing definitions and perceptions of child labor:
  — Levi Strauss says child labor is not acceptable and defines a "child" as a person under the age of fourteen or who is under the compulsory schooling age.

—Wal-Mart will not accept the use of child labor in the manufacture of goods that it sells. Suppliers/subcontractors must not recruit persons under the age of fifteen, or below the compulsory schooling age. If national legislation includes higher criteria, these must be applied.

—JC Penney will not allow the importation into the U.S. of merchandise manufactured by illegal child labor.

—The Gap states that no person under the age of fourteen may be allowed to work in a factory that produces Gap goods and that vendors must comply with local child labor laws.

—The FIFA (soccer ball governing body) code refers to child labor in the terms of ILO Convention 138 (i.e., children under fifteen years of age, as well as provisions for younger children in certain countries).

- *In word only, not in deed:* Despite the introduction of codes of conduct, company implementation has been ill conceived and ill executed. Media reports, worker complaints, and persistent consumer concerns have underscored the ineffectiveness of the company-monitored codes of conduct. It has become evident that words on paper and even the best-intentioned internal monitoring is unreliable and inadequate.

- *Lack of transparency:* Without assurances from independent monitors and publicly available reports, consumers have little guarantee that company codes of conduct are being meaningfully implemented and overseen.

### The Apparel Industry Code of Conduct
### An Overview of One Global Problem Addressed: Child Labor

Child labor exploitation is a global issue, with problems evident in over two-thirds of all nations. According to a 1997 report by the International Labor Organization, more than 250 million children between the ages of five and fourteen are forced to work in one hundred countries, most performing dangerous tasks. Ninety-five percent of all child workers live in developing countries. In some regions, as many as 25 percent of children between the ages of ten and fourteen are estimated to be working. The Department of State's 1991 and 1992 Human Rights Reports and a 1992 ILO report attest to the growing numbers of children in servitude and their worsening conditions of work.

The problem is growing along with the expansion of the global marketplace. Child labor is cheap labor. Children are targeted for nonskilled, labor-intensive work. Because children are docile and easily controlled, employers have no fear of them demanding rights or organizing. Child employment instead of adult employment creates a climate where many children support their unemployed or underemployed parents, and the entire family and their future families remain in poverty, ignorance, and exploitation.

Child labor flourishes under many conditions: cultural traditions; prejudice and discrimination based on gender, ethnic, religious, or racial issues; unavailability of educational and other alternatives for working children; and no or weak enforcement of compulsory education and child labor laws. Globalization is strengthening child labor through providing ready access to areas of cheap labor that are rife with the above-described conditions. Child labor increasingly offers an attractive incentive to keep labor costs down in a highly competitive global market.

Many U.S. companies have included child labor in their codes of conduct, due to persistent evidence of child exploitation in the industry. Although no definitive figures are available on the number of children working in the garment industry, the U.S. Department of Labor's Child Labor Study (1994) identified children working in the garment industry in most of the countries they reviewed. A direct connection was evident between these countries' exports and the United States, the world's largest importer of garments from 168 countries. "Child labor" does not refer to children working on the family farm or in the family business. It refers to employment that prevents school attendance, and which is often performed under conditions that are hazardous or harmful to children.

## Apparel Industry Code of Conduct

In 1996, President Clinton convened a meeting at the White House, inviting apparel industry leaders, unions, and nongovernmental organizations to form a task force on sweatshops. The president charged the group to determine appropriate steps for the industry to take "to ensure that the products they make and sell are manufactured under decent and humane working conditions." He also charged the group to "develop options to inform consumers that the products they buy are not produced under those exploitative conditions."

The Apparel Industry Partnership's negotiations and first report revolved around the development of an industry standard code of conduct. The code blends elements of existing corporate codes into a set of standards, which may be adopted by the apparel industry as a whole. Definitions of each prohibition related to child labor, maximum workweeks, harassment and abuse, forced labor, and other issues, were hammered out. Integral to the code is definitive monitoring, including both internal and external (i.e., independent) evaluations of compliance.

The partnership is working on forming a permanent association that will provide membership to companies that adopt the code of conduct, as well as setting the parameters of monitoring. It will also standardize and control the use of any symbol, label, or other mechanism employed to provide information to the consumer about decent working conditions.

To ensure consumer confidence and the integrity of the governing association, several elements must be maintained in this initiative:

- Consumers want a "sweatshop-free," "good labor practices," or "member of" claim that applies to both domestic and international production. Consumers are not going to react favorably to a company that is applauded for a sweatshop-free stand in the U.S. while doing business overseas with sweatshops.
- Consumers want a claim that is credible. Legitimate external, independent monitoring is essential for consumers to have confidence in any company claim.
- Consumers want the industry to work with their subcontractors who are found to be out of compliance with the code of conduct to assure that the problems are solved and restitution to the workers is made. Canceling contracts does not help workers.
- Easy consumer access to information to enable ethical decision-making, preferably at point of purchase.
- Full disclosure of manufacturers' performance in relation to the code of conduct.

### Labels: Easy Access to Information for Consumers

Consumers have expanding choices in the global marketplace. Savvy shoppers ask questions and the answers often are the foundation for their purchasing decisions. Many consumers want to know what they are getting—and what they are supporting—when they buy.

The most obvious response of savvy shoppers is their burgeoning demand for labels. Consumers wanted more nutrition labeling on food and got it. The ever-evident recycling symbol was a response to consumer concerns about environmental issues. Some consumers wanted dolphin-safe tuna or products not tested on animals, and the affected industries scrambled to provide assurances to consumers.

In the last few years, there has been a resurgence in interest for a label that identifies decent labor conditions. "Country of origin" and "Made in USA" labeling is an important beginning point. But such labels do not provide the complete story behind the labor. Consumers want information, guarantees, and a choice in products made under decent conditions.

Whether to educate consumers about nutrition, environmental impact, product testing, or labor conditions, consumers expect labels to be meaningful and honest. A meaningful label for products made under decent labor conditions must delineate precisely what is meant and met by the use of the label. Consumers expect an honest label, where the veracity of the claim is assured through independent evaluation and oversight of the company or industry using the label.

One of the most credible labeling programs is RUGMARK. This trail-blazing initiative certifies carpet manufacturers who meet stringent requirements to assure that no child labor is used in handmade carpets from India and Nepal. Consumer confidence in the label is gained through systematic, independent monitoring and unannounced inspections of manufacturers by nonindustry RUGMARK representatives. There are more than a thousand children in RUGMARK-supported schools in India and Nepal. RUGMARK carpets represent nearly 15 percent of all Indian production and nearly 70 percent of Nepalese production. Pakistan is expected to form a RUGMARK program.

### Other Consumer Efforts

An informed, empowered, and energized consumer movement is responsible for much of the progress against sweatshops and child labor abuses. Last January, the National Consumers League and UNITE launched a Stop Sweatshop campaign, targeting both domestic and international sweatshops. The campaign's combined outreach represents over fifty million consumers. One goal of the Stop Sweatshops campaign is to equip consumers with the tools they need to send a "No Sweatshop" message to retailers and manufacturers.

"No Sweatshop" has gained new energy as public officials, city councils, and united consumers force the issue into the limelight in their hometown. Recognizing the advantages of citizen action and the greater responsiveness of local government, a new pressure point has been added to end sweatshop abuses. "If we can envision ourselves as a community of consumers rather than autonomous shoppers," says the Clean Clothes Campaign, "some remarkable things can happen."

### Bangor's Clean Clothes Campaign

A city of nearly thirty-one thousand residents, Bangor, Maine, is working toward "sweatshop free" clothing within its city limits. Led by Peace through Inter-American Community Action, the Clean Clothes Campaign wants the city of Bangor to support a simple principle: Clothes sold in our community should not be supplied by manufacturers who violate established international standards regarding forced labor, child labor, poverty wages, and decent working conditions. They accomplished this in 1997 by banning the sale in Bangor of any item of clothing produced in violation of these most basic standards of ethical practice.

The campaign will next build upon the community consensus against sweatshops with a retailer campaign. Retailers will be pressed to take a pledge of corporate and social accountability to the Bangor community. The Clean Clothes Campaign insists that "ordinary people should have something to say about the behavior of businesses, large or small, that operate in our community. We would never permit local vendors to sell us rotten meat, or stolen property, or illicit drugs because such behavior offends our community values. Likewise, we do not condone international corporations supplying our retailers with items made under conditions that equally offend our sense of decency."

### "Foul Ball" Spurs Los Angeles

The City Council of Los Angeles approved a resolution in December 1996 requiring the city to only purchase sporting goods that have been certified by a reputable independent organization as having been manufactured without the illegal use of child labor. The resolution has received tremendous support from youth soccer leagues, parents, and schools. The effort was a response to the Foul Ball Campaign to end the exploitation of children in the manufacture of sports equipment. It has become a model resolution for other cities.

### Innovative Law in North Olmsted, Ohio

In February 1996, the North Olmsted City Council approved an ordinance forbidding the purchase, rent, or lease of goods which have been manufactured under sweatshop conditions. The law refers to the following when determining sweatshop conditions: child labor, forced labor, wages and benefits, hours of work, worker rights, and health and safety. A Cleveland suburb with a population of thirty-five thousand, North Olmsted's purchasing amounts to approximately $150,000 per year on items commonly produced in sweatshops.

Suppliers must sign a new clause on all contracts and purchase requisitions stating that their products are not made in sweatshops. If the city discovers a supplier does sell sweatshop products, the contract will be canceled or other appropriate action taken.

Twelve other cities in Ohio, including Cleveland and Dayton, have passed the same resolution. In Pennsylvania, Allentown has passed a law and Pittsburgh and Philadelphia are pending. Cities elsewhere that have the same law are San Francisco and Lansing, Michigan. The North Olmsted model was to be presented as a resolution urging all cities to adopt this policy at the annual U.S. Conference of Mayors meeting in January 1998.

### A Look Ahead

The FY 1998 Treasury-Postal Appropriations, passed in the U.S. Congress, contains a clarification of the Tariff Act of 1930. The law bans the import of items manufactured by "prison," "forced," or "indentured" labor. Congress has clarified in the appropriations legislation that this prohibition includes forced and indentured child labor, as well as bonded child labor.

The clarifying language and subsequent enforcement by U.S. Customs is expected to affect nearly $100 million of imports. The effect it will have on the garment industry—and other industries—remains to be seen. There is not doubt, however, that this clarification poses a significant first step in closing down the U.S. market to products made through child labor exploitation.

Meanwhile, two other bills have been introduced in Congress related to imports of products made by children. The Child Labor Free Consumer Information Act of 1997 (H.R. 1301 and S. 554) establishes a *voluntary* labeling system for wearing apparel and sporting goods made without child labor. The Child Labor Deterrence Act (H.R. 1328 and S. 332) would prohibit the importation of manufactured and mined goods into the United States that are produced by children under the age of fifteen.

### Conclusion

The heart and soul of the consumers movement is social responsibility. Sweatshops and child labor are not new concerns or a new battle for consumers. Our expectations in company conduct are reasonable and attainable, despite the complexities of global sourcing. And, like our predecessors, we will not give up the fight until consumers—at a minimum—are given a clear and credible choice in the marketplace for products made under decent conditions. No excuses accepted.

## Notes

1. Editorial excerpt on the NCL from the *New York Times,* December 9, 1949.
2. Editorial Notebook, *New York Times,* June 28, 1997.

# 16

# Voting with Their Pocketbooks

## The Strengths and Limits of Consumer-Driven Codes of Conduct

### KEVIN J. SWEENEY

Patagonia, Inc., is a California-based company that designs and distributes high-quality outdoor clothing and gear. Our roots are in the climbing industry: our founder is a blacksmith who forged the first readily available hard-steel pitons for climbers. We've branched out into other sports beyond climbing and alpinism, and we now outfit paddlers, anglers, mountain bikers, surfers, and others. Our climbing roots led us to retain an unrelenting commitment to the highest possible quality. Our clothing is often used in situations where, if the gear fails, the user dies—an incentive for quality, particularly if the designer is the user, as is often the case in our company.

We sell products through our own retail stores, through a mail-order catalog and through more than a thousand specialty outdoor shops. We sell our products on five continents. In our most recent fiscal year, we had sales of approximately $160 million. As a company, we're in very good shape: we have grown when we've wanted to grow and we've consciously slowed our growth when we've wanted to do that, which is more often than not.

While our reputation with our customers is based solidly in a commitment to quality, much of our public reputation is based on how we conduct our business. We have an on-site child care center and innovative family leave policies, including parental leave for new mothers and new fathers. We have a very informal work atmosphere.

Most significant is the company's strong commitment to environmental protection and restoration. We give one percent of sales to environmental groups. We grant leaves of up to two months for employees to work for non-profit environmental organizations while still receiving their full compensation from Patagonia. Our retail stores are used as host sites for numerous environmental events. We make synthetic fleece—Synchilla—from recycled plastic soda bottles. Two years ago, after years of research convinced us of the devastating impact of the synthetic pesticides used to produce conventional cotton, we shifted our entire line of sportswear to organic cotton. We also announced at the time that our shift was permanent, that there was no going back—that if we could not make and sell organic cotton sportswear successfully, we would never make cotton products again.

The fact is, over the years, our focus on environmental issues has been nearly singular. And as a result, we gave little, if any, direct attention to the issues of international human rights. My colleagues at Patagonia are compassionate, humane individuals, and the overwhelming majority of them are well informed on these issues. But as a company, we took no conscious steps in this area.

## Avoiding Sweatshops: A Focus on Quality

That said, we've had no instances whatsoever that would link us in any way to a sweatshop. This, again, was not by design. We had a strong human rights record because of our commitment to quality, which we believe is not something that can be pursued piecemeal. You either believe in quality, or you don't; it shows up everywhere, or it doesn't show up at all. There are important linkages: quality products, quality workplace, quality of life for your employees, even a respect for quality of life on earth. If a company's goal is to make the best products, it must pursue quality everywhere. If the goal is to make the best alpine jackets, as we claim to do, one has no alternative but to source in a high-quality factory using a well-trained and stable workforce.

Quality is best achieved not by focusing on the bottom of the funnel—in a quality control department that searches for defects—but at the top of the funnel where the ingredients are selected. It's about the process of quality. At least twice a year our internal field auditors are at every factory that helps make our gear; at most facilities, it's much closer to once every two months. What they look for is whether or not a company is managing for quality, whether or not the process is one that will naturally lead to a quality product.

So we had avoided human rights abuses not by focusing on them but by committing to quality.

In 1996, however, we added a layer to this process by committing to regular, independent human rights audits of any facility making Patagonia products. The auditors looked to see if the facilities were in compliance with all local laws regarding such issues as wages, age of workers, and hours worked. We did this despite the fact that we had no concerns whatsoever that any of the factories where we did business resembled anything like a sweatshop. We did this because we wanted to have a defense ready should we be surprised by any allegations that we were connected to sweatshops. We know, at some point, that one of our auditors or contract managers could make a mistake. We also know that there are counterfeit Patagonia products being made, and that a reporter or activist finding such products in a sweatshop might not stop to ask us for—or listen to—an explanation. The investment in these audits is, pure and simple, insurance against a public attack on our credibility as a company. They do nothing to eliminate sweatshops because we are dealing with high-quality firms who in fact treat their employees well on a relative scale. They represent, for good or bad, how money often gets spent these days.

We did make one significant change in company policy in 1996 as a response to the public exposure of sweatshop issues. We decided that we would no longer tolerate indirect relationships. In very rare cases, some of our accessories had been produced with the help of an agent, an intermediary business that would find a facility that made the products to our specifications. In 1996, it was one factory making one product, but we terminated that relationship, and committed to the policy of moving forward.

It should be obvious from this introduction that we had not had a great deal of experience, and had shown little leadership, in dealing with sweatshop issues. We also have never considered ourselves part of the fashion industry, or even the conventional clothing industry. Rather, we think of ourselves as making outdoor gear. So we were surprised to be invited to speak at the Fashion Industry Forum, convened at Marymount University in July 1996. And we were even more surprised by the invitation to participate in the White House meeting that led to the formation of the Apparel Industry Partnership (AIP).

### Choosing Involvement: The Apparel Industry Partnership

We were hesitant to participate because it would imply that we presumed to be leaders in this area, when we have no such presumption. We were also, frankly, not excited about having our company name and the term "sweatshop" used in the same media stories, a concern I know other companies felt as well. But we chose to get involved.

We chose to get involved in the issue because we felt, once invited and once very clearly conscious of the problems, it would be wrong to say no. Many organizations, among them the Lawyers Committee for Human Rights and the Interfaith Center for Corporate Responsibility, have helped to expose the inhumane conditions under which clothing is made in far too many countries, including our own. Wages that are far too low, work weeks that are far too long, forced labor—all of these woes are tied to our industry. Perhaps worst of all, ILO estimates suggest that nearly a quarter of a billion children may be working today.

We chose to get involved because of the holistic nature of many global problems—and many potential solutions. More and more, it is becoming clear to activists that the many progressive movements ongoing today are in fact one movement. Some come to it because of a love for nature; others come to it because they see injustice more clearly than others do. They can be seen as different approaches to the same fundamental issue of how we treat the land and each other. The environmental crisis will not be solved without resolving difficult issues of class and economic justice. And issues of economic and social justice are inherently linked to the kind of respect that is required to preserve and protect natural resources.

We chose to get involved because we want high standards. We want credible entities to set standards for competition. We were angered when domestic business groups fought, under the General Agreement on Trade and Tariffs (GATT), an effort by German consumers to set voluntary standards for the manufacture of clothing. We wondered why strong businesses or a strong nation would be afraid of high standards. High standards are a way of rewarding those companies and those countries with smart, dedicated workers and courageous, visionary leaders. We think that's true of Patagonia and we think it's true of the United States. So an effort to raise the standards seemed like a reasonable risk.

That said, it is important to note that setting and meeting high standards, admittedly, may be easier for Patagonia than it is for most other companies. We make high-end products, and our customers have shown a willingness to pay for quality and for values. We also have a unique relationship with our customers, a relationship built on a common appreciation of quality and, increasingly, on a set of shared environmental values. The fact is, our customers trust us already.

The challenge of living up to high standards, and successfully selling the product, is far more difficult for those who make commodity products or clothing and fashion items for which quality expectations are quite low. Adding seventy-five cents to a garment's sewing cost in order to meet a higher ethical standard can, in many cases, add more than two dollars to the retail price. On $20 children's pants, that is no small increase, and it may lead shoppers to look further down the retail rack.

### The Partnership on the Brink of Success

Now, we find ourselves many months after the AIP was founded. We are on the brink of a tremendous success. Human rights organizations, religious partnerships, trade unions and several corporations have signed on to a Workplace Code of Conduct, which would require both internal and external monitoring. The agreement could, if implemented in its current form, take great strides towards eliminating those factories that clearly fit the common description of a sweatshop. The measure would place a cap on the number of work hours each week and provide for mandatory days off. It would ensure that local wage standards are met. It would be a major help in ridding the industry of child labor. It would require the participating companies to internally monitor manufacturing facilities, in addition to engaging outside entities to provide independent monitoring. It would establish an association that could serve as the credible entity that could serve consumers by telling them which companies were manufacturing under the code of conduct and which ones were not. It would give consumers a way of knowing that the clothes they wear were not made by children or by others who were working in sweatshops.

Human rights organizations and others have roundly criticized the agreement. But the agreement, objectively, was historic, and my own view is that it still has a chance to make a difference.

It can make a difference—a positive difference—if the partnership grows beyond its current membership. Currently, there are but a handful of corporations participating. If the group focuses very clearly and exclusively on the goal of eliminating sweatshops, the number of participating companies can grow substantially. Because of the growing number of bankruptcies and consolidations in the retail sector, there is a growing concentration of large corporations at the retail level; the five largest retail companies now account for more than 50 percent of total retail sales in the U.S. This could mean that the partnership may be only five commitments—admittedly not easy ones to gain—from affecting an overwhelming majority of the garments sold in the U.S. With increased visibility, and pressure applied by the participating NGOs, the partnership's allies could focus on each of those major retail chains—one by one—to bring them into the fold. In five years, it is quite possible that nearly every garment sold in a retail chain of any reasonable size would be made under the proposed code of conduct. That would be a great accomplishment.

### Obstacles on the Path to Progress

Despite these prospects for success, however, I am not currently optimistic about the future of the partnership.

I'm not optimistic because this is a very difficult time for public discourse and for any agreement on a public solution. NGOs and others gain media visibility by making negative attacks, and their ability to raise funds is often linked to the perceived depth of their opponent's evil. Demonizing of a perceived adversary has become a useful tool these days, and it's a habit that is not easily lost. And so there are groups who will continue to attack the partnership and its approach, in part because the AIP can legitimately be attacked and in part out of old habits. When a group has made its name attacking Nike, it's difficult for that group to say anything positive about an effort in which Nike is playing a major role. (And I would add that I find the improvements Nike is making in its practices to be impressive.) And many reporters, in the pursuit of the kind of fairness that always allows one positive and one negative quote for each sensitive topic, seek out these groups and legitimize their attacks, occasionally giving disproportionate emphasis. But these continued attacks on AIP member companies continue to stop other companies from joining.

After its initial accomplishments, the group has done very little since the White House press conference announcing agreement on the code of conduct. It is a long time to go without momentum. The different factions inside the group will give different reasons for the lack of movement. Some will say this is because the corporations are not interested in moving beyond the minimum requirements and will not, ultimately, sign onto an operational plan that does not allow them to fully control and substantially limit the external monitoring component. Others say the human rights organizations are focused on how their organizations can make money by providing the external monitoring functions. And others will say it is being dragged out by a split in the NGO community, and that it is impossible to expect a major U.S. trade union to allow the process to succeed, given that this process might ultimately allow an American consumer to feel good about buying a product made overseas. There is still a great deal of the skepticism that reigned when we started this process;

I'm hopeful that a renewed focus on what we were asked to do by the president can help us look beyond our differences to see the many issues on which we in fact agree. I'm also hopeful that some positive encouragement from consumers will bring new energy to the process and move us toward success.

I am concerned about issues of cost. We've not yet determined the extent of external monitoring that will ultimately be required. One assumption holds that a model based on generally accepted accounting practices would suffice: a statistically valid sample would be reviewed unless or until irregularities were discovered. Another assumption holds that a much larger percentage of contractors—or even 100 percent of all contractors—must have an annual independent audit. In either case, the audits will be expensive. And what marketplace advantage does that additional expense bring? At this point, it looks like very little. None of the companies currently participating intend to attach a "No Sweat" label to their garments. None have given serious consideration to aggressive in-store or point-of-sale marketing efforts. To the extent that they are participating in self-interest (as all of us are in some way), they arc looking to show that they are working in good faith to meet a high human rights standard. If the additional costs brought on by external monitoring end up being very substantial, they might dwarf the potential marketplace advantage of joining. The prospect of applying a label to individual garments must be retained as a means of attracting future members to the partnership. But it is important to recognize that, while it is clear there could be substantial economic costs for joining the partnership, the economic benefits of joining are not yet evident.

### Taking on the Living Wage Issue

Lastly, and most importantly, I am concerned about the issue of a "living wage." There is an ongoing effort, run in part by one of the NGOs in the partnership, to alter the AIP agreement to require participating companies to go beyond paying workers the legal minimum, and instead "tie wages to the basic cost of living in each country." Massive public relations efforts are seeking to gain visibility for this demand; they had a series of rallies—called "A National Day of Conscience to End Sweatshops"—in cities across the country. A petition circulated before and during these rallies suggested that this increase in wages is something "the multinationals can easily afford." (Their petition also proposed to change the AIP agreement by insisting that "corporations must open their plants to independent monitoring by respected local religious and human rights organizations.")

Joining together to bring a genuine living wage to workers around the world is an important goal and one that is far more ambitious than the AIP's original task of eliminating those facilities that anyone would describe as sweatshops. The elusiveness of a living wage holds hundreds of millions of workers in lives of poverty, even though those workers regularly put in far more hours than the average American does. A living wage must, ultimately, be the goal of those who strive for justice; those who are forcing this issue onto the international social and political agenda clearly have justice in mind and are among the most thoughtful advocates of impoverished workers.

If the National Day of Conscience to End Sweatshops were based on one issue or another—eliminating sweatshops or guaranteeing a living wage for all workers—its chances of success would increase dramatically. But such is not the case.

The petition associated with the Day of Conscience is targeted at the Apparel Industry Partnership, directly challenging the group to take on this issue of a living wage. As important as this issue is, as horrid as the wage conditions are for hundreds of millions of workers around the world, the partnership is simply not the vehicle to achieve such a goal. Demanding that it do so will lead to the failure of the partnership before its work to end sweatshops has hardly begun.

Sticking to the original goal—the elimination of sweatshops—is the only method by which the partnership can succeed. The apparel industry has been home to sweatshops for more than a century; indeed, when most people think of sweatshops, they likely picture a garment factory. With a focus on this one major problem in the very industry known for the biggest abuses, we actually have a chance of success. But that chance disappears if we are expected to also tackle the issue of a living wage. The living wage issue goes well beyond our industry, touching nearly every industry in every part of the globe. It is an appropriate battle for governments and trade unions to lead; it is simply too massive of a goal for a partnership that currently has half a dozen companies in one industry.

Adding the issue of a living wage will lead to the collapse of the partnership. To succeed, the partnership must grow beyond its current membership. We need hundreds of companies involved, not the current small group. This growth will not happen if new and more controversial issues are constantly added to the agenda. Nor will it happen if the group continues its divisive tactics. The participating companies, unions, and activist organizations all agreed on a set of criteria—the Workplace Code of Conduct. We stood with the president and together said that meeting the standards in the code would make a difference for millions of workers around the world. But when the White House press conference ends and partnership members then begin applying very public pressure to reopen the code of conduct, it tells prospective corporate members that the group's work is not settled, that the partnership is not moving forward cohesively. That makes a pup tent out of what should be a big tent.

Ridding the world of sweatshops would of course not rid the world of poverty. But it would be a significant contribution to working conditions around the world. Indeed, it would likely be the greatest accomplishment any partnership member would ever be part of. By keeping our focus on sweatshops, we can dramatically reduce the number of children working, again, likely to be a quarter of a billion children today.

The partnership's chances of success increase exponentially if our membership grows quickly. If the National Day of Conscience instead put pressure on other companies to join the partnership, we would begin to make quick progress in chasing sweatshop owners down and driving them out of business. Bringing in to the partnership, through persuasion or through public pressure, dozens of major clothing manufacturers would send a clear signal to sweatshop owners. Bringing in the five major retail chains would be an even greater step. But these additions will work only if the partnership takes the "big tent" approach. That is, we can only succeed by recognizing that we need to have hundreds of partners working with us. And that won't happen if we keep changing the rules or if we keep raising the standards even before we've taken real steps.

The living wage issue is, again, a vital one. But the partnership is not the group that can successfully advance this issue. At least today it can't. But look ahead five years. If the partnership at that stage has hundreds of members, if we've made significant progress in dramatically reducing child labor and forced overtime, and if consumers are joining with us in the battle to end sweatshops, those who seek justice in the workplace might have much more visible and much more powerful allies. But we can only build that power and that momentum if we choose our goals carefully at the outset.

## The Long Term Focus: Changing the Trade Regimes

The challenges I've raised thus far may stop the partnership from making any real progress. But they are short-term problems; ones that can in fact be addressed by the partnership members themselves. A much bigger challenge is one posed by the existing international trade regimes.

If the Apparel Industry Partnership is successful, it will most certainly be challenged as a de facto trade barrier under GATT. That specter looms on the horizon, and the group's fate may well be determined by a small group of World Trade Organization (WTO) judges.

But more important is the fact that existing trade regimes require that this continues to be a voluntary, consumer-driven effort—and I have doubts as to the long-term potential of such efforts. As noted earlier, the marketplace benefits of participation are limited at best. The most effective benefit may be the opportunity to avoid negative attention. A major retail chain, for example, might want to avoid being the target of boycotts or negative media attention if it is one of the few major chains to stay outside of the partnership. A corporation might gain short-term promotional benefits upon joining the group or in making certain policy changes to come into compliance. But these benefits will last only so long as the issue retains public and media attention.

To be effective in the long term, these improvements must have the full force and effect of law. Having the force of law in the country of manufacture would require no changes in international trade laws, but it is unlikely that such legal changes would occur on a scale that would significantly alter international working conditions. Alternatively, applying the force of law in the country of sale would require significant changes in the trade regime, but this is a required step if the standards are to be raised permanently. Applying the force of law in the country of sale would allow us to move beyond the "lowest common denominator" approach to trade standards. It would allow individual countries or groups of countries to raise the standards in such a way that all nations wanting to sell their products globally would need to meet that higher standard.

Currently, the GATT prevents nations from trying to raise standards as they apply to both domestically produced and imported products. As a recent *Economist* article noted, "If anyone was in any doubt as to the true nature of the WTO, its action in the three years since it was created paint a depressingly clear picture. As feared, in every case brought before it to date, the WTO has ruled in favor of corporate interests, striking down national and sub-national legislation protecting the environment and public health at every turn."

In 1996, Venezuela and Brazil filed a challenge to prevent the U.S. Environmental Protection Agency from raising clean air standards for gasoline sold in the U.S. The standards were too high for Venezuelan and Brazilian exporters to meet without making significant improvements in their refining capabilities. The WTO ruled that the higher standards discriminated against the polluting nations. A year later, the U.S. EPA changed the clean air regulations to comply with the WTO.

In another case, the U.S. Marine Mammal Protection Act placed an embargo on tuna caught using methods that commonly killed dolphins. Rather than leading to the protection of a charismatic aquatic species, the measure was challenged as a projectionist trade weapon, and the law was declared illegal under GATT.

In the third case, the WTO declared that a European Union ban on imports of beef raised with artificial growth hormones violated the trade regimes and was therefore illegal.

Three efforts to legally raise standards—to protect air quality, to ensure the safety of foods, and to save a species from reckless poaching—all have been struck down by the World Trade Organization.

But the very extreme nature of these decisions is in part what makes me optimistic that these trade regimes will not last much longer than this century. People in this country and elsewhere want clean air, they want safe foods and they want to see nature preserved. When they find out that a small group of faceless judges and trade lawyers is preventing them from attaining these goals, they will be justifiably angry, and they will take steps to dismantle these trade regimes. In Europe, chronic high unemployment is already leading political leaders to seek scapegoats; the trade regimes, which limit domestic political options, are an obvious and growing target. In the U.S., populist or charismatic candidates for national office will continue to use the trade regimes as a foil; they will likely find increasing success, because the trade regimes are stopping the American people from reaching goals on which there is in fact a rare consensus.

On both continents, more citizens are aware of the fact that their own nation's democracies now have less power than another nation's corporations. As governments cede authority to international corporations and institutions, the power to set a nation's standards and to define the quality of life within its borders—a power that not long ago rested with voters—now lies in the hands of a select group: corporate shareholders. A new poll tax: This issue can, and I believe will, be used successfully by emerging leaders on both continents, leading to a breakdown in the existing trade regimes and a wave of national or regional trade standards. Some of these standards will be undeniably projectionist. But many of them can be successful attempts to improve the quality of life in a nation and on earth.

Nations and businesses that try to deny this trend will suffer; those that embrace it will flourish. Those that seek out the highest standards, and meet them, will be able to sell their products in the broadest range of markets.

While the long-term focus must be on changing the international trade regimes, I want to close by returning to the Apparel Industry Partnership and its role today. Even if my assumption is true that the long-term focus for our efforts must be on attaining the full force and effect of law, voluntary measures such as this one play an essential short-term role. By "short-term," I mean roughly the length of a childhood. With a quarter of a billion children working today, waiting for a long-term solution would deprive them of one of the most fundamental of human rights: the right to a childhood. And that is why the partnership—with a useful life that will likely be the length of a childhood—needs support.

— ✺ —

# Global Codes
# of Conduct
# and the
# Environment

# 17

# Who Speaks for the Trees?

## Consideration for Any Transnational Code

LISA H. NEWTON

If ethical considerations are to have any place in the economic activity of the next millennium, they must address a world without political boundaries, whose actors are trans-national companies—literally, economic enterprises that transcend nations, becoming laws unto themselves, dealing equally with peoples all over the earth. We will require new corporate codes of ethics, that honor the human rights of all whose rights are affected by the operation, irrespective of local law or practice, and that provide for the sustainable protection of noneconomic as well as economic values into the future. I will argue that whatever means we may have in hand to recognize and protect human rights in all economic contexts (even as political obstacles complicate their implementation), environmental sustainability, as a criterion of ethically acceptable operations, is not sufficiently addressed in this new transnational ethics initiative. I examine the possibility that the concept of *kyosei*, newly emerged as a conceptual player in the business ethics field, may contain an environmental imperative sufficient as a governing principle for global business.

## Free Markets Across the World

### Hurrah for the Market

"With the collapse of communism," Gerald Cavanagh points out, "and the advance of communications and transportation, the market system has rapidly become both global and dominant in our world."[1] We capitalists are the only game in town: what, exactly, does the town have a right to expect of us?

First and foremost, the town, in this case the world, has a right to expect that we will give the market a chance to show what it can do to improve human welfare through the exercise of human freedom. It may be noted that of the three major imperatives of ethics—beneficence (avoiding harm, and seeking the greatest happiness of the greatest number in the long run), justice (preserving human equality through rectification of wrongs and fair distribution of benefits and burdens), and respect for persons (their autonomy, moral agency, privacy, and dignity)—the market only claims to serve two of them. It serves liberty, free choice, in allowing participants to chose their personal favorites among the economic options offered them, and because (in theory) the sum of all personal choices will secure the wealth of the nation, it serves beneficence. It never claimed that it would serve justice, especially if justice is expected to rectify the limitation of options that luck and genetic endowment may dictate, or achieve anything like equality of result for its buyers and its sellers. When the injustice becomes extreme, nonmarket forces like community boycott and government regulation have a tendency to step in and freeze the market; the same forces, of course, can preempt otherwise reasonable market decisions in order to forbid the trade in heroin, child prostitutes, or ivory. (The ivory is problematic; more on that below.) But as far as possible, until the injustice cries to heaven, we should let the market work its wealth-producing magic: a world that has been alternately terrorized and micro-mismanaged by presidential Big Brothers of socialist persuasions is starved for personal opportunity and the freedom to go after it.

### First Limits: Three Moves to Preserve the Market

That said, some practices that have so far emerged in the new global free market do indeed cry to heaven, or at least to Adam Smith, for remedy, and have already attracted the attention of governments and ethicists alike.

First of all, we need to be able to formulate and defend a distinction between the valid and the corrupt market transaction. I have a tendency to defend the proposition that there is no distinction at all between bribery and other market transactions, save as law intervenes in the market to separate sheep (legitimate payments) from goats (bribes). In theory, every good and every service could be sold at auction to the highest bidder; if we want policemen and customs officers to refrain from such auctions for their services, we will have to regulate police and customs by law and enforce the law. Most especially, if we respect the free market and wish to keep competition honest, we will have to rely on the umpires, rulebooks, and adjudicatory panels needed for all fair competitions. There is powerful motivation to sew up the market share you want by a few well-placed bribes, which practice, where successful, would surely increase your happiness but would negate the Greatest Happiness for Greatest Number results predicted by market theory.[2]

Much of the world winks at simple bribery—not the huge payoffs to prime ministers, but the "tips" and "facilitating payments" to the "little men doing little jobs in a big world."[3] Yet as Thomas Donaldson points out, even routine bribery "undermines market efficiency and predictability" and ultimately "undermines essential social and economic systems."[4] Never mind whether bribery in fact takes rewards away from the deserving, favors the worse rather than the better deal, and buys promotions that should have gone to others, although Donaldson argues that it does all that; the fact that potential investors *perceive* the system as unjust is sufficient to make sure that it does not function. We appeal to the greatest happiness principle only, without introducing justice: bribery, a free market institution if ever there was one, fails by free market standards alone.

Second, we need to articulate principles that reserve liberty for the lowest in society. The first defense of the free market is, after all, its freedom. If we find that our freedom to buy a soccer ball at an extraordinarily low price is purchased with the freedom of eight- and ten-year-old children to live their lives outside of an abusive factory, then surely the freedom won is nowhere near the value of the freedom lost, and the arrangement should be renegotiated. The opposition to sweatshops rests on two moral pillars: our warmhearted natural sympathy, human sentiment (cited by David Hume as the only and sufficient source of morality) that will not allow our consciences to rest in the contemplation of suffering children, and the cold-eyed market of the day after tomorrow, foreseeing that such uses of young humanity are nowhere near as efficient as schools and summer camps in producing the upscale consumers that guarantee profits into the future. Today and maybe tomorrow, child slavery is profitable; after that, the used-up slave becomes a burden and the economy stagnates. Appealing directly to the consumers, through the contagious fury of Kathy Lee Gifford, outraged at the discovery that her fashionable line of clothing is being crafted by children brutalized in foreign sweatshops, organizing that outrage into the Apparel Industry Partnership to ban all trade in the products of sweatshops, the convergence of sympathy and the market results in firm and sensible limits on the choice of workers and the conditions under which they may work.[5]

Third, we need to control the pirates. Piracy—appropriating for yourself what someone else owns or has created, especially software—is classified by Aristotle as a type of "hunting," and therefore one of the honorable professions (as opposed to retail trade).[6] Piracy has had a long and distinguished history, and has many defenders to this day, under the age of twelve. Past that age, "asked whether one should use software without paying for it, most people, including people in Italy and Hong Kong, say no."[7] But that answer does not describe their practice, any more than the general acceptance of standards of justice kept the pirates of the Barbary Coast from preying on the merchants who ventured into their area.

Piracy is now what it was in the days of the Barbary scourge or the Wild West—an indulgence of a penchant for getting something for nothing, usually by violence, that is unproductive, needlessly painful, and above all hostile to investment, production, and the growth and stability of markets. It is incompatible with the global free market. It survives now as a throwback to an earlier age, a practice tolerated only because it is just beyond the reach of the free market powers. It deserved an entire box of condemnation in Thomas Donaldson's essay on global business ethics. It has to go. As the European Union standardizes its practices, and Asia is drawn into the market, go it will.

### Next Limits: The Areas that Challenge the Market

So there is a morality built into the market: in order to keep the money flowing easily across borders and secure a base of customers across the globe, we must support honesty in word and deed, and a decent wage for the worker. But what of the larger problems that attend the market when it is working well? We cannot use free market justifications for remedying injustice of result in the grim competitive atmosphere (we cannot extend an infinite safety net for all losers in the contest), we cannot find an economic reason to preserve cultures whose demands are incompatible with the market (the indigenous peoples of the Americas, Africa, or the South Pacific Islands, for instance, who want only to be left alone in the vast tracts of land they have occupied for eons), and we cannot preserve the natural environment. Let us sketch these problems briefly, then turn to the possibility that an international code of ethics, the Caux Principles, may provide the protections needed by the noncompetitive sectors of this world.

### Where Markets Destroy

The purpose of this section is only to call to mind the limits of market values in a pluralistic world. There is no suggestion that these are the only areas where the whole free market mentality is the problem; indeed, to read some of the current tracts, the free market and its consumer temptations will cost us all our families, our sanity, and our souls.[8] Nor, emphatically, is there any suggestion that some other standard mentality—socialist, perhaps—holds answers that the market does not. Indeed, in the three areas that are most troublesome—the safety net for those who fail to compete successfully in the new global economy, the preservation of the culture of the indigenous peoples, and the preservation of the environment—socialism in its heyday only claimed superiority to capitalism in the first of them. For the other two, socialist nations have exhibited the same insensitivities as the capitalist ones, and have often been significantly more destructive (witness Tibet and Romania). If these areas are going to be addressed at all effectively, they will be addressed in the larger context of a global system dominated by global business.

The problem shared by these areas is that the logic of the market simply does not include them as terms: they evade its preconditions, they do not quantify easily, or at all, and therefore to mention them in the context of business activity seems always to change the subject. We shall cover them very briefly in this section, showing only that market-oriented analysis has no solution for them, and go on in the next section to consider the possibility that *kyosei* may do a better job than "human rights" in addressing them.

### The People Who Aren't in It

This is not the forum to rehearse the miseries of those who lose the rat race, or to condemn the callous winners. We are all aware that in this booming economy the pain of the poor is especially acute, and that the cuts in welfare payments have struck with particular cruelty in areas of high endemic unemployment (like the Mississippi Delta), which inevitably turn out to be areas of high concentrations of minorities. Simply let it be pointed out that the poor we always will have with us—business cycles and other rising tides will not raise them up, gentrification will not get rid of them, and prisons are the most expensive public housing we have. Now that our worldwide commerce moves the market race to an international track, the problems of noncompetitive populations have expanded exponentially. Eventually, we will be expected to address them.

The problem with the market is that, like the lottery, you have to be in it to win it, or even to carve out a nice niche to survive in. The world contains many categories of those who are losing at the market game. Some, the "market poor," cyclically or accidentally unemployed, are very much in the game, and will continue to participate in the economy even in their losing periods—by continuing to consume while on unemployment, by going back to school to acquire market-oriented skills, by taking lower-paying jobs to keep paying the mortgage, and so on. We can help these people and get them back into the action so they will not need any more help—by forgiving mortgages for a period of time, by making expenses so they can move where the jobs are. Incidentally, we can do this worldwide, for these people exist on every continent. They may not achieve "success," but they will survive in the market economy for the entirety of their working lives. These constitute a first category of the market losers. The other two are not in the market at all, and addressing their problems requires more imagination.

There are, for a secondary category, the low-skilled "migrant poor," uneducated, capable of only the lowest-skilled (and least needed) places in a market economy, but entirely aware of the richer world that surrounds them, and capable of taking action instrumental to partaking in that prosperity. We have many in this country, in the rural South especially, where their farm labor is no longer needed, south of our border in Mexico and on throughout South America, in Haiti, all through Africa, in the former communist-bloc nations, and all through Asia. They cannot make a living where they are, so they move. They move from where the conditions are bad (Mississippi, Mexico, Haiti, the South of the world, rural villages anywhere) to where conditions are better (New York, the United States, the North of the world, cities anywhere). Some are born or trained entrepreneurs and fit in anywhere; much of our recent Asian immigration fits into this pattern. But for the displaced peasantry and menial labor of this migration, entrepreneurial opportunities are no help. Unlike the market poor, they cannot easily be prepared by available education and job-skills programs to join the economic activity of the nation or the world. It is doubtful that we could muster the political will to pour out the educational, housing, nutrition, and health care resources that would be necessary to raise their skills, lifestyle, and outlook to the point where they would compete successfully. And any place that began to make such an effort would immediately become a world magnet for more of this category of needy people. Ultimately, we may end by viewing them as a hostile horde, made enemies by their simple desire to enjoy what we enjoy.[9]

A third category of the world's poor are precisely those who do not, as long as they can avoid it, want what we enjoy. The "indigenous poor" want to be left alone on their own land, and since it *is* their own land, there seems to be a prima facie reason to honor their request. The problem is, that there are others who want that land, and the indigenous people have few resources, military or other, to keep them out—as ever, where the imbalance of power is extreme, a prima facie reason does not have very much staying power. This, of course, was the condition of the Native Americans when the Europeans came; to this day, save in Connecticut in the vicinity of Foxwoods Casino, integrating

Native Americans into the economy is not an easy task. It remains the condition of many tribal settlements in Brazil; the battle to save the tropical rainforest in Brazil is at least as much a battle to save the endangered tribes that live, entirely sustainably, within it.[10] Unlike the migrant poor, these peoples do not move to more favorable economic climates; like the trees and the wildlife on which they depend, they stay where their way of life has evolved, at the mercy of the market forces moving in. There are gallant efforts by conscientious businesses to let the market save both the forest and its peoples, as in the marketing of "Rainforest Crunch" ice cream by Ben & Jerry's, the introduction of "ecotourism" in Ecuador, and the use of tropical rainforest products in soaps and cosmetics by the Body Shop.[11] These efforts are not likely to succeed against the persistent pressure of political and economic power in the country to "open up" the forest to "productive use," i.e., cut it down and use the land for a few years before it turns to desert.[12] There is similar pressure, not all of it from people greedy for land, to open schools and teach the children the skills they will need to become part of the economy of the twenty-first century. Their parents often do not want them to go to such schools. They want the children to live as the tribe has always lived, and schools with foreign teachers are not necessary for that; further, the schools take the children away from learning what they must learn, namely, the ways of the forest. If the tribe is to endure, the children must know how to live in the forest. If they do not, they will have to leave it, and the tribal culture will disappear forever.[13]

### The Land

And that brings us to the forest itself. Famously, the market has not been able to see the forest for the trees—the trees cut down, rendered into board lumber (or worse, sold as whole logs to Japan for storage until the price goes up), replanted only if a sure profit will follow replanting. The market looks at Nature and sees "raw material," resources to be transformed into goods and services. The only protection for the great forests from the time of market ascendancy was their inaccessibility and the availability of beautiful wood from nearer places. So Sarawak's forests had been left alone until the last fifteen years or so; the Amazonian rainforests were difficult to clear, the virgin forests of Africa were in districts difficult to access. But with falling world supply, advanced transportation technology, and enthusiastically cooperative governments, these last forests have been falling to the oldest of purposes—they are being cut down for their wood.

Recently, with the support of somewhat more enlightened forest services, the market has been reintroduced on the other side of the equation. Noting the damage done by mudslides down deforested mountains, fish stocks depleted in clogged streams at the bottom of those mountains and in ocean waters off of filled-up salt marshes, some attempts have been made to calculate the economic value of environmental features left in place, not transformed into other goods. If a forest is controlling rain runoff, and preventing floods and mudslides, it stands to reason that it is worth in place at least what flood control devices would cost, if they had to be brought in to do the same thing. So there should be at least some instances where we can show that the destruction of the forest, or field, or marsh, or mountain, is economically inadvisable. (A solid effort of this kind is found in Janet Abramovitz' article, "Valuing Nature's Services.")[14]

Over the vast majority of instances where this counterweight might be useful, it does not work well because there are no people to be flooded out, or because if there are, we don't care about them. Or, as is usually the case, we have no idea what services are being performed by the ecosystem until after it has been irreparably destroyed. So we have attempted to introduce other economic counterweights, in the form of the educational, scientific, and recreational uses of the forest. These defenses are not strong in market terms: the money is difficult to count in advance, the jobs supplied are nowhere near the level of pay of the jobs of the loggers or construction workers, and educational and recreational values are a very difficult sell. The major disadvantage of asserting these "values," of course, is that they do have to be "sold." It takes an act of the public, and the expenditure of public tax funds, to create a national park (for instance), and must be accomplished over the objections of the private wealth that presently holds the land and would increase if it could sell the lumber. An act of political will is required each and every time the forest is to be moved from commercial extractive status to recreational status, and that takes more effort than we can muster very often.

### From Anthropocentricity to Ecocentricity

What will save the forest? Nothing short of a radical change in perspective. As Aldo Leopold pointed out half a century ago:

> There is as yet no ethic dealing with man's relation to the land and to the animals and plants which grow upon it. Land, like Odysseus' slave girls, is still property. The land-relation is still strictly economic, entailing privileges but not obligations.[15]

We cannot hang the slave girls on a single rope anymore; we cannot execute people without due process of law and we cannot have slaves. Both limits are a function of mandatory respect of humans and their rights. Humans used to be of two kinds, persons and property. Now we recognize all humans as part of a single human community.

> All ethics so far rest upon a single premise: that the individual is a member of a community of interdependent parts. . . . The land ethic simply enlarges the boundaries of the community to include soils, waters, plants, and animals, or collectively: the land.[16]

The land ethic drops the economic out of the picture altogether and sees Nature whole, as something that must be stewarded, protected, and preserved, as an end in itself, like humans of the community, not merely as means to some human's ends. We need to re-value Nature, not as raw material, not as performing services, but as itself the standard of the good and the acceptable. Leopold continues:

> [Quit] thinking about decent land use as solely an economic problem. Examine each question in terms of what is ethically and aesthetically right, as well as what is economically expedient. A thing is right when it tends to preserve the integrity, stability and beauty of the biotic community. It is wrong when it tends otherwise.[17]

Until very recently, no ethic that purported to apply to business (or any human practice) really took the land seriously. How could it? Although we can all admit that, on a dead planet, no business will prosper and though we may all agree that the environment today is indeed threatened, so that we might end up with a dead planet if we do not act to preserve its life, there is a tremendous difference between a utilitarian imperative for the very long term, and a human rights imperative right now. There really is a fundamental opposition between honoring human rights and honoring Nature: if and wherever the question of preservation of the ecosystem has come up, it is because some constellation of human rights (property rights in the North, development rights in the South) may be exercised to destroy it. Protecting the land has always required the limitation in some part of human rights, and always will. How can we make sense of an ethic, or code of ethics, that simultaneously insists on human rights and dignity and on the necessity of limiting those rights for the land? Is it possible to have a code of ethics that permits ecocentric perspectives?

### The Caux Principles: A Glimmer of Hope

The Caux Round Table (CRT) was established in 1986 by an unusual assortment of eminent world business executives: Frederick Philips, former president of Philips Electronics, Olivier Giscard d'Estaing, vice-chairman of France's leading business school, the then-CEO Ryuzaburo Kaku of Canon in Japan, and an assortment of other Europeans and Americans. The topic of conversation around the table was business ethics, ethics for a global economy. When they decided to issue a set of moral principles in 1992, they were presented with a tried-and-true model by the American contingent. Known as the Minnesota Principles, the Minneapolis-centered group had based them on the experience of Dayton Hudson and other American firms with an excellent reputation for ethical care and conduct, and simply expanded that experience to a global context. The efforts to fit the American principles, essentially a commitment to honesty and human rights, with Japanese communitarian presuppositions, in a European context, did not always go smoothly but were ultimately successful. As Kenneth Goodpaster, discussion leader for the group, summed it up,

> There were some tender moments when a few members felt the work they had done wasn't being recognized. . . . A breakthrough came when Jean-Loup Dherse of France argued forcefully for the Japanese communitarian concept of *kyosei* being supplemented by the Western European notion of the dignity of the human person. The healthy dynamic tension between *kyosei* and human dignity would underpin the whole document. And then we brought in The Minnesota Principles as the body of the CRT Principles document.[18]

The Caux Principles are reproduced elsewhere in this volume for your inspection. You will note that section 3, Stakeholder Principles, reads very much like the very best of the American codes of business ethics, with wording changed to reflect the global obligations the companies are assuming. This part, essentially the Minnesota Principles, is familiar. What is new is *kyosei*. What does it mean?

The word is put together from two Japanese terms, *kyo* (working together) and *sei* (life), and is translated as "the working-together life," or (in Chairman Kaku's understanding) "the spirit of cooperation," or "working together for the common good."[19] The preamble of the CRT Principles draws the first implications in its understanding of the term: "living and working together for the common good—enabling cooperation and mutual prosperity to coexist with healthy and fair competition." *Kyosei* captures the notion of community, cooperation, as a good in itself, not as simply instrumental to other goods. But service to community—to the common good, to the long run, to the morale of the group—can require that individuals both abstain from exercising their rights (without losing them) and set aside, for the moment, their individual interests. This principle, then, is not limited by the requirement that any action done in observance of it must respect an individual human right, serve a human interest, or both; this principle can extend to the land.

*Kyosei,* then, is the immediate and natural extension of Leopold's notion of "community," which begins with family, extends to the tribe, eventually includes all human beings including slave girls, and then takes in the entire living physical basis of human existence—the earth and all that is in it. And it has been adopted by some of the most prominent business executives in the world as the foundation for an ethic of global business. If there is hope for the global environment in the new global free market, it comes from this fact.

The CRT Principles for Business continue to spell out their fundamental moral commitments—kyosei and human dignity—in the second section, the seven general principles. The seriousness with which the participants took their moral obligations is immediately apparent. They identify a series of stakeholders, not just shareholders, as within the ambit of the moral community of business. They commit themselves to the use of business to foster innovation, justice, and world community. They commit themselves to respect rules even as they aspire to go beyond rules to foster trust, and they pledge to avoid illicit operations. The sixth general principle is Respect for the Environment, committing the signatories to protecting "and, where possible, improv[ing] the environment," preventing waste and promoting environmental sustainability. This principle, and the stakeholder principles that follow from it, will commit any signatory to go well beyond the demands of most codes of ethics. Twice in the stakeholder principles, once in the provisions for customers and once in the provisions for "communities," the CRT principles require the signatories to protect the natural environment: they are required to make environment-friendly products, to promote sustainable development, even required to "play a leading role in preserving and enhancing the physical environment and conserving the earth's resources." In the same two places they are required to respect "cultures": might this provision extend to the rainforest tribes now being obliterated by the attacks upon the rainforest?

This last point raises an interesting possibility. In the path of the triumphant market there are three mute victims—the refugee, the tribesman, and the land itself. If *kyosei* can extend to a commitment to preserve the land, it can surely extend to cover the others. The key is community, the community of all.

## Notes

1. Gerald F. Cavanagh, S.J., "Executives' Code of Business Conduct: Prospects for the Caux Principles," chapter 10 of this volume.

2. See, on these points, ibid., and Kathleen A. Getz, chapter 9 of this volume.

3. A beautiful characterization of the not-quite-innocent hand extended from a thousand offices all over the world, from a presentation on bribery and corruption by Igor Grazin, at the Global Codes of Conduct Conference, Notre Dame, Indiana, October 7, 1997.

4. Thomas Donaldson, "Values in Tension: Ethics Away from Home," *Harvard Business Review,* September–October 1996:48–62, p. 58.

5. For an account of that partnership, see Kevin Sweeney's "Voting with Their Pocketbooks: The Strengths and Limits of Consumer-Driven Codes of Conduct," chapter 16 in this volume.

6. Aristotle, *Politics,*Book 1, Chapter VIII, Article8, 1256B.

7. Donaldson, "Values in Tension."

8. See Robert J. Samuelson, *The Good Life and Its Discontents: The American Dream in the Age of Entitlement* (New York: Times Books [Random House], 1995; Vintage edition with a new afterword, 1997). If you can find a copy, there's a hilarious movie named *Affluenza* (Bullfrog Productions) that makes all the same points in an entertaining hour's time.

9. See P. Kennedy and M. Connelly, "Must It Be the Rest against the West?" *Atlantic Monthly,* volume 274, number 6, p. 61, Dec. 1994.

10. See Augusta Dwyer, *Into the Amazon: The Struggle for the Rain Forest* (San Francisco: Sierra Club Books, 1990), for a nice account of several of these indigenous tribes in the region of the Amazon River.

11. The worth of these efforts, even on their own terms, is not unquestioned. See Jon Entine, "Shattered Image: Is the Body Shop Too Good to Be True?" *Business Ethics* volume 8, number 5, pp. 23–28, Sept/Oct 1994.

12. See Norman Myers, *The Primary Source: Tropical Forest and Our Future* (New York: Norton, 2nd ed., 1992).

13. A noteworthy discussion of the ethics and politics of the confrontation of market and primitive peoples was presented by Benjamin R. Barber, in "Jihad Vs. McWorld," *The Atlantic Monthly,* March, 1992. See also Stephen Mills, "Last Chance for First People," *Omni Magazine* 17(6) March 1995, pp. 62ff; see also Mac Chapin, "Disappearing Forests: Disappearing Peoples," *Cultural Survival Quarterly,* Fall 1992, pp. 63–66.

Mark Sagoff points out that much of this debate follows the insights of Karl Polanyi, in his *The Great Transformation* (Boston: Beacon Press, 1944) in which he discusses the transformation of land and work from resources dedicated to traditional communities and activities into commodities that could be bought and sold on the open market.

14. Janet Abramovitz, "Valuing Nature's Services," in *State of the World 1997,* ed. Lester R. Brown, Christopher Flavin, and Hillary French (New York: WW Norton, 1997), pp. 95–114.

15. Aldo Leopold, *A Sand County Almanac* (New York: Oxford University Press, 1949), p. 203.

16. Ibid., pp. 203–4.

17. Ibid., p. 225.

18. Joe Skelly, "The Caux Round Table Principles for Business: The Rise of International Ethics," *Business Ethics,* March/April 1995, Supplement, pp. 2–5. Professor Kenneth Goodpaster is Koch Chair in Business Ethics at the Graduate School of Business, University of St. Thomas in Minneapolis.

19. See his own exposition on the subject: Ryuzaburo Kaku, "The Path of Kyosei," *Harvard Business Review,* July–August 1997, pp. 55–63.

# 18

# Effective Codes of Conduct

## *Lessons from the Sullivan and CERES Principles*

ROBERT KINLOCH MASSIE

### Codes in Context

Corporate principles or codes of conduct are a special configuration of articulated values embedded in extremely complex systems of human behavior.[1] They constitute a subset of a much broader network of social codes that vary along four dimensions: from the implicit to the explicit, from small to large, from informal to formal, and from duties to goals.

- Implicit to Explicit: Human behavior is defined by a large web of values and expectations, which range from unspoken (but well understood) social codes to highly explicit rules.
- Small to Large: Social codes vary according to the number of people to which they apply, ranging from the rules that guide a family to those that govern nations.
- Informal to Formal: Informal codes have weak and variable systems of evaluation, commendation, and discipline. Formal codes become highly stylized, with elaborately developed mechanisms for evaluation and adjudication, punishment and reward.
- Duties to Goals: Social codes vary along the spectrum from the teleological to deontological, that is from those that emphasize goals to those that stress duties.

Corporate codes of conduct occupy the middle of each of these spectra. They represent a mix of implicit and explicit values. They apply usually to a large social group that is itself embedded in still larger systems. Codes of conduct attempt to find a balance between informal and formal structures of evaluation, recognition, and reward. Finally, they are often a mix of means and ends, duties and goals. This middle position is the source of both the support and the suspicion such codes attract.

This chapter is a set of preliminary reflections about the effectiveness of corporate codes of conduct. The observations are drawn from the Sullivan Principles, first drafted in 1976 to guide the employment practices of American firms in South Africa[2] (see Appendix 27), and the CERES Principles (see Appendix 2), created in 1989 to urge companies to commit to a program of continuous environmental improvement.[3] I intend not to provide a detailed account of these examples but to offer some comparative comments and questions about the structural characteristics of these and other codes.

## General Purposes of Codes

The first question to address is: what is the purpose of a code of conduct? Or, put differently, what is the problem for which codes of conduct are seen as the answer?

### Clarified Frame of Reference

Codes of conduct have risen in popularity as a mechanism of accountability for multinational companies because changes in markets, technology, and social conditions have undermined the older methods of providing meaning and order. The relentless effect of global capitalism has pushed human communities toward larger spheres of interaction and to bring groups and organizations with markedly different cultures and values into greater contact and competition. Such circumstances have bred uncertainty, misunderstanding, and conflict. As the number and complexity of interactions expand, the desire also arises to reduce confusion by clarifying expectations. Implicit, informal structures of class and culture must be supplemented by more explicit rules of behavior.

This need has been particularly acute for the business firm. Over the last century, corporations have dramatically expanded their power, complexity, and scope. Laws and regulations that provided guidance within one geographic sphere often do not have jurisdiction in others. As corporations have become more powerful, the confusion over the boundaries of their freedom and responsibility has intensified. As they have become more complicated, the task of management—of setting rules and direction—has become more difficult. And as they have steadily expanded within and beyond national borders, they have been subjected to a blizzard of new cultural values and political expectations.

Such confusion has led to a cacophony of claims, both inside and outside firms, about the responsibilities of the firm. The debate over the effect of multinationals on their employees, customers, communities, and environment has steadily intensified. Stakeholder organizations, now better linked through information technology, are applying their pressures with greater sophistication. They are increasingly determined to get managers to acknowledge, measure, and disclose their broader social responsibilities. Managers, who watch with dismay as new demands accumulate on top of the already huge challenge of international competition, are reluctant to take on new tasks unless they have been carefully specified.

In short, the expansion of power, complexity, and scope of corporate influence has produced a search for mechanisms of delineation, simplification, and clarification. Codes of conduct are attempts to create a common language or frame of reference for the discussion and evaluation of corporate behavior. As such, they are often seen as a compromise that meets very different needs for each of their endorsing parties. External stakeholders often see the articulation of responsibilities in codes as a means of specifying duties that managers might otherwise evade. Managers in turn see them as a way to guide their firms while limiting the escalation and unpredictability of external demands.

### From Constraints to Goals

Indeed, codes of conduct are often intended to shift a conflictual relationship from resistance to movement, from clashing duties to common goals. Disagreements between stakeholders and managers often begin as an argument about the cessation of some activity. Activists want a company to stop polluting a river, exploiting child labor, or building a plant. Such activists rarely consider what positive steps a firm might have taken in the past or be willing to take in the future. Managers often spend their early interactions with stakeholders explaining why they are obliged or have a right to keep doing whatever they have been asked to stop.

One can see this is the experience of the Sullivan and CERES Principles. Prior to the creation of the Sullivan Principles, the debate had focused on whether companies should withdraw from South Africa. Shareholder activists presented one resolution after another asking companies to stop doing business with the apartheid government, and boards of directors consistently refused. The only exception was the Reverend Leon Sullivan, who had been appointed as the first African-American member of the General Motors board in 1971 and who voted with the shareholder activists for five straight years with no effect. By 1976 Sullivan had tired of the stalemate and decided to shift the debate by crafting a statement of affirmative duties for corporations. Though activists angrily (and correctly) predicted that his efforts would draw energy away from the drive to force companies to leave South Africa, his initiative drew support from a cluster of previously resistant companies and launched a ten-year transformation of corporate practices.

Similarly, at the time of the creation of the CERES Principles, managers viewed environmental issues as matters of cost and compliance. Because, in their view, such controls were expensive, executives argued for the standards to be as low as possible. In other words, business accepted environmental restrictions as a set of negative duties. The coalition of large environmental groups and institutional investors that created CERES wanted to find a way to get companies to move to a more affirmative set of goals—to say what they would do rather than what they would not.

### Changed Behavior and Increased Goodwill

Finally, a code of conduct implies, by its very nature, that the organization has set a high standard that it intends to meet and maintain. Most codes of conduct are aspirational in tone and content and imply that the signatory is committed to making substantive progress. Codes obtain a portion of their moral credibility from human patience and goodwill, that is, from the understanding that even though deeds may not yet match the words, a good-faith effort is being made toward progress. If such trust is rewarded, observers and stakeholders will often extend this trust. If, on the other hand, people inside or outside the firm suspect that the aspiration has actually been embraced as a strategy to avoid change, the resulting disillusionment and backlash can be strong.

### Structural Characteristics of Effectiveness

As noted earlier, changing global conditions have led a wide array of people to the same idea of articulating corporate responsibilities in a code of conduct—with the sometimes self-defeating consequence that multiple standards arise simultaneously. In some cases one set of codes is designed specifically to parry the momentum of another. During the time of the South African divestment movement, there were the European Community Charter, the

Sullivan Principles, and eventually the Tutu Principles. Within the field of environment and sustainability, there have been the CERES Principles, the ICC Charter of Sustainable Development, the Environmental Justice Principles, the Hanover Principles, and the "system conditions" of the Natural Step. In the general field of corporate social responsibility we have seen the creation of the Caux Principles, and the ICCR Global Principles, and a new set of Global Sullivan Principles. The range and diversity of such principles have, by the sheer number of them, undermined the effort to create a common language and define mutually agreed upon goals. Often the debate has turned into a complicated version of "my principles are better than yours."

Experience with the creation and implementation of these and other principles has generated a range of questions about the effectiveness of the mechanism.[4] The achievement of the goals mentioned above—a clarified frame of reference, a shift to affirmative goals, a record of changed behavior, and a system that increases goodwill—requires that codes exhibit certain structural features.

For the remainder of the chapter I intend to explore these features through a series of diagnostic questions that can be asked of any code.

### Who was involved in the formation of the code?

Codes of conduct face a difficult balance between alienating blandness and offending specificity. The most common mistake that people setting out to create codes of conduct is that they write codes that appeal only to one of the contending communities. An elaborate political process may unfold, in which people argue over every jot and tittle of the text, yet when the process is completed, the document has little legitimacy for or appeal to the people who were excluded from its formation. One classic example is the industry association that decides, usually under the pressure of some embarrassing event, to form a voluntary industry code of conduct. The industry representatives huddle in secret and hash out a document, which, because it is designed to win acceptance with every industry performer, becomes waterlogged with every company's anxieties and objections. The end result is usually a short, safe restatement of the obvious, without goal or mechanisms of accountability. Those who have forged it view the result of industry agreement as a major achievement while external stakeholders tend to see this as a defensive maneuver to elude accountability.

The flip side of the industry-generated code is that created solely by activists. In this case, the code becomes a repository for the frustrations and anger of activists. Such codes become long lists of aspirations and grievances dressed up as goals, as every group with a complaint is granted space on the page. Those who have forged this form of code of conduct also tend to see this as a major achievement while managers see it as a comprehensive attack on everything they do.

If codes of conduct that are written exclusively by one set of parties have difficulty winning support and credibility from the other, what about negotiating in the middle? That is, what if one were to take an equal number of participants from each "side" and have them draw up a common understanding? While promising in theory, this approach doesn't usually work in practice, in part because of the very gulf in perspectives and unarticulated values the code is supposed to overcome.

It is interesting to note that the Sullivan and CERES Principles, both reasonably successful efforts in spanning the gulf, started from a more subtle position. The Sullivan Principles were drafted by a small number of corporate executives under the direct guidance and influence of a corporate critic, Leon Sullivan. The CERES Principles were written by a combination of environmentalists and investor activists who wanted to craft something that business would be willing to support. In the case of CERES, though there were not business executives involved in the actual writing of principles, the presence of the investor community—whose knowledge of business behavior and whose interest in the economic success of the firm overlap with the interests of business—allowed the language to be shaped and tempered.

Even though both the Sullivan and CERES Principles were written by one set of contending parties in a manner they hoped would appeal to the other, they were initially rejected. The Sullivan Principles were immediately attacked from both sides—by executives as a subversion of their responsibilities in a manner that might bring them into conflict with the laws of a foreign country, and by activists as an incrementalist distraction that would divert attention from the critical support that American firms provided to the South African government through their material goods, taxes, and physical presence. Similarly, the CERES Principles were universally rejected as too radical by large American companies for the first four years of the principles' existence, while at the same time being criticized by some environmental activists as not being bold enough.

### How widely and deeply is the code accepted?

Acceptance is both an external concept and internal concept. A code of conduct like the ICC Charter for Sustainable Development might be widely accepted by one community (more than two thousand businesses have subscribed) but it is viewed as almost completely irrelevant by environmentalists. Similarly a code of conduct might be publicly embraced by the chief executive but never work its way deeply into the corporate culture.

More effective codes of conduct are accepted widely enough to create a critical mass of groups committed to change and deeply enough to create change within a specific organization.

### How are the results measured and to whom are they disclosed?

From the historical experience with codes of conduct, disclosure and transparency emerge as necessary but not sufficient conditions of effectiveness. In the early life of a code of conduct, the articulation of a set of duties and goals may seem like an achievement in itself, but soon the question arises, both inside and outside the organization, whether the firm is complying with its duties and making progress toward its goals. The popularity of the adage that "what gets measured, gets managed," points to the intuitive recognition that both executives and external stakeholders need feedback loops to determine what kinds of outcomes the commitments embodied in the codes of conduct are generating.

Codes of conduct that have no systems of measurement at all pop up from time to time in response to external pressures; the EC Charter on South Africa was one, the ICC Charter on Sustainable Development is another. Even if such codes of conduct produced some changes in corporate behavior—a contention that few would support—those examples remain invisible. Codes of conduct without any systems of measurement or feedback are not only ineffective, they actually undermine confidence in the entire approach to corporate accountability, since they give the impression that corporations sign on to such codes largely to deflect and ignore the concerns of external critics.

Even if a corporation has a system of measurement and feedback in place, there is tremendous variation in the degree of transparency or disclosure that the firm selects. Some firms, for example, have created ethics codes and set up internal officers who measure compliance, but these data are never released to anyone by senior management. Under other schemes, such as the Responsible Care program created by the Chemical Manufacturers Association, the information is gathered and then sent to an industry association or other third party, who then aggregate and release the data for the total industry. This system allows the coordinating body to give private information to firms that they are operating outside industry norms, but it prevents external stakeholders from evaluating anything other than the industry as a whole.

In the case of both the Sullivan and CERES Principles, measurement and disclosure were built into the codes of conduct from the start. During the creation of the Sullivan Principles, company representatives vigorously fought the creation of a measurement or grading system on performance but were forced to accept it when Sullivan threatened to withdraw his support for the entire project and denounce the firms publicly unless one was put in place.[5] Sullivan then worked with corporate representatives to create an elaborate structure of funding and accountability that allowed corporate money to pass from an "industry support unit" through a group controlled by Sullivan and other clergy to the Arthur D. Little company, whose consultants gathered the corporate performance data and released the results. Sullivan also pushed hard for the companies to set numeric goals against which to measure, for example, their progress toward nondiscriminatory hiring. Some of the targets were selected arbitrarily, and in at least one case when the companies discovered that they were already meeting the target, they did nothing to raise the bar.

Nonetheless, the measurement of outcomes—and particularly the summation of the results into broader categories of performance such as "Improving Steadily"—had a huge impact on both corporate and stakeholder behavior. Some of the companies that had opposed any system of grading actually came to support it when it became clear that otherwise their conscientious efforts might be indistinguishable from those of the laggards. Corporate executives in South Africa who had, up until that point, been relatively insulated from the stakeholder concerns in the United States, suddenly found their performance being evaluated by outsiders and scrutinized by their superiors. Most important, large investors gradually shifted their requests to companies from simply signing the Sullivan Principles to showing improvement; toward the end of the divestment debate, for example, several large pension funds required firms to have received at least a Category I or II rating from Arthur D. Little for them to retain the stock in their portfolios.

When the CERES Principles were originally drafted, the founders gave some thought to following the Sullivan pattern and requiring companies not only to report but also be graded on their performance relative to each principle. This approach proved to be impossible in the early stages for a variety of reasons, including the primitive state of environmental reporting at the time, the large expense such a requirement would have entailed, and the vociferous opposition from industry to the idea of any environmental code of conduct at all. Indeed, it is remarkable to look back today, when environmental reporting is concerned standard practice for leadership firms in all industries, to that earlier period. In 1989, the only firms who were willing to endorse the CERES Principles and commit to a process of measurement and disclosure were smaller firms led by entrepreneurs with deep environmental commitments. There were only a tiny handful of environmental reports released by large companies. Today, the debate has shifted substantially; reporting has become standard practice for all leadership firms in all industries; the discussion is not about whether to report but how. This discussion has in turn lead CERES to create the Global Reporting Initiative, an international effort involving dozens of groups from around the world to harmonize environmental and sustainability reporting standards.

In contrast to the Sullivan Principles, the CERES coalition has not chosen to group or grade the companies, but instead to push for the endorsement of the principles through shareholder activism and for the disclosure of information which others, such as the Council on Economic Priorities, the Investor Responsibility Research Center, and the ever-expanding group of environmental analysts, can use for their evaluations. Now that dozens of companies have endorsed the CERES Principles and are using the CERES report format, CERES has found it difficult to tap enough environmental expertise to provide the kind of detailed feedback that companies would like. Still, there is no question that the process of completing a public report sends a clear signal to the internal segments of firms that the information, and the process of improvement that is supposed to undergird it, is an important part of the company's internal management and external relations.

### Are there mechanisms for dialogue, learning, and improvement?

Unlike certain categories of regulatory or legal compliance, where the task might be to avoid exceeding a fixed standard, codes of conduct are intended to move companies along a path of continuous improvement in which each year's performance becomes, ideally, a benchmark to be surpassed the next year. For example, in the CERES Principles, the overall goal under the first principle is to reduce the impact on the biosphere; the practical consequence would be to measure and reduce greenhouse gas emissions on an annual basis. In order to meet such systematically moving targets, the organization must have an internal structure of learning that pushes environmental and sustainability thinking outside of the confines of environmental, health, and safety management (which has traditionally been focused only on compliance) and into other corporate functions such as process and product design, supplier relations, marketing, and so forth. This can be difficult. Corporations, like other human communities, often develop powerful internal cultures. These cultures develop recognizable features—some are open to new thoughts and responsive to criticism, others are closed and defensive. Some embrace change while others fear it.

Among the most striking features of the CERES Principles are the channels of dialogue and learning that have been created between firms and outside stakeholders, allowing all parties to gain new information and perspectives. Executives accustomed to thinking along traditional environment, health, and safety lines are introduced to new realms of activity and thought, such as environmental justice or sustainable design. Similarly, environmental activists who have maintained a simplified view of the structure and function of companies gain new appreciation for the complexity and creativity of corporate life.

Most important, these mechanisms for dialogue and learning allow the interpretation of the code of conduct—and sometimes the code of conduct itself—to be reviewed and recalibrated. Thus the feedback loop for information and growth is not restricted solely to the firms to which the code is intended to apply, but it also influences the original proponents.

## Is Effectiveness the Same as Success?

Even as we seek to identity the structural dimensions of effectiveness in codes of conduct, we should not forget that the original point, that codes of conduct are but one component in a complex system of organizational values and behaviors. There is, for example, a complicated relationship between the notions of *effectiveness* and *success*.

This distinction was developed by Gary Hufbauer and Jeffrey Schott of the Institute for International Economics. In the mid-1980s they published a lengthy study of the history of economic sanctions in the twentieth century in which they distinguished the effectiveness and the success of such sanctions.[6] Sanctions were effective, they said, if the actions taken by the sending countries could be shown to have had material consequences for the target, such as, for example, a reduction in foreign trade and investment. Sanctions were considered a success if the policy goals of the sending country were attained.

Thus, sanctions could sometimes be effective without being successful. One might argue, for example, that the current U.S. sanctions against Iraq were having a material impact on the country without obtaining the intended policy result. Conversely, sanctions can also be successful without being effective; that is, the sender country could achieve its policy goal without the sanctions ever having had a demonstrable impact on the target.

The distinction between effectiveness and success is important for codes of conduct. In the case of the Sullivan Principles, the effectiveness of the proponents in changing employment practices within specific firms may not have ultimately been as effective as the success they had in changing thinking about apartheid in the halls of the American corporate and investor elite.

Similarly, though the number of large corporations that have endorsed the CERES Principles has risen modestly and the coalition can point to improvements in corporate performance and transparency, the impact of the principles more broadly in the corporate world—sparking preemptive moves by corporations, legitimizing the whole field of environmental reporting, shifting the terms of the debate—has been even broader.

There are a host of reasons for the differences between effectiveness and success. To measure effectiveness one must be able to show fairly tight causal connections. Particular changes must be linked to particular actions. To isolate such impacts within a complex organization that is responding to millions of ideas and stimuli can be difficult. The task is made even more arduous if parts of the target organization are reluctant to embrace change and protective of their independence.[7] One can see this tension in both the Sullivan and CERES experiences. Though the speed, depth, and effectiveness of change varied enormously within the endorsing companies, the Sullivan Principles succeeded in shifting the terms of the debate from whether U.S. companies had the right to operate anywhere they chose to whether the presence of U.S. corporations was beneficial to South African blacks. Similarly, the CERES coalition has generally found it easier to track larger policy successes—the decision by hundreds of companies to publish annual environmental reports and to issue public statements about their environmental commitments—than to identify which of these decisions result specifically from an intervention by CERES.

## Conclusion

In summary, codes of conduct are forms of articulation and compromise that attempt to balance explicitness, scale, formality, constraint, and creativity. They provide a clarified frame of reference and an opportunity to shift the energy of conflict from arguments about positions at the margin to the possibility of joint gains.

Their effectiveness—that is, the ability of codes of conduct to meet their expectations and to produce change both inside and outside the organization—depends on the presence of certain structural characteristics, though effectiveness is not always identical with success. As long as the material conditions to which they are a response exist, codes of conduct will continue to be invented. if they are used to create the illusion of commitment and change where none exists they will breed only disillusionment and anger. If they are used in good faith to build learning, trust, and commitment, they can help to create networks of understanding and cooperation that would be new to the history of the world.

## Notes

1. I use the term "codes of conduct" broadly to include sets of principles, ethics statements, credos, and other explicit, written statements through which one organization, or particularly for the purposes of this chapter a group of organizations, specifies the relationship between values and behavior.

2. For more information on the Sullivan Principles, see Robert Kinloch Massie, *Loosing the Bonds: The United States and South Africa in the Apartheid Years* (New York: Doubleday, 1998).

3. Originally known as the Valdez Principles, the CERES Principles were formed by a coalition of national environmental groups such as the Sierra Club, National Wildlife Federation, Friends of the Earth, and Natural Resources Defense Council who formed an alliance with a large consortium of large public and religious investors. For more information, see the CERES website at www.ceres.org.

4. Effectiveness is defined as "having the intended or expected effect, serving the purpose. Producing or adapted to produce the desired impression or response. These adjectives mean having the capacity to produce an effect or a result. *Effective* and *effectual* may imply *proven* capacity for doing the job in question." *American Heritage Dictionary.*

5. See *Loosing the Bonds,* pp. 448ff.

6. See Gary Clyde Hufbauer and Jeffrey J. Schott, *Economic Sanctions in Support of Foreign Policy Goals* (Washington, D.C.: Institute for International Economics, 1983); also *Economic Sanctions Reconsidered: History and Current Policy* (Washington, D.C.: Institute for International Economics, 1985).

7. The apartheid government, for example, went to extreme lengths to conceal the material impact of sanctions on the South African economy.

PART VIII

— ❋ —

# What Remains to Be Done

# 19

# Corporate Ethics Statements

## *An Update*

PATRICK E. MURPHY

### Background

Many large companies first found the necessity for publishing their ethical guidelines in the 1970s. A bribery scandal involving a defense contractor and a foreign government made firms realize that they needed to promulgate ethics statements and communicate them to their employees. Most of these ethics statements were what we know as codes of ethics or codes of conduct. Several other companies, most notably J. C. Penney, formulated their ethical principles near the time of the founding of the firm. The Penney Idea was instituted in 1913 (Oliverio 1989).

As U.S. companies grew and expanded internationally, most decided the ethics policy they had in place should apply wherever they operated. Another stimulus for a single set of ethical operating principles was the Foreign Corrupt Practices Act, passed in the late 1970s as a further reaction to the bribery scandals. In the 1980s and 1990s virtually all large U.S.-based multinationals have some type of written ethics policy in place. They explicitly recognize that global issues need to be addressed in such documents (Cottril 1996; Payne et al. 1997).

One method for understanding global codes of conduct is to benchmark ethics statements from other major corporations. The study reported in this chapter represents an update of a project conducted in 1992 whose results were published previously (Murphy 1995). After five years, it seemed to be an appropriate time to examine how companies are progressing in developing, revising, and promoting their ethics statements.

The major premise of this research is that each company has to develop and implement the type of ethics statement that works for that firm. For example, Johnson and Johnson has produced a widely publicized credo (Nash

1988), while the Co-Operative Bank in England developed an ethics policy with fifteen one-sentence statements. Caterpillar, on the other hand, has a much more extensive twenty-page code of ethics and, as one executive told the author, it serves as our "Bible." Company ethics statements should capture the essence of the corporate stance on this important topic. Academics and outside critics often suggest to a firm what it should do regarding ethics, but it is ultimately the company and its leadership who must implement and live with any ethics policy.

## Types of Ethics Statements

Although ethics statements can be classified into several types, three appear to dominate. They are: values statements, corporate credo/creed, and codes of ethics. This section describes each of these and presents a rationale for them. Recognition is also made of their limitations, and, in the spirit of full disclosure, criticisms are recounted.

### Values Statements

Many companies have set out their corporate values in a systematic manner that makes reference to quality, customers, the environment, and a range of employee issues such as diversity, teamwork, and respect. Values statements often stem from the company's mission and give direction to it. While these statements are not exclusively devoted to ethics, they do provide insight to how companies integrate ethical issues with their operating principles. A number of values statements speak of a firm's being ethical and fair, with an emphasis on integrity, commitment, trustworthiness, and openness in communication.

Values statements are intended to set out the guiding principles of the firm. Many organizations list them in concert with their mission statement. Some companies even make reference to the values espoused by its founder as ones that have withstood the test of time. For example, the Golden Rule appears as a core value in a number of firms.

The most frequent criticism of values statements is that companies do not live up to them or that they have no practical impact on the organization. Prospective employees are also encouraged to prioritize their personal values and may have to compromise with the company on some of the less important ones.

### Corporate Credos

A corporate credo delineates a firm's ethical responsibility to its stakeholders. It is often somewhat longer than the values statement and is usually written in paragraph form. Among the stakeholders commonly listed in most corporate credos are customers, employees, suppliers, shareholders, communities, and the environment.

Corporate credos can serve as a benchmark document for companies that desire a cohesive corporate culture. A spirit of strong communication is essential if the credo's ideals are to be transmitted throughout the firm. Corporate credos are often not precise enough to offer guidance for large multinational companies facing complex ethical issues unless those credos have been extensively communicated over time. Recently merged companies also have difficulty meshing their corporate cultures and coming up with a unified corporate credo.

### Codes of Ethics

These ethical statements represent more detailed discussions of a firm's ethical policies. Codes commonly address issues like conflict of interest, relationships with competitors and suppliers, privacy matters, gift giving and receiving, and political contributions. The vast majority of large, U.S.-based companies have ethics codes in place and have revised them in recent years. Codes increasingly contain examples or short scenarios to illustrate how firms expect employees to react when faced with an ethical dilemma. Codes of ethics range in length from a pamphlet-sized document of two or three pages to extensive booklets of over fifty pages.

Codes of ethics have long been criticized for several reasons. First, many of the earliest codes were too platitudinous or were meant to be exclusively public relations statements. A second criticism focuses on the general nature of some codes that cover topics not especially pertinent to the company or industry. Third, no code can account for every conceivable ethical violation. Fourth, another criticism is that codes tend to be too legalistic and just codify rules and regulations rather than provide guidance. A final criticism about codes is that they are not enforced. Twenty percent of the respondents to my 1992 survey did not include sanctions for violating the code. Although this number may seem high, it is lower than the 30 percent number that this author found in earlier research (Murphy 1995).

## Exemplary Ethics Statements

Companies can learn from one another when it comes to developing and implementing ethics statements. Smaller and medium-size firms can use the experience of large corporations. In the spirit of benchmarking mentioned at the outset of this chapter, this writer (Murphy 1998) reprinted and commented on exemplary ethics statements of major organizations. In the opening chapter of that book several principles were advanced for organizations to follow in developing an effective ethics statement. They are as follows.

*Write it.* Top management or owners of any organization should write down the guiding philosophy or values of the firm. These principles can then be conveyed to all stakeholders, especially to the employees. Written ethics statements clarify the rules of the organization and/or the ideals to which it aspires.

*Tailor it.* Ideally, ethics statements should be tailored to the industry or line of business in which the firm operates. Although it is more difficult for short statements to be tailored, certainly codes of ethics can contain information relevant to the firm and its industry practices. The common criticisms of longer codes is that they are very similar. Tailoring a code allows an organization to differentiate its ethical position from that of its competitors.

*Communicate it.* An ethics statement should be communicated to both internal and external stakeholders. Companies always distribute these documents to employees but often do not make a conscious effort to provide them to suppliers, customers, and other interested stakeholders.

*Promote it.* It is not enough to just communicate ethics statements. They should be actively promoted. Companies should take every opportunity to make the code or other statements widely available. Some of the techniques used to promote ethics statements are laminated cards, backs of business cards, and framed statements in lobbies of corporate headquarters and its subsidiaries in distant locations. An increasing number of companies have begun actively promoting their ethics position, including ones regarding privacy, on their website.

*Revise it.* All ethics statements should be subject to revision once every few years. Similar to a mission document, ethics codes, credos, and values statements should be frequently updated. Companies ideally should revisit their ethics statements on a regular basis so that they represent the latest thinking on any particular topic and incorporate emerging ethical concerns.

*Live it.* The litmus test for any ethics document is whether members of the organization follow it on a daily basis. It is hard to determine whether companies do so from a vantage point outside the firm. Top managers are instrumental in two ways. First, they must make a concerted effort to reward employees who follow the principles listed in the ethics statement. Second, they are role models to whom others look for guidance. For example, Levi Strauss's Aspiration Statement says that management should exhibit "leadership that epitomizes stated standards of ethical behavior."

*Enforce/Reinforce it.* Enforcement or reinforcement is critical to gain the respect of managers and all employees in any organization. For codes of ethics, sanctions must be specified and punishment, when necessary, should be carried out. Companies either take a strong stance (violators will be terminated) or a middle ground (punishment depends on severity of violation) in their discussion of code enforcement. For the values statements or corporate credo, the reinforcement of the ideals and principles are essential for the document to have impact on the members of the firm.

These seven principles do not address several relevant questions dealing with global codes of conduct. For instance:

- Are these global codes? The ones reprinted in my 1998 book are largely international codes and have been translated into a number of other languages. The values and principles reflect primarily those of the U.S. culture, but multinationals are increasingly attempting to be as inclusive as possible regarding the wording of their ethics statements.

- Who writes the codes? The principles do not specifically address the actual writing of ethics statements. Traditionally, top management, owners, or the leadership group tend to be the drafters of any ethics statements. However, more and more companies are putting out their ethics statement for comment by employees and within their subsidiaries whether located in the United States or elsewhere in the world.

- Who should communicate the ethics statement? This is a philosophical point that companies must address. A number of firms have the CEO or managing director or a single high-level manager act as the spokesperson for its ethics position. However, some companies who take more of a compliance orientation utilize the legal department as the primary communicator about the code and its implementation. Still others use the human resources department as the major point of contact for its ethics statement since it is usually charged with employee training.

## 1992 Survey

The purpose of the 1992 survey (Murphy 1995) was to gain insight into the status of ethics statements and training programs in large U.S.-based companies. The sample was drawn from the *Forbes 500* list of firms which contained about eight hundred companies. The rationale for selecting these large firms was that they should be on the forefront of ethical thinking because of their size and scope of operations. Two hundred and thirty-five completed surveys were used for analytical purposes. The response rate was approximately 30 percent.

This research attempted to gain information about the three types of ethics statements: corporate credo, values statements, and codes of ethics. Furthermore, a number questions about the ethics training program which was in place at the firm were also asked. The instrument used to collect the information was a four-page mail survey sent to the CEO of the company, who was requested to route the survey to the appropriate manager in charge of the ethics program.

Table 1 depicts the results of the 1992 (and 1997) study. About one-third of the companies had a formal written corporate credo, and just half had drafted a values statement, while over 90 percent had a code of ethics in place. The code tended to be the oldest document, while the values statements were relatively recent, with over half being introduced in the late '80s or early '90s. The survey also found that over 80 percent of these statements had been revised in the last several years. Somewhat surprisingly, only 47 percent of the statements were communicated to both internal and external stakeholders. Although not indicated in the table, 64 percent of the firms emphasized information pertinent to their industry and 80 percent include sanctions for violating the code and specific guidance on gift giving and receiving.

The overall sentiment regarding corporate ethics statements in the early 1990s was largely favorable. These companies had statements in place, regularly revised them, and appeared to use systems to make them effective. However, ethics policies were not widely disseminated beyond the firm and most codes were not tailored to deal with ethical issues facing a particular industry.

## 1997 Survey

The purpose of the 1997 study was to update and extend the one conducted in 1992. Both the conference on global codes of conduct and the five-year interval from the first study were stimuli to undertake this extension. The focus of the project was the same as before—ethics statements and ethics training programs. The instrument was again a mail survey sent to the CEO of large firms. The questionnaire was only two pages in length and contained less detail on training programs and more detail on ethics statements.

The sampling frame was again the *Forbes 500* companies. Each April the magazine publishes its list of top firms and this time there were 785 firms on it. One hundred and ninety-eight surveys were returned for a response rate of approximately 25 percent. Although the response was slightly lower than in the 1992 study, companies are being increasingly bombarded with requests for information, and the response rate for a mail survey (without follow-up contact) seemed quite acceptable. In addition, over a dozen letters were received from companies stating that they do not respond to any such survey or request for information.

TABLE 1.   *Corporate Ethics Statements in U.S. Firms*

| *Does your company have a formal written* | | | | | *1997* | *1992* |
|---|---|---|---|---|---|---|
| Corporate Credo | | | | | 43% | 34% |
| Code of Ethics | | | | | 93% | 91% |
| Values Statement | | | | | 63% | 53% |

| | *Credo* | | *Code* | | *Values Statement* | |
|---|---|---|---|---|---|---|
| *When were these documents first introduced?* | *1997* | *1992* | *1997* | *1992* | *1997* | *1992* |
| Less than 5 years ago | 30% | 41% | 18% | 18.5% | 31% | 51.0% |
| 5–10 years ago | 34% | 23% | 37% | 34.5% | 40% | 27.5% |
| 11–20 years ago | 20% | 14% | 27% | 31.5% | 18% | 13.5% |
| Over 20 years ago | 16% | 22% | 18% | 15.5% | 11% | 8% |

*What percentage of these documents have been revised in the last five years?*

| | |
|---|---|
| Corporate Credo | 58% |
| Code of Ethics | 80% |
| Values Statement | 62% |

| *Were these "major" or "minor" changes?* | *Major* | *Minor* | *Unspecified* |
|---|---|---|---|
| Corporate Credo | 38% | 59% | 3% |
| Code of Ethics | 50% | 47% | 3% |
| Values Statement | 54% | 40% | 6% |

| *How are they communicated?* | *1997* | *1992* |
|---|---|---|
| Only to employees | 57% | 53% |
| Both internally and externally | 38% | 47% |
| Unspecified | 5% | 0% |

| *Are they promoted in any way?* | |
|---|---|
| Yes | 74% |
| No | 23% |

Table 1 also depicts the results for the 1997 study. The number of firms with ethics statements were higher in all three categories compared to 1992. Over 93 percent of the firms have a code in place, while almost two-thirds have formal values statements and 43 percent now indicate they have a corporate credo. While these differences are not statistically significant, they do represent an even greater emphasis on ethics by large corporations in the ensuing five years. Although not shown on the table, the absolute number of firms with one, two, or three of these statements is instructive. Sixty-two (of the 198) companies have all three types of ethics statements; fifty-five have both a code and values statement, and fifty have only a code of ethics.

The introduction of the credo, code, and values statement tracks rather closely the 1992 data with the code being the oldest of the three and the values statement the most recent. Not surprisingly, codes were revised more frequently than the other two types of ethics statements. This likely reflects the more legalistic and compliance orientation of codes which must be kept up to date and follow the most recent legal precepts.

Regarding the other principles for effective ethics statements discussed earlier in the chapter, a couple of interesting findings surfaced. Somewhat surprisingly, an even smaller percentage than in 1992 (38 percent versus 47 percent) of companies communicate their codes both internally and externally. One interpretation of this is that companies do not go out of their way to communicate their code beyond the firm. Some might even argue that companies are even more secretive or sensitive to legal concerns than before. However, 74 percent actively promote the ethics statement (bottom of Table 1), which indicates that many firms do in fact promote their code rather widely. While these results might seem to be a contradiction, it does appear that companies are serious about making their codes widely available.

Table 2 shows several areas where the codes of ethics may contain specific guidance. Respondents were asked to circle the areas where their code provides some explicit direction. Of several areas of interest in the global arena, for example, bribery and grease payments represent the second highest category with over 86 percent of the respondents indicating that their company and its ethics statements provide specific guidance on how to deal with this issue. Other areas of interest include working conditions, with 58 percent stating that they have specific policies dealing with it. On human rights and international issues, about 40 percent of the companies provide direction in these areas. Although the exact percentage of the responding firms that are multinational corporations is unknown, these are large firms and many do in fact have specific statements regarding global issues such as human rights and international topics.

Interestingly, one area shown in Table 2 actually declined in importance from '92 to '97. The violations/sanctions category was noted by 74 percent of the respondents in '97, but in '92 80 percent of the companies said their firms included sanctions in the code. Part of this decline may be attributed to the method of asking the questions. In the '92 survey, it was a separate question, while in '97 this was one of fifteen issues listed.

At the bottom of Table 2, the total number of categories mentioned by each firm is included. As can be seen, the vast majority of the companies included between five and ten categories. Therefore, codes do appear to contain

TABLE 2.  *Code Containing Specific Guidance*
         n= 117

|  |  |
|---|---|
|  | *1992* |
| Gift Giving/Receiving—109 (93.6%) | 84% |
| Bribery/Grease Payments—101 (86.3%) | |
| | |
| Violations/Sanctions—87 (74.4%) | 80% |
| Workforce Diversity—83 (70.9%) | |
| | |
| Selling Practices—73 (62.4%) | |
| Competitive Intelligence—72 (61.5%) | |
| | |
| Working Conditions—68 (58.1%) | |
| Environmental Problems—67 (57.3%) | |
| Relationship with Dealers—65 (55.5%) | |
| | |
| Pertinent Industry Issues—51 (43.6%) | 36% |
| Human Rights—46 (39.3%) | |
| International Issues—43 (36.8%) | |
| | |
| Advertising—36 (30.8%) | |
| Product Safety—36 (30.8%) | |
| | |
| Other–34 (29.1%) | |

Number of Mentions
(Out of 15)

1–4 categories—11

5–7 categories—42

8–11 categories—41

12–15 categories—22

specific guidance in a number of areas. However, a minority of firms give explicit direction on many potentially troublesome ethical issues.

## Conclusion

The current status of ethics statements is that they have become even more pervasive (see Table 1) with many companies now having multiple ones in place. Furthermore, global issues are increasingly being treated in codes of ethics. Issues such as bribery, working conditions, and human rights have now been incorporated into the ethics policies of multinational corporations. The extensiveness of the commitment to these emerging areas both within the codes themselves and in the daily operating procedures of the firms represents a needed extension to this research project.

Finally, actions speak louder than words. Companies need to live up to the values they profess, the credo they espouse, and the code they set down. The results of this work indicate that we can be encouraged with the emphasis being placed on the various ethics statements. These efforts should go some distance in strengthening the moral climate of large firms. Thus, we appear to have reason for cautious optimism regarding corporate ethics as we approach the new millennium.

## Bibliography

Cottril, Ken (1996), "Global Codes of Conduct," *Journal of Business Strategy*, May/June, 55–59.

Murphy, Patrick. E. (1995), "Corporate Ethics Statements: Current Status and Future Prospects," *Journal of Business Ethics*, 14: 727–40.

Murphy, Patrick E. (1998), *Eighty Exemplary Ethics Statements*, Notre Dame: University of Notre Dame Press.

Nash, Laura N. (1988), "Johnson & Johnson Credo," in *Corporate Ethics: A Prime Business Asset,* J. Keogh, ed. New York: The Business Roundtable, 93–104.

Oliverio, M. E. (1989), "The Implementation of a Code of Ethics: The Early Effort of One Entrepreneur," *Journal of Business*, 8: 367–74.

Payne, Dinah, Cecily Raiborn, and Jorn Askvik (1997), "A Global Code of Business Ethics," *Journal of Business Ethics*, 16: 1727–35.

# Appendices

APPENDIX 1

## THE BUSINESS CHARTER FOR SUSTAINABLE DEVELOPMENT
(Produced by the International Chamber of Commerce)

### Principles for Environmental Management

**1. Corporate priority**
To recognize environmental management as among the highest corporate priorities and as a key determinant to sustainable development; to establish policies, programs and practices for conducting operations in an environmentally sound manner.

**2. Integrated management**
To integrate these policies, programs and practices fully into each business as an essential element of management in all its functions.

**3. Process of improvement**
To continue to improve corporate policies, programs and environmental performance, taking into account technical developments, scientific understanding, consumer needs and community expectations, with legal regulations as a starting point; and to apply the same environmental criteria internationally.

**4. Employee education**
To educate, train and motivate employees to conduct their activities in an environmentally responsible manner.

**5. Prior assessment**
To assess environmental impacts before starting a new activity or project and before decommissioning a facility or leaving a site.

**6. Products and services**
To develop and provide products or services that have no undue environmental impact and are safe in their intended use, that are efficient in their consumption of energy and natural resources, and that can be recycled, reused, or disposed of safely.

### 7. Customer advice

To advise, and where relevant educate, customers, distributors and the public in the safe use, transportation, storage and disposal of products provided; and to apply similar considerations to the provision of services.

### 8. Facilities and operations

To develop, design and operate facilities and conduct activities taking into consideration the efficient use of energy and materials, the sustainable use of renewable resources, the minimization of adverse environmental impact and waste generation, and the safe and responsible disposal of residual wastes.

### 9. Research

To conduct or support research on the environmental impacts of raw materials, products, processes, emissions and wastes associated with the enterprise and on the means of minimizing such adverse impacts.

### 10. Precautionary approach

To modify the manufacture, marketing or use of products or services or the conduct of activities, consistent with scientific and technical understanding, to prevent serious or irreversible environmental degradation.

### 11. Contractors and suppliers

To promote the adoption of these principles by contractors acting on behalf of the enterprise, encouraging and, where appropriate, requiring improvements in their practices to make them consistent with those of the enterprise; and to encourage the wider adoption of these principles by suppliers.

### 12. Emergency preparedness

To develop and maintain, where significant hazards exist, emergency preparedness plans in conjunction with the emergency services, relevant authorities and the local community, recognizing potential transboundary impacts.

### 13. Transfer of technology

To contribute to the transfer of environmentally sound technology and management methods throughout the industrial and public sectors.

### 14. Contributing to the common effort

To contribute to the development of public policy and to business, governmental and intergovernmental programs and educational initiatives that will enhance environmental awareness and protection.

### 15. Openness to concerns

To foster openness and dialogue with employees and the public, anticipating and responding to their concerns about the potential hazards and impacts of operations, products, wastes or services, including those of transboundary or global significance.

### 16. Compliance and reporting

To measure environmental performance; to conduct regular environmental audits and assessments of compliance with company requirements, legal requirements and these principles; and periodically to provide appropriate information to the Board of Directors, shareholders, employees, the authorities and the public.

*Adopted by the International Chamber of Commerce at the 64th Session of its Executive Board on 27th November 1990 and first published by the JCC In April 1991.*

The International Chamber of Commerce can be contacted at
38, Cours Albert ler, 75008 PARIS. France

## APPENDIX 2

### THE CERES PRINCIPLES
(Produced by the Coalition for Environmentally Responsible Economics)

*The CERES Principles, as the name which they were first given (the Valdez Principles) shows, arose in North America after the fateful accident to the "Exxon Valdez"—the oil tanker which ran aground in Alaska and destroyed the wild life. In Britain, they are, as yet, little heard of, but it may be that their time is coming. On February 3, 1994, the giant American company, General Motors, adopted the CERES Principles and may well be followed, even by some British companies, in due course.*

### Introduction
By adopting these Principles, we publicly affirm our belief that corporations have a responsibility for the environment, and must conduct all aspects of their business as responsible stewards of the environment by operating in a manner that protects the Earth. We believe that corporations must not compromise the ability of future generations to sustain themselves.

We will update out practices continually in light of advances in technology and new understandings in health and environmental science. In collaboration with CERES, we will promote a dynamic process to ensure that the Principles are interpreted in a way that accommodates changing technologies and environmental realities. We intend to make consistent, measurable progress in implementing these Principles and to apply them in all aspects of our operations throughout the world.

### 1. Protection of the Biosphere
We will reduce and make continual progress toward eliminating the release of any substance that may cause environmental damage to the air, water, or the earth or its inhabitants. We will safeguard all habitats affected by our operations and will protect open spaces and wilderness, while preserving biodiversity.

### 2. Sustainable Use of Natural Resources
We will make sustainable use of renewable natural resources such as water, soils and forests. We will conserve nonrenewable natural resources through efficient use and careful planning.

### 3. Reduction and Disposal of Wastes
We will reduce and where possible eliminate waste through source reduction and recycling. All waste will be handled and disposed of through safe and responsible methods.

#### 4. Energy Conservation

We will conserve energy and improve the energy efficiency of our internal operations and of the goods and services we sell. We will make every effort to use environmentally safe and sustainable energy sources.

#### 5. Risk Reduction

We will strive to minimize the environmental, health and safety risks to our employees and the communities in which we operate through safe technologies, facilities and operating procedures, and by being prepared for emergencies.

#### 6. Safe Products and Services

We will reduce and where possible eliminate the use, manufacture, or sale of products and services that cause environmental damage or health or safety hazards. We will inform our customers of the environmental impacts of our products or services and try to correct unsafe use.

#### 7. Environmental Restoration

We will promptly and responsibly correct conditions we have caused that endanger health, safety or the environment. To the extent feasible, we will redress injuries we have caused to persons or damage we have caused to the environment and will restore the environment.

#### 8. Informing the Public

We will inform in a timely manner everyone who may be affected by conditions caused by our company that might endanger health, safety or the environment. We will regularly seek advice and counsel through dialogue with persons in communities near our facilities. We will not take any action against employees for reporting dangerous incidents or conditions to management or to appropriate authorities.

#### 9. Management Commitment

We will implement these Principles and sustain a process that ensures that the Board of Directors and Chief Executive Officer are fully informed about pertinent environmental issues and are fully responsible for environmental policy. In selecting our Board of Directors, we will consider demonstrated environmental commitment as a factor.

#### 10. Audits and Reports

We will conduct an annual self-evaluation of our progress in implementing these Principles. We will support the timely creation of generally accepted environmental audit procedures. We will annually complete the CERES Report, which will be made available to the public.

#### Disclaimer

These Principles establish an environmental ethic with criteria by which investors and others can assess the environmental performance of companies. Companies that sign these Principles pledge to go voluntarily beyond the requirements of the law. These Principles are not intended to create new legal liabilities, expand existing rights or obligations, waive legal defenses, or otherwise affect the legal position of any signatory company, and are not intended to be used against a signatory in any legal proceeding for any purpose.

*The CERES Principles in this form were adopted on April 28, 1992.*

The Coalition for Environmentally Responsible Economies (CERES),
711 Atlantic Avenue, BOSTON, Massachusetts 02111. USA

## APPENDIX 3

### PRINCIPLES AND CRITERIA FOR FOREST STEWARDSHIP
(Proposed by the Forest Stewardship Council—FSC)

#### PRINCIPLE #1: COMPLIANCE WITH LAWS AND FSC PRINCIPLES
*Forest management shall respect all applicable laws of the country in which they occur, and international treaties and agreements to which the country is a signatory, and comply with all FSC Principles and Criteria.*

1.1 Forest management shall respect all national and local laws and administrative requirements.

1.2 All applicable and legally prescribed fees, royalties, taxes and other charges shall be paid.

1.3 In signatory countries, the provisions of all binding international agreements such as CITES, ILO Conventions, ITTA, and Convention on Biological Diversity, shall be respected.

1.4 Conflicts between laws, regulations and the FSC Principles and Criteria shall be evaluated for the purposes of certification, on a case by case basis, by the certifiers and the involved or affected parties.

1.5 Forest management areas should be protected from illegal harvesting, settlement and other unauthorized activities.

1.6 Forest managers shall demonstrate a long-term commitment to adhere to the FSC Principles and Criteria.

#### PRINCIPLE #2: TENURE AND USE RIGHTS AND RESPONSIBILITIES
*Long-term tenure and use rights to the land and forest resources shall be clearly defined, documented and legally established.*

2.1 Clear evidence of long-term forest use rights to the land (e.g. land title, customary rights, or lease agreements) shall be demonstrated.

2.2 Local communities with legal or customary tenure or use rights shall maintain control, to the extent necessary to protect their rights or resources, over forest operations unless they delegate control with free and informed consent to other agencies.

2.3 Appropriate mechanisms shall be employed to resolve disputes over tenure claims and use rights. The circumstances and status of any outstanding disputes will be explicitly considered in the certification evaluation. Disputes of substantial magnitude involving a significant number of interests will normally disqualify an operation from being certified.

## PRINCIPLE #3: INDIGENOUS PEOPLES' RIGHTS
*The legal and customary rights of indigenous peoples to own, use and manage their lands, territories, and resources shall be recognized and respected.*

3.1 Indigenous peoples shall control forest management on their lands and territories unless they delegate control with free and informed consent to other agencies.

3.2 Forest management shall not threaten or diminish, either directly or indirectly, the resources or tenure rights of indigenous peoples.

3.3 Sites of special cultural, ecological, economic or religious significance to indigenous peoples shall be clearly identified in cooperation with such peoples, and recognized and protected by forest managers.

3.4 Indigenous peoples shall be compensated for the application of their traditional knowledge regarding the use of forest species or management systems in forest operations. This compensation shall be formally agreed upon with their free and informed consent before forest operations commence.

## PRINCIPLE #4: COMMUNITY RELATIONS AND WORKERS' RIGHTS
*Forest management operations shall maintain or enhance the long-term social and economic well-being of forest workers and local communities.*

4.1 The communities within, or adjacent to, the forest management area should be given opportunities for employment, training, and other services.

4.2 Forest management should meet or exceed all applicable laws and/or regulations covering health and safety of employees and their families.

4.3 The rights of workers to organize and voluntarily negotiate with their employers shall be guaranteed as outlined in Conventions 87 and 98 of the International Labor Organization (ILO).

4.4 Management planning and operations shall incorporate the results of evaluations of social impact. Consultations shall be maintained with people and groups directly affected by management operations.

4.5 Appropriate mechanisms shall be employed for resolving grievances and for providing fair compensation in the case of loss or damage affecting the legal or customary rights, property, resources, or livelihoods of local peoples. Measures shall be taken to avoid such loss or damage.

## PRINCIPLE #5: BENEFITS FROM THE FOREST
*Forest management operations shall encourage the efficient use of the forest's multiple products and services to ensure economic viability and a wide range of environmental and social benefits.*

5.1 Forest management should strive toward economic viability, while taking into account the full environmental, social, and operational costs of production, and ensuring the investments necessary to maintain the ecological productivity of the forest.

5.2 Forest management and marketing operations should encourage the optimal use and local processing of the forest's diversity of products.

5.3 Forest management should minimize waste associated with harvesting and on-site processing operations and avoid damage to other forest resources.

5.4 Forest management should strive to strengthen and diversify the local economy, avoiding dependence on a single forest product.

5.5 Forest management operations shall recognize, maintain, and, where appropriate, enhance the value of forest services and resources such as watersheds and fisheries.

5.6 The rate of harvest of forest products shall not exceed levels which can be permanently sustained.

## PRINCIPLE #6: ENVIRONMENTAL IMPACT

*Forest management shall conserve biological diversity and its associated values, water resources, soils, and unique and fragile ecosystems and landscapes, and, by so doing, maintain the ecological functions and the integrity of the forest.*

6.1 Assessment of environmental impacts shall be completed—appropriate to the scale, intensity of forest management and the uniqueness of the affected resources—and adequately integrated into management systems. Assessments shall include landscape level considerations as well as the impacts of on-site processing facilities. Environmental impacts shall be assessed prior to commencement of site-disturbing operations.

6.2 Safeguards shall exist which protect rare, threatened and endangered species and their habitats (e.g. nesting and feeding areas). Conservation zones and protection areas shall be established, appropriate to the scale and intensity of forest management and the uniqueness of the affected resources. Inappropriate hunting, fishing, trapping and collecting shall be controlled.

6.3 Ecological functions and values shall be maintained intact, enhanced, or restored, including:

(a) Forest regeneration and succession.
(b) Genetic, species and ecosystem diversity.
(c) Natural cycles that affect the productivity of the forest ecosystem.

6.4 Representative samples of existing ecosystems within the landscape shall be protected in their natural state and recorded on maps, appropriate to the scale and intensity of operations and the uniqueness of the affected resources.

6.5 Written guidelines shall be prepared and implemented to: control erosion; minimize forest damage during harvesting, road construction, and all other mechanical disturbances; and protect water resources.

6.6 Management systems shall promote the development and adoption of environmentally friendly non-chemical methods of pest management and strive to avoid the use of chemical pesticides. World Health Organization Type 1A and 1B and chlorinated hydrocarbon pesticides; pesticides that are persistent, toxic, or whose derivatives remain biologically active and accumulate in the food chain beyond their intended use; as well as any pesticides banned by international agreement, shall be prohibited. If chemicals are used, proper equipment and training shall be provided to minimize health and environmental risks.

6.7 Chemicals, containers, liquid and solid non-organic wastes including fuel and oil shall be disposed of in an environmentally appropriate manner at off-site locations.

6.8 Use of biological control agents shall be documented, minimized, monitored and strictly controlled in accordance with national laws and internationally accepted scientific protocols. Use of genetically modified organisms shall be prohibited.

6.9 The use of exotic species shall be carefully controlled and actively monitored to avoid adverse ecological impacts.

## PRINCIPLE #7: MANAGEMENT PLAN

*A management plan—appropriate to the scale and intensity of the operations—shall be written, implemented, and kept up to date. The long-term objectives of management, and the means of achieving them, shall be clearly stated.*

7.1 The management plan and supporting documents shall provide:

(a) Management objectives.

(b) Description of the forest resources to be managed, environmental limitations, land use and ownership status, socio-economic conditions, and a profile of adjacent lands.

(c) Description of silvicultural and/or other management system, based on the ecology of the forest in question and information gathered through resource inventories.

(d) Rationale for rate of annual harvest and species selection.

(e) Provisions for monitoring of forest growth and species dynamics.

(f) Environmental safeguards based on environmental assessments.

(g) Plans for the identification and protection of rare, threatened and endangered species.

(h) Maps describing the forest resource base including protected areas, planned management activities and land ownership.

(i) Description and justification of harvesting techniques and equipment to be used.

7.2 The management plan shall be periodically revised to incorporate the results of monitoring or new scientific and technical information, as well as to respond to changing environmental, social and economic circumstances.

7.3 Forest workers shall receive adequate training and supervision to ensure proper implementation of the management plan.

7.4 While respecting the confidentiality of information, forest managers shall make publicly available a summary of the primary elements of the management plan, including those listed in Criterion 7.1.

## PRINCIPLE #8: MONITORING AND ASSESSMENT

*Monitoring shall be conducted—appropriate to the scale and intensity of forest management—to assess the condition of the forest, yields of forest products, chain of custody, management activities and their social and environmental impacts.*

8.1 The frequency and intensity of monitoring should be determined by the scale and intensity of forest management operations as well as the relative complexity and fragility of the affected environment. Monitoring procedures should be consistent and replicable over time to allow comparison of results and assessment of change.

8.2 Forest management should include the research and data collection needed to monitor, at a minimum, the following indicators:

(a) Yield of all forest products harvested.

(b) Growth rates, regeneration and condition of the forest.

(c) Composition and observed changes in the flora and fauna.

(d) Environmental and social impacts of harvesting and other operations.

(e) Costs, productivity, and efficiency of forest management.

8.3 Documentation shall be provided by the forest manager to enable monitoring and certifying organizations to trace each forest product from its origin, a process known as the "chain of custody." *

8.4 The results of monitoring shall be incorporated into the implementation and revision of the management plan.

8.5 While respecting the confidentiality of information, forest managers shall make publicly available a summary of the results of monitoring indicators, including those listed in Criterion 8.2.

## PRINCIPLE #9: MAINTENANCE OF NATURAL FORESTS

*Primary forests, well-developed secondary forests and sites of major environmental, social or cultural significance shall be conserved. Such areas shall not be replaced by tree plantations or other land uses.*

9.1 Trees planted in natural forests may supplement natural regeneration, fill gaps or contribute to the conservation of genetic resources. Such plantings shall not replace or significantly alter the natural ecosystem.

9.2 The use of replanting as a technique for regenerating stands of certain natural forest types may be appropriate under certain circumstances. Guidelines on the acceptable intensity and spatial extent of tree planting will be addressed in national and regional forest stewardship standards to be approved by FSC. In the absence of such national or regional standards, guidelines developed by the certifier and approved by FSC will prevail.

## PRINCIPLE #10: PLANTATIONS

*Plantations shall be planned and managed in accordance with Principles and Criteria 1–9, and Principle 10 and its Criteria. While plantations can provide an array of social and economic benefits, and can contribute to satisfying the world's needs for forest products, they should complement the management of, reduce pressures on, and promote the restoration and conservation of natural forests.*

---

* "Chain of Custody": The channel through which products are distributed from their origin in the forest to their end-use.

10.1 The management objectives of the plantation, including natural forest conservation and restoration objectives, shall be explicitly stated in the management plan, and clearly demonstrated in the implementation of the plan.

10.2 The design and layout of plantations should promote the protection, restoration and conservation of natural forests, and not increase pressures on natural forests. Wildlife corridors, streamside zones and a mosaic of stands of different ages and rotation periods, shall be used in the layout of the plantation, consistent with the scale of the operation. The scale and layout of plantation blocks shall be consistent with the patterns of forest stands found within the natural landscape.

10.3 Diversity in the composition of plantations is preferred, so as to enhance economic, ecological and social stability. Such diversity may include the size and spatial distribution of management units within the landscape, number and genetic composition of species, age classes and structures.

10.4 The selection of species for planting shall be based on their overall suitability for the site and their appropriateness to the management objectives. In order to enhance the conservation of biological diversity, native species are preferred over exotic species in the establishment of plantations and the restoration of degraded ecosystems. Exotic species, which shall be used only when their performance is greater than that of native species, shall be carefully monitored to detect unusual mortality, disease, or insect outbreaks and adverse ecological impacts.

10.5 A proportion of the overall forest management area, appropriate to the scale of the plantation and to be determined in regional standards, shall be managed so as to restore the site to a natural forest cover.

10.6 Measures shall be taken to maintain or improve soil structure, fertility, and biological activity. The techniques and rate of harvesting, road and trail construction and maintenance, and the choice of species shall not result in long-term soil degradation or adverse impacts on water quality, quantity or substantial deviation from stream course drainage patterns.

10.7 Measures shall be taken to prevent and minimize outbreaks of pests, diseases, fire and invasive plant introductions. Integrated pest management shall form an essential part of the management plan, with primary reliance on prevention and biological control methods rather than chemical pesticides and fertilizers. Plantation management should make every effort to move away from chemical pesticides and fertilizers, including their use in nurseries. The use of chemicals is also covered in Criteria 6.6 and 6.7.

10.8 Appropriate to the scale and diversity of the operation, monitoring of plantations shall include regular assessment of potential on-site and off-site ecological and social impacts (e.g. natural regeneration, effects on water resources and soil fertility, and impacts on local welfare and social well-being), in addition to those elements addressed in Principles 8, 6 and 4. No species should be planted on a large scale until local trials and/or experience have shown that they are ecologically well-adapted to the site, are not invasive, and do not have significant negative ecological impacts on other ecosystems. Special attention will be paid to social issues of land acquisition for plantations, especially the protection of local rights of ownership, use or access.

*Principles 1–9 were ratified by the FSC Founding Members and Board of Directors in September 1994.*
*Principle 10 was ratified by the FSC Members and Board of Directors in February 1996.*

The Forest Stewardship Council. A.C. Avenida Hidalgo 502,68000 OAXACA. Mexico

## APPENDIX 4

### BELLAGIO PRINCIPLES
#### Guidelines for the Practical Assessment of Progress
#### Toward Sustainable Development
(Proposed at the Rockefeller Foundation's Study and Conference Center in 1996)

#### 1. Guiding Vision and Goals
Assessment of progress toward sustainable development should be guided by a clear vision of sustainable development and goals that define that vision.

#### 2. Holistic Perspective
Assessment of progress toward sustainable development should:

- include review of the whole system as well as its parts
- consider the well-being of social, ecological, and economic sub-systems, their state as well as the direction and rate of change of that state, of their component parts, and the interaction between parts
- consider both positive and negative consequences of human activity, in a way that reflects the costs and benefits for human and ecological systems, in monetary and non-monetary terms

#### 3. Essential Elements
Assessment of progress toward sustainable development should:

- consider equity and disparity within the current population and between present and future generations, dealing with such concerns as resource use, over-consumption and poverty, human rights, and access to services, as appropriate
- consider the ecological conditions on which life depends
- consider economic development and other, non-market activities that contribute to human/social well-being

#### 4. Adequate Scope
Assessment of progress toward sustainable development should:

- adopt a time horizon long enough to capture both human and ecosystem time scales thus responding to needs of future generations as well as those current to short-term decision-making

- define the space of study large enough to include not only local but also long distance impacts on people and ecosystems
- build on historic and current conditions to anticipate future conditions—where we want to go, where we could go

### 5. Practical Focus
Assessment of progress toward sustainable development should be based on:

- an explicit set of categories or an organizing framework that links vision and goals to indicators and assessment criteria
- a limited number of key issues for analysis
- a limited number of indicators or indicator combinations to provide a clearer signal of progress
- standardizing measurement wherever possible to permit comparison
- comparing indicator values to targets, reference values, ranges, thresholds, or direction of trends, as appropriate

### 6. Openness
Assessment of progress toward sustainable development should:

- make methods and data that are used accessible to all
- make explicit all judgments, assumptions, and uncertainties in data and interpretations

### 7. Effective Communication
Assessment of progress toward sustainable development should:

- be designed to address the needs of the audience and set of users
- draw from indicators and other tools that are stimulating and serve to engage decision-makers
- aim, from the outset, for simplicity in structure and use of clear and plain language

### 8. Broad Participation
Assessment of progress toward sustainable development should:

- obtain broad representation of key grass-roots, professional, technical and social groups, including youth, women, and indigenous people—to ensure the recognition of diverse and changing values
- ensure the participation of decision-makers to secure a firm link to adopted policies and resulting action

### 9. On-going Assessment
Assessment of progress toward sustainable development should:

- develop a capacity for repeated measurement to determine trends
- be iterative, adaptive, and responsive to change and uncertainty because systems are complex and change frequently
- adjust goals, frameworks, and indicators as new insights are gained
- promote development of collective learning and feedback to decision-making

## 10. Institutional Capacity

Continuity of assessing progress toward sustainable development should be assured by:

- clearly assigning responsibility and providing on-going support in the decision-making process
- providing institutional capacity for data collection, maintenance, and documentation
- supporting development of local assessment capacity

*These 'Bellagio Principles' were composed in November 1996 at the Rockefeller Foundation's Study and Conference Center in Bellagio, Italy, by an international group of measurement practitioners and researchers from five continents.*

## APPENDIX 5

## THE INTERNATIONAL LABOR ORGANIZATION CONVENTION CONCERNING INDIGENOUS AND TRIBAL PEOPLES IN INDEPENDENT COUNTRIES (CONVENTION 169)

### PART 1
### *General Policy*

#### Article 1

1. This Convention applies to:
   a. tribal peoples in independent countries whose social, cultural and economic conditions distinguish them from other sections of the national community, and whose status is regulated by their own customs or traditions or by special laws or regulations;
   b. peoples in independent countries who are regarded as indigenous on account of their descent from the populations which inhabited the country, or a geographical region to which the country belongs, at the time of conquest or colonization or the establishment of present state boundaries and who, irrespective of their legal status retain some or all of their own social, economic, cultural and political institutions.
2. Self-identification as indigenous or tribal shall be regarded as a fundamental criterion for determining the groups to which the provisions of this Convention apply.
3. The use of the term "peoples" in this Convention shall not be construed as having any implications as regards the rights which may attach to the term under international law.

#### Article 2

1. Governments shall have the responsibility for developing, with the participation of the peoples concerned, coordinated and systematic action to protect the rights of these peoples and to guarantee respect for their integrity.

2. Such action shall include measures for:
   a. ensuring that members of these peoples benefit on an equal footing from the rights and opportunities which national laws and regulations grant to other members of the population;
   b. promoting the full realization of the social, economic and cultural rights of these peoples with respect for their social and cultural identity, their customs and traditions and their institutions;
   c. assisting the members of the peoples concerned to eliminate socio-economic gaps that may exist between indigenous and other members of the national community, in a manner compatible with their aspirations and ways of life.

### Article 3

1. Indigenous and tribal peoples shall enjoy the full measure of human rights and fundamental freedoms without hindrance or discrimination. The provisions of the Convention shall be applied without discrimination to male and female members of these peoples.
2. No form of force or coercion shall be used in violation of the human rights and fundamental freedoms of the peoples concerned, including the rights contained in this Convention.

### Article 4

1. Special measures shall be adopted as appropriate for safeguarding the persons, institutions, property, labor, cultures and environment of the peoples concerned.
2. Such special measures shall not be contrary to the freely-expressed wishes of the peoples concerned.
3. Enjoyment of the general rights of citizenship, without discrimination, shall not be prejudiced in any way by such special measures.

### Article 5

In applying the provisions of this Convention:
   a. the social, cultural, religious and spiritual values and practices of these peoples shall be recognized and protected, and due account shall be taken of the nature of the problems which face them both as groups and as individuals;
   b. the integrity of the values, practices and institutions of these peoples shall be respected;
   c. the policies aimed at mitigating the difficulties experienced by these peoples in facing new conditions of life and work shall be adopted, with the participation and cooperation of the peoples affected.

### Article 6

1. In applying the provisions of this Convention, governments shall:
   a. consult the peoples concerned, through appropriate procedures and in particular through their representative institutions, whenever consideration is being given to legislative or administrative measures which may affect them directly;
   b. establish means by which these peoples can freely participate, to at least the same extent as other sectors of the population, at all levels of decision-making in elective institutions and administrative and other bodies responsible for policies and programs which concern them;

c.  establish means for the full development of these peoples' own institutions and initiatives, and in appropriate cases provide the resources necessary for this purpose.

2.  The consultations carried out in application of this Convention shall be undertaken, in good faith and in a form appropriate to the circumstances, with the objective of achieving agreement or consent to the proposed measures.

## Article 7

1.  The peoples concerned shall have the right to decide their own priorities for the process of development as it affects their lives, beliefs, institutions and spiritual well-being and the lands they occupy or otherwise use, and to exercise control, to the extent possible, over their own economic, social and cultural development. In addition, they shall participate in the formulation, implementation and evaluation of plans and programs for national and regional development which may affect them directly.

2.  The improvement of the conditions of life and work and levels of health and education of the peoples concerned, with their participation and cooperation, shall be a matter of priority in plans for the overall economic development of areas they inhabit. Special projects for development of the areas in question shall also be so designed as to promote such improvement.

3.  Governments shall ensure that, whenever appropriate, studies are carried out, in cooperation with the peoples concerned, to assess the social, spiritual, cultural and environmental impact on them of planned development activities. The results of these studies shall be considered as fundamental criteria for the implementation of these activities.

4.  Governments shall take measures, in cooperation with the peoples concerned, to protect and preserve the environment of the territories they inhabit.

## Article 8

1.  In applying the national laws and regulations to the peoples concerned, due regard shall be had to their customs or customary laws.

2.  These peoples shall have the right to retain their own customs and institutions, where these are not incompatible with fundamental rights defined by the national legal system and with internationally recognized human rights. Procedures shall be established, whenever necessary, to resolve conflicts which may arise in the application of this principle.

3.  The application of paragraphs 1 and 2 of this Article shall not prevent members of these peoples from exercising the rights granted to all citizens and from assuming the corresponding duties.

## Article 9

1.  To the extent compatible with the national legal system and internationally recognized human rights, the methods customarily practiced by the peoples concerned for dealing with offences committed by their members shall be respected.

2.  The customs of these peoples in regard to penal matters shall be taken into consideration by the authorities and courts dealing with such cases.

## APPENDIX 6

## AMOCO CANADA PETROLEUM COMPANY LTD
## ABORIGINAL* POLICY

### Mission

In support of our business objectives to become a premier company with a competitive advantage, Amoco will establish long term mutually beneficial relationships based on trust, respect and understanding with the aboriginal people of Canada.

### Vision

Amoco will pro-actively promote opportunities for aboriginal people which establish sustainable self-sufficiency through employment, education, business development and community involvement.

### Values

- We value diversity and respect and honor traditional aboriginal values and individual differences.
- We will be honest, fair and trustworthy.
- We share a pledge with aboriginal people to respect the environment.

Amoco Native Affairs operates within the Amoco corporate structure to advise, educate and assist in the development and implementation of programs whereby aboriginal communities and Amoco can constructively work together.

### Policy Guidelines

**Employment**

Objective
- Pro-actively develop and increase the opportunity for employment of aboriginal people in all phases of Amoco operations.

*Opportunities for Dialogue*
- Recruit qualified aboriginal people.
- Promote aboriginal employee career management.
- Provide internship opportunities.
- Provide summer employment and temporary employment for qualified aboriginal people.

Objective
- Build a work environment that is diverse and culturally aware.

*Opportunities for Dialogue*
- Develop on-going strategic alliances with other companies and organizations to enhance the opportunities for aboriginal people.
- Develop an aboriginal employee support network.
- Develop an aboriginal element in our orientation program.

**Education**

Objective
- Create a climate of opportunity for aboriginal people to further their education, skills development, and experience.

---

* Aboriginal includes first nations, M01s, Inuit and non-status.

*Opportunities* • Offer scholarships/award programs.
*for Dialogue* • Work with the local community to conduct workshops, open houses and career fairs.
• Support specialized programs with local educational institutions.
• Promote stay-in-school incentives.
• Support and promote traditional values textbooks written by the local communities.

**Cross-Cultural Awareness**

Objective • Encourage Amoco employees to obtain an understanding of the aboriginal culture, treaties, history and current issues.

*Opportunities* • Organize and participate in speaker forums.
*for Dialogue* • Provide cross-cultural workshops on issues of mutual concern.
• Organize and participate in cross-cultural social and athletic events.

**Aboriginal Business Development**

Objective • Develop joint working agreements with aboriginal communities to build business relationships and commitment.

*Opportunities* • Support life skills programs.
*for Dialogue* • Support pre-employment seminars.

Objective • Invite aboriginal businesses and contractors to participate in Amoco activities.

*Opportunities* • Identify a liaison person in operating centers.
*for Dialogue* • Provide lead time to aboriginal businesses to enable them to mobilize resources and bid on items of work or services.
• Facilitate the timely payment of invoices.

**Community Involvement**

Objective • Maintain "good corporate citizenship" within aboriginal communities in Amoco's core areas.

*Opportunities* • Support events and programs organized by the aboriginal com-
*for Dialogue* munity.
• Support initiatives and partnerships with aboriginals that promote self-sustainability.
• Support aboriginal involvement in events and programs organized outside the aboriginal community.

**Public Consultation**

Objective • Ensure aboriginal communities and Amoco have a clear understanding of each other's plans and needs and communicate these plans and needs on a timely basis.

*Opportunities* • Develop a process to involve aboriginal people from the very
*for Dialogue* early planning stages of exploration through production to post-production restoration.

- Ongoing dialogue and consultation on concerns specific to aboriginal communities.
- Initiate discussions with aboriginal communities to establish a mutually beneficial partnership.

Produced by Amoco Canada Petroleum Company Ltd., October 17, 1994.


## APPENDIX 7

## INTERNATIONAL CODE OF ETHICS FOR CANADIAN BUSINESS

### Vision

Canadian business has a global presence that is recognized by all stakeholders as economically rewarding to all parties, acknowledged as being ethically, socially and environmentally responsible, welcomed by the communities in which we operate, and that facilitates economic, human resource and community development within a stable operating environment.

### Beliefs

We believe that:
- we can make a difference within our sphere of influence (our stakeholders)
- business should take a leadership role through establishment of ethical business principles
- national governments have the prerogative to conduct their own government and legal affairs in accordance with their sovereign rights
- all governments should comply with international treaties and other agreements that they have committed to, including the areas of human rights and social justice
- while reflecting cultural diversity and differences, we should do business throughout the world consistent with the way we do business in Canada
- the business sector should show ethical leadership
- we can facilitate the achievement of wealth generation and a fair sharing of economic benefits
- our principles will assist in improving relations between the Canadian and host governments
- open, honest and transparent relationships are critical to our success
- local communities need to be involved in decision-making for issues that affect them
- multi-stakeholder processes need to be initiated to seek effective solutions
- confrontation should be tempered by diplomacy
- wealth maximization for all stakeholders will be enhanced by resolution of outstanding human rights and social justice issues

- doing business with other countries is good for Canada and vice versa

### Values

We value:
- Human rights and social justice
- Wealth maximization for all stakeholders
- Operation of a free market economy
- A business environment which militates against bribery and corruption
- Public accountability by governments
- Equality of opportunity
- A defined code of ethics and business practice
- Protection of environmental quality and sound environmental stewardship
- Community benefits
- Good relationships with all stakeholders
- Stability and continuous improvement within our operating environment

### Principles

A. Concerning Community Participation and Environmental Protection, we will:
- strive within our sphere of influence to ensure a fair share of benefits to stakeholders impacted by our activities
- ensure meaningful and transparent consultation with all stakeholders and attempt to integrate our corporate activities with local communities as good corporate citizens
- ensure our activities are consistent with sound environmental management and conservation practices
- provide meaningful opportunities for technology cooperation, training and capacity building within the host nation

B. Concerning Human Rights, we will:
- support and promote the protection of international human rights within our sphere of influence
- not be complicit in human rights abuses

C. Concerning Business Conduct, we will:
- not make illegal and improper payments and bribes and will refrain from participating in any corrupt business practices
- comply with all applicable laws and conduct business activities in a transparent fashion
- ensure contractors', suppliers' and agents' activities are consistent with these principles

D. Concerning Employee Rights and Health and Safety, we will:
- ensure health and safety of workers is protected
- strive for social justice and promote freedom of association and expression in the workplace

- ensure consistency with universally accepted labor standards, including those related to exploitation of child labor

## Application

The signatories of this document are committed to implementation with their individual firms through the development of operational codes and practices that are consistent with the vision, beliefs, values and principles contained herein.

*This Code of Ethics was launched by the Department of Foreign Affairs and
International Trade of the Canadian Government on September 5, 1997.*


# APPENDIX 8

## GM BOARD GUIDELINES ON CORPORATE GOVERNANCE ISSUES

### 1. Selection of chairman and CEO
The board should be free to make this choice any way that seems best for the company at a given point in time. Therefore, the board does not have a policy, one way or the other, on whether or not the role of the CEO and chairman should be separate and, if it is to be separate, whether the chairman should be selected from the non-employee directors or be an employee.

### 2. Lead director concept
The board adopted a policy that it have a director selected by the outside directors who will assume the responsibility of chairing the regularly scheduled meetings of outside directors or other responsibilities which the outside directors as a whole might designate from time to time. Currently this role is filled by the non-executive chairman of the board. Should the company be organized in such a way that the chairman is an employee of the company, another director would be selected for this responsibility.

### 3. Number of committees
The current committee structure of the company seems appropriate. There will, from time to time, be occasions on which the board may want to form a new committee or disband a current committee, depending upon the circumstances. The current six committees are Audit, Capital Stock, Director Affairs, Finance, Incentive and Compensation, and Public Policy.

### 4. Assignment & rotation of committee members
The committee on Director Affairs is responsible, after consultation with the CEO and with consideration of the desires of individual board members, for the assignment of board members to various committees. It is the sense of the board that consideration should be given to rotating committee members periodically at about a five-year interval, but the board does not feel that such a rotation should be mandated as policy since there may be reasons at a given point in time to maintain an individual director's committee membership for a longer period.

### 5. Frequency & length of committee meetings
The committee chairman, in consultation with committee members, will determine the frequency and length of the meetings of the committee.

### 6. Committee agenda
The chairman of the committee, in consultation with the appropriate members of management and staff, will develop the committee's agenda. Each committee will issue a schedule of agenda subjects to be discussed for the ensuing year at the beginning of each year (to the degree these can be foreseen). This forward agenda will also be shared with the board.

### 7. Selection of agenda items for board meetings
The chairman of the board and the CEO (if the chairman is not the CEO) will establish the agenda for each board meeting. Each board member is free to suggest the inclusion of item(s) on the agenda.

### 8. Board materials distributed in advance
It is the sense of the board that information and data that is important to the board's understanding of the business be distributed in writing to the board before the board meets. The management will make every attempt to see that this material is as brief as possible while still providing the desired information.

### 9. Presentations
As a general rule, presentations on specific subjects should be sent to the board members in advance so that board meeting time may be conserved and discussion time focused on questions that the board has about the material. On those occasions in which the subject matter is too sensitive to put on paper, the presentation will be discussed at the meeting.

### 10. Regular attendance of non-directors at board meetings
The board is comfortable with the regular attendance at each board meeting of non-board members who are members of the President's Council. Should the CEO want to add additional people as attendees on a regular basis, it is expected that this suggestion would be made to the board for its concurrence.

### 11. Executive sessions of outside directors
The outside directors of the board will meet in executive session three times each year. The format of these meetings will include a discussion with the CEO on each occasion.

### 12. Board access to senior management
Board members have complete access to GM's management. It is assumed that board members will use judgment to be sure that this contact is not distracting to the business operation of the company and that such contact, if in writing, be copied to the CEO and the chairman. Furthermore, the board encourages the management to, from time to time, bring managers into board meetings who: (a) can provide additional insight into the items being discussed because of personal involvement in these areas, and/or (b) represent managers with future potential that the senior management believes should be given exposure to the board.

### 13. Board compensation review
It is appropriate for the staff of the company to report once a year to the Committee on Director Affairs the status of GM board compensation in relation to other large US companies. Changes in board compensation, if any, should come at the suggestion of the Committee on Director Affairs, but with full discussion and concurrence by the board.

### 14. Size of the board

The board presently has 14 members. It is the sense of the board that a size of 15 is about right. However, the board would be willing to go to a somewhat larger size in order to accommodate the availability of an outstanding candidate(s).

### 15. Mix of inside and outside directors

The board believes that as a matter of policy there should be a majority of independent directors on the GM board (as stipulated in Bylaw 2.12). The board is willing to have members of management, in addition to the CEO, as directors. But the board believes that management should encourage senior managers to understand that board membership is not necessary or a prerequisite to any higher management position in the company. Managers other than the CEO currently attend board meetings on a regular basis even though they are not members of the board. On matters of corporate governance, the board assumes decisions will be made by outside directors.

### 16. Board definition of what constitutes independence for outside directors

GM's bylaw defining independent directors was approved by the board in January 1991. The board believes there is no current relationship between any outside director and GM that would be construed in any way to compromise any board member being designated independent. Compliance with the bylaw is reviewed annually by the Committee on Director Affairs.

### 17. Former CEO's board membership

The board believes this is a matter to be decided in each individual instance. It is assumed that when the CEO resigns from the position, he/she should offer his/her resignation from the board at the same time. Whether the individual continues to serve on the board is a matter for discussion at that time with the new CEO and the board. A former CEO serving on the board will be considered an inside director for purposes of corporate governance.

### 18. Board membership criteria

The Committee on Director Affairs is responsible for reviewing with the board on an annual basis the appropriate skills and characteristics required of board members in the context of the current makeup of the board. This assessment should include issues of diversity, age, skills such as understanding of manufacturing technologies, international background etc.—all in the context of an assessment of perceived needs of the board at that point in time.

### 19. Selection of new director candidates

The board itself should be responsible, in fact as well as procedure, for selecting its own members. The board delegates the screening process involved to the Committee on Director Affairs, with direct input from the chairman of the board as well as the CEO.

### 20. Extending the invitation to a new potential director to join the board

The invitation to join the board should be extended by the board itself, by the chairman of the Committee on Director Affairs (if the chairman and CEO hold the same position), the chairman of the board and the CEO of the company.

### 21. Assessing the board's performance

The Committee on Director Affairs is responsible to report annually to the board an assessment of the board's performance. This will be discussed with the full board. This should be done following the end of each fiscal year and at the same time as the report on board membership criteria. This assessment should be of the board's contribution as a whole and specifically review areas in which the board and/or the management believes a better contribution could be made. Its purpose is to increase the effectiveness of the board, not to target individual board members.

### 22. Directors who change their present job responsibility

It is the sense of the board that individuals who change the responsibility they had when they were elected to the board should volunteer to resign from the board. It is not the sense of the board that the directors who retire or change from the position they held when they came on the board should necessarily leave the board. There should, however, be an opportunity for the board via the Committee on Director Affairs to review the continued appropriateness of board membership under these circumstances.

### 23. Term limits

The board does not believe it should establish term limits. While term limits could help ensure that there are fresh ideas and viewpoints available to the board, they hold the disadvantage of losing the contribution of directors who have been able to develop, over a period of time, increasing insight into the company and its operations and, therefore, provide an increasing contribution to the board as a whole. As an alternative to term limits, the Committee on Director Affairs, in consultation with the CEO and the chairman of the board, will review each director's continuation on the board every five years. This will allow each director the opportunity to confirm his/her desire to continue as a member of the board.

### 24. Retirement age

It is the sense of the board that the current retirement age of 70 is appropriate.

### 25. Formal evaluation of the CEO

The full board (outside directors) should make this evaluation annually, and it should be communicated to the CEO by the (non-executive) chairman of the board or the lead director. The evaluation should be based on objective criteria including performance of the business, accomplishment of long-term strategic objectives, development of management, etc. The evaluation will be used by the Incentive and Compensation Committee in the course of its deliberations when considering the compensation of the CEO.

### 26. Succession planning

There should be an annual report by the CEO to the board on succession planning. There should also be available, on a continuing basis, the CEO's recommendation as to his successor should he/she be unexpectedly disabled.

### 27. Management development

There should be an annual report to the board by the CEO on the company's program for management development. This report should be given to the board at the same time as the succession planning report, noted above.

**28. Board interaction with institutional investors, the press, customers, etc.**
The board believes that the management speaks for General Motors. Individual board members may, from time to time, meet or otherwise communicate with various constituencies that are involved with General Motors. But it is expected that the board members would do this with the knowledge of the management and, in most instances, at the request of management.

## APPENDIX 9

### THE CODE OF BEST PRACTICE
(The Cadbury Code)

#### 1. The Board of Directors
1.1 The board should meet regularly, retain full and effective control over the company and monitor the executive management.

1.2 There should be a clearly accepted division of responsibilities at the head of a company, which will ensure a balance of power and authority, such that no one individual has unfettered powers of decision. Where the chairman is also the chief executive, it is essential that there should be a strong and independent element on the board, with a recognized senior member.

1.3 The board should include non-executive directors of sufficient caliber and number for their views to carry significant weight in the board's decisions.

1.4 The board should have a formal schedule of matters specifically reserved to it for decision to ensure that the direction and control of the company is firmly in its hands.

1.5 There should be an agreed procedure for directors in the furtherance of their duties to take independent professional advice if necessary, at the company's expense.

1.6 All directors should have access to the advice and services of the company secretary, who is responsible to the board for ensuring that board procedures are followed and that applicable rules and regulations are complied with. Any question of the removal of the company secretary should be a matter for the board as a whole.

#### 2. Non-Executive Directors
2.1 Non-executive directors should bring an independent judgement to bear on issues of strategy, performance, resources, including key appointments, and standards of conduct.

2.2 The majority should be independent of management and free from any business or other relationship which could materially interfere with the exercise of their independent judgement, apart from their fees and shareholding. Their fees should reflect the time they commit to the company.

2.3 Non-executive directors should be appointed for specified terms and reappointment should not be automatic.

2.4 Non-executive directors should be selected through a formal process and both this process and their appointment should be a matter for the board as a whole.

### 3. Executive Directors

3.1 Directors' service contracts should not exceed three years without shareholders' approval.

3.2 There should be full and clear disclosure of directors' total emoluments and those of the chairman and the highest-paid UK director, including pension contributions and stock options. Separate figures should be given for salary and performance-related elements and the basis on which performance is measured should be explained.

3.3 Executive directors' pay should be subject to the recommendations of a remuneration committee made up wholly or mainly of non-executive directors.

### 4. Reporting and Controls

4.1 It is the board's duty to present a balanced and understandable assessment of the company's position.

4.2 The board should ensure that an objective and professional relationship is maintained with the auditors.

4.3 The board should establish an audit committee of at least 3 non-executive directors with written terms of reference which deal clearly with its authority and duties.

4.4 The directors should explain their responsibility for preparing the accounts next to a statement by the auditors about their reporting responsibilities.

4.5 The directors should report on the effectiveness of the company's system of internal control.

4.6 The directors should report that the business is a going concern, with supporting assumptions or qualifications as necessary.

*The Code of Best Practice proposed by The Committee on Financial Aspects of Corporate Governance (known as the Cadbury Committee) was published in 1992.*

It is available from Gee Publishing Ltd, 100 Avenue Road,
Swiss Cottage, LONDON. NW3 3PG. UK


### APPENDIX 10

## INTERNATIONAL LABOR ORGANIZATION
## (ILO) STANDARDS *(extracts)*
A summary of selected passages from the tripartite declaration

This declaration, officially called the Tripartite Declaration of Principles Concerning Multinational Enterprises and Social Policy, was approved by the ILO in 1977. It is one of the few internationally recognized standards designed specifically to control the conduct of multinational corporations. It is not a convention and therefore is not ratified by member governments; however, the principles described in the declaration should be respected by all international corporations and by the countries in which they operate. The Declaration is summarized.

## Introduction
1. Multinational corporations, by virtue of their concentration of economic power and ability to operate beyond the capacities of local governments, can help develop countries both economically and socially. They can also abuse this power by operating in a way that conflicts with the worker's and country's best interests. Due to the size and complexity of their operations, MNCs can cause concern both in their home and host countries.

2. The Tripartite Declaration aims to encourage the positive side of international investment and to minimize the negative aspects.

3. The governments, workers, and employers should further this aim through laws and policy.

6. The Declaration applies to, but is not limited to, the following multinational enterprises: private and publicly owned corporations which own or control production, distribution services or other facilities outside the country in which they are based.

## General Policies
8. MNCs should respect the laws and customs of the host country in which they are operating. They should also respect internationally recognized standards, including the Universal Declaration of Human Rights and the corresponding international covenants adopted by the General Assembly of the United Nations. MNCs should honor all commitments they have made both to the host government and internationally.

10. The activities of MNCs should not conflict with the development policy and social aims of the host country. MNCs, host governments, and worker and employer organizations should consult together to make sure their policies are harmonious.

11. Multinational and local businesses should be held to the same standards regarding their treatment of workers and general conduct.

12. The governments of both host country and home country should be prepared to meet with each other regarding the conduct of the MNCs at the request of either government.

## Employment
16. MNCs in developing countries should try to increase the availability of secure jobs and emphasize the long-term development of their enterprise. They should cooperate with the employment objectives of the host government.

17. Before an MNC begins its operations it should consult with the local worker and employer organizations so that its hiring plans are in harmony with local policies. Consultations should continue after operations have begun.

18. Citizens of the host country should be given priority in hiring and promotions.

19. When possible, MNCs should use technologies that create jobs. They should also develop appropriate technology in the host country.

20. To increase employment in developing countries, MNCs should try to obtain parts and equipment manufactured by local businesses. They should also attempt to use local raw materials and promote the local processing of those materials.

22. MNCs should promote equal opportunity and nondiscrimination but should also abide by government policies (such as the establishment of racial quotas) to correct historical patterns of discrimination.

23. Host governments should not encourage or require MNCs to discriminate when hiring or promoting workers.

25. MNCs should provide stable, long-term employment and should respect obligations and agreements concerning employment that they have made with host countries and worker organizations.

26. In the event that the MNC decides to close or lay-off workers for any reason, it should provide reasonable notice to the host government and worker representatives.

28. Governments together with MNCs should provide some form of support for workers who have been laid-off or fired.

### Training
29. Governments should create a national policy for worker training. MNC training programs should operate within this policy.

30. Training of employees by the MNC should be appropriate for both the enterprise and the overall development of the country. It should teach generally useful skills and provide opportunities for promotion within the enterprise. Training should be designed in consultation with local government, worker and employer organizations.

31. MNCs in developing countries should participate in and provide funds for training programs to improve the technical skills of workers. They should make their skilled personnel available for these programs.

### Conditions of Life and Work
33. Wages, benefits and working conditions in MNCs must be equal to those of other comparable businesses operating in the country.

34. MNCs in developing countries should offer the best possible wages, benefits, and work conditions "within the framework of government policies." They should at least support the basic needs of workers and their families. If the MNCs provide housing, medical care, or food they should be "of a good standard."

35. Governments should try to ensure that lower income groups and less developed areas benefit from the activities of MNCs.

36. Governments should require MNCs to respect ILO guidelines on safety and health in the workplace.

37. MNCs' health and safety standards should not only conform with those of the host country but should take into account their experiences in other countries.

*MNCs should provide information on the safety and health standards they maintain in other countries to representatives of workers in the host countries. Upon request, they should also make this information available to worker and employer organizations in all countries in which they operate.* MNCs *"should make known any special hazards and related protective measures associated with new products and processes."* MNCs should *"play a leading role"* in finding the causes and preventing the occurrence of *industrial accidents.*

38. MNCs should cooperate with international organizations in the creation of safety and health standards.

39. MNCs should cooperate with local health and safety authorities and worker representatives. Health and safety should be part of agreements made between MNCs and worker representatives.

### Industrial Relations

41. Workers for MNCs should have the same freedom to organize unions, federations or other groups as do workers for local businesses.

45. Governments should not suppress workers' right to organize as an incentive for MNC investment.

47. Governments should not restrict representatives of workers from other countries from visiting workers in the host country.

51. MNCs should allow worker representatives from every country in which they operate to negotiate with management.

52. MNCs should not threaten to move all or part of their operations in an attempt to influence negotiations with workers, nor should they transfer workers from other countries in order to influence negotiations.

54. MNCs should provide information about the operations of the company in order to negotiate fairly with workers.

55. Governments should provide information on the relevant industry to worker representatives to help achieve meaningful negotiations. MNCs should cooperate with government requests for this information.

57. MNCs should allow workers to express their complaints and problems to the appropriate authority without fear of reprisal.

*Quoted from the "Field Guide to Labor Rights."*

### APPENDIX 11

### THE CONVENTION ON THE RIGHTS OF THE CHILD *(an extract)*

#### ARTICLE 32

1. States Parties recognize the right of the child to be protected from economic exploitation and from performing any work that is likely to be hazardous or to interfere with the child's education, or to be harmful to the child's health or physical, mental, spiritual, moral or social development.

2. States Parties shall take legislative, administrative, social and educational measures to ensure the implementation of the present article. To this end, and having regard to the relevant provisions of other international instruments, States Parties shall in particular:

(a) Provide for a minimum age or minimum ages for admission to employment;
(b) Provide for appropriate regulation of the hours and conditions of employment;
(c) Provide for appropriate penalties or other sanctions to ensure the effective enforcement of the present article.

## APPENDIX 12

### INTERNATIONAL CONVENTION ON THE ELIMINATION OF ALL FORMS OF RACIAL DISCRIMINATION (*extracts*)

**Article 5**
In compliance with the fundamental obligations laid down in article 2 of this Convention, States Parties undertake to prohibit and to eliminate racial discrimination in all its forms and to guarantee the right of everyone, without distinction as to race, color, or national or ethnic origin, to equality before the law, notably in the enjoyment of the following rights:

a. The right to equal treatment before the tribunals and all other organs administering justice;
b. The right to security of person and protection by the State against violence or bodily harm, whether inflicted by government officials or by any individual group or institution;
c. Political rights, in particular the rights to participate in elections—to vote and to stand for election—on the basis of universal and equal suffrage, to take part in the Government as well as in the conduct of public affairs at any level and to have equal access to public service;
d. Other civil rights, in particular:

(i) The right to freedom of movement and residence within the border of the State;
(ii) The right to leave any country, including one's own, and to return to one's country;
(iii) The right to nationality;
(iv) The right to marriage and choice of spouse;
(v) The right to own property alone as well as in association with others;
(vi) The right to inherit;
(vii) The right to freedom of thought, conscience, and religion;
(viii) The right to freedom of opinion and expression;
(ix) The right to freedom of peaceful assembly and association;

e.  Economic, social and cultural rights, in particular:

    (i)    The rights to work, to free choice of employment, to just and favorable con-
ditions of work, to protection against unemployment, to equal pay for
equal work, to just and favorable remuneration;

    (ii)   The right to form and join trade unions;

    (iii)  The right to housing;

    (iv)  The right to public health, medical care, social security and social services;

    (v)   The right to education and training;

    (vi)  The right to equal participation in cultural activities;

f.  The right of access to any place or service intended for use by the general public,
such as transport, hotels, restaurants, cafes, theatres and parks.

*Adopted and opened for signature, ratification and accession by United Nations
General Assembly, resolution 2106 A (XX) on 21 December 1965.*

*Entered into force on 4 January 1969 in accordance with article 19.*

## APPENDIX 13

### THE WOOD-SHEPPARD PRINCIPLES FOR RACE EQUALITY IN EMPLOYMENT

Companies wishing to support Race Equality in Employment are asked to give a general endorsement to these principles, to work progressively towards their implementation and to be willing to provide a modest response annually on their progress.

1. Adopt a detailed equal opportunities policy (EOP), preferably with assistance from the Commission for Racial Equality (CRE) or a similar body.

2. Declare a clear intention to increase the representation of black and minority ethnic groups in their workforce, wherever these are under-represented in relation to the local community.

3. Undertake positive action to improve, where appropriate, the representation of minorities in the workforce, to offset any imbalance caused by previous discrimination.

4. Practice effective ethnic monitoring of the policy, with a regular review.

5. Use fair recruitment and selection processes, with clear objective criteria, avoiding reliance on "word-of-mouth" or family contact methods.

6. Evolve comprehensive training opportunities both for those carrying out the policy, and also for potential recruits and employees from the black communities, integrated where possible but separate if necessary, and focused on enabling them to fulfil their potential.

7. Designate an Equal Opportunities Manager who, until all departments or divisions of the company or group have EOP fully operational, shall be responsible for assisting

line managers to draw up an action plan both linked to business need and aimed at maximizing the benefits of a diverse workforce, and for ensuring the policy, its monitoring and the related practices are carried through.

8. Make racial harassment and racial discrimination—verbal, non-verbal or physical— serious offences under the firm's disciplinary code, to be fully and properly investigated by a panel which includes black representation wherever possible, this information to be clearly publicized in the company's terms and conditions of employment.

9. Publish an annual employee profile by race, gender and grade within the company as part of the Annual Report, and use this to enhance the company's image as a progressive employer.

10. Consider making one Board member responsible for EOP and Monitoring and seek actively for a suitably qualified black Board member who may or may not oversee EOP, but who can be regularly consulted on the issue.

The Rt Revd David Sheppard      The Rt Revd Wilfred Wood
The Bishop of Liverpool      The Bishop of Croydon

*Formulated by the Race Equality Employment Project of the Ecumenical Council
for Corporate Responsibility (ECCR) December 1993.*

## APPENDIX 14

### INTERNATIONAL COVENANT ON ECONOMIC, SOCIAL, AND CULTURAL RIGHTS

**Preamble**
*The States Parties to the present Covenant,*

*Considering* that, in accordance with the principles proclaimed in the Charter of the United Nations, recognition of the inherent dignity and of the equal and inalienable rights of all members of the human family is the foundation of freedom, justice and peace in the world,

*Recognizing* that these rights derive from the inherent dignity of the human person,

*Recognizing* that, in accordance with the Universal Declaration of Human Rights, the ideal of free human beings enjoying freedom from fear and want can only be achieved if conditions are created whereby everyone may enjoy his economic, social and cultural rights, as well as his civil and political rights,

*Considering* the obligations of States under the Charter of the United Nations to promote universal respect for, and observance of, human rights and freedoms,

*Realizing* that the individual, having duties to other individuals and to the community to which he belongs, is under a responsibility to strive for the promotion and observance of the rights recognized in the present Covenant,

*Agree* upon the following articles:

## Part I
### Article 1

1. All peoples have the right of self-determination. By virtue of that right they freely determine their political status and freely pursue their economic, social and cultural development.

2. All peoples may, for their own ends, freely dispose of their natural wealth and resources without prejudice to any obligations arising out of international economic cooperation, based upon the principle of mutual benefit, and international law. In no case may a people be deprived of its own means of subsistence.

3. The States Parties to the present Covenant, including those having responsibility for the administration of Non-Self-Governing and Trust Territories, shall promote the realization of the right of self-determination, and shall respect that right, in conformity with the provisions of the Charter of the United Nations.

## Part II
### Article 2

1. Each State Party to the present Covenant undertakes to take steps, individually and through international assistance and cooperation, especially economic and technical, to the maximum of its available resources with a view to achieving progressively the full realization of the rights recognized in the present Covenant by all appropriate means, including particularly the adoption of legislative measures.

2. The States Parties to the present Covenant undertake to guarantee that the rights enunciated in the present Covenant will be exercised without discrimination of any kind as to race, color, sex, language, religion, political or other opinion, national or social origin, property, birth or other status.

3. Developing countries, with due regard to human rights and their national economy, may determine to what extent they would guarantee the economic rights recognized in the present Covenant to non-nationals.

### Article 3

The States Parties to the present Covenant undertake to ensure the equal right of men and women to the enjoyment of all economic, social and cultural rights set forth in the present Covenant.

### Article 4

The States Parties to the present Covenant recognize that, in the enjoyment of those rights provided by the State in conformity with the present Covenant, the State may subject such rights only to such limitations as are determined by law only in so far as this may be compatible with the nature of these rights and solely for the purpose of promoting the general welfare in a democratic society.

### Article 5

1. Nothing in the present Covenant may be interpreted as implying for any State, group or person any right to engage in any activity or to perform any act aimed at the destruction of any of the rights or freedoms recognized herein, or at their limitation to a greater extent than is provided for in the present Covenant.

2. No restrictions upon or derogation from any of the fundamental human rights recognized or existing in any country in virtue of law, conventions, regulations or

custom shall be admitted on the pretext that the present Covenant does not recognize such rights or that it recognizes them to a lesser extent.

## Part III
### Article 6

1. The States Parties to the present Covenant recognize the right to work, which includes the right of everyone to the opportunity to gain his living by work which he freely chooses or accepts, and will take appropriate steps to safeguard this right.

2. The steps to be taken by a State Party to the present Covenant to achieve the full realization of this right shall include technical and vocational guidance and training programs, policies and techniques to achieve steady economic, social and cultural development and full and productive employment under conditions safeguarding fundamental political and economic freedoms to the individual.

### Article 7

The States Parties to the present Covenant recognize the right of everyone to the enjoyment of just and favorable conditions of work which ensure, in particular:

a.  Remuneration which provides all workers, as a minimum, with:

  (i) Fair wages and equal remuneration for work of equal value without distinction of any kind, in particular women being guaranteed conditions of work not inferior to those enjoyed by men, with equal pay for equal work;

  (ii) A decent living for themselves and their families in accordance with the provisions of the present Covenant;

b.  Safe and healthy working conditions;

c.  Equal opportunity for everyone to be promoted in his employment to an appropriate higher level, subject to no considerations other than those of seniority and competence;

d.  Rest, leisure and reasonable limitation of working hours and periodic holidays with pay, as well as remuneration for public holidays.

*Adopted and opened for signature, ratification, and accession by United Nations General Assembly resolution 2200 A (XXI) on 16 December 1966. Entered into force on 3 January 1976 in accordance with article 27.*

## APPENDIX 15

### CONVENTION ON THE ELIMINATION OF ALL FORMS OF DISCRIMINATION AGAINST WOMEN

*The States Parties to the present Convention,*

*Noting* that the Charter of the United Nations reaffirms faith in fundamental human rights, in the dignity and worth of the human person and in the equal rights of men and women,

*Noting* that the Universal Declaration of Human Rights affirms the principle of the inadmissibility of discrimination and proclaims that all human beings are born free and equal in dignity and rights and that everyone is entitled to all the rights and freedoms set forth therein, without distinction of any kind including distinction based on sex,

*Noting* that the States Parties to the International Covenants on Human Rights have the obligation to ensure the equal rights of men and women to enjoy all economic, social, cultural, civil and political rights,

*Considering* the international conventions concluded under the auspices of the United Nations and the specialized agencies promoting equality of rights of men and women,

*Noting* also the resolutions, declarations and recommendations adopted by the United Nations and the specialized agencies promoting equality of rights of men and women,

*Concerned,* however, that despite these various instruments extensive discrimination against women continues to exist,

*Recalling* that discrimination against women violates the principles of equality of rights and respect for human dignity, is an obstacle to the participation of women, on equal terms with men, in the political, social, economic and cultural life of their countries, hampers the growth of the prosperity of society and the family and makes more difficult the full development of the potentialities of women in the service of their countries and of humanity,

*Concerned,* that in situations of poverty women have the least access to food, health, education, training and opportunities for employment and other needs,

*Convinced* that the establishment of the new international economic order based on equity and justice will contribute significantly towards the promotion of equality between men and women,

*Emphasizing* that the eradication of apartheid, all forms of racism, racial discrimination, colonialism, neo-colonialism, aggression, foreign occupation and domination and interference in the internal affairs of States is essential to the full enjoyment of the rights of men and women,

*Affirming* that the strengthening of international peace and security, the relaxation of international tension, mutual cooperation among all States irrespective of their social and economic systems, general and complete disarmament in particular nuclear disarmament under strict and effective international control, the affirmation of the principles of justice, equality and mutual benefit in relations among countries and the realization of the right of peoples under alien and colonial domination and foreign occupation to self-determination and independence as well as respect for national sovereignty and territorial integrity will promote social progress and development and as a consequence will contribute to the attainment of full equality between men and women,

*Convinced* that the full and complete development of a country, the welfare of the world and the cause of peace require the maximum participation of women on equal terms with men in all fields,

*Bearing* in mind the great contribution of women to the welfare of the family and to the development of society, so far not fully recognized, the social significance of maternity and the role of both parents in the upbringing of children, and aware that the role of women in procreation should not be a basis for discrimination but that the upbringing of children requires a sharing of responsibility between men and women and society as a whole,

*Aware* that a change in the traditional role of men as well as the role of women in society and in the family is needed to achieve full equality between men and women,

*Determined* to implement the principles set forth in the Declaration on the Elimination of Discrimination against Women and, for that purpose, to adopt the measures required for the elimination of such discrimination in all its forms and manifestations,

*Have agreed* on the following:

## Part I
### Article I

For the purposes of the present Convention, the term "discrimination against women" shall mean any distinction, exclusion or restriction made on the basis of sex which has the effect or purpose of impairing or nullifying the recognition, enjoyment or exercise by women, irrespective of their marital status, on a basis of equality of men and women, of human rights and fundamental freedoms in the political, economic, social, cultural, civil or any other field.

### Article II

States Parties condemn discrimination against women in all its forms, agree to pursue by all appropriate means and without delay a policy of eliminating discrimination against women and, to this end, undertake:

a.   To embody the principle of the equality of men and women in their national constitutions or other appropriate legislation if not incorporated therein and to ensure, through law and other appropriate means, the practical realization of this principle;

b.   To adopt appropriate legislative and other measures, including sanctions where appropriate, prohibiting all discrimination against women;

c.   To establish legal protection of the rights of women on an equal basis with men and to ensure through competent national tribunals and other public institutions the effective protection of women against any act of discrimination;

d.   To refrain from engaging in any act or practice of discrimination against women and to ensure that public authorities and institutions shall act in conformity with this obligation;

e.   To take all appropriate measures to eliminate discrimination against women by any person, organization or enterprise;

f.   To take all appropriate measures, including legislation, to modify or abolish existing laws, regulations, customs and practices which constitute discrimination against women;

g. To repeal all national penal provisions which constitute discrimination against women.

*Adopted and opened for signature, ratification and accession by United Nations General Assembly resolution 34/180 on 18 December 1979. Entered into force on 3 September 1981 in accordance with article 27 (I).*

## APPENDIX 16

### BEIJING DECLARATION

1. We, the Governments participating in the Fourth World Conference on Women,
2. Gathered here in Beijing in September 1995, the year of the fiftieth anniversary of the founding of the United Nations,
3. Determined to advance the goals of equality, development and peace for all women everywhere in the interest of all humanity,
4. Acknowledging the voices of all women everywhere and taking note of the diversity of women and their roles and circumstances, honoring the women who paved the way and inspired by the hope present in the world's youth,
5. Recognize that the status of women has advanced in some important respects in the past decade but that progress has been uneven, inequalities between women and men have persisted and major obstacles remain, with serious consequences for the well-being of all people,
6. Also recognize that this situation is exacerbated by the increasing poverty that is affecting the lives of the majority of the world's people, in particular women and children, with origins in both the national and international domains,
7. Dedicate ourselves unreservedly to addressing these constraints and obstacles and thus enhancing further the advancement and empowerment of women all over the world, and agree that this requires urgent action in the spirit of determination, hope, cooperation and solidarity, now and to carry us forward into the next century.

**We reaffirm our commitment to:**
8. The equal rights and inherent human dignity of women and men and other purposes and principles enshrined in the Charter of the United Nations, to the Universal Declaration of Human Rights and other international human rights instruments, in particular the Convention on the Elimination of All Forms of Discrimination against Women and the Convention on the Rights of the Child, as well as the Declaration on the Elimination of Violence against Women and the Declaration on the Right to Development;
9. Ensure the full implementation of the human rights of women and of the girl child as an inalienable, integral and indivisible part of all human rights and fundamental freedoms;
10. Build on consensus and progress made at previous United Nations conferences and summits—on women in Nairobi in 1985, on children in New York in 1990,

on environment and development in Rio de Janeiro in 1992, on human rights in Vienna in 1993, on population and development in Cairo in 1994 and on social development in Copenhagen in 1995 with the objective of achieving equality, development and peace;

11. Achieve the full and effective implementation of the Nairobi Forward-looking Strategies for the Advancement of Women;

12. The empowerment and advancement of women, including the right to freedom of thought, conscience, religion and belief, thus contributing to the moral, ethical, spiritual and intellectual needs of women and men, individually or in community with others and thereby guaranteeing them the possibility of realizing their full potential in society and shaping their lives in accordance with their own aspirations.

**We are convinced that:**

13. Women's empowerment and their full participation on the basis of equality in all spheres of society, including participation in the decision-making process and access to power, are fundamental for the achievement of equality, development and peace;

14. Women's rights are human rights;

15. Equal rights, opportunities and access to resources, equal sharing of responsibilities for the family by men and women, and a harmonious partnership between them are critical to their well-being and that of their families as well as to the consolidation of democracy;

16. Eradication of poverty based on sustained economic growth, social development, environmental protection and social justice requires the involvement of women in economic and social development, equal opportunities and the full and equal participation of women and men as agents and beneficiaries of people-centered sustainable development;

17. The explicit recognition and reaffirmation of the right of all women to control all aspects of their health, in particular their own fertility, is basic to their empowerment;

18. Local, national, regional and global peace is attainable and is inextricably linked with the advancement of women, who are a fundamental force for leadership, conflict resolution and the promotion of lasting peace at all levels;

19. It is essential to design, implement and monitor, with the full participation of women, effective, efficient and mutually reinforcing gender-sensitive policies and programs, including development policies and programs, at all levels that will foster the empowerment and advancement of women;

20. The participation and contribution of all actors of civil society, particularly women's groups and networks and other non-governmental organizations and community-based organizations, with full respect for their autonomy, in cooperation with Governments, are important to the effective implementation and follow-up of the Platform for Action;

21. The implementation of the Platform for Action requires commitment from Governments and the international community. By making national and international commitments for action, including those made at the Conference, Governments

and the international community recognize the need to take priority action for the empowerment and advancement of women.

**We are determined to:**

22. Intensify efforts and actions to achieve the goals of the Nairobi Forward-looking Strategies for the Advancement of Women by the end of this century;
23. Ensure the full enjoyment by women and the girl child of all human rights and fundamental freedoms and take effective action against violations of these rights and freedoms;
24. Take all necessary measures to eliminate all forms of discrimination against women and the girl child and remove all obstacles to gender equality and the advancement and empowerment of women;
25. Encourage men to participate fully in all actions towards equality;
26. Promote women's economic independence, including employment, and eradicate the persistent and increasing burden of poverty on women by addressing the structural causes of poverty through changes in economic structures, ensuring equal access for all women, including those in rural areas, as vital development agents, to productive resources, opportunities and public services;
27. Promote people-centered sustainable development, including sustained economic growth, through the provision of basic education, lifelong education, literacy and training, and primary health care for girls and women;
28. Take positive steps to ensure peace for the advancement of women and, recognizing the leading role that women have played in the peace movement, work actively towards general and complete disarmament under strict and effective international control, and support negotiations on the conclusion, without delay, of a universal and multilaterally and effectively verifiable comprehensive nuclear-test-ban treaty which contributes to nuclear disarmament and the prevention of the proliferation of nuclear weapons in all its aspects;
29. Prevent and eliminate all forms of violence against women and girls;
30. Ensure equal access to and equal treatment of women and men in education and health care and enhance women's sexual and reproductive health as well as education;
31. Promote and protect all human rights of women and girls;
32. Intensify efforts to ensure equal enjoyment of all human rights and fundamental freedoms for all women and girls who face multiple barriers to their empowerment and advancement because of such factors as their race, age, language, ethnicity, culture, religion, or disability, or because they are indigenous people;
33. Ensure respect for international law, including humanitarian law, in order to protect women and girls in particular;
34. Develop the fullest potential of girls and women of all ages, ensure their full and equal participation in building a better world for all and enhance their role in the development process.

**We are determined to:**

35. Ensure women's equal access to economic resources, including land, credit, science and technology, vocational training, information, communication and mar-

kets, as a means to further the advancement and empowerment of women and girls, including through the enhancement of their capacities to enjoy the benefits of equal access to these resources, *inter alia,* by means of international cooperation;

36. Ensure the success of the Platform for Action, which will require a strong commitment on the part of Governments, International organizations and institutions at all levels. We are deeply convinced that economic development, social development and environmental protection are interdependent and mutually reinforcing components of sustainable development, which is the framework for our efforts to achieve a higher quality of life for all people. Equitable social development that recognizes empowering the poor, particularly women living in poverty, to utilize environmental resources sustainably is a necessary foundation for sustainable development. We also recognize that broad-based and sustained economic growth in the context of sustainable development is necessary to sustain social development and social justice. The success of the Platform for Action will also require adequate mobilization of resources at the national and international levels as well as new and additional resources to the developing countries from all available funding mechanisms, including multilateral, bilateral and private sources for the advancement of women; financial resources to strengthen the capacity of national, subregional, regional and International institutions; a commitment to equal rights, equal responsibilities and equal opportunities and to the equal participation of women and men in all national, regional and international bodies and policy-making processes; and the establishment or strengthening of mechanisms at all levels for accountability to the world's women;

37. Ensure also the success of the Platform for Action in countries with economies in transition, which will require continued International cooperation and assistance;

38. We hereby adopt and commit ourselves as Governments to implement the following Platform for Action, ensuring that a gender perspective is reflected in all our policies and programs. We urge the United Nations system, regional and international financial Institutions, other relevant regional and International institutions and all women and men, as well as non-governmental organizations, with full respect for their autonomy, and all sectors of civil society, in cooperation with Governments, to fully commit themselves and contribute to the implementation of this Platform for Action.

## APPENDIX 17

### EQUAL OPPORTUNITY OF EMPLOYMENT FOR WOMEN

*Opportunity 2000 is a campaign to increase the quality and quantity of women's participation in the workforce. The campaign is a result of work by the Opportunity 2000 Target Team, chaired by Lady Howe and set up by Business in the Community. The team feels that British business is not taking full advantage of the economic potential of women in the workforce.*

*The purpose of Opportunity 2000 is to encourage companies to take up the challenge and set programs and goals necessary for improvement.*

*Campaign members accept that in the long term their companies will be best served by a balance of women and men in the workforce in all areas and at all levels, especially in management, that reflects the abilities of the labor force as a whole.*

*As a first step, campaign companies will voluntarily set their own goals for increasing opportunity for women in the workforce by the year 2000. Each company's goals will be based on its own particular starting point, its specific circumstances and business needs with progress monitored regularly and reported on. Above all, the goals will clearly signal a public commitment to ensure that in all areas and at all levels, women have the opportunity to make progress according to their abilities.*

### The Opportunity 2000 Approach

Opportunity 2000 invites organizations to increase opportunities for women in the workforce and membership of the campaign offers a range of information and support to bring this about. Making any change requires an accurate view of the current situation, a clear vision of the desired outcome, a plan of actions and a means of measuring progress.

The Opportunity 2000 approach therefore involves:

- The development of challenging but achievable goals based on an assessment of each organization's current situation and future needs.
- A public statement of commitment to the organization's specific Opportunity 2000 goals and publications of progress at agreed intervals.
- An active, ongoing program of initiatives which will provide a measurable improvement in each participating organization.

Opportunity 2000 is able to provide help in each of these stages. In particular by stimulating and supporting board level initiatives, providing practical publications, exchange of information and local forums for human resource specialists and line managers.

It is only by promoting effective initiatives in all three levels that measurable change will be achieved.

## APPENDIX 18

### THE UNITED NATIONS DRAFT DECLARATION ON GENDER EQUITY (*extracts*)

**Paragraph 119**
It is vital that the link between the advancement of women and socio-economic and political development be emphasized for the effective mobilization of resources for women.

**Paragraph 120**
The remunerated and, in particular, the unremunerated contributions of women to all aspects and sectors of development should be recognized, and appropriate efforts should be made to measure and reflect these contributions in national accounts and economic statistics and in the gross national product. Concrete steps should be taken to quantify the unremunerated contribution of women to agriculture, food production, reproduction and household activities.

**Paragraph 132**
Special measures aimed at the advancement of women in all types of employment should be consistent with the economic and social policies promoting full productive and freely chosen employment.

**Paragraph 133**
Policies should provide the means to mobilize public awareness, political support, and institutional and financial resources to enable women to obtain jobs involving more skills and responsibility, including those at the managerial level, in all sectors of the economy. These measures should include the promotion of women's occupational mobility, especially in the middle and lower levels of the work-force, where the majority of women work.

**Paragraph 134**
Governments that have not yet done so should ratify and implement the Convention on the Elimination of All Forms of Discrimination against Women and other international instruments relating to the improvement of the condition of women workers.

**Paragraph 135**
Measures based on legislation and trade union action should be taken to ensure equity in all jobs and avoid exploitative trends in part-time work, as well as the tendency towards the feminization of part-time, temporary and seasonal work.

**Paragraph 136**
Flexible working hours for all are strongly recommended as a measure for encouraging the sharing of parental and domestic responsibilities by women and men, provided that such measures are not used against the interests of employees. Re-entry programs, complete with training and stipends, should be provided for women who have been out of the labor force for some time. Tax structures should be revised so that the tax liability on the combined earnings of married couples does not constitute a disincentive to women's employment.

**Paragraph 137**
Eliminating all forms of employment discrimination, *inter alia* through legislative measures, especially wage differentials between women and men carrying out work of equal value, is strongly recommended to all parties concerned. Additional programs should help to overcome still existing disparities in wages between women and men. Differences in the legal conditions of work of women and men should also be eliminated, where there are disadvantages to women, and privileges should be accorded to male and female parents. Occupational desegregation of women and men should be promoted.

**Paragraph 138**
The public and private sectors should make concerted efforts to diversify and create new employment opportunities for women in the traditional, non-traditional and high productivity areas and sectors in both rural and urban areas through the design and implementation of incentive schemes for both employers and women employees and through widespread dissemination of information. Gender stereotyping in all areas should be avoided and the occupational prospects of women should be enhanced.

**Paragraph 139**
The working conditions of women should be improved in all formal and informal areas by the public and private sectors. Occupational health and safety and job security should be enhanced and protective measures against work-related health hazards effectively implemented for women and men. Appropriate measures should be taken to prevent sexual harassment on the job or sexual exploitation in specific jobs, such as domestic service. Appropriate measures for redress should be provided by Governments and legislative measures guaranteeing these rights should be enforced. In addition, Governments and the private sector should put in place mechanisms to identify and correct harmful working conditions.

**Paragraph 140**
National planning should give urgent consideration to the development and strengthening of social security and health schemes and maternity protection schemes in keeping with the principles laid down in the ILO maternity protection convention and maternity protection recommendation and other relevant ILO conventions and recommendations as a prerequisite to the hastening of women's effective participation in production, and all business and trade unions should seek to promote the rights and compensations of working women and to ensure that appropriate infrastructures are provided. Parental leave following the birth of a child should be available to both women and men and preferably shared between them. Provision should be made for accessible child-care facilities for working parents.

**Paragraph 141**
Governments and non-governmental organizations should recognize the contribution of older women and the importance of their input in those areas that directly affect their well-being. Urgent attention should be paid to the education and training of young women in all fields. Special retraining programs including technical training should also be developed for young women in both urban and rural sectors who lack qualifications and are ill-equipped to enter productive employment. Steps should be taken to eliminate exploitative treatment of young women at work, in line with ILO Convention No. 111 concerning discrimination in respect of employment and occupation, 1958, and ILO Convention No. 122 concerning employment policy, 1964.

**Paragraph 142**
National planning, programs and projects should launch a twofold attack on poverty and unemployment. To enable women to gain access to equal economic opportunities, Governments should seek to involve and integrate women in all phases of the planning, delivery and evaluation of multisectoral programs that eliminate income generation.

An increased number of women should be hired in national planning mechanisms. Particular attention should be devoted to the informal sector since it will be the major employment outlet of a considerable number of underprivileged urban and rural women. The cooperative movement could play an indispensable role in this area.

### Paragraph 143
Recognition and application should be given to the fact that women and men have equal rights to work, and, on the same footing, to acquire a personal income on equal terms and conditions, regardless of the economic situation. They should be given opportunities in accordance with the protective legislation of each country and especially in the labor market, in the context of measures to stimulate economic development and to promote employment growth.

### Paragraph 144
In view of the persistence of high unemployment levels in many countries, Governments should endeavor to strengthen the efforts to cope with this issue and provide more job opportunities for women. Given that in many cases women account for a disproportionate share of total unemployment, that their unemployment rates are higher than those of men and that, owing to lower qualifications, geographical mobility and other barriers, women's prospects for alternative jobs are mostly limited, more attention should be given to unemployment as it affects women. Measures should be taken to alleviate the consequences of unemployment for women in declining sectors and occupations. In particular, training measures must be instituted to facilitate the transition.

### Paragraph 145
Although general policies designed to reduce unemployment or to create jobs may benefit both men and women, by their nature they are often of greater assistance to men than to women. For this reason, specific measures should be taken to permit women to benefit equally with men from national policies to create jobs.

### Paragraph 146
As high unemployment among youth, wherever it exists, is a matter of serious concern, policies designed to deal with this problem should take into account that unemployment rates for young women are often much higher than those for young men. Moreover, measures aimed at mitigating unemployment among youth should not negatively affect the employment of women in other age groups—for example, by lowering minimum wages. Women should not face any impediment to employment opportunities and benefits in cases where their husbands are employed.

### Paragraph 147
Governments should also give special attention to women in the peripheral or marginal labor market, such as those in unstable temporary work or unregulated part-time work, as well as to the increasing number of women working in the informal economy.

*These extracts are taken from a document entitled "Nairobi Forward-Looking Strategies for the Advancement of Women" (July 1985) and provided as an insight to the questions under negotiation in the compilation of the draft declaration.*

## APPENDIX 19

## A CODE OF PRACTICE FOR THE EMPLOYMENT
## OF DISABLED PEOPLE *(extracts)*

*In October 1984 the British government agency then known as the Manpower Services Commission produced a new guide. It was entitled "Code of Practice on the Employment of Disabled People." As well as defining the legal position about the employment of people who are disabled, it lists what it calls "Suggested objectives for companies in employing disabled people."*

- The company should be recognized by the community as one which provides good employment opportunities to disabled people.
- Disabled people who apply for jobs with the company should know that they will receive fair treatment and be considered solely on their ability to do the job.
- The company should have a policy of looking after employees who become disabled and the norm should be to retain them in suitable employment.
- Disabled people who join the company or employees who become disabled should be integrated smoothly into work and any special needs they may have concerning work or the working environment should be examined thoroughly.
- The company should develop the skills and potential of disabled employees to the full and offer them training and promotion opportunities according to their abilities.
- All employees in the company should accept disabled colleagues as readily as able-bodied colleagues.
- The company should ensure that it is meeting its legal obligations towards employing disabled people.

*The document goes on to spell out ways in which a company can seek to achieve these objectives.*

Whatever the size and structure of the company, the best way of achieving its objectives is to have a sound and effective policy towards employing disabled people. A policy will:

- draw together firm and realistic objectives which fit the circumstances of a particular company;
- involve all managers and staff, through appropriate consultation, in considering the right attitude and approach for them and their company to adopt;
- set out for all managers, particularly those responsible for recruitment and employment matters, what they should be achieving in respect of disabled workers, and
- identify clearly the practical means, financial and other assistance which managers should know about and use to help achieve the company's objectives.

## APPENDIX 20

## INTERNATIONAL LABOR ORGANIZATION (ILO) CONVENTIONS

### 29 Forced Labor Convention (1930)

Each Member of the International Labor Organization which ratifies this Convention undertakes to suppress the use of forced or compulsory labor in all its forms within the shortest possible period. With a view to this complete suppression recourse to forced or compulsory labor may be had during the transitional period, for public purposes only and as an exceptional measure, subject to the conditions and guarantees hereinafter provided. (Article 1)

For the purposes of this Convention the term "forced or compulsory labor" shall mean work or service which is exacted from any person under the menace of any penalty and for which the said person has not offered himself voluntarily. (Article 2)

The competent authority shall not impose or permit the imposition of forced or compulsory labor for the benefit of private individuals, companies or associations. (Article 4)

### 87 Freedom of Association and Protection of the Right to Organize Convention (1948)

Workers and employers, without distinction whatsoever, shall have the right to establish and, subject only to the rules of the organization concerned, to join organizations of their own choosing without previous authorization. (Article 2)

The public authorities shall refrain from any interference which would restrict this right or impede the lawful exercise thereof. (Article 3)

Workers' and employers' organizations shall not be liable to be dissolved or suspended by administrative authority. (Article 4)

Workers' and employers' organizations shall have the right to establish and join federations and confederations and any such organization, federation or confederation shall have the right to affiliate with international organizations of workers and employers. (Article 5)

The law of the land shall not be such as to impair, nor shall it be so applied as to impair, the guarantees provided for in this Convention. (Article 8)

Each Member of the International Labor Organization for which this Convention is in force undertakes to take all necessary and appropriate measures to ensure that workers and employers may exercise freely the right to organize. (Article 11)

### 98 Right to Organize and Collective Bargaining Convention (1949)

Workers shall enjoy adequate protection against acts of anti-union discrimination in respect of their employment. (Article 1)

Workers' and employers' organizations shall enjoy adequate protection against any acts of interference by each other or each other's agents or members in their establishment, functioning or administration. In particular, acts which are designed to promote the establishment of workers' organizations under the domination of employers or employers' organizations, or to support workers' organizations by financial or other means, with the object of placing such organizations under the control of employers or employers' organizations, shall be deemed to constitute acts of interference within the meaning of this Article. (Article 2)

Measures appropriate to national conditions shall be taken where necessary, to encourage and promote the full development and utilization of machinery for voluntary negotiation between employers or employers' organizations and workers' organizations, with a view to the regulation of terms and conditions of employment by means of collective agreements. (Article 4)

### 100 Equal Remuneration Convention (1951)

For the purpose of this convention—

(a) the term "remuneration" includes the ordinary, basic or minimum wage or salary and any additional emoluments whatsoever payable directly or indirectly, whether in cash or in kind, by the employer to the worker and arising out of the worker's employment;

(b) the term "equal remuneration for men and women workers for work of equal value" refers to rates of remuneration established without discrimination based on sex. (Article 1)

Each Member shall, by means appropriate to the methods in operation for determining rates of remuneration, promote and, in so far as is consistent with such methods, ensure the application to all workers of the principle of equal remuneration for men and women workers for work of equal value. (Article 2)

Differential rates between workers which correspond, without regard to sex, to differences, as determined by such objective appraisal, in the work to be performed, shall not be considered as being contrary to the principle of equal remuneration for men and women workers for work of equal value. (Article 3)

### 105 Abolition of Forced Labor Convention (1957)

Each Member of the International Labor Organization which ratifies this Convention undertakes to suppress and not to make use of any form of forced or compulsory labor—

(a) as a means of political coercion or education or as a punishment for holding or expressing political views or views ideologically opposed to the established political, social or economic system;

(b) as a method of mobilizing and using labor for purposes of economic development;

(c) as a means of labor discipline;

(d) as a punishment for having participated in strikes;

(e) as a means of racial, social, national or religious discrimination. (Article 1)

Each Member of the International Labor Organization which ratifies this Convention undertakes to take effective measures to secure the immediate and complete abolition of forced or compulsory labor as specified in Article 1 of this Convention. (Article 2)

**111 Discrimination (Employment and Occupation) Convention (1958)**
For the purpose of this Convention the term "discrimination" includes—

(a) any distinction, exclusion or preference made on the basis of race, color, sex, religion, political opinion, national extraction or social origin which has the effect of nullifying or impairing equality of opportunity or treatment in employment or occupation;

(b) such other distinction, exclusion or preference which has the effect of nullifying or impairing equality of opportunity or treatment in employment or occupation as may be determined by the Member concerned after consultation with the representative employers' and workers' organizations, where such exist, and with other appropriate bodies.

Any distinction, exclusion or preference in respect of a particular job based on the inherent requirements thereof shall not be deemed to be discrimination. (Article 1)

Each Member for which this Convention is in force undertakes to declare and pursue a national policy designed to promote, by methods appropriate to national conditions and practice, equality of opportunity and treatment in respect of employment and occupation, with a view to eliminating any discrimination in respect thereof. (Article 2)

Any Member may, after consultation with representative employers' and workers' organizations, where such exist, determine that other special measures designed to meet the particular requirements of persons who, for reasons such as sex, age, disablement, family responsibilities or social or cultural status, are generally recognized to require special protection or assistance, shall not be deemed to be discrimination. (Article 5)

**122 Employment Policy Convention (1964)**
With a view to stimulating economic growth and development, raising levels of living, meeting manpower requirements and overcoming unemployment and underemployment, each Member shall declare and pursue, as a major goal, an active policy designed to promote full, productive and freely chosen employment. The said policy shall aim at ensuring that—

(a) there is work for all who are available for and seeking work;

(b) such work is as productive as possible;

(c) there is freedom of choice of employment and the fullest possible opportunity for each worker to qualify for, and to use his skills and endowments in, a job for which he is well suited, irrespective of race, color, sex, religion, political opinion, national extraction or social origin.

The said policy shall take due account of the stage and level of economic development and the mutual relationships between employment objectives and other economic and social objectives, and shall be pursued by methods that are appropriate to national conditions and practices. (Article 1)

Each Member shall, by such methods and to such extent as may be appropriate under national conditions—

(a)  decide on and keep under review, within the framework of a co-ordinated economic and social policy, the measures to be adopted for attaining the objectives specified in Article 1;

(b)  take such steps as may be needed, including when appropriate the establishment of programs, for the application of these measures. (Article 2)

In the application of this Convention, representatives of the persons affected by the measures to be taken, and in particular representatives of employers and workers, shall be consulted concerning employment policies, with a view to taking fully into account their experience and views and securing their full cooperation in formulating and enlisting their support for such policies. (Article 3)

### 138 Minimum Age Convention (1973)

Each Member for which this Convention is in force undertakes to pursue a national policy designed to ensure the effective abolition of child labor and to raise progressively the minimum age for admission to employment or work to a level consistent with the fullest physical and mental development of young persons. (Article 1)

The minimum age shall not be less than the age of completion of compulsory schooling and, in any case, shall not be less than 15 years.

A Member whose economy and educational facilities are insufficiently developed may, after consultation with the organizations of employers and workers concerned, where such exist, initially specify a minimum age of 14 years. (Article 2)

## APPENDIX 21

### THE MACBRIDE PRINCIPLES FOR NORTHERN IRELAND

In light of decreasing employment opportunities in Northern Ireland and on a global scale, and in order to guarantee equal access to regional employment the undersigned propose the following equal opportunity/affirmative action principles:

- Increasing the representation of individuals from under-represented religious groups in the workforce including managerial, supervisory, administrative, clerical and technical jobs.
- Adequate security for the protection of minority employees both at the workplace and while traveling to and from work.
- The banning of provocative religious or political emblems from the workplace.
- All job openings should be publicly advertised and special recruitment efforts should be made to attract applicants from under-represented religious groups.
- Layoff, recall, and termination procedures should not in practice favor particular religious groupings.
- The abolition of job reservations, apprenticeship restrictions, and differential employment criteria, which discriminate on the basis of religion or ethnic origin.
- The development of training programs that will prepare substantial numbers of current minority employees for skilled jobs, including the expansion of existing

programs and the creation of new programs to train, upgrade, and improve the skills of minority employees.

- The establishment of procedures to assess, identify, and actively recruit minority employees with potential for further advancement.
- The appointment of a senior management staff member to oversee the company's affirmative action efforts and the setting up of timetables to carry out affirmative action principles.

Sean MacBride—Dublin, Ireland

Dr. John Robb—Ballymoney, Northern Ireland

Inez McCormack—Belfast, Northern Ireland

Fr. Brian Brady—Belfast, Northern Ireland

## APPENDIX 22

### President Clinton's
### WHITE HOUSE APPAREL INDUSTRY PARTNERSHIP
### WORKPLACE CODE OF CONDUCT &
### PRINCIPLES OF MONITORING

#### Workplace Code of Conduct

The Apparel Industry Partnership has addressed issues related to the eradication of sweatshops in the United States and abroad. On the basis of this examination, the Partnership has formulated the following set of standards defining decent and humane working conditions. The Partnership believes that consumers can have confidence that products that are manufactured in compliance with these standards are not produced under exploitative or inhumane conditions.

*Forced Labor.* There shall not be any use of forced labor, whether in the form of prison labor, indentured labor, bonded labor or otherwise.

*Child Labor.* No person shall be employed at an age younger than 15 (or 14 where the law of the country of manufacture[1] allows) or younger than the age for completing compulsory education in the country of manufacture where such age is higher than 15.

*Harassment or Abuse.* Every employee shall be treated with respect and dignity. No employee shall be subject to any physical, sexual, psychological or verbal harassment or abuse.

*Nondiscrimination.* No person shall be subject to any discrimination in employment, including hiring, salary, benefits, advancement, discipline, termination or retirement, on the basis of gender, race, religion, age, disability, sexual orientation, nationality, political opinion, or social or ethnic origin.

---

[1] All references to local law throughout this Code shall include regulations implemented in accordance with applicable local law.

*Health and Safety.* Employers shall provide a safe and healthy working environment to prevent accidents and injury to health arising out of, linked with, or occurring in the course of work or as a result of the operation of employer facilities.

*Freedom of Association and Collective Bargaining.* Employers shall recognize and respect the right of employees to freedom of association and collective bargaining.

*Wages and Benefits.* Employers recognize that wages are essential to meeting employees' basic needs. Employers shall pay employees, as a floor, at least the minimum wage required by local law or the prevailing industry wage, whichever is higher, and shall provide legally mandated benefits.

*Hours of Work.* Except in extraordinary business circumstances, employees shall (i) not be required to work more than the lesser of (a) 48 hours per week and 12 hours overtime or (b) the limits on regular and overtime hours allowed by the law of the country of manufacture or, where the laws of such country do not limit the hours of work, the regular work week in such country plus 12 hours overtime and (ii) be entitled to at least one day off in every seven day period.

*Overtime Compensation.* In addition to their Compensation for regular hours of work, employees shall be compensated for overtime hours at such premium rate as is legally required in the country of manufacture or, in those countries where such laws do not exist, at a rate at least equal to their regular hourly compensation rate.

• • •

Any company that determines to adopt the Workplace Code of Conduct shall, in addition to complying with all applicable laws of the country of manufacture, comply with and support the Workplace Code of Conduct in accordance with the attached Principles of Monitoring and shall apply the higher standard in cases of differences or conflicts. Any company that determines to adopt the Workplace Code of Conduct also shall require its contractors and, in the case of a retailer, its suppliers to comply with applicable local laws and with this Code in accordance with the attached Principles of Monitoring and to apply the higher standard in cases of differences or conflicts.

## Principles of Monitoring

### *1. Obligations of Companies**

**A. Establish Clear Standards**
- Establish and articulate clear, written workplace standards[2]

---

* It is recognized that implementation by companies of internal monitoring programs might vary depending upon the extent of their resources but that any internal monitoring program adopted by a company would be consistent with these Principles of Monitoring. If companies do not have the resources to implement some of these Principles as part of an internal monitoring program, they may delegate the implementation of such Principles to their independent external monitors.

[2] Adoption of the Workplace Code of Conduct would satisfy the requirement to establish and articulate clear written standards. Accordingly, all references to the "workplace standards" and the

- Formally convey those standards to company factories as well as to contractors and suppliers[3]
- Receive written certifications, on a regular basis, from company factories as well as contractors and suppliers that standards are being met, and that employees have been informed about the standards
- Obtain written agreement of company factories and contractors and suppliers to submit to periodic inspections and audits, including by independent external monitors, for compliance with the workplace standards

**B. Create An Informed Workplace**
Ensure that all company factories as well as contractors and suppliers inform their employees about the workplace standards orally and through the posting of standards in a prominent place (in the local languages spoken by the employees and managers) and undertake other efforts to educate the employees about the standards on a regular basis

**C. Develop An Information Database**
- Develop a questionnaire to verify and quantify compliance with the workplace standards
- Require company factories and contractors and suppliers to complete and submit the questionnaire to the company on a regular basis

**D. Establish Program to Train Company Monitors**
Provide training on a regular basis to company monitors about the workplace standards and applicable local and international law, as well as about effective monitoring practices, so as to enable company monitors to be able to assess compliance with standards

**E. Conduct Periodic Visits and Audits**
- Have trained company monitors conduct periodic announced and unannounced visits to an appropriate sampling of company factories and facilities of contractors and suppliers to assess compliance with the workplace standards
- Have company monitors conduct periodic audits of production records and practices and of wage, hour, payroll and other employee records and practices of company factories and contractors and suppliers

**F. Provide Employees With Opportunity to Report Noncompliance**
Develop a secure communications channel, in a manner appropriate to the culture and situation, to enable company employees and employers of contractors and suppliers to report to the company on noncompliance with the workplace standards, with security that they will not be punished or prejudiced for doing so

---

"standards" throughout this document could be replaced with a reference to the Workplace Code of Conduct.

[3]These Principles of Monitoring should apply to contractors where the company adopting the workplace standards is a manufacturer (including a retailer acting as a manufacturer) and to suppliers where the company adopting the standards is a retailer (including a manufacturer acting as a retailer). A "contractor" or a "supplier" shall mean any contractor or supplier engaged in a manufacturing process, including cutting, sewing, assembling and packaging, which results in a finished product for the consumer.

### G. Establish Relationships with Labor, Human Rights, Religious or other Local Institutions

- Consult regularly with human rights, labor, religious or other leading local institutions that are likely to have the trust of workers and knowledge of local conditions and utilize, where companies deem necessary, such local institutions to facilitate communication with company employees and employees of contractors and suppliers in the reporting of noncompliance with the workplace standards
- Consult periodically with legally constituted unions representing employees at the worksite regarding the monitoring process and utilize, where companies deem appropriate, the input of such unions
- Assure that implementation of monitoring is consistent with applicable collective bargaining agreements

### H. Establish Means of Remediation

- Work with company factories and contractors and suppliers to correct instances of noncompliance with the workplace standards promptly as they are discovered and to take steps to ensure that such instances do not recur
- Condition future business with contractors and suppliers upon compliance with the standards

### *II. Obligations of Accredited External Monitors*

### A. Establish Clear Evaluation Guidelines and Criteria

Establish clear, written criteria and guidelines for evaluation of company compliance with the workplace standards

### B. Review Company Information Database

Conduct independent review of written data obtained by company to verify and quantify compliance with the workplace standards

### C. Verify Creation of Informed Workplace

Verify that company employees and employees of contractors and suppliers have been informed about the workplace standards orally, through the posting of standards in a prominent place (in the local languages spoken by employees and managers) and through other educational efforts

### D. Verify Establishment of Communications Channel

Verify that the company has established a secure communications channel to enable company employees and employees of contractors and suppliers to report to the company on noncompliance with the workplace standards, with security that they will not be punished or prejudiced for doing so

### E. Be Given Independent Access to, and Conduct Independent Audit of, Employee Records

- Be given independent access to all production records and practices and wage, hour, payroll and other employee records and practices of company factories and contractors and suppliers
- Conduct independent audit, on a confidential basis, of an appropriate sampling of production records and practices and wage, hour, payroll, and other employee records and practices of company factories and contractors and suppliers

## F. Conduct Periodic Visits and Audits

Conduct periodic announced and unannounced visits, on a confidential basis, of an appropriate sampling of company factories and facilities of contractors and suppliers to survey compliance with the workplace standards

## G. Establish Relationships with Labor, Human Rights, Religious or Other Local Institutions

- In those instances where accredited external monitors themselves are not leading local human rights, labor rights, religious or other similar institutions, consult regularly with human rights, labor, religious or other leading local institutions that are likely to have the trust of workers and knowledge of local conditions
- Assure that implementation of monitoring is consistent with applicable collective bargaining agreements and performed in consultation with legally constituted unions representing employees at the worksite

## H. Conduct Confidential Employee Interviews

- Conduct periodic and confidential interviews, in a manner appropriate to the culture and situation, with a random sampling of company employees and employees of contractors and suppliers (in their local languages) to determine employee perspective on compliance with the workplace standards
- Utilize human rights, labor, religious or other leading local institutions to facilitate communication with company employees and employees of contractors and suppliers, both in the conduct of employee interviews and in the reporting of noncompliance

## I. Implement Remediation

Work, where appropriate, with company factories and contractors and suppliers to correct instances of noncompliance with the workplace standards

## J. Complete Evaluation Report

Complete report evaluating company compliance with the workplace standards

*Workplace Code of Conduct & Principles of Monitoring Announced 14 April 1997.*

*For information, contact the Lawyers Committee for Human Rights,*
*New York City; TEL: 212-845-5225.*

*The full text of the Agreement is available on the Internet: http://www./chr/sweatshop/aipfull.htm*

# APPENDIX 23

## ADVERTISING CODE

From the British Codes of Advertising and Sales Promotion

*These are produced by the Committee of Advertising Practice (CAP) which is a self-regulatory body that devises and enforces the Codes. The members of the committee include organizations which represent advertising sales promotion and media businesses. The Advertising Standards Authority (ASA) is the independent body responsible for ensuring that the system works in the public interest. It investigates complaints relating to the Codes.*

*Many of the things referred to in the Codes are also part of British law but not all of them.*

## Principles

2.1 All advertisements should be legal, decent, honest and truthful.

2.2 All advertisements should be prepared with a sense of responsibility to consumers and to society.

2.3 All advertisements should respect the principles of fair competition generally accepted in business.

2.4 No advertisement should bring advertising into disrepute.

2.5 Advertisements must conform with the Codes. Primary responsibility for observing the Codes falls on advertisers. Others involved in preparing and publishing advertisements such as agencies, publishers and other service suppliers also accept an obligation to abide by the Codes.

2.6 Any unreasonable delay in responding to the ASA's enquiries may be considered a breach of the Codes.

2.7 The ASA will on request treat in confidence any private or secret material supplied unless the Courts or officials acting within their statutory powers compel its disclosure.

2.8 The Codes are applied in the spirit as well as in the letter.

## Substantiation

3.1 Before submitting an advertisement for publication, advertisers must hold documentary evidence to prove all claims, whether direct or implied, that are capable of objective substantiation.
Relevant evidence should be sent without delay if requested by the ASA. The adequacy of evidence will be judged on whether it supports both the detailed claims and the overall impression created by the advertisement.

3.2 If there is a significant division of informed opinion about any claims made in an advertisement they should not be portrayed as universally agreed.

3.3 If the contents of non-fiction books, tapes, videos and the like have not been independently substantiated, advertisements should not exaggerate the value or practical usefulness of their contents.

3.4 Obvious untruths or exaggerations that are unlikely to mislead and incidental minor errors and unorthodox spellings are all allowed provided they do not affect the accuracy or perception of the advertisement in any material way.

## Legality

4.1 Advertisers have primary responsibility for ensuring that their advertisements are legal. Advertisements should contain nothing that breaks the law or incites anyone to break it, and should omit nothing that the law requires.

## Decency

5.1 Advertisements should contain nothing that is likely to cause serious or widespread offence. Particular care should be taken to avoid causing offence on the grounds of race, religion, sex, sexual orientation or disability. Compliance with the Codes will be judged on the context, medium, audience, product and prevailing standards of decency.

5.2 Advertisements may be distasteful without necessarily conflicting with 5.1 above. Advertisers are urged to consider public sensitivities before using potentially offensive material.

5.3 The fact that a particular product is offensive to some people is not sufficient grounds for objecting to an advertisement for it.

## Honesty

6.1 Advertisers should not exploit the credulity, lack of knowledge or inexperience of consumers.

## Truthfulness

7.1 No advertisement should mislead by inaccuracy, ambiguity, exaggeration, omission or otherwise.

## Matters of opinion

8.1 Advertisers may give a view about any matter, including the qualities or desirability of their products, provided it is clear that they are expressing their own opinion rather than stating a fact. Assertions or comparisons that go beyond subjective opinions are subject to 3.1 above.

## Fear and distress

9.1 No advertisement should cause fear or distress without good reason. Advertisers should not use shocking claims or images merely to attract attention.

9.2 Advertisers may use an appeal to fear to encourage prudent behavior or to discourage dangerous or ill-advised actions; the fear likely to be aroused should not be disproportionate to the risk.

## Safety

10.1 Advertisements should not show or encourage unsafe practices except in the context of promoting safety. Particular care should be taken with advertisements addressed to or depicting children and young people.

10.2 Consumers should not be encouraged to drink and drive. Advertisements, including those for breath testing devices, should not suggest that the effects of drinking alcohol can be masked and should include a prominent warning on the dangers of drinking and driving.

## Violence and anti-social behavior

11.1 Advertisements should contain nothing that condones or is likely to provoke violence or anti-social behavior.

## Political advertising

12.1 Any advertisement whose principal function is to influence opinion in favor of or against any political party or electoral candidate contesting a UK, European parliamentary or local government election, or any matter before the electorate for a referendum, is exempt from clauses 3.1, 7.1, 14.3, 19.2 and 20.1. All other rules in the Codes apply.

12.2  The identity and status of such advertisers should be clear. If their address or other contact details are not generally available they should be included in the advertisement.

12.3  There is a formal distinction between government policy and that of political parties. Advertisements by central or local government, or those concerning government policy as distinct from party policy, are subject to all the Codes' rules.

## Protection of privacy

13.1  Advertisers are urged to obtain written permission in advance if they portray or refer to individuals or their identifiable possessions in any advertisement. Exceptions include most crowd scenes, portraying anyone who is the subject of the book or film being advertised and depicting property in general outdoor locations.

13.2  Advertisers who have not obtained prior permission from entertainers, politicians, sportsmen and others whose work gives them a high public profile should ensure that they are not portrayed in an offensive or adverse way. Advertisements should not claim or imply an endorsement where none exists.

13.3  Prior permission may not be needed when the advertisement contains nothing that is inconsistent with the position or views of the person featured. Advertisers should be aware that individuals who do not wish to be associated with the advertised product may have a legal claim.

13.4  References to anyone who is deceased should be handled with particular care to avoid causing offence or distress.

13.5  References to members of the Royal Family and the use of the Royal Arms and Emblems are not normally permitted; advertisers should consult the Lord Chamberlain's Office. References to Royal Warrants should be checked with the Royal Warrant Holders' Association.

## Testimonials and endorsements

14.1  Advertisers should hold signed and dated proof, including a contact address, for any testimonial they use. Testimonials should be used only with the written permission of those giving them.

14.2  Testimonials should relate to the product being advertised.

14.3  Testimonials alone do not constitute substantiation and the opinions expressed in them must be supported, where necessary, with independent evidence of their accuracy. Any claims based on a testimonial must conform with the Codes.

14.4  Fictitious endorsements should not be presented as though they were genuine testimonials.

14.5  References to tests, trials, professional endorsements, research facilities and professional journals should be used only with the permission of those concerned. They should originate from within the European Union unless otherwise stated in the advertisement. Any establishment referred to should be under the direct supervision of an appropriately qualified professional.

## Prices

15.1  Any stated price should be clear and should relate to the product advertised. Advertisers should ensure that prices match the products illustrated.

15.2 Unless addressed exclusively to the trade, prices quoted should include any VAT payable. It should be apparent immediately whether any prices quoted exclude other taxes, duties or compulsory charges and these should, wherever possible, be given in the advertisement.

15.3 If the price of one product is dependent on the purchase of another, the extent of any commitment by consumers should be made clear.

15.4 Price claims such as "up to" and "from" should not exaggerate the availability of benefits likely to be obtained by consumers.

### Free offers

16.1 There is no objection to making a free offer conditional on the purchase of other items. Consumers' liability for any costs should be made clear in all material featuring the offer. An offer should only be described as free if consumers pay no more than:

    a. the current public rates of postage

    b. the actual cost of freight or delivery

    c. the cost, including incidental expenses, of any travel involved if consumers collect the offer.

    Advertisers should make no additional charges for packing and handling.

16.2 Advertisers must not attempt to recover their costs by reducing the quality or composition or by inflating the price of any product that must be purchased as a precondition of obtaining another product free.

### Availability of products

17.1 Advertisers must make it clear if stocks are limited. Products must not be advertised unless advertisers can demonstrate that they have reasonable grounds for believing that they can satisfy demand. If a product becomes unavailable, advertisers will be required to show evidence of stock monitoring, communications with outlets and the swift withdrawal of advertisements whenever possible.

17.2 Products which cannot be supplied should not normally be advertised as a way of assessing potential demand.

17.3 Advertisers must not use the technique of switch selling, where their sales staff criticize the advertised product or suggest that it is not available and recommend the purchase of a more expensive alternative. They should not place obstacles in the way of purchasing the product or delivering it promptly.

### Guarantees

18.1 The full terms of any guarantee should be available for consumers to inspect before they are committed to purchase. Any substantial limitations should be spelled out in the advertisement.

18.2 Advertisers should inform consumers about the nature and extent of any additional rights provided by the guarantee, over and above those given to them by law, and should make clear how to obtain redress.

18.3 "Guarantee" when used simply as a figure of speech should not cause confusion about consumers' legal rights.

## Comparisons

19.1 Comparisons can be explicit or implied and can relate to advertisers' own products or to those of their competitors; they are permitted in the interests of vigorous competition and public information.

19.2 Comparisons should be clear and fair. The elements of any comparison should not be selected in a way that gives the advertisers an artificial advantage.

## Denigration

20.1 Advertisers should not unfairly attack or discredit other businesses or their products.

20.2 The only acceptable use of another business's broken or defaced products in advertisements is in the illustration of comparative tests, and the source, nature and results of these should be clear.

## Exploitation of goodwill

21.1 Advertisers should not make unfair use of the goodwill attached to the trademark, name, brand, or the advertising campaign of any other business.

## Imitation

22.1 No advertisement should so closely resemble any other that it misleads or causes confusion.

## Identifying advertisers and recognizing advertisements

23.1 Advertisers, publishers and owners of other media should ensure that advertisements are designed and presented in such a way that they can be easily distinguished from editorial.

23.2 Features, announcements or promotions that are disseminated in exchange for a payment or other reciprocal arrangement should comply with the Codes if their content is controlled by the advertisers. They should also be clearly identified and distinguished from editorial (see clause 41).

23.3 Mail order and direct response advertisements and those for one day sales, homework schemes, business opportunities and the like should contain the name and address of the advertisers. Advertisements with a political content should clearly identify their source. Unless required by law, other advertisers are not obliged to identify themselves.

In addition the Codes include:

*Specific Rules relating to —*

Alcoholic Drinks
Children
Motoring
Environmental Claims
Health & Beauty Products and Therapies
Slimming
Distance Selling
List and Database Practice

Employment and Business Opportunities
Financial Services and Products

and a

**Cigarette Code**

*The Code is produced by the Committee of Advertising Practice, 2 Torrington Place, London WC1E 7HW. UK and was revised and re-issued to take effect on 1st February 1995.*

## APPENDIX 24

### PURCHASING POWER INDEX (PPI)
CREA: A Center for Reflection, Education and Action, Inc.

*The Purchasing Power Index provides data regarding the ability of workers anywhere in the world to meet their own needs and those of their families. It accurately measures the intersection of prices, wages and inflation while providing data that allows for comparison:*

a)   *Transtemporally: Purchasing Power can be compared over time for a given group of workers;*

b)   *Transculturally: Purchasing Power can be compared for different groups of workers within a given area, region or country; and*

c)   *Transnationally: Purchasing Power can be compared for workers doing the same work in different countries.*

#### Advantages of the Purchasing Power Index

1. The PPI establishes a basis of comparison over time. For example, how many minutes of work are required (at a given wage level) to purchase a kilogram (2.2 lb.) of rice in January 1998. The PPI also allows us to compare purchasing power after three months or six months as a way of determining the effects of inflation, currency revaluation and/or new contracts.

2. It establishes a basis of comparison between one location and another. Different locations can be any combination of different free trade zone areas within a country, different countries, or urban, suburban and rural locations. The conditions of workers at different plants operating for the same company can be monitored.

3. It allows for the assessment of wage levels without the need to price every item a person might ever need to purchase. By knowing the purchasing power, in minutes of work necessary, to provide basic commodities as well as household expenses, the possibility of meeting basic needs through the normal workweek can be assessed.

4. It removes the question of judgment normally involved in decisions as to how one spends one's money. The PPI states what is possible in terms of the purchasing power that accrues as a result of the normal workweek. Questions as to whether a person

spends money in a manner that another person might consider "frivolous" is no longer relevant. What is affordable is emphasized. With 60 minutes in an hour and approximately 40 hours in an average workweek, any person, at any wage level, earns 2400 minutes of purchasing power each week (50 hours=3000 minutes). What changes are the "prices in purchasing power minutes" or the "cost in work minutes" according to the varied wage levels.

5. The PPI creates the ability to compare the effects of earned purchasing power at different wage levels.

### Wages, Prices, and Locations

Analysis and discussion of wages and benefits can be misleading if they are not set within the context of prices at any particular time and in given places. For example, if wages increase at the same time that prices increase, the overall effect of wage increases is often non-existent. For persons living in any particular place, items are cheaper only if (a) wages increase while prices remain the same or (b) wages remain the same while prices decrease. Similarly, if an exchange rate changes, persons using the currency that has increased in comparative value will experience the items being purchased in another country as being "cheaper." The person earning the lesser-valued currency experiences the same items as being more expensive.

What will be seen as beneficial to one stakeholder within a community can often be harmful, or at least not beneficial, to another stakeholder in the same community at the same time. By using minutes of purchasing power (minPP) required for purchase, the question moves from "what is cheaper or more expensive and for whom?" to the real question: "what is affordable and for whom?"

For information, contact: CREA Inc., PO Box 2507, Hartford, CT 06146-2507, TEL: 860-586-0705, FAX: 860-233-4673, e-mail: crea-inc@concentric.net; website: www.crea-inc.org

## APPENDIX 25

### PRINCIPLES FOR GLOBAL CORPORATE RESPONSIBILITY:
Bench Marks For Measuring Business Performance

#### The Context of Faith

The purpose of the Principles for Global Corporate Responsibility is to promote positive corporate social responsibility consistent with the responsibility to sustain the human community and all creation.

From a perspective of faith, the context for all human activity is the totality of creation. Therefore we need to use our power to live in harmony with creation, affirm the interdependence of everything on earth and the dignity of all parts of creation.

Faith communities evaluate companies, not only by what they produce and their impact on the environment, but also by how companies contribute to sustainable community and protect or undermine the dignity of the human person. We believe these companies carry responsibility for the human and moral consequences of their economic decisions.

We believe the challenge for both companies and individuals in the global economy is to ensure that the distribution of economic benefits is equitable, supports sustainable community and preserves the integrity of creation.

We believe the promotion and protection of human rights—civil, political, social, religious, cultural and economic—are minimum standards for all social institutions, including companies.

We believe all people and institutions have a responsibility to work for a just society marked by love, compassion and peace. Justice requires that we stand with those oppressed by poverty and exploitation and we work to change the structures and policies which support their oppression. Justice also requires that the allocation of income, wealth and power be evaluated in the light of their impact on the poorest and most vulnerable in the world.

Our religious institutions as shareholders have an obligation to take into account not only the financial return but also the impact of a company's activities on the human community and all creation.

## Preamble

The Principles brought together in this document have been drawn up by collaborating agencies of certain faith communities in Canada, the United Kingdom and the United States. They are the Taskforce on the Churches and Corporate Responsibility (TCCR) in Canada, the Ecumenical Council for Corporate Responsibility (ECCR) in the UK, and the Interfaith Center on Corporate Responsibility (ICCR) in the US. These agencies have worked for over two decades on corporate responsibility issues.

In this document, by *Principles* we mean a statement of business philosophy fundamental to a responsible company's actions. By *Criteria* we mean particular company policies and practices that can be compared for consistency with the Principles. By *Bench Marks* we mean suggested specific reference points of measurement to be used in assessing the company's performance in relation to the Criteria. For reasons of clarity the categories under which the Principles are defined are divided into two groupings: The Wider Community and the Corporate Business Community.

The Principles are offered as an ethical standard of measurement on which to base decisions about global corporate social responsibility. They arise from jointly held beliefs which are based on the faiths of the participant groups, communities, denominations and traditions. The concepts stem from an understanding of the ethical value of creation, humanity and the nature of society.

In our understanding of global corporate responsibility, the community rather than the company is the starting point of economic life.[1] For the community to be sustain-

---

[1] Corporate language generally uses the word "stakeholder" to include only those who benefit from the company's activities. In the corporate context the company, rather than the community, is the starting point of economic life.

able, all members need to be recognized, i.e., consumers, employees, shareholders, the community at large and corporations. Respect for each group's essential role in the economic and social life of the community will facilitate more just relationships locally and globally.

## The Wider Community

### Section 1.1—Ecosystems
*Principles*

1.1.P.1   Careful attention is paid to ensure that the company's actions do not damage the global environment. Issues such as climate change, bio-diversity and pollution prevention are central to this. The company adopts high standards and ensures that they are implemented universally regardless of any legal enforcement or lack thereof in any jurisdiction and continually seeks to improve its performance.

1.1.P.2   To minimize environmental degradation and health impacts, the precautionary principle,[2] is the overriding principle guiding action, shifting the burden of proof from one of proving environmental harm to one of proving environmental safety.

1.1.P.3   The presence of unused, unexploited, non-renewable, natural resources within a particular area is recognized as an asset of the community of that area.

1.1.P.4   The company has responsibility for the environmental impact of its products and services throughout the life cycle of these products and services.

*Criteria*

1.1.C.1   A company-wide environmental code has been adopted and implemented.

1.1.C.2   An active environmental committee has been established by and reports to the Board of Directors.

1.1.C.3   The company has in place appropriate management systems to implement its policies.

1.1.C.4   Environmental assessments are completed by the company in which the unused, unexploited natural resources are stated as assets of the community.

1.1.C.5   The company provides to the public regular reports on its environmental performance and future plans. These are based on a pattern of environmental auditing and reporting according to a recognized standard (such as CERES, ICC Business Charter for Sustainable Development or any other appropriate standardized format) and include data for each facility.

1.1.C.6   The company holds public consultations and seeks collaboration from interested individuals and groups to review both its past performance and its future plans, including the location of new facilities.

---

[2] Precautionary principle: Where there are threats of serious or irreversible damage, lack of full scientific certainty should not be used as a reason for postponing cost-effective measures to prevent environmental degradation. (Agenda 21, Principle 15)

1.1.C.7  Where environmental damage does occur, every effort is made by the company to reduce its impact immediately, to provide technical data to those working on the containment and repair, to restore the damaged ecosystem and to ensure appropriate measures are taken to redress injuries to persons caused by environmental hazards created by the company.

1.1.C.8  The company has policies, practices and procedures to prevent pollution, reduce resource and energy use in each stage of the product or service life-cycle.

*Bench Marks*

1.1.B.1  Natural resources which become an asset to the company are stated as a debit to the community.

1.1.B.2  Environmental assessments are made periodically and include, but are not limited to:

—environmental impact
—physical infrastructure impact
—social infrastructure impact
—cumulative (synergistic) impacts.

1.1.B.3  The company has a policy which includes performance standards relating to:

—protection of the biosphere
—sustainable use of natural resources
—reduction and disposal of wastes
—reduction of anthropogenic greenhouse gas emissions
—energy conservation
—risk reduction
—safe products and services
—environmental restoration
—informing the public.

The company has adopted and implemented at least one or more of the recognized environmental monitoring programs. *(See Appendices)*

1.1.B.4  Environmental performance standards are set and applied on a comparable basis throughout the company's operations.

1.1.B.5  The company is in full compliance with all international, national, and subnational environmental regulations, and breaches are recorded.

1.1.B.6  The company discloses for each of its operations the same categories and levels of information as are required in their "home" country.

1.1.B.7  An annual, standardized, environmental report, including data on the extent to which performance goals have been met, is publicly issued and its contents are verified by an independent authority.

1.1.B.8  On-going environmental performance evaluation is conducted and the results are periodically audited by an independent auditor. The results of the audit are reported to the stakeholders.

1.1.B.9  Employee remuneration/compensation packages, especially those of senior executives, are linked to corporate environmental performance.

1.1.B.10   The company introduces changes in product design and process technology in order to reduce life cycle impacts.

## Section 1.2—National Communities
*Principles*

1.2.P.1   The company values being a good corporate citizen in all its locations and holds it to be the responsibility of every employee to ensure that there is full compliance with all internationally recognized labor, health, environment and safety standards.

1.2.P.2   The company makes a commitment to be a good corporate citizen in each and every country in which it operates.

1.2.P.3   The company contributes in a responsible and transparent way to each society's efforts to promote full human development for all its members.

1.2.P.4   The company respects the political jurisdiction of national communities.

1.2.P.5   The company is fully committed to respecting internationally recognized human rights standards, including the Universal Declaration of Human Rights, International Covenant on Economic, Social and Cultural Rights, corresponding international covenants adopted by the General Assembly of the United Nations, and International Labor Organization Conventions. *(See Appendices)*

1.2.P.6   The company does not use the mobility of capital and the immobility of labor as a tool against workers.

*Criteria*

1.2.C.1   The company pays appropriate taxes and uses no covert means (such as inflated internal or transfer prices) for removing profits from a host jurisdiction.

1.2.C.2   In instances where legislation or the actual practices of any public institution violate fundamental human rights, the company does everything in its power to maintain respect for those fundamental rights in its own operations. The company also seeks to exercise its corporate influence to contribute to the establishment of such fundamental rights.

1.2.C.3   The company has a policy that it will withdraw from a country in instances where there are gross and systematic violations of human rights and when there is a recognized movement from within the country calling for withdrawal.

1.2.C.4   An active human rights committee has been established by and reports to the Board of Directors.

*Bench Marks*

1.2.B.1   A senior executive in each operation is responsible for all matters of human rights.

1.2.B.2   All contraventions of health and safety laws are reviewed and recorded, and corrective action is taken.

1.2.B.3   Taxes are paid by the company within the appropriate jurisdictions.

1.2.B.4   Operations in countries which consistently violate the UN Charter of Human Rights are reviewed annually by the Board of Directors.

1.2.B.5 The company discloses labor and human rights tribunal cases and lawsuits settled or decided against the company, in addition to any pending lawsuits that might have a significant material effect on the company.

1.2.B.6 The company subscribes to the principles expressed in the 1977 International Labor Organization Tripartite Declaration of Principles Concerning Multinational Enterprises and Social Policy. *(See Appendices)*

## Section 1.3—Local Communities
*Principles*

1.3.P.1 The company recognizes its political and economic impact on local communities especially where it is the principal or key employer. Its program, policies and practices help promote a broad spectrum of human rights within each community where it operates.

1.3.P.2 The company takes account of local culture in its decision-making processes while not condoning cultural patterns which denigrate human beings on the basis of gender, class, race, culture, ethnicity, religion, tribe or disability.

1.3.P.3 The company strives to contribute to the long-term environmental, social, cultural, and economic sustainability of the local communities in which it operates.

*Criteria*

1.3.C.1 Respect is shown by the company for the local community, especially with regard to water, land, air, food, energy, religion, and culture.

1.3.C.2 The company consults with the local community and gives support for activities which enhance the quality of community life.

1.3.C.3 Employees are encouraged to participate in local community activities and organizations.

1.3.C.4 The company seeks to develop long-term business relationships in local communities and does not terminate its operations without assessing the social, economic and environmental impact on the local community.

1.3.C.5 The company is careful of the impact of its power and influence especially in its use of the local media and its advertising strategies.

*Bench Marks*

1.3.B.1 The company decisions are made in accord with the UN Declaration of Human Rights, the Convention on the Elimination of All Forms of Discrimination Against Women and the International Convention on the Elimination of All Forms of Racial Discrimination. *(See Appendices)*

1.3.B.2 Community consultation mechanisms are established and used.

1.3.B.3 The company has a plant closure policy which provides for proper notice and transitional arrangements for employees.

1.3.B.4 Donations of money, service and assistance are made to community and charitable organizations.

## Section 1.4—Indigenous Communities
*Principles*

1.4.P.1 The company only pursues economic development upon prior resolution and completion of the settlement of land claims between the indigenous people (or First Nation) and the appropriate government(s).

1.4.P.2   The company is committed to respecting fully the rights of indigenous peoples as they are recognized by the appropriate jurisdictions and laws.

1.4.P.3   Indigenous peoples, by virtue of their inherent rights, are entitled to full participation in the business decisions which pertain to their ancestral lands and their way of life.

1.4.P.4   The company respects the cultural, religious and social customs and traditional knowledge of members of indigenous communities.

1.4.P.5   The development of joint working agreements between indigenous communities and companies is a prerequisite to building business relationships and commitments.

1.4.P.6   The company respects the bio-cultural integrity of indigenous peoples and their lands.

*Criteria*

1.4.C.1   The company communicates its business plans in a way that the local indigenous community can understand.

1.4.C.2   The company seeks and receives approval from the legitimate local indigenous leadership prior to beginning any business activities.

1.4.C.3   The company, with the cooperation of the indigenous peoples concerned, performs a holistic comprehensive study of its potential environmental, physical, social, economic, cultural and spiritual impact on the community and modifies its business plan to ameliorate potential harm.

1.4.C.4   The company provides employment and training opportunities to, and actively recruits from, indigenous communities for all levels of employment.

1.4.C.5   The company's employment policies and practices fully accommodate the cultural, spiritual and social needs of employees who are members of indigenous communities.

1.4.C.6   The company develops a transparent process for the inclusion of indigenous peoples as full participants in business decisions.

1.4.C.7   The company negotiates a just and equitable economic settlement with the indigenous community(ies) involved.

1.4.C.8   The company provides opportunities for all its employees to obtain an understanding of indigenous culture, treaties, history and current issues.

*Bench Marks*

1.4.B.1   The company, through its programs, policies, practices, and communications implements the principles expressed in the International Conventions on Human Rights, Agenda 21 and the International Labor Organization Convention Concerning Indigenous and Tribal Peoples in Independent Countries, Convention 169. *(See Appendices)*

1.4.B.2   The company, together with the legitimate representatives of the indigenous community jointly establishes clear decision-making processes and structures.

1.4.B.3   The company's business plans, and its employment policies and practices are communicated clearly and are available in indigenous languages in both written and oral form.

1.4.B.4    The company adheres to the International Convention on Bio-Diversity and ensures the protection of bio-cultural integrity and intellectual property rights of the indigenous community(ies). *(See Appendices)*

1.4.B.5    The company, as a matter of policy, refrains from litigation that obstructs the implementation of the recognized rights of indigenous peoples.

## The Corporate Business Community

### Section 2.1—The Employed—Conditions
*Principles*

2.1.P.1    The company values all its employees and their contributions in every sector of its operations.

2.1.P.2    The company ensures that each employee is treated with respect and dignity.

2.1.P.3    The company has a global standard governing its employment practices and industrial relations. This standard includes genuine respect for employees' right to freedom of association, labor organization, free collective bargaining, non-discrimination in employment and a safe and healthy working environment provided for all employees.

2.1.P.4    The company does not discriminate on the basis of gender, race, social or ethnic origin, culture, religion, age, disability, sexual orientation, nationality, citizenship or political opinion.

2.1.P.5    The company ensures its labor force is proportionally representative of the communities in which its operations are located.

2.1.P.6    The company seeks to maximize long-term contractual relationships with its employees and to safeguard employees' future employability.

2.1.P.7    The company pays sustainable community wages which enable employees to meet the basic needs of themselves and their families, as well as to invest in the on-going sustainability of local communities through the use of discretionary income.

2.1.P.8    The company provides equal pay for work of equal value.

2.1.P.9    The company ensures work schedules that are reasonable and enable employees and their families to live in a sustained and healthful manner; the company does not rely on production based on unpaid labor.

2.1.P.10   The company recognizes the need for supporting and/or providing the essential social infrastructure of child care, elder care and community service in order to facilitate access to employment and the full participation of employees in the workplace.

*Criteria*

2.1.C.1    The company ensures that no person is subject to any discrimination in employment, including recruitment, hiring, remuneration, benefits, advancement, discipline, termination, or retirement, on the basis of gender, race, social or ethnic origin, culture, religion, age, disability, sexual orientation, nationality or political opinion.

2.1.C.2    The company accommodates the cultural, religious and social needs of employees.

2.1.C.3    The company ensures that no employee is subject to any physical, sexual, psychological or verbal harassment or abuse.

2.1.C.4    The company has a policy which prohibits pregnancy testing as a condition of employment.

2.1.C.5    The company actively recruits and employs for all positions at all levels, including management, from the local population.

2.1.C.6    Training, development, promotion and advancement opportunities within the company are available to all employees of the company regardless of status whether full-time, part-time, short-term, permanent, or with any other contracts of employment.

2.1.C.7    All who work within and on the company's premises, whether permanent, temporary or contracted employees, including those engaged in day labor, receive equal protection especially in provision of equipment, and information concerning their health and safety at work. This information is provided in the languages of the workers.

2.1.C.8    The company recognizes the responsibilities of all workers to their families, and provides for maternity leave, paternity leave, family leave, compassionate leave.

2.1.C.9    The company supports and/or provides the essential social infrastructure of child care, elder care and community services which allow workers, especially women who have traditionally done this work as unpaid labor, to participate as employees.

2.1.C.10    Employees are free to organize and join workers' organizations without discrimination or interference and to engage freely in collective negotiations to regulate the terms and conditions of employment. No employee is discriminated against for engaging in union organizing and collective bargaining activities.

2.1.C.11    The company has in place programs, policies and practices with specific goals and time lines to ensure equal pay for work of equal value.

2.1.C.12    The company ensures that, at a minimum, all employees are paid a wage which, at least, provides sufficient purchasing power to enable employees to meet the basic needs of themselves and their families.

2.1.C.13    The company uses an established process to calculate a sustainable living wage. The process to determine a sustainable living wage is used in each of the geographic areas where workers live.

2.1.C.14    The company pays all legally mandated benefits as a minimum standard.

2.1.C.15    The company limits overtime work to a level that ensures humane working conditions.

2.1.C.16    In situations where corporate restructuring is taking place, the company provides the opportunity for redeployment and retraining of employees in order to offer sustainable patterns of employment. Formal redundancy/layoff policies are only adopted as a last resort.

*Bench Marks*

2.1.B.1 The company adheres to international accords, conventions and covenants regarding basic employment practices, equality of opportunity, and the elimination of all forms of discrimination. *(See Appendices 10–21)*

2.1.B.2 The company adheres to the principles set out in the International Labor Organization Conventions on Freedom of Association and Free Collective Bargaining.

2.1.B.3 The company makes available to independent monitors the work records of employees when there is question of discrimination against labor organizing or other collective bargaining activities.

2.1.B.4 The company arranges for regular health and safety inspections by qualified inspectors. The company agrees to take action to rectify any problems in a timely fashion.

2.1.B.5 The company conducts regular health and safety training for its employees.

2.1.B.6 The company does not require employees to work overtime on a regular basis. Employees may refuse overtime without any threat of penalty, punishment, demotion or dismissal.

2.1.B.7 The company uses a process, such as the Purchasing Power Index Study or other equally exact method, that can measure the effects of changes in wages, prices and inflation; the process is geographic area-specific, and is implemented on a regular basis in order to adjust wages to provide adequate purchasing power to meet basic needs.

## Section 2.2—The Employed—Persons
### *Subsection 2.2a—Women in the Workforce*

*Principles*

2.2a.P.1 The company values women as a vital group of employees who have a significant contribution to make to the work of all companies.

2.2a.P.2 The company is aware that the rights of women are often violated by business policies and practices which contribute to the "feminization of poverty" and exacerbate gender inequalities. It seeks to neutralize the impact of any such policies or practices on their employees.

2.2a.P.3 The company ensures that there is equal remuneration for work of equal value.

2.2a.P.4 The company ensures that the social and biological determinants that affect women because of gender, are addressed by appropriate policies within the work place, including, but not limited to, pregnancy leave, maternity leave, medical leave.

*Criteria*

2.2a.C.1 The company recognizes that there may be particular barriers to the full participation of women and takes positive action to diminish these barriers within the company.

2.2a.C.2 The company has in place a ranking of work situations to ensure pay parity among workers.

2.2a.C.3   The company works to provide resources of social support to enhance women's economic empowerment.

*Bench Marks*

2.2a.B.1   The company has in place effective and appropriate policies and statements of equality of opportunity for women in the workforce and these are monitored and maintained throughout all levels of employment. These are available to all workers in the languages of the workers.

2.2a.B.2   The company develops specific goals and measurable objectives to provide women with true and equal participation in decision-making.

2.2a.B.3   The company provides adequate technical training which contributes to the advancement of all workers, especially women.

2.2a.B.4   The company has a policy of responding flexibly to the needs of women regarding pregnancy and family care without detriment to their employment.

2.2a.B.5   The company encourages or participates in the creation of child care centers and centers for the elderly and persons with disabilities where appropriate.

### Subsection 2.2b—Minority Groups

*Principles*

2.2b.P.1   The company does not discriminate on grounds of race, ethnicity, or culture.

*Criteria*

2.2b.C.1   The company has an employment policy which enables people from minority groups to be recruited to the company, to achieve progression in employment in the company and to receive training and promotional opportunities without discrimination.

2.2b.C.2   The company recognizes that there may be particular barriers to the full participation of people from minority groups and takes positive action to diminish these barriers within the company.

2.2b.C.3   The company has a policy that its work force reflects the racial, ethnic and cultural composition of the local population at all levels.

*Bench Marks*

2.2b.B.1   The company complies with the Wood-Sheppard Principles on equal opportunity of employment for people from minority groups or an equally rigorous code. *(See Appendices)*

2.2b.B.2   The company complies with the International Convention on the Elimination of all Forms of Racial Discrimination. *(See Appendices)*

### Subsection 2.2c—Persons with Disabilities

*Principles*

2.2c.P.1   The company ensures that persons with disabilities who apply for jobs with the company receive fair treatment and are considered solely on their ability to do the job with or without workplace modifications.

2.2c.P.2   The company values persons with physical and/or mental disabilities as full participants in the company workforce.

*Criteria*

2.2c.C.1     The company has in place an operative anti-discrimination policy vis-à-vis persons with physical and/or mental disabilities, with provisions for the monitoring of compliance with the policy. *(See Appendices)*

2.2c.C.2     The company has a policy of employing people with disabilities and of providing the resources and facilities which enable them to achieve progression in employment in the company and to receive training and promotional opportunities without discrimination.

2.2c.C.3     When a worker employed by the company becomes disabled, the company continues to employ that person and provides the modifications necessary to enable the worker to continue at the previous status. If a worker requires transfer to another position within the company because of disability, wherever possible this new job is at the same level; where not possible, existing remuneration is protected for a specified period.

2.2c.C.4     The company provides training to all employees about hiring and accommodating persons with physical and/or mental disabilities.

2.2c.C.5     The company recognizes that there may be particular barriers to the full participation of people with disabilities and takes positive action to diminish these barriers within the company.

*Bench Marks*

2.2c.B.1     The company periodically assesses its hiring and employment practices of persons with physical and/or mental disabilities and makes necessary correction in a specified period.

2.2c.B.2     The company regularly consults with organizations with experience and expertise regarding the employment of persons with physical and/or mental disabilities.

2.2c.B.3     The company makes the particular accommodations necessary for persons with disabilities to be able to function in the workplace.

### Subsection 2.2d—Child Labor

*Principles*

2.2d.P.1     The company does not exploit children as workers.

2.2d.P.2     The company guarantees that neither it nor its contractors employ children in conditions that violate the rights of the child.

2.2d.P.3     The company:

    — does not interfere with the right of a child to an education

    — agrees to abide by minimum age requirements for admission of children to employment as stated in the International Convention on the Rights of the Child

    — accepts appropriate regulation of hours and conditions regarding employment of children

    — safeguards the health, safety and morals of child workers.

2.2d.P.4     The company does not employ persons under the age of majority as a means of avoiding the payment of the full adult wage for doing the same work.

*Criteria*

2.2d.C.1  The company does not employ, in a full-time capacity, in its own work-places or in that of its subsidiaries and suppliers, any child under the age of completion of compulsory schooling and, in any case, less than the age of 15 years. In countries where the economy and educational facilities are insufficiently developed, companies may, after consultation with the young workers, worker associations, and organizations concerned with children's rights, labor rights and human rights, initially specify a minimum age of 14 years.

2.2d.C.2  The company, when it has taken advantage of the above exception to 14 years has made a specific public declaration of the reasons for this exception and has determined a date by which it will cease to avail itself of the provisions of this policy.

2.2d.C.3  The company works with organizations concerned with children's rights, human rights and labor rights and within the country of production to ensure that young workers are not exploited.

2.2d.C.4  The company has a precise statement regarding the employment of children and young people. This policy is publicly available throughout the company and its suppliers in the languages of any and all workers. It is clearly communicated to all employees in a manner which can be understood, and includes verbal communications for employees lacking adequate reading skills.

2.2d.C.5  The company has a clearly stated policy and monitoring program in regard to the employment of children.

*Bench Marks*

2.2d.B.1  The company has in place a monitoring and auditing program to ensure compliance with its corporate code of conduct. This program includes internal monitoring and auditing as well as independent monitoring.

2.2d.B.2  The company has a precise standard of recording and measurement in place which enables it to monitor the significance of all exceptions to the pattern of child employment below the age of 16 years. In addition, the company has a precise standard and measurement of any exposure to a potentially hazardous environment for anyone aged 18 or below. These records are available for public scrutiny, especially by those groups responsible for human rights, labor rights and children's rights.

2.2d.B.3  If monitoring reveals that children are being exploited, immediate steps are taken to rectify the practice and to provide for the rehabilitation of the children involved. The company does not solve the problem by the dismissal of the children affected.

2.2d.B.4  The company regularly consults with country-specific knowledgeable organizations regarding programs and practices to remove children from work sites and reintegrate them into home, school and community.

### Subsection 2.2e—Forced Labor

*Principles*

2.2e.P.1  The company employs workers who choose to be employed by that company. The company does not use any forced labor, whether in the forms of prison labor, indentured labor, bonded labor, slave labor or any other non-voluntary labor.

*Criteria*

2.2e.C.1   The company has a clearly stated policy in regard to the monitoring of the employment of people under duress. If it is discovered in such monitoring that any workers have been employed under duress, immediate steps are taken to rectify the practice and to provide for the rehabilitation of the workers involved. The company does not solve the problem by the dismissal of the workers involved.

*Bench Marks*

2.2e.B.1   The company adheres to International Labor Organization Convention Number 29 on Forced Labor. *(See Appendices)*

## Section 2.3—Suppliers

*Principles*

2.3.P.1   The company accepts responsibility for all those whom it employs either directly or indirectly through contract suppliers, sub-contractors, vendors or suppliers.

2.3.P.2   The company is responsible for the labor conditions under which and in which its products and services are produced, provided, advertised or marketed under licensing agreement.

*Criteria*

2.3.C.1   The company has a strong code of conduct for vendors and suppliers which includes, but is not limited to, child labor, forced labor, harassment, nondiscrimination, healthy and safe workplace, freedom of association and right to bargain collectively, sustainable living wages and benefits, hours of work, the environment, supportive social and physical community infrastructure and monitoring mechanisms for compliance.

*Bench Marks*

2.3.B.1   The company clearly communicates to its suppliers, vendors and licensees the company's code of vendor/supplier conduct and its process of enforcement. Violations of the code are effectively addressed. Cancellation of contract is used only as a last resort.

2.3.B.2   The company has an effective internal compliance process of training, on-site inspections and audits of suppliers and vendors.

2.3.B.3   To supplement its internal monitoring of code compliance, the company accepts independent monitoring of its suppliers and/or vendors. Sources of independent monitoring include non-governmental organizations, local community groups, religious, human rights, children's rights and labor groups.

2.3.B.4   The company has clear guidelines for the investigation of possible code of conduct violations which include a safe, confidential process of interviewing employees without penalizing them or jeopardizing their jobs or safety.

2.3.B.5   The company, along with its vendors and suppliers, has a plan of action with specific time lines to address code violations. The company has guidelines to terminate its contract if identified code violations are not dealt with in a reasonable period of time.

2.3.B.6  The company adopts a transparent policy to make the internal investigation of complaints, and the results of internal and independent monitoring, available to the public.

## Section 2.4—Financial Integrity
*Principles*

2.4.P.1  The company insists on honesty and integrity in all aspects of its business, wherever business is conducted.

2.4.P.2  The company does not offer, pay, solicit or accept bribes in any form.

*Criteria*

2.4.C.1  All transactions on behalf of the company are appropriately described in the accounts of the company in accordance with established procedures and are subject to audit.

2.4.C.2  All employees are required to avoid conflicts of interest between their private financial activities and their part in the conduct of company business.

*Bench Marks*

2.4.B.1  As part of their reporting responsibilities, the company's auditors indicate the amount of any consultancy fees incurred, and/or commission payments made, in respect of any contract and the percentage which these fees bear to the total gross value of such contract.

2.4.B.2  The senior administrative officer of each significant unit of the company, as well as the company Chief Executive Officer, is required annually to sign a letter containing the following representations:

— that neither the company (unit) nor any of its authorized representatives has been party to the offering, paying or receiving of bribes
— that no payments have been made which knowingly violate the laws of the countries in which the company operates
— that no receipts or payments of monies or other assets derived from the company (unit) have been either unrecorded or falsified when described in the relevant books and records and no other improper accounting practice has been adopted in the period under review.

## Section 2.5—Ethical Integrity
*Principles*

2.5.P.1  The company recognizes that its directors and employees have a central role in upholding the company's ethical standards and codes of conduct.

2.5.P.2  The company actively seeks to participate in all voluntary codes and standards that pertain to its operations.

*Criteria*

2.5.C.1  The company provides training for its directors and employees regarding ethical issues and codes of conduct.

2.5.C.2 The company has a mechanism to address ethical issues of concern raised by employees.

*Bench Marks*

2.5.B.1 The company ensures that employees who raise issues of concern do not suffer negative repercussions.

2.5.B.2 The company ensures that, should the mechanism fail and the employee raises the issue outside the company, there are no negative repercussions on their employment.

## Section 2.6—The Shareholders
*Principles*

2.6.P.1 The company's corporate governance policies balance the interests of managers, employees, shareholders, and other interested and affected parties.

2.6.P.2 Information which enables shareholders to understand corporate compliance with these Principles of Global Corporate Responsibility as evidenced in the Criteria and Bench Marks of this document is fully available.

2.6.P.3 The company neither restricts nor obstructs the legal rights of shareholders.

*Criteria*

2.6.C.1 The company ensures shareholders' participation and rights to information while protecting other interested and affected parties.

2.6.C.2 The company respects the right of shareholders to submit proposals for vote and to ask questions at the annual meeting.

2.6.C.3 The company is committed to meet with shareholders to address issues of concern.

*Bench Marks*

2.6.B.1 The company observes a code or codes of best practice or has drawn up its own comprehensive corporate code which includes guidelines for corporate governance. *(See Appendices)*

2.6.B.2 Shareholders are informed through reports and meetings about significant and material violations of corporate policies, including codes of conduct, adverse decisions by tribunals or courts, and the results of internal audits or analyses of corporate activity.

2.6.B.3 Shareholder proposals and questions are welcomed at the company's annual meeting.

## Section 2.7—Joint Ventures / Partnerships / Subsidiaries
*Principles*

2.7.P.1 When entering into and throughout the duration of joint ventures and partnerships, the company takes into account the ethical implications as well as the financial implications of those relationships.

2.7.P.2 All parts of the company, associated companies, divisions and units and subsidiary companies abide by the same codes of ethics and conduct as the parent company as a minimum standard.

2.7.P.3 The company accepts a responsibility to promote its codes of ethics and of conduct with licensees and franchisees.

*Criteria*

2.7.C.1   The company recognizes that unethical behavior by joint venture and other partners reflects on its own reputation and integrity, and the company has a mechanism to address such unethical behavior.

2.7.C.2   The company has a clearly stated policy in regard to the monitoring of the application of codes of ethics and conduct by licensees and franchisees.

*Bench Marks*

2.7.B.1   The company has guidelines to assess and determine its course of action when a violation of ethical codes is perpetrated by a partner or subsidiary. These guidelines include, but are not limited to, challenging the partner or terminating the relationship.

2.7.B.2   The company takes immediate steps to address violations of codes of ethics and conduct by licensees and franchisees. The company only terminates the relationship as a last resort.

**Section 2.8—Customers & Consumers**

*Principles*

2.8.P.1   The company adheres to international standards and protocols relevant to its products and services.

2.8.P.2   The company ensures that its products and services meet customer requirements and product specification.

2.8.P.3   The company is committed to marketing practices which protect consumers and which ensure the safety of all products.

2.8.P.4   The company is fully committed to fair trading practices.

*Criteria*

2.8.C.1   All advertisement and labeling of products is complete, fair and honest. Only claims which can be substantiated and fulfilled are made by the company, its employees and its agents.

2.8.C.2   The company does not market products which denigrate or supplant sustainable natural products in such a way as to cause harm to the environment or to consumers.

2.8.C.3   The company does not market products in other countries which have been found to be harmful in any country.

2.8.C.4   The company does not engage in cartels, spheres of influence or patent protections which are deliberately designed to denigrate the rights of others.

2.8.C.5   The company ensures that products marketed globally have clear, specific warnings in the appropriate local language, about their possible dangers to the consumer.

2.8.C.6   The company does not take advantage of vulnerable groups through inappropriately directed marketing.

*Bench Marks*

2.8.B.1   The company's activities and products have received positive evaluations from independent consumer organizations.

2.8.B.2   Relevant consumer codes are followed by the company in such a way as to protect vulnerable groups. *(See Appendices)*

2.8.B.3   Where either advertising standards legislation, international standards and protocols, product safety legislation or recognized codes exist they are complied with and this compliance is regularly disclosed. *(See Appendices)*

2.8.B.4   There is no evidence of the participation of the company in cartels, spheres of influence or unfair patent protections.

## GLOSSARY OF TERMS

The following is by no means an exhaustive list but is an attempt to provide an introduction to the underlying thinking behind some of the language which is used in appendix 25 or which is associated with the concepts of corporate activity and responsibility. The definitions have been culled from various sources and these are, where possible, indicated in square brackets [ ].

[AICoC]  = Apparel Industry Codes of Conduct of the US Dept. of Labor
[CEP]    = Council on Economic Priorities
[EIRIS]  = Ethical Investment Research Service
[FSC]    = Forest Stewardship Council

*Associated companies*
Those companies in which aggregate interest in the equity share capital held by the parent company and its direct and indirect subsidiaries amounts to 20%–50% inclusive. [EIRIS]

*Biological diversity*
The variability among living organisms from all sources including, *inter alia,* terrestrial, marine and other aquatic ecosystems and the ecological complexes of which they are a part; this includes diversity within species, between species and of ecosystems. (see Convention on Biological Diversity, 1992) [FSC]

*Company*
A company is an organization or business entity including all its personnel (i.e. directors, executives, management, supervisors, and non-management staff, whether directly employed, contracted or otherwise representing the company). [CEP]

*Company group*
A company whose shares are quoted on the Stock Exchange and all other parts of the company. [EIRIS]

*Corporate citizenship*
Corporate citizenship is about a new contract between business and society, a vision of partnership between different sections of community which allies profitable companies with healthy communities because what happens to societies happens to business. [CEP]

*Customary rights*
Rights which result from a long series of habitual or customary actions, constantly repeated, which have, by such repetition and by uninterrupted acquiescence, acquired the force of law within a geographical or sociological unit. [FSC]

*Ecosystem*
A community of all plants and animals and their physical environment, functioning together as an independent unit. [FSC]

*Indigenous lands and territories*
The total environment of the lands, air, water, sea, sea-ice, flora and fauna, and other resources which indigenous peoples have traditionally owned or otherwise occupied or used. [FSC]

*Indigenous peoples*
The existing descendants of the peoples who inhabited the present territory of a country wholly or partially at the time when persons of a different culture or ethnic origin arrived there from other parts of the world, overcame them and, by conquest, settlement, or other means reduced them to a non-dominant or colonial situation; who today live more in conformity with their social, economic and cultural customs and traditions than with the institutions of the country of which they now form a part, under a State structure which incorporates mainly the national, social and cultural characteristics of other segments of the population which are predominant. (Working definition adopted by the UN Working Group on Indigenous Peoples) [FSC]

*Local laws*
Includes all legal norms given by organisms of government whose jurisdiction is less than the national level, such as departmental, municipal and customary norms. [FSC]

*Monitoring*
Four patterns of monitoring have been defined:

*Internal Monitoring* conducted by local or regional company personnel or headquarters personnel or a combination of employees from each group.

*External Monitoring* using the activity of buying agents to monitor compliance with a corporate code.

*Outside Audits,* now a service offered by some accounting and auditing firms to add to their normal service functions and define corporate code compliance.

*Independent Monitoring by NGOs* is a system now being utilized by some companies using local and international NGOs, or religious and human rights groups to conduct or assist in monitoring. [AICoC]

*Parent company*
The company quoted on the Stock Exchange. [EIRIS]

*Parts of a company*
Direct and indirect subsidiaries, associated companies, divisions and units. [EIRIS]

*Precautionary Principle*
Where there are threats of serious or irreversible damage, lack of full scientific certainty should not be used as a reason for postponing cost-effective measures to prevent environmental degradation. (Agenda 21, Principle 15)

### Purchasing Power Index (PPI)

The PPI is a transnational, transcultural and transtemporal index which brings together wages, prices and inflation to accurately measure the ability of the wages a worker earns to meet the needs of that worker as well as the worker's family. The PPI is culturally specific. In addition, it allows for the monitoring of the effects of the movement/migration of jobs around the world on the lives of workers who are left behind as well as the lives of newly hired workers. [Ruth Rosenbaum, 1996]

### Stakeholder

Corporate language generally uses the word "stakeholder" to include only those who benefit from the company's activities. In the corporate context the company, rather than the community, is the starting point of economic life. The proposers of these Principles believe that the community rather than the company is the starting point of economic life.

### Subsidiary companies

A company is a subsidiary if another company holds more than 50% of its equity share capital. [EIRIS]

### Wage levels

Level 1: Marginal survival: Wage does not provide for adequate nutritional needs. Starvation is prevented.

Level 2: Basic survival: Wage allows for meeting immediate survival needs including basic food, used clothing, minimal shelter, fuel for cooking.

Level 3: Short Range Planning Wage: Wage meets basic survival needs. Possibility of small amount of discretionary income allows for minimal planning beyond living from paycheck to paycheck. Allows for occasional purchase of needed item(s) as small amounts can be set aside from meeting basic survival needs.

Level 4: Long Range Planning Wage: Wage meets basic survival needs. Also allows for the setting aside of small amounts of money (savings) to allow for planning for the future purchase of items and meeting of needs.

Level 5: Sustainable Community Wage: In addition to meeting basic needs and allowing the worker to set aside money for future purchases, allows for the availability of enough discretionary income to allow the worker to support the development of small businesses in a local community including the support of cultural and civic needs of the community. Wage allows for long range planning and participation. [Ruth Rosenbaum, 1994]

*Appendices 1 to 25 were originally published by the ICCR and are reproduced
here with permission. For information, contact:
ICCR, 475 Riverside Drive, Suite 550, New York, NY 10115,
TEL: (212) 870-2295; FAX: (212) 870-2023; e-mail: info@iccr.org*

## APPENDIX 26

### THE CAUX PRINCIPLES
Business Behavior for a Better World

**Introduction.** This document has been developed by the Caux Round Table, an international group of business executives from Japan, Europe, and the United States who meet each year in Caux, Switzerland, and who believe that the world business community should play an important role in improving economic and social conditions. As a statement of aspirations, it is not meant to mirror reality but to express a world standard against which corporate performance can be held accountable. In the end, members seek to begin a process that identifies shared values and reconciles differing values so we may move toward developing a shared perspective on business behavior that is acceptable to and honored by all.

These principles are rooted in two basic ethical ideals: the Japanese concept of "kyosei" and the more Western concept of "human dignity." "Kyosei" means living and working together for the common good—in a way that enables cooperation and mutual prosperity to coexist with healthy and fair competition. "Human dignity" refers to the sacredness or value of each human person as an end, not simply as a means to others' purposes or even—in the case of basic human rights—majority prescription. The intermediate General Principles in Section 2 help to clarify the spirit of "kyosei" and "human dignity," while the more specific Stakeholder Principles in Section 3 represent a practical way to apply the ideals of kyosei and human dignity.

Business behavior can affect relationships among nations and the prosperity and well-being of us all. Business is often the first contact between nations and, by the way in which it causes social and economic changes, has a significant impact on the level of fear as well as confidence felt by people worldwide. Members of the Caux Round Table place their first emphasis on putting one's own house in order, seeking what is right not who is right.

### Section 1. PREAMBLE

The mobility of employment and capital is making business increasingly global in its transactions and its effects. Laws and market forces in such a context are necessary but insufficient guides for conduct. Responsibility for a corporation's actions and policies and respect for the dignity and interests of its stakeholders are fundamental. And shared values, including a commitment to shared prosperity, are as important for a global community as for communities of smaller scale. For all of the above reasons, and because business can be a powerful agent of positive social change, we offer the following principles as a foundation for dialogue and action by business leaders in search of corporate responsibility. In so doing, we affirm the legitimacy and centrality of moral values in economic decision making because, without them, stable business relationships and a sustainable world community are impossible.

## Section 2. GENERAL PRINCIPLES

### Principle 1. The Responsibilities of Corporations:
### Beyond Shareholders toward Stakeholders.

The role of a corporation is to create wealth and employment and to provide marketable products and services to consumers at a reasonable price commensurate with quality. To play this role, the corporation must maintain its own economic health and viability, but its own survival is not an end in itself. The corporation also has a role to play in improving the lives of all of its customers, employees, and shareholders by sharing with them the wealth it has created. Suppliers and competitors as well should expect businesses to honor their obligations in a spirit of honesty and fairness. And as responsible citizens of the local, national, regional, and global communities in which they operate, corporations share a part in shaping the future of those communities.

### Principle 2. The Economic and Social Impact of Corporations:
### Toward Innovation, Justice and World Community.

Corporations established in foreign countries to develop, produce, or sell should also contribute to the social advancement of those countries by creating jobs and helping to raise their purchasing power. They should also give attention to and contribute to human rights, education, welfare, vitalization of communities in the countries in which they operate. Moreover, through innovation, effective and prudent use of resources, and free and fair competition, corporations should contribute to the economic and social development of the world community at large, not only the countries in which they operate. New technology, production, products, marketing, and communication are all means to this broader contribution.

### Principle 3. Corporate Behavior:
### Beyond the Letter of Law toward a Spirit of Trust.

With the exception of legitimate trade secrets, a corporation should recognize that sincerity, candor, truthfulness, the keeping of promises, and transparency contribute not only to the credit and stability of business activities but also to the smoothness and efficiency of business transactions, particularly on the international level.

### Principle 4. Respect for Rules: Beyond Trade Friction toward Cooperation.

To avoid trade frictions and promote freer trade, equal business opportunity, and fair and equitable treatment for all participants, corporations should respect international and domestic rules. In addition, they should recognize that their own behavior, although legal, may still have adverse consequences.

### Principle 5. Support for Multilateral Trade:
### Beyond Isolation toward World Community.

Corporations should support the multilateral trade system of GATT/World Trade Organization and similar international agreements. They should cooperate in efforts to promote the judicious liberalization of trade and to relax those domestic measures that unreasonably hinder global commerce.

**Principle 6. Respect for the Environment: Beyond Protection toward Enhancement.**
A corporation should protect, and where possible, improve the environment, promote sustainable development, and prevent the wasteful use of natural resources.

**Principle 7. Avoidance of Illicit Operations: Beyond Profit toward Peace.**
A corporation should not participate in or condone bribery, money laundering, and other corrupt practices. It should not trade in arms or materials used for terrorist activities, drug traffic or other organized crime.

### Section 3. STAKEHOLDER PRINCIPLES

**CUSTOMERS.** We believe in treating customers with dignity and that our customers are not only those who directly purchase our products and services but also those who acquire them through authorized market channels. In cases where those who use our products and services do not purchase them directly from us, we will make our best effort to select marketing and assembly/manufacturing channels that accept and follow the standards of business conduct articulated here. We have a responsibility:

- to provide our customers with the highest quality products and services consistent with their requirements;
- to treat our customers fairly in all aspects of our business transactions, including a high level of service and remedies for customer dissatisfaction;
- to make every effort to ensure that the health and safety (including environmental quality) of our customers will be sustained or enhanced by our products or services;
- to avoid disrespect for human dignity in products offered, marketing, and advertising;
- to respect the integrity of the cultures of our customers.

**EMPLOYEES.** We believe in the dignity of every employee and we therefore have a responsibility:

- to provide jobs and compensation that improve and uplift workers' circumstances in life;
- to provide working conditions that respect employees' health and dignity;
- to be honest in communications with employees and open in sharing information, limited only by legal and competitive constraints;
- to be accessible to employee input, ideas, complaints, and requests;
- to engage in good faith negotiations when conflict arises;
- to avoid discriminatory practices and to guarantee equal treatment and opportunity in areas such as gender, age, race, and religion;
- to promote in the corporation itself the employment of handicapped and other disadvantaged people in places of work where they can be genuinely useful;
- to protect employees from avoidable injury and illness in the workplace;
- to be sensitive to the serious unemployment problems frequently associated with business decisions and to work with governments and other agencies in addressing these dislocations.

**OWNERS/INVESTORS.** We believe in honoring the trust our investors place in us. We therefore have a responsibility:

- to apply professional and diligent management in order to secure a fair and competitive return on our owners' investment;
- to disclose relevant information to owners/investors subject only to legal and competitive constraints;
- to conserve and protect the owners/investors' assets;
- to respect owner/investor requests, suggestions, complaints, and formal resolutions.

**SUPPLIERS.** We begin with the conviction that our relationship with suppliers and subcontractors, like a partnership, must be based on mutual respect. As a result, we have a responsibility:

- to seek fairness in all our activities including pricing, licensing, and rights to sell;
- to ensure that our business activities are free from coercion and unnecessary litigation, thus promoting fair competition;
- to foster long-term stability in the supplier relationship in return for value, quality and reliability;
- to share information with suppliers and integrate them into our planning processes in order to achieve stable relationships;
- to pay suppliers on time and in accordance with agreed terms of trade;
- to seek, encourage, and prefer suppliers and subcontractors whose employment practices respect human dignity.

**COMPETITORS.** We believe that fair economic competition is one of the basic requirements for increasing the wealth of nations and ultimately for making possible the just distribution of goods and services. We therefore have responsibilities:

- to foster open markets for trade and investment;
- to promote competitive behavior that is socially and environmentally beneficial and demonstrates mutual respect among competitors;
- to refrain from either seeking or participating in questionable payments or favors to secure competitive advantages;
- to respect both material and intellectual property rights;
- to refuse to acquire commercial information by dishonest or unethical means, such as industrial espionage.

**COMMUNITIES.** We believe that as global corporate citizens we can contribute, even to a small extent, to such forces of reform and human rights as are at work in the communities in which we operate. We therefore have responsibilities in the communities in which we do business:

- to respect human rights and democratic institutions, and to promote them wherever practical;
- to recognize government's legitimate obligation to the society at large and to support public policies and practices that promote human development through harmonious relations between business and other segments of society;
- to collaborate in countries and areas which struggle in their economic development with those forces which are dedicated to raising standards of health, education, and workplace safety;

- to promote and stimulate sustainable development;
- to play a lead role in preserving the physical environment and conserving the earth's resources;
- to support peace, security, and diversity in local communities;
- to respect the integrity of local cultures;
- to be a good citizen by supporting the communities in which we operate; this can be done through charitable donations, educational and cultural contributions, and employee participation in community and civic affairs.

## APPENDIX 27

### THE SULLIVAN PRINCIPLES
Statement of Principles of U.S. Firms with Affiliates in the Republic of South Africa

**Principle I. Non-Segregation of the races in all eating, comfort and work facilities.**
Each signator of the Statement of Principles will proceed immediately to:
- Eliminate all vestiges of racial discrimination.
- Remove all race designation signs.
- Desegregate all eating, comfort and work facilities.

**Principle II. Equal and fair employment practices for all employees.**
Each signator of the Statement of Principles will proceed immediately to:
- Implement equal and fair terms and conditions of employment.
- Provide non-discriminatory eligibility for benefit plans.
- Establish an appropriate and comprehensive procedure for handling and resolving individual employee complaints.
- Support the elimination of all industrial racial discriminatory laws which impede the implementation of equal and fair terms and conditions of employment, such as abolition of job reservations, job fragmentation, and apprenticeship restrictions for Blacks and other non-whites.
- Support the elimination of discrimination against the rights of Blacks to form or belong to government registered and unregistered unions and acknowledge generally the rights of Blacks to form their own unions or be represented by trade unions which already exist.
- Secure rights of Black workers to the freedom of association and assure protection against victimization while pursuing and after attaining these rights.
- Involve Black workers or their representatives in the development of programs that address their educational and other needs and those of their dependents and the local community.

**Principle III. Equal pay for all employees doing equal or comparable work for the same period of time.**
Each signator of the Statement of Principles will proceed immediately to:

- Design and implement a wage and salary administration plan which is applied equally to all employees, regardless of race, who are performing equal or comparable work.
- Ensure an equitable system of job classifications, including a review of the distinction between hourly and salaried classifications.
- Determine the extent upgrading of personnel and/or jobs in the upper echelons is needed, and accordingly implement programs to accomplish this objective in representative numbers, insuring the employment of Blacks and other non-whites at all levels of company operations.
- Assign equitable wage and salary ranges, the minimum of these to be well above the appropriate local minimum economic living level.

**Principle IV. Initiation of and development of training programs that will prepare, in substantial numbers, Blacks and other non-whites for supervisory, administrative, clerical and technical jobs.**
Each signator of the Statement of Principles will proceed immediately to:

- Determine employee training needs and capabilities, and identify employees with potential for further advancement.
- Take advantage of existing outside training resources and activities, such as exchange programs, technical colleges, and similar institutions or programs.
- Support the development of outside training facilities, individually or collectively—including technical centers, professional training exposure, correspondence and extension courses, as appropriate, for extensive training outreach.
- Initiate and expand inside training programs and facilities.

**Principle V.  Increasing the number of Blacks and other non-whites in management and supervisory positions.**
Each signator of the Statement of Principles will proceed immediately to:

- Identify, actively recruit, train and develop a sufficient and significant number of Blacks and other non-whites to assure that as quickly as possible there will be appropriate representation of Blacks and other non-whites in the management group of each company at all levels of operations.
- Establish management development programs for Blacks and other non-whites, as needed, and improve existing programs and facilities for developing management skills of Blacks and other non-whites.
- Identify and channel high management potential Blacks and other non-white employees into management development programs.

**Principle VI. Improving the quality of employees' lives outside the work environment in such areas as housing, transportation, schooling, recreation and health facilities.**
Each signator of the Statement of Principles will proceed immediately to:

- Evaluate existing and/or develop programs, as appropriate, to address the specific needs of Black and other non-white employees in the areas of housing, health care, transportation and recreation.

- Evaluate methods for utilizing existing, expanded or newly established in-house medical facilities or other medical programs to improve medical care for all non-whites and their dependents.
- Participate in the development of programs that address the educational needs of employees, their dependents, and the local community. Both individual and collective programs should be considered, in addition to technical education, including such activities as literacy education, business training, direct assistance to local schools, contributions and scholarships.
- Support changes in influx control laws to provide for the right of Black migrant workers to normal family life.
- Increase utilization of and assist in the development of Black and other non-white owned and operated business enterprises including distributors, suppliers of goods and services and manufacturers.

**Principle VII. Working to eliminate laws and customs which impede social, economic and political justice.**

Each signator of the Statement of Principles must proceed immediately to:

- Press for a single education system common to all races.
- Use influence and support the unrestricted rights of Black businesses to locate in the urban areas of the nation.
- Influence other companies in South Africa to follow the standards of equal rights principles.
- Support the freedom of mobility of Black workers, including those from *so-called* independent homelands, to seek employment opportunities wherever they exist and make possible provisions for adequate housing for families of employees within the proximity of workers' employment.
- Use financial and legal resources to assist Blacks, Coloreds and Asians in their efforts to achieve equal access to all health facilities, educational institutions, transportation, housing, beaches, parks and all other accommodations normally reserved for Whites.
- Oppose adherence to all apartheid laws and regulations.
- Support the ending of all apartheid laws, practices and customs.
- Support full and equal participation of Blacks, Coloreds and Asians in the political process.

With all the foregoing in mind, it is the objective of the companies to involve and assist in the education and training of large and telling numbers of Blacks and other non-whites as quickly as possible. The ultimate impact of this effort is intended to be of massive proportion, reaching and helping millions.

**Periodic Reporting**

The Signatory Companies of the Statement of Principles will proceed immediately to:

- Report progress on an annual basis through the independent administrative unit established.
- Have all areas specified audited by a certified public accounting firm.
- Inform all employees of the company's annual periodic report rating and invite their input on ways to improve the rating.

# The Center for Ethics and
# Religious Values in Business

The Notre Dame Center for Ethics and Religious Values in Business seeks to build bridges among business, business studies, and the humanities. Its programs are designed to strengthen the Judeo-Christian ethical foundations in business and public policy decisions by fostering dialogue between academic and corporate leaders, and by research and publications. The academic director of the Center is Oliver F. Williams, c.s.c., associate professor of management, College of Business Administration; the program director is Bonnie Fremgen, associate professional specialist in the College. The Center was founded in 1978 by John W. Houck, who died in 1996 and who was a professor of management for forty years, and Oliver F. Williams, c.s.c.

Publications by the Center include:

*Full Value: Cases in Christian Business Ethics* (1978)
"Quite successfully juxtaposes the power of the Christian story, in its biblical immediacy, to concrete problems Christians in the world of business are likely to meet."
—Michael Novak

"Religious traditions provide, as these writers observe, a story, for example the Christian story, which informs our moral outlook, creates our moral vision, sustains our moral loyalties, and nurtures our moral character."
—James M.Gustafson

*The Judeo-Christian Vision and the Modern Corporation* (1980)
In 1980 the Center hosted a national symposium bearing the same name as this work, about which the *New York Times* reported, "there would be no facile resolution to the conflict between the values of a just society and the

sharply opposing values of successful corporations." Further, the *Los Angeles Times* contrasted "the competitive success-oriented style necessary to corporate promotion with the traditional Christian view of the virtuous person."

*Co-Creation and Capitalism: John Paul II's "Laborem Exercens"* (1983)

The symposium "Co-creation: A Religious Vision of Corporate Power" was presented in 1982, focusing on Pope John Paul II's encyclical letter, *Laborem Exercens. Newsweek* characterized the conference as a "free marketplace of ideas" exploring a religious vision of corporate power.

*Catholic Social Teaching and the U.S. Economy* (1984)

In December 1983, the Center assisted the U.S. Bishops' Committee charged to write a pastoral letter on the economy by convening a three-day symposium, "Catholic Social Teaching and the American Economy." The *Los Angeles Times* observed: "About one-third of the major speakers represented conservative viewpoints, the remainder voiced moderate-to-liberal positions." The *New York Times* reported that "contentiousness is commonplace here at Notre Dame . . . and when dozens of business leaders, theologians and academics lined up against each other at the university this week, the debate over the economy was fought as hard as any gridiron encounter." More than two hundred and fifty people attended the meeting, including the five bishops who were to draft the letter.

*The Common Good and U.S. Capitalism* (1987)

"Catholic Social Teaching and the Common Good" was the theme of a 1986 symposium to explore the possible retrieval of the notion of "the common good" in philosophical-economic discourse. Ralph McInerny saw the concept of the common good as needed "to draw attention to flaws in our economic thinking and policies as well as to make positive suggestions that will be manifestly in line with our tradition." *New Catholic World* wrote: "a collection of eighteen essays . . . by social scientists, theologians, philosophers, business faculty, and television producers. The essays represent different points of view from both theoretical and practical perspectives. . . . It would be a valuable contribution to Catholic social teaching if all it did was to make people aware that a concept of the common good once was alive and well. It does much more than that."

*Ethics and the Investment Industry* (1989)

The 1987 symposium focused on ethics in the investment industry. Much has been written in the eighties about the misdeeds of actors in the investment community; suggestions for legislative reform abound. Very little has been said about the ethical vision and institutional bonding that form the context for a humane capitalism. It is these themes, as well as the appropriate market and legal aspects, that were explored at Notre Dame. *America* said of *Ethics and the Investment Industry* that it "will be an important reference for future participants in the international business community."

*A Virtuous Life in Business: Stories of Courage and Integrity in the Corporate World* (1992)

"I highly recommend *A Virtuous Life in Business: Stories of Courage and Integrity in the Corporate World. . . .* This book is not only valuable, it is readable and gets progressively better."

—*Commonweal*

*Catholic Social Thought and the New World Order: Building on One Hundred Years* (1993)

"With the recent demise of the Marxist alternative to capitalism, Catholic social teaching has assumed the role of the major international force challenging free enterprise to be more humane."

—*National Catholic Register*

Other publications by the Center include:

*The Moral Imagination: How Literature and Films Can Stimulate Ethical Reflections in the Business World* (1998)

*Is the Good Corporation Dead? Social Responsibility in a Global Economy* (1996)

*The Making of an Economic Vision* (1991)

*The Apartheid Crisis* (1986)

*Matter of Dignity: Inquiries into the Humanization of Work* (1977)

as well as articles appearing in *California Management Review, Business Horizons, Theology Today, Business and Society Review, Horizons, Journal of Business Ethics,* and the *Harvard Business Review.*

*A New Activity*
The Center inaugurated an Executive-in-Residence Program in the fall of 1996. In this program, a senior executive comes to campus for a period of time and shares his or her experience of the ethical dimension of business with our students. David Collins, a former Vice Chairman of Johnson and Johnson was the first executive, and he taught two seminars. In the fall of 1997 there were four executives-in-residence: J. Neil Statler, former Vice President for Public Affairs, Campbell Soup Company; Joseph W. Keating, former President, Merck Pharmaceutical Manufacturing Division

of Merck and Co., Inc.; Alfred C. DeCrane, J., former Chairman of the Board and C.E.O., Texaco, Inc.; and F. Byron Nahser, President and C.E.O., Frank C. Nahser Advertising Company. In the fall of 1998 there were five executives-in-residence: Buzz McCoy, former Managing Partner of Morgan Stanley; Brian Levey, Law/Policy Officer of MCI; Joseph Maciariello, Horton Professor of Management at Claremont Graduate School; David E. Collins, former Vice Chair of Johnson and Johnson; and Thomas M. Chappell, President of Tom's of Maine.

# Contributors

GERALD F. CAVANAGH, S.J., holds the Charles T. Fisher Chair of Business Ethics and is a professor of management at the University of Detroit Mercy. He is the author of numerous articles and five books, including *American Business Values: With Global Perspectives,* 4th edition. He has lectured internationally, consulted with business firms, governments, and universities, and has given workshops on business ethics and the role of the business firm in society. He holds a B.S. in engineering; graduate degrees in philosophy, theology, and education; a doctorate in management from Michigan State University; and is an ordained Catholic priest in the Society of Jesus.

GEORGES ENDERLE is the Arthur and Mary O'Neil Professor of International Business Ethics at the University of Notre Dame and vice president of the International Society of Business, Economics, and Ethics (ISBEE). He has taught business ethics in Europe for over ten years and was cofounder of the European Business Ethic Network (EBEN). Since 1994 he has been involved in numerous research and teaching activities in China. His research focuses on understanding the ethical challenges of international business for corporate decision-making; he has authored and edited many books and articles on this subject.

KATHLEEN A. GETZ is associate professor of management and international business at the Kogod College of Business Administration of the American University. She won the 1991 Best Dissertation Award and the 1991 Best Paper Award from the Social Issues in Management Division of the Academy of Management for research on corporate political activity related to the Montreal Protocol on Substances that Deplete the Ozone Layer, and is the author of numerous articles on corporate political activity, international codes of conduct, and regulation. She received her doctorate from the University of Pittsburgh.

LINDA F. GOLODNER is president of the National Consumers League and cochairs the White House Apparel Industry Partnership. She has served as chair of the

U.S. Department of Labor Child Labor Advisory Committee and is a former commissioner and chair of the Fairfax Country Commission for Women. Before joining the League in 1983 she was president of her own public affairs firm, representing nonprofit institutions, associations, and political organizations. She received the American Pharmaceutical Association's Hugh Schaefer Award in 1997 and her doctorate from the University of Maryland in 1975.

KENNETH E. GOODPASTER is the Koch Professor of Business Ethics at the University of St. Thomas Graduate School of Business in Saint Paul, Minnesota. He taught philosophy at the University of Notre Dame throughout the 1970s before joining the Harvard Business School faculty in 1980. He is the author of many articles and several books on applied philosophy, including *Policies and Persons: A Casebook in Business Ethics*. He earned his A.B. in mathematics from the University of Notre Dame and his A.M. and Ph.D. in philosophy from the University of Michigan.

JOHN M. KLINE is director of the Landegger Program in International Business Diplomacy at the Georgetown University School of Foreign Service. Before joining the faculty in 1979 he was director of the International Economic Policy at the National Association of Manufacturers. He is the author of several books, including *Foreign Investment Strategies in Restructuring Economies: Learning from Corporate Experiences in Chile*, and has conducted studies for the United Nations, the Inter-American Development Bank, and the U.S. Advisory Committee on Intergovernmental Relations. He received his Ph.D. in political science from the George Washington University and an M.S. in international relations from the Johns Hopkins University School of Advanced International Studies.

ROBERT KINLOCH MASSIE received his master of divinity from Yale University in 1982 and his doctorate in business administration from Harvard Business School in 1989. He is executive director of the Coalition for Environmentally Responsible Economies (CERES) and the author of *Loosing the Bonds: The United States and South Africa in the Apartheid Years,* which won the Lionel Gelber prize for the best book on international relations in 1998.

GARTH MEINTJES is associate director of the Center for Civil and Human Rights at the University of Notre Dame Law School where he teaches international law and human rights. Previously, he taught constitutional law and criminal law at the University of the Western Cape in South Africa. He received his B.A. in law from Stellenbosch University and his LL.B. from the University of Cape Town. The recipient of a Bradlow Foundation Scholarship, he received his LL.M. degree in international human rights from the University of Notre Dame in 1991.

PATRICK E. MURPHY is professor and chair of the Department of Marketing at the University of Notre Dame. During the 1993-94 academic year he was a Fulbright Scholar in the Department of Management and Marketing at University College in Cork, Ireland. He is the author of *Eighty Exemplary Ethics Statements* and a number of articles on business and marketing ethics. In 1992 he received the Reinhold Niebuhr Award, given annually by Notre Dame to a faculty member whose writings promote the areas of ethics and social justice. He holds a Ph.D. from the University of Houston, an M.B.A. from Bradley University, and a B.B.A. from the University of Notre Dame.

LISA H. NEWTON is professor of philosophy and director of the Program in Applied Ethics at Fairfield University in Fairfield, Connecticut. She has authored or coauthored several textbooks in the fields of Ethics and Environmental Studies, including *Wake Up Calls: Classic Cases in Business Ethics* (1996), *Watersheds: Cases in Environmental Ethics* (2d ed. 1997), and *Taking Sides: Controversial Issues in Business Ethics and Society* (5th ed. 1998); she has authored over seventy articles on ethics in politics, law, medicine, and business, and was the writer and ethics consultant for Media and Society's 1990 series, *Ethics in America*, still occasionally aired on public television. She has been president of the Society for Business Ethics and the American Society for Value Inquiry, and made numerous presentations on current issues in business ethics, including the International Conference on Business Ethics in Milan, 1992. She consults with several regional health care providers, corporations, and professional associations.

JAMES E. POST is professor of management and public policy at Boston University where he serves as faculty director of the Program in Public and Non-Profit Management, and is director of the Public Affairs Research Group. He also serves as a trustee of the Foundation for Public Affairs in Washington, D.C. He is the author of over one hundred publications and is the author or coauthor of fourteen books, including *Private Management and Public Policy.* He has been a worldwide consultant, in particular with several United Nations agencies on business practices, and was a member of the Nestlé Audit Commission which monitored the company's compliance with the World Health Organization international marketing code of conduct. He holds J.D., M.B.A., and Ph.D. degrees and teaches global strategic management, business-government relations, and corporate public affairs.

RUTH ROSENBAUM, T.C., has been part of the founding of the Center for Reflection, Education and Action, Inc. (CREA, Inc.) where she serves as executive director. She is responsible for the development of the Purchasing Power Index (PPI), the first transnational, transcultural and transtemporal index which allows for analysis of the combined effects of wages, prices, and inflation on the purchasing power of workers worldwide. For the past ten years she has also been director of the Research and Report Service for Ethical and Socially Responsible Investing, an organization that monitors the activities of corporations worldwide, and she chairs the Global Corporate Accountability Issue Group at the Interfaith Center on Corporate Responsibility (ICCR). She holds B.A. degrees in biology and chemistry from Hunter College of CUNY, an M.A. in both biology and theology from Manhattan College, and her Ph.D. in social economics and social justice from Boston College.

DAVID M. SCHILLING, an ordained United Methodist minister, is director of the Global Corporate Accountability Programs at the Interfaith Center on Corporate Responsibility (ICCR) and works with religious shareholders on issues of human rights, labor rights, sustainable wages, and codes of conduct. He served as codirector of the Riverside Church Disarmament Program and program director at the Fellowship of Reconciliation. He is a member of the Coalition for Justice in the Maquiladoras, of President Clinton's Anti-Sweatshop Task Force, and of the Independent Monitoring Working Group that monitors the Gap's San Salvador supplier, Mandarin International; he has written extensively on these issues.

S. PRAKASH SETHI is Academic Director/Executive Education at Baruch College School of Business, the City University of New York. Prior to joining Baruch College he was professor of international business and social policy at the University of Texas at Dallas. He is well known for his research and writings in business ethics, corporate social responsibility, corporate strategy and public policy, international business, and private enterprise and Third World economic development, and has had a long involvement in the international sociopolitical arena pertaining to the role of multinational corporations. His latest book is *Multinational Corporations and the Impact of Public Advocacy on Corporate Strategy: Nestlé and the Infant Formula Controversy*.

KEVIN J. SWEENEY, as one of the seven-member Patagonia management team, overseas most of the company's environmental programs, and supervises Patagonia's art department, the public affairs staff, and the core customer service division. He was an original member of the Apparel Industry Partnership. Appointed by President Clinton to be assistant to the Secretary of the Interior in 1993, he helped shape a wide range of U.S. environmental policies. He serves on the board of directors for the Sierra Nevada alliance and the Ojai Valley Land Conservancy. He was press secretary to U.S. Senator Gary Hart, appeared as a guest on *Nightline*, the *McNeil/Lehrer News Hour*, and *Larry King Live*, and has published numerous articles on environmental and social topics.

WINTHROP M. SWENSON is the managing director of the Business Ethics Services for KPMG Peat Marwick LLP. This service provides organizations with advice on how to establish effective ethics/compliance systems as well as how to systematically measure, evaluate, and verify effective operations. From 1990 to 1996 he served as deputy general counsel, U.S. Sentencing Commission. In this role, he chaired the interdisciplinary staff task force that developed the organizational sentencing guidelines. Author of numerous works on the organizational sentencing guidelines and compliance/ethics programs, Swenson also serves as associate editor of *Corporate Conduct Quarterly*.

LEE A. TAVIS is the C. R. Smith Professor of Business Administration, founding director of the Program on Multinational Managers and Developing Country Concerns at the University of Notre Dame, and Faculty Fellow of the Helen Kellogg

Institute for International Studies and the Joan B. Kroc Institute for International Peace Studies. His work focuses on the trade-off between corporate economic optimization and the contribution to development in the poor countries of Africa, Asia, Latin America, and Central Europe. He is the editor of four volumes, the latest being *Power and Responsibility*, and coeditor of another. He received his B.S. from the University of Notre Dame, his M.B.A. from Stanford University, and his D.B.A. from Indiana University.

ANN E. TENBRUNSEL is assistant professor in the College of Business Administration at the University of Notre Dame, teaching management and negotiation courses. Her research interests focus on decision-making and negotiations, with a specific emphasis on ethics; she is the coeditor of two books on these subjects. Prior to joining the faculty, she was a sales force and marketing consultant for ZS Associates, a sales support analyst and engineer for S. C. Johnson and Son, and a negotiation consultant/trainer to several other companies, including Ernst and Young and the National Association of Broadcasters. She received her B.S.I.O.E. from the University of Michigan and her M.B.A. and Ph.D. from Northwestern University.

OLIVER F. WILLIAMS, C.S.C., is associate professor of management and academic director of the Notre Dame Center for Ethics and Religious Values in Business. He was associate provost of the university from 1987 to 1994. He served as a member of the United Nations Observations Mission for South Africa's first post-apartheid national elections in 1994, and has studied the South African business and political landscape for many years. He was a member of the National Advisory Council to U.S. firms with business operations in South Africa from 1987 to 1994 (the Sullivan Principles). He is the chairman of the board of the United States-South Africa Leadership Development Program. He facilitated a landmark 1991 meeting at Notre Dame between U.S. corporate and government officials and representatives of the African National Congress, the Inkatha Freedom Party, and the Pan-Africanist Congress. He was a visiting professor at the University of Cape Town, Graduate School of Business, during the 1995–96 academic year and returns there each year for two months. He has published and lectured extensively in the field of business ethics, is the author of *The Apartheid Crisis* and coeditor of ten books, including *A Virtuous Life in Business* and *The Moral Imagination: How Literature and Films Can Stimulate Ethical Reflection in the Business World*. He received his B.A. in chemical engineering and M.A. in theology from the University of Notre Dame and his doctorate from Vanderbilt University. He was ordained a Catholic priest in 1970.

# Index

— ✳ —